'I suspect it may well be the best overview of *Doctor Who* that I have ever read . . . If you're keen to understand why this wonderful show has been such a success and have it set in context, now is your chance to enter the world of academia and see *Doctor Who* from a new and rewarding perspective.'

Andrew Pixley, *Doctor Who Magazine*

'Chapman's approach is unpretentious, readable, solidly authoritative and self-consciously anti-theoretical . . . Chapman's nook is an extremely good starting point for anyone wishing to think seriously about *Doctor Who.'*

Matthew Sweet, *The Independent*

'A serious-minded "cultural history" which sets out to examine how the series "maps the shifting cultural landscape of Britain . . . Illuminating".'

Jon Barnes, *Times Literary Supplement*

'*Inside the Tardis* is a sideways look at the history of broadcasting since the 1960s. As the show skips from crabbit William Hartnell to David Tennant, Paisley's first Time Lord, we see how changes at the BBC affected the show.'

Sunday Herald

'A genuinely worthwhile addition to the library-full of books about the series.'

Starburst

'James Chapman has written an absorbing, highly readable account of the series. This is an intelligent, well-balanced work, that thanks to the BBC archives, brings something genuinely new to the party.'

SFX Magazine

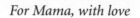

For Mama, with love

INSIDE THE
TARDIS

THE WORLDS OF
DOCTOR WHO

A Cultural History

JAMES CHAPMAN

I.B. TAURIS

LONDON · NEW YORK

New revised edition published in 2013 by I.B.Tauris & Co Ltd
6 Salem Road, London W2 4BU
175 Fifth Avenue, New York NY 10010
www.ibtauris.com

Distributed in the United States and Canada
Exclusively by Palgrave Macmillan
175 Fifth Avenue, New York NY 10010

First published in 2006 by I.B.Tauris & Co Ltd

ISBN: 978 1 78076 140 4

A full CIP record for this book is available from the British Library
A full CIP record is available from the Library of Congress

Library of Congress Catalog Card Number: available

Printed and bound in Great Britain by Page Bros, Norwich

Contents

Acknowledgements

This book would have been impossible to research were it not for the BBC Written Archives Centre at Caversham, Reading, a delightful archive in which to work, and I am indebted to its staff, most especially to Jacqueline Kavanagh, Julie Snelling and Karen White, who did so much to make my extended research into the *Doctor Who* production files throughout the long hot summer of 2003 such a pleasurable and rewarding experience. Other libraries that I have used in the preparation of this book are the National Library of the British Film Institute and the Open University Library. Many of the ideas explored in this book have taken shape through conversation with friends, colleagues, fellow *Doctor Who* aficionados and casual acquaintances in the Caversham tea room, including, but not limited to, Philip Chaston, John Cook, Nicholas Cull, Steven Gregory, Matthew Hilton, Nathalie Morris, Eric Peterson, Thomas Ribbits, Oliver Redmayne, Jeffrey Richards, Susan Sydney Smith and Michael Williams. A special note of thanks to Steve Tribe for his eagle-eyed copy-editing, and for saving my blushes regarding certain fan myths.

It was my commissioning editor at I.B.Tauris, Philippa Brewster, who suggested I should write this book – an offer I was delighted to accept – and do for 'The Doctor' what I had already done for James Bond (*Licence To Thrill*) and the British adventure series of the 1960s (*Saints and Avengers*). In this sense *Inside the Tardis* completes a triptych of studies of British fantasy-adventure narratives in which I have argued that popular culture can be taken seriously without recourse to the impenetrable critical language of high theory. The Doctor may have conquered Daleks, Cybermen and Ice Warriors, but would he survive an encounter with Foucault, Derrida or Deleuze?

This book will also be the last I write while teaching at The Open University. It seems an appropriate time to acknowledge the role of my colleagues in the History Department in fostering a climate in which I have been able to pursue my own research interests and for tolerating my obsession with secret agents, *Avengers* heroines and Time Lords. For their friendship, as much as for their generous support at the outset of my academic career, I am particularly indebted to Tony Aldgate and Arthur Marwick.

This book is dedicated, with love, to the memory of my grandmother, Priscilla Mary Ruthven (1911–2004).

Preface to the Second Edition

The opportunity to publish a second edition of *Inside the Tardis* is welcome for many reasons – not least of which is that 23 November 2013 marks the fiftieth anniversary of *Doctor Who* and I have been able to bring the history of the series up to date (at least almost up to date – the cut-off point for publication of this edition was the 2012 Christmas special). Moreover, in the seven years since the first edition of this book, the field of *Doctor Who* scholarship has expanded almost as fast as the universe itself following the 'Big Bang'. At the time of writing the first edition of *Inside the Tardis*, the only real academic study of *Doctor Who* – other than a few journal articles here and there – was John Tulloch and Manuel Alvorado's seminal *Doctor Who: The Unfolding Text* (1983). In recent years, however, there have been several additions to the field that have added significantly to our knowledge and understanding of *Doctor Who* and its place in popular culture. If I were to pick out two texts that should be on the shelf of anyone interested in *Doctor Who* they would be David Butler's edited volume *Time and Relative Dissertations in Space: Critical Perspectives on 'Doctor Who'* (2007) – a wide-ranging and eclectic collection focusing mostly on what is now generally known as 'the classic series', but also including the first scholarly work on *Doctor Who* in other media such as continuation novels and audios – and Matt Hills's *Triumph of a Time Lord: Regenerating 'Doctor Who' in the Twenty-First Century* (2010), the first study of the production practices and discourses of 'New *Who*', an equivalent of *The Unfolding Text* for the new series but thankfully without recourse to the same level of theoretical jargon. And honourable mentions must also be afforded to Piers D. Britton's

TARDISbound: Navigating the Universes of 'Doctor Who' (2011), Andrew Ireland's edited collection *Illuminating 'Torchwood'* (2010) – the first study of *Doctor Who*'s 'adult' spin-off – Jim Leach's *Doctor Who* (2009) for the 'TV Milestones' series and Kim Newman's *Doctor Who* (2005) for the BFI 'Television Classics' series. All these offer a great deal of critical insight, and have prompted me to reflect on my own interpretation of *Doctor Who*. And the success of new *Doctor Who* has spawned a mini-industry of *Who*-related fan publishing in both print and online media: the expanded bibliography includes some of the best work in this genre.

For this second edition I have entirely revised Chapter 9 (on the Christopher Eccleston series of 2005, which I wrote more or less concurrently with its original broadcast on BBC1: a degree of critical distance now allows me to appreciate more fully the extent to which its success was no happy accident) and have added four new chapters: one each on the Russell T. Davies/David Tennant and Steven Moffat/Matt Smith 'eras' of *Doctor Who*, and one each on the spin-off series *Torchwood* and *The Sarah Jane Adventures*.

My appreciation of *Doctor Who* deepens all the time through discussion, debate and engagement with other scholars and fans. Thank you to Steven Peacock and Kim Akass for inviting me to deliver the opening keynote of the fiftieth anniversary *Doctor Who* conference 'Walking in Eternity' at the University of Hertfordshire in September 2013. And to the acknowledgements listed in the first edition of *Inside the Tardis*, I should like to add the names of Jonathan Bignell, Victoria Byard, David Ekserdjian, Tobias Hochscherf, Claire Jenkins, James Leggott, Laura Mayne and Andrew Pixley (who reviewed the first edition so kindly in *Doctor Who Magazine*). Splendid fellows – all of them!

Introduction

Let me get this straight. A thing that looks like a police box, standing in a junk-yard, it can move anywhere in time and space?

Ian Chesterton (William Russell) in 'An Unearthly Child'

In a 1999 British Film Institute poll of television critics and professionals, *Doctor Who* was voted the third-best British television programme of all time.[1] While this is testimony to the series' special place in British television history, the fact that *Doctor Who* should be chosen ahead of more ostensibly prestigious fare such as *Boys from the Blackstuff*, *Brideshead Revisited* and *I, Claudius* is also indicative of the growing legitimation of popular culture as a subject worthy of serious attention. *Doctor Who* belongs to the genre of science fiction (SF), which remains largely beyond the pale of critical respectability. Can we really take seriously a series in which a benevolent alien travels around the universe in a space-and-time machine that outwardly resembles an obsolete Prussian blue police telephone box? No less remarkable about the BFI's selection of *Doctor Who* as the third-best series is that at the time of the poll it had not been in regular production for a decade and appeared to all intents and purposes to be consigned forever to that ethereal afterlife of 'classic' television that is the cable channel UKTV Gold. The BBC's announcement in the autumn of 2003 that *Doctor Who* was to return in a new series – and, furthermore, that it would be accorded the level of production resources that it had always deserved but had rarely received – was greeted with much jubilation by the series' legions of fans.

Doctor Who is often described in such terms as the 'longest-running TV SF series' in television history.[2] It may even be the longest-running popular drama series, other than soap operas, ever made. *Doctor Who* was in continuous production at the BBC for some twenty-six years, from 1963 to 1989, running longer than the police series *Dixon of Dock Green* (1955–1976) and the American Western series *Gunsmoke* (1955–1975) – probably its closest two rivals in terms of longevity – and over-taken in recent years only by the comedy series *Last of the Summer Wine* (beginning in 1972), which, however, has been produced in shorter seasons and has notched up barely a third of *Doctor Who*'s 695 episodes. Certainly in comparison to *Star Trek* – which remains the only SF adventure series to rival it in international popularity and the extent of its fan base – *Doctor Who* was both the first and the longest in production.

How can we account for the longevity of *Doctor Who*? To answer this question we need to consider both the series' production strategies and its content. In their cultural studies analysis of the series, *Doctor Who: The Unfolding Text*, John Tulloch and Manuel Alvarado describe *Doctor Who* as 'a text that unfolds according to a wide range of institutional, professional, public, cultural and ideological forces'.[3] These include, but are not limited to, the production practices of the BBC, the competing demands of 'educational' and 'popular' television, the narrative and discursive strategies of the SF genre and the different modes of performance associated with the various 'stars' who have appeared in the series. Tulloch and Alvarado argue that 'in terms of the production context, range of characters and characterisations, generic form, range and size of audience, *Doctor Who* represents a site of endless transformations and complex weavings as well as a programme of increasing institutional stability and public popularity.'[4] Ironically, those words were written just as the popularity of *Doctor Who* began to decline in the mid 1980s. Within a few years, the hostility towards the series of Michael Grade, at the time Controller of BBC1, would reveal a level of institutional *in*stability that Tulloch and Alvarado could not have foreseen. Although, on that occasion, *Doctor Who* was spared extermination, its eventual demise in 1989 – and its successful resurrection in 2005 – are useful reminders that the history of any long-running television series involves not just the internal history of the programme itself but also the external history of the television industry that produces it.

Perhaps the key to the longevity of *Doctor Who* has been its format, which has proved malleable enough to respond flexibly both to changing broadcasting ecologies and to cultural determinants from inside and outside the BBC. *Doctor Who* is – or rather was for most of its history – a hybrid of the episodic series (like the police or Western series) and the continuous serial (like the soap opera) in that it was a series of serials: each production season comprised a number of different individual stories that would run for, typically, four or six weeks. This format allows greater flexibility than either an episodic series (where each episode has to be more or less complete in itself) or a continuous serial (where individual storylines remain subordinate to the overall narrative). *Doctor Who* has thus been able to utilise a wider range of narrative devices and thematic motifs than most other SF adventure series. During its first three production seasons, indeed, *Doctor Who* alternated SF adventures with historical stories. It is not tied to the space opera format of, say, *Star Trek* or *Babylon 5*, or to the existential 'human nature' theme of other time-travel series such as *Quantum Leap*. It is coded neither as 'serious' SF in the tradition of *The Quatermass Experiment* nor as comedy in the manner of *The Hitchhiker's Guide to the Galaxy* or *Red Dwarf*. The fact that *Doctor Who* is able to be all of these things at different moments indicates the flexibility of its format in exploring a wide range of narrative possibilities and genre templates.

The longevity of *Doctor Who* is due in large measure, therefore, to the series' ability to renew and refresh its own format. Nowhere is this more apparent than in the 'regeneration' of the lead character, who is capable, quite literally, of becoming an entirely different person. This was originally a short-term solution to the deteriorating health of the first 'Doctor Who', actor William Hartnell, but it developed into part of the series' mythos and became a strategy for renewal. Each new actor cast as the Doctor has brought a different characterisation and style of performance to the part. Hartnell (1963–1966) had been a grumpy old man whose irritability with his companions was matched only by his insatiable scientific curiosity. His dress suggested a late-Victorian or Edwardian gentleman and his habit of holding his lapels whilst delivering a moralising monologue imbued him with the authority of a schoolmaster. Patrick Troughton (1966–1969), who took over after three years, played the Doctor as a Chaplinesque clown with baggy trousers and a recorder. His three years in the role saw a shift in the series' production strategy towards younger companions and more monster and invasion stories. The next incumbent was Jon Pertwee (1970–1974), whose arrival coincided with the series' shift to colour. His Doctor was a dandy gentleman adventurer in a ruffled shirt and velvet jacket who belonged to the same heroic pedigree as John Steed and Adam Adamant. He spent much of his time marooned on Earth at the behest of his own people, who, it now transpired, were a powerful race known as the Time Lords. The fourth incarnation, Tom Baker (1974–1981), was the most eccentric 'Doctor Who' of all, a bohemian middle-aged student-type whose floppy hat and absurdly long scarf were suggestive of counter-cultural associations. His quirk was to carry a bag of jelly babies that he would offer to bewildered aliens unaccustomed to the delights of British confectionery. The Fifth Doctor, Peter Davison (1981–1984), was a younger, more vulnerable but nobly heroic character whose mode of dress, Edwardian cricket attire, asserted his association with a particular 'heritage' image of Englishness. Doctor No. 6, Colin Baker (1984–1986), brought an edginess to the role that had been absent since Hartnell's time, while the seventh incarnation, Sylvester McCoy (1987–1989, 1996), restored the mystery of the Doctor's origins by suggesting he was a manipulator of events and people for his own ends. The short-lived Eighth Doctor, Paul McGann, who starred in a one-off television film in 1996, was a Romantic hero in the mould of Percy Bysshe Shelley, while the 2005 revival of the series brought us a crop-haired, leather-jacketed Doctor with a northern accent in the person of Christopher Eccleston. At the time of writing Doctor No. 10 has recently been announced as David ('Casanova') Tennant, whose ill-fitting pinstripe suit and loose tie give him a contemporary but casual, rather louche, appearance.[5]

The changing face and characterisation of the Doctor is the most visible sign of the series' strategy of periodic renewal, though there are many others. These include the different 'companions' who travel with him (preferably, though not exclusively, young and female), the occasional revisions to the series' signature music and title sequence and even changes to the interior design of the Doctor's time-and-space machine the TARDIS (though its exterior appearance – the result of a broken 'chameleon circuit' – has remained constant throughout). These changes to the internal history of the series often reflect external factors. The ability of *Doctor Who* to respond to social and cultural change is another explanation for its longevity. In this regard it is difficult to agree with Piers D. Britton and Simon J. Barker, in their otherwise admirable study of design and visual style in British telefantasy, that *Doctor Who* 'largely ignored contemporary social change' or that it 'derived its subtlety in part from being out of touch with the changing realities of life in postcolonial Britain'.[6] Rather, as Nicholas J. Cull has persuasively argued, *Doctor Who* should be seen as a 'text of its time' that 'became an arena for exploring emerging issues in British life between 1963 and 1989'.[7] These issues include, but are not limited to, the decline of British power, the retreat from empire, the rise of technocracy, environmentalism, industrial unrest and changes in the role and status of women in society. To this extent, *Doctor Who* demonstrates the potential of SF for allegory: ostensibly concerned with projecting images of what the future might be like, SF narratives in literature, film and television may also offer commentaries on the present.[8]

The format of *Doctor Who* places it directly in the historical lineage of British literary SF. Indeed, it draws explicitly upon two of the founding texts of the genre. The influence of H.G. Wells's *The Time Machine* (1895) is evident not only in the time-travel premise but also in the series' frequently dystopian vision of the future. Numerous *Doctor Who* serials employ Wells's motif of societies where the moral distinctions between civilisation and savagery (the Eloi and the Morlocks in Wells's novel) are often confused. And the SF template that *Doctor Who* employs most frequently – the invasion narrative – can be traced back directly to Wells's *The War of the Worlds* (1898), in which the Martians first land in Woking. One of the quaint conventions of classic *Doctor Who* is that alien invasions of the Earth invariably centre on London and the Home Counties – though the reason for this probably has more to do with production economies than it does with the strategic significance of south-eastern England. The invasion narrative reflects a contradictory sense of national awareness. On the one hand, it expresses a sense of paranoia and insecurity: the nation is vulnerable to alien (for which read foreign) invasion and proves unable to resist a technologically superior force until it is saved by the advanced scientific knowledge of the Doctor. On the other hand, it also suggests a perverse sense of national self-importance and prestige: as long as alien invaders deem it necessary to take over the British Isles as a prelude to their conquest of the Earth, the illusion of Britain as a great power is maintained. (It is significant in this regard that American adaptations of *The War of the Worlds* for radio, film and television tend to transpose the invasion to the USA.) To this extent, *Doctor Who* is informed by, and draws upon, post-war British anxieties about decline and the nation's place on the world stage.

A criticism that has been made of *Doctor Who* – as it has of popular television drama generally – is that it is conservative in terms of both its aesthetics and its politics. Tulloch and Alvarado suggest that 'one of the major disappointments of the series ... [is that] it ultimately is narratively highly conventional,' while Britton and Barker argue that it 'grew steadily more conservative ... novelty was stifled and fantasy circumscribed.'[9] Neither charge stands up to close scrutiny. First, *Doctor Who* should not be compared to more obviously innovative television drama such as *The Wednesday Play* or the work of writers such as Dennis Potter or Stephen Poliakoff: it is genre fiction and should be compared to other examples of its own kind, in which context it emerges as rather more progressive than its critics have allowed. Second, it needs to be seen historically. The mutability of its form and the narratively bold device of replacing its central character was very far from 'conventional' when *Doctor Who* began in the 1960s and is still an exception rather than the norm, even today. Third, as Britton and Barker themselves demonstrate, *Doctor Who* 'was graced by some of the most inventive scenic and costume design work ever contributed to television or film drama, much of which has never been surpassed'.[10] Two designs in particular – the TARDIS and the Daleks – have been so visually successful that they are indelibly inscribed upon the popular imagination of the British public. The first appearance of the Daleks was voted one of television's greatest moments by Channel 4 viewers and the Daleks themselves have become, in one recent commentator's apt phrase, 'the godfathers of British robotic villainy'.[11]

The charge that *Doctor Who* is conservative, even reactionary, in its social politics is perhaps best exemplified in its representation of women. The gender politics of *Doctor Who* demonstrate both the potential and the limitations of popular culture as a vehicle for responding to social change. There has always been a perception that the Doctor's female companions, like James Bond's women, have been cast largely for their sex appeal. The production discourse of *Doctor Who* – as exemplified in interviews and writings by those involved in making it – repeatedly asserts that the role of the female companion in *Doctor Who* is twofold: she is there to provide 'something for the dads' (hence the necessity that all space-and-time travelling heroines should wear revealing clothes) and she is there to act as a 'lady-in-jeopardy' who is menaced by the monster. Several *Who* companions, indeed, have since claimed that their auditions involved showing how well they could scream.[12] To be fair to *Doctor Who*, the series has made repeated attempts to challenge this stereotype: one of the very first companions was a woman schoolteacher who was not easily frightened and represented a challenge to the Doctor's (male) authority, while later TARDIS crewmembers included two 'brainy' scientists, an investigative journalist, a pre-*Xena* Amazonian warrior, two incarnations of an intellectually superior Time Lady, a 'pushy' Australian air stewardess and a streetwise teenager. For all these valiant attempts to offer more positive female roles, however, most companions eventually slipped back into the traditional mould of 'screamers'. Ultimately, perhaps, this is a function of form in a series where much of the drama arises from the companion getting into jeopardy. It also reflects the (perceived) interests of its (male) viewers. As one critic put it: 'The real fans of *Dr Who* are not children at all. They are middle-aged men who enjoy watching half-naked girls being chased by space monsters.'[13]

As for the charge that *Doctor Who* is politically conservative, this merely recalls the discredited critique of popular culture by the Frankfurt School and their disciples who aver that all popular culture is reactionary because it encourages standardisation, uniformity and conformity. The cultural politics and narrative ideologies of *Doctor Who*, however, serve to encourage difference and non-conformity. This is evident not only in the characterisation of the Doctor himself as an eccentric and a social outsider, but also in his companions who embrace class and regional (and finally, in the 1996 film, ethnic) diversity. The entire series, moreover, is imbued with an unmistakably liberal ethos. The Doctor stands for the values of liberty, freedom, equality, justice and tolerance; he is implacably opposed to totalitarianism, slavery, inequality, injustice and prejudice. This reading, certainly, informs the critical response to *Doctor Who*: after the series' tenth anniversary, for example, one commentator remarked that the Doctor had spent the last ten years 'battling against interplanetary power maniacs and upholding decent liberal values throughout the universe'.[14]

We might just as easily substitute 'liberal' with 'British', for another characteristic of *Doctor Who* is its distinctively British flavour. *Doctor*

Who asserts its Britishness through a range of cultural associations and archetypes. It is surely no accident, for example, that this Time Lord's beverage of choice is a cup of tea or that he should demonstrate his prowess on the cricket field as a 'first-class bat and a demon bowler'. In his various incarnations, the Doctor assumes character traits reminiscent of Sherlock Holmes, Professor Quatermass and James Bond. The series is replete with visual signifiers of Britishness: the TARDIS exterior, for example, which remained consistent long after the police telephone box had been phased out, might be seen as 'a metaphor for the persistence of mid-twentieth-century British-ness within the series'.[15] The exterior locations are mostly British (despite occasional excursions to Paris, Amsterdam, Lanzarote, Seville and San Francisco) and, while many alien landscapes conveniently resemble a quarry or sand pit, the series has also pulled off powerful and culturally resonant images of alien creatures against the backdrop of famous landmarks: Daleks gliding over Westminster Bridge and Cybermen on the steps of St Paul's Cathedral.

This emphasis on the Britishness of *Doctor Who* is perhaps only to be expected given its parentage although, in an increasingly globalised and transnational television culture where modern production trends seek to emulate the glossy visual style and slick professionalism of US television series, *Doctor Who*'s insistence upon an almost parochial sense of Britishness is unusual. The difference in production values between *Doctor Who* and rival American television and film SF such as *Star Trek* or *Star Wars* further invokes an idea of Britishness: the notion that small is beautiful and that British ingenuity is superior to American technological hardware. *Doctor Who*, the argument goes, is about ideas rather than action and its strength lies in its scripts rather than its special effects. The popular discourse of *Doctor Who* – that reflected in the fan literature – makes a virtue out of its Heath Robinson production values. One of the criticisms made of the 1996 television film, for example, was that its slick visual effects seemed 'unBritish' in comparison to the fondly remembered wobbly sets and rubber monsters of yore. In fact the set design and visual effects of *Doctor Who* were state-of-the-art for what could be accomplished on video (rather than on film) during the 1960s and 1970s, and it was only in the age of what John Thornton Caldwell has since called 'televisuality' – where technological advances made possible a more sophisticated visual representation of SF fantasy on television, which can be dated quite specifically to the mid 1980s

– that *Doctor Who* began to look inferior in comparison.[16] A view has always persisted, however, that the Doctor is somehow, as A.A. Gill put it, 'a Bakelite and Spam spaceman'.[17]

There is, of course, an extensive popular historiography of *Doctor Who*. In addition to the many books devoted to the *Doctor Who* phenomenon, the series has sustained its own dedicated magazine since 1979 (originally *Doctor Who Weekly*, now *Doctor Who Magazine*), while its production history has been documented in an on-going sequence of 'making of' publications (*In Vision*). This book is not, therefore, yet another internal history of *Doctor Who*, recounting the Doctor's many adventures and listing all his foes and companions. It is, rather, a cultural history of *Doctor Who* that places the series in several different contexts. It really comprises three separate, though overlapping, histories: the institutional history of the BBC throughout the period that the series has been in production; a critical history of British science fiction over the same period; and a wider social history of how *Doctor Who* has been informed by and responded to developments in British society and culture since 1963.

This is the first history of *Doctor Who* to draw extensively upon the full riches of the BBC Written Archives (Tulloch and Alvarado's 1983 book, in contrast, was based largely on interviews with production personnel). The production and correspondence files reveal how the series was conceived, its uncertain and ad hoc origins, the vicissitudes of its production and the various tensions that arose between the production team, the senior management of the BBC and external pressure groups such the National Viewers' and Listeners' Association. Particularly valuable is the evidence of the series' popular reception, which takes two forms. There is the quantitative evidence of the BBC's 'viewing barometers', which express the size of the audience as a percentage of the estimated total United Kingdom audience excluding children under five. (In 1981 the BBC and the independent television companies jointly set up BARB – the Broadcasters' Audience Research Board – which has become the industry's standard for monitoring the size and demographic make-up of its audiences.)[18] Perhaps more revealing of popular attitudes towards the series, however, is the qualitative evidence of its reception. This is to be found both in the BBC's own surveys of its volunteer viewing panels from which a 'reaction index' is calculated (surprisingly, *Doctor Who* rarely scored as highly as one might have expected for such a long-running series) and in unsolicited letters from children (and from some older viewers) describing their responses to particular episodes. At the time of conducting my research, however, the BBC Written Archives were open only until the end of the 1970s, and for the later chapters, therefore, I have been dependent upon published sources. Thus the 'inside story' of the troubled 1980s and the events that led first to the series' suspension and then to its cancellation – at least as far as the internal paper trails are concerned – remains, for the time being, secret knowledge concealed within the legendary Black Scrolls of Rassilon.

The book is written chronologically, so as to demonstrate how *Doctor Who* has changed over time, though I have not divided the series' history into artificial 'eras' defined by the personality of the incumbent Doctor. While the character and performance style of each 'star' has done much to influence the nature of the series, the role of key production personnel, particularly the producer and script editor, is even more significant in shaping the content of the series. For example, it was the series' first producer, Verity Lambert, who oversaw the original blend of historical and science fiction stories – something to which William Hartnell's didactic authority was eminently suited – and the third producer, Innes Lloyd, who steered *Doctor Who* decisively towards the monster and invasion narratives that predominated from the autumn of 1966. Sometimes the 'era' of a particular Doctor coincides with a production regime: during Jon Pertwee's five years, for example, the same producer (Barry Letts) and script editor (Terrance Dicks) remained at the helm throughout. Tom Baker's seven-year stint, by contrast, included three distinct production regimes: the Philip Hinchcliffe-Robert Holmes 'Gothic' period, the 'camp' period of Graham Williams, and the beginning of John Nathan-Turner's long period in charge of the series throughout the 1980s. The twenty-first-century revival of the series clearly carries the imprint of executive producer and writer-in-chief Russell T. Davies, whose creative control over the series has been exerted to a much greater extent than any of his predecessors.

At the same time as approaching *Doctor Who* from the perspective of a professional historian, however, I am also writing this book as a fan. Like so many British children of the 1970s, some of my earliest memories revolve around watching *Doctor Who* in a state of nervous anticipation, not least insisting that my father should be there to hold his hand over my eyes when the monster appeared. I still remember the psychological effect exerted by the music and opening titles in rooting me to the sofa. For the record my clear memory of *Who* begins with 'The Time Warrior' – the first adventure of the last Jon Pertwee season. (This may also help to explain why Elisabeth Sladen was the object of my first-ever boyhood crush: there is still something very sexy about the way she pronounces 'Doc-tor'.) My hope in writing this book is that readers may rekindle their own passion for *Doctor Who*, whilst at the same time appreciating the series not just as the continuing saga of a mysterious Time Lord and his many adventures in time and space, but also as a reflection of some of the issues that have affected British television and society over the five decades during which 'The Doctor' has been a part of British cultural life.

1

A Space-Age Old Curiosity Shop

1963–1966

Have you ever thought what it's like to be wanderers in the fourth dimension?
Have you? To be exiles... Susan and I are cut off from our own planet, without
friends or protection. But one day we shall get back. Yes, one day, one day...

The Doctor (William Hartnell) in 'An Unearthly Child'

The origins of *Doctor Who* have become the subject of almost as many
different narratives as the mythology of the Time Lords or the history of
the Daleks. It has been claimed, variously, that 'the late Sydney Newman
effectively invented *Doctor Who*' and that it was devised 'not by any
one person, but by the collaboration of several'; that it was conceived
as a short-term solution to a gap in the television schedules and that it
was part of a long-term BBC strategy of 'populism' in the corporation's
battle for ratings against its commercial rival ITV; that it was intended
primarily as an educational series 'for children' and that it 'was never
designed to be just a children's programme but was intended to cater for
a broad audience'; that it was never intended as 'hard' science fiction but
that '[from] the start it appealed to considerable sections of the science
fiction reading public'.[1] To sift through these different narratives and to
establish the institutional and cultural contexts in which *Doctor Who*
was created, we have recourse to the BBC Written Archives, where the
evidence contained in copious memoranda and discussion documents
reveals a history more complex than even the Laws of Time.

Like any television series, *Doctor Who* was the product of a particular
set of historical circumstances and determinants. It appeared at a critical

moment in the history of British broadcasting precisely when television was establishing itself as the dominant mass medium. Television broadcasting, which had begun in the late 1930s but had been suspended upon the outbreak of the Second World War, had resumed in 1946, but for a decade or so thereafter it had remained, at best, a poor third to radio and cinema in both its cultural respectability and its mass appeal. In 1955, for example, the year in which the independent television network was launched, there were still over twice as many radio licences issued (9.5 million) as there were combined 'sound and vision' licences (4.5 million). It was not until the late 1950s that television surpassed radio as the pre-eminent broadcasting medium: 1958 was the first year in which the number of combined licences (8.1 million) exceeded radio licences (6.5 million). Thereafter the expansion of television was rapid: by 1963, the year in which *Doctor Who* was first broadcast, there were four times as many combined licences (12.4 million) as there were radio licences (3.3 million).[2] As television surpassed radio, so, too, it overtook cinema. The decline of cinema attendances in Britain from their peak in the mid 1940s correlates with the increase in the issue of television licences. There was a slow decline in the number of annual paid cinema admissions throughout the late 1940s and early 1950s – 1.6 million in 1945, 1.5 million in 1950, 1.2 million in 1955 – but a precipitous decline in the late 1950s and early 1960s during which over half the cinema audience disappeared. Thus in 1960 there were only 500,000 annual admissions and in 1963 only 357,000.[3]

While the early 1960s marked a watershed in the relationship between television and other mass media, moreover, this was also an important period for the structure and cultural politics of the television industry itself. The advent of ITV in 1955 marked the end of the BBC's monopoly and the beginning of the era of competition. The differences between the two rivals have generally, if rather too simplistically, been categorised as, on the one hand, the ethos of 'public service broadcasting' (represented by the BBC) and, on the other, an ideology of 'populism' (exemplified by ITV). In fact ITV also had a public service remit, while the BBC had always been alert to the desirability of providing audiences with popular light entertainment alongside its more serious fare. The youth-oriented pop music revue *Juke Box Jury*, for example, was the BBC's highest-rated series of the early 1960s. It was ITV, however, which by the early 1960s was winning the battle for ratings when it had a lead of roughly two-to-one over the BBC in terms of their share of the viewing public.[4]

In this context *Doctor Who* needs to be understood as part of the BBC's campaign to claw back its diminishing audience share through the commissioning of different programme forms and genres. A major aspect of this campaign was the shift in television drama output, hitherto dominated by the single play, towards the episodic series. The single play did not disappear – many would argue, indeed, that it enjoyed its heyday with *The Wednesday Play*, which began in 1964 – but the episodic series became more prominent in the BBC schedules. It was exemplified in the early 1960s by *Maigret* (based on Georges Simenon's novellas and a rare example of a BBC drama series produced on film rather than videotape), *Z Cars* (police series) and *Dr Finlay's Casebook* (medical drama). A symptom, rather than a cause, of this shift in policy was the resignation in 1962 of Michael Barry, the Head of Television Drama since 1950, and his replacement by Sydney Newman.

Newman, arguably, is the most important single figure in the history of the golden age of television drama in Britain.[5] A Canadian, Newman had worked under John Grierson at the National Film Board of Canada during the 1940s before moving into television in the 1950s. In 1958 he joined the British independent television company ABC and took over as producer of its *Armchair Theatre*, a strand of single plays broadcast on Sunday evenings that was one of ITV's top-rated programmes, acclaimed for providing serious drama with popular appeal and influenced to some extent by the realist theatre of the 1950s and the vogue for 'kitchen sink' films in the early 1960s. It was Newman whom BBC Director-General Hugh Carleton Greene 'poached' to replace Barry in 1962, though due to ABC's insistence that he serve out the full term of his contract it was not until April 1963 that Newman formally took up his appointment as Head of Drama Group (Television) at the BBC. The Drama Group was reorganised into three units – Series, Serials and Single Plays – each with its own head, responsible in the first instance to Newman, and then up the chain of command to Donald Baverstock (Controller of Programmes BBC1) and Kenneth Adam (Controller of Television). *Doctor Who* happened to be the first major new series launched following the reorganisation of the Drama Group. Before its first episode, the trade paper *Kine Weekly* predicted that 'the BBC Drama Group should be making its first major ratings breakthrough against ITV'.[6]

As Head of Drama Group, it was Newman who actually commissioned *Doctor Who*, though the initiative to develop a science fiction serial pre-dated his arrival at the BBC. It was early in 1962, a whole year before Newman took up his post, that Eric Maschwitz, the Head of Television Light Entertainment, instructed the Script Department 'to survey the field of published science fiction, in its relevance to BBC Television Drama'. Maschwitz himself played no further part in the process, though he may be credited with originating the initiative that ultimately led to *Doctor Who*. The resulting report, by two staff writers, Donald Bull and Alice Frick, was described by Donald Baverstock as 'exactly the kind of hard thinking over a whole vein of dramatic material that is most useful to us'.[7] They surveyed the field of recent SF literature and consulted Brian Aldiss, honorary secretary of the British Science Fiction Association. Bull and Frick reported that 'SF is overwhelmingly American in bulk' and that, if they were looking for British writers to adapt, 'our field is exceptionally narrow'. Their views on individual SF writers were nothing if not opinionated: C.S. Lewis was dismissed as 'clumsy and old-fashioned in his use of the SF apparatus', Arthur C. Clarke was 'a modest writer, with a decent feeling for his characters, able to concoct a good story, and a master of the ironmongery department', while John Wyndham was the 'best practitioner' of what they termed the 'Threat and Disaster' school. Interestingly, given the sort of series that *Doctor Who* would become, Bull and Frick were dismissive of Charles Eric Maine, who 'is too much a fantasist: he is obsessed with the Time theme, time-travel, fourth dimensions and so on – and we consider this indigestible stuff for the audience.' The report concluded that 'the vast bulk of SF literature is by nature unsuitable for translation to TV' and recommended that 'television science fiction drama must be written not by SF writers, but by TV dramatists ... There is a wide gulf between SF as it exists, and the present tastes and needs of the TV audience, and this can only be bridged by writers deeply immersed in the TV discipline.'[8]

This verdict was based on the fact that the most notable British attempts at the genre for television had been in the form of serials by television dramatists rather than SF authors. Nigel Kneale, a young BBC staff writer, had written the three successful *Quatermass* serials of the 1950s. The *Quatermass* serials demonstrated the potential of SF for dealing with wider social, political and moral issues and demonstrated that, conceived with due regard for the aesthetic possibilities as well as the technical limitations of live television, SF could win both popular and critical acclaim. Set in a Britain of the near-future, the serials exemplified many of the tropes of contemporary SF, including 'first contact' with an alien life form (*The Quatermass Experiment*, 1953), the infiltration and invasion narrative (*Quatermass II*, 1955) and a socio-political allegory of racial hatred and social disintegration (*Quatermass and the Pit*, 1958–1959).[9] The BBC's next serious attempt at the genre was *A for Andromeda* (1961), written jointly by Cambridge astronomer Fred Hoyle and television dramatist John Elliott. This serial and its sequel, *The Andromeda Breakthrough* (1962), were based on the premise of a super-computer that takes over the body of a laboratory assistant (played in the first serial by Julie Christie and in the sequel by Susan Hampshire) and explored the 'hard SF' themes of technological advancement and artificial intelligence.[10] Bull and Frick observed that both *Quatermass* and *Andromeda*

> belong to the Threat and Disaster school, the type of plot in which the whole of mankind is threatened, usually from an 'alien' source ... Apart from the instinctive pull of such themes, the obvious appeal of these TV SF essays lies in the ironmongery – the apparatus, the magic – and in the excitement of the unexpected.

The principal difficulty of adapting science fiction for television has always been that, in its literary form, SF is more about ideas than drama. Bull and Frick remarked: 'Audiences – we think – are not as yet interested in the mere exploitation of ideas – the "idea as hero" aspect of SF. They must have something to latch on to. The apparatus must be attached to the current human situation, and identification must be offered with recognisable human beings.' This problem was demonstrated by ABC's *Out of This World*, a thirteen-part anthology series produced in 1962 by Irene Shubik, which included adaptations of classic SF stories including John Wyndham's 'Dumb Martian', Isaac Asimov's 'Little Lost Robot', Rog Phillips's 'The Yellow Pill' and Philip K. Dick's 'The Impostor' (the latter adapted by future *Doctor Who* writer Terry Nation). *Out of This World* is a series whose reputation has grown in hindsight, though at the time little faith was placed in it by ABC, which, feeling that the plays were not strong enough in their own right, recruited Boris Karloff to introduce them.

Despite the acknowledged problems of television science fiction, however, there was evidently sufficient support within the BBC for the idea to be given further consideration. To this end, another report was commissioned, this time from Frick and another staff writer, John Braybon. Braybon and Frick read 'some hundreds of science fiction stories' and in July 1962 they produced a shortlist of five novels that were deemed 'potentially suitable for adaptation to television'. The criteria for selection were that '[they] do not include Bug-Eyed Monsters' (demonstrating that this phrase, often attributed to Newman, had been coined well before his arrival at the corporation), that '[the] central characters are never Tin Robots', and that they 'do not require large and elaborate science fiction type settings'. Braybon and Frick felt that a combination of these elements had 'already resulted in a failure in the current ITV series'. They provided synopses of the five novels: *Guardians of Time* by Poul Anderson, which posited the notion of a futuristic Time Patrol 'set up to stop anyone from tampering with the past'; *Three to Conquer* by Eric Frank Russell, about a telepath who detects an alien invasion ('Written with a fair degree of humour and not, for once, populated by bad-tempered scientists and inefficient politicians'); *Eternity Lost* by Clifford Simak, posited on the notion of a futuristic World House of Representatives whose members are entitled to stand election for eternal life; *Pictures Don't Lie* by Catherine Maclean, about a friendly alien species who land on the Earth but are nearly killed when their microscopic spaceship sinks in a puddle on the tarmac; and *No Woman Born* by C.L. Moore about a robot with a human brain ('an exception to our rule about robots'). Braybon and Frick felt that *Three to Conquer* and *Guardians of Time* offered the best opportunities for adaptation. 'This latter one is particularly attractive as a series,' they suggested, 'since individual plots can easily be tackled by a variety of script-writers; it's the *Z Cars* of science fiction.'[11] *Guardians of Time* was not the blueprint for *Doctor Who*, but it would seem to have planted the idea of a time-travel theme, something about which the earlier report had been rather dismissive.

As it happened, the idea for a science fiction series then stalled for several months. It was resurrected in March 1963 when Donald Wilson, Head of Serials, convened a meeting between Braybon, Frick and writer Cecil 'Bunny' Webber to devise 'a "loyalty programme"', lasting at least 52 weeks, consisting of various dramatised SF stories, linked to form a continuous serial, using basically a few characters who continue through all the stories'. The concept of a 'loyalty programme' was that it 'must attract and hold the audience'. In this particular case the series was designed to bridge a gap in the late Saturday afternoon schedule between the sports magazine programme *Grandstand*, which ended at 5.15 pm, and *Juke Box Jury*, which began at around six o'clock. The first consideration was to devise 'suitable characters for the five o'clock Saturday audience'. Much consideration was given to the age and gender profile of the likely audience:

> Child characters do not command the interest of children older than themselves. Young heroines do not command the interest of boys. Young heroes do command the interest of girls. Therefore, the highest coverage amongst children and teenagers is got by:- THE HANDSOME YOUNG MAN HERO (First character). A young heroine does not command the full interest of older women; our young hero has already got the boys and girls; therefore we can consider the older woman by providing:- THE HANDSOME WELL-DRESSED HEROINE AGED ABOUT 30 (Second character). Men are believed to form an important part of the 5 o'clock Saturday (post-*Grandstand*) audience. They will be interested in the young hero; and to catch them firmly we should add:- THE MATURER MAN, 35–40, WITH SOME 'CHARACTER' TWIST. Nowadays, to satisfy grown women, Father-Figures are introduced into loyalty programmes at such a rate that TV begins to look like an Old People's Home: let us introduce them ad hoc, as our stories call for them. We shall have no child protagonists, but child characters may be introduced ad hoc, because story requires it, not to interest children.[12]

This highly schematic breakdown of 'loyalty' characters is a revealing insight into the BBC's assumptions about the interests and tastes of its viewers. As for the format of the programme, it was Wilson who suggested the idea of a machine 'not only for going forward and backward in time, but into space'. Frick's suggestion of a flying saucer was ruled out as 'not based in reality – or too Sunday press'. Braybon suggested that the series should be set in the future 'and that a good device would be a world body of scientific trouble-shooters, established to keep scientific experiments under control for political or humanistic reasons'. This idea was rejected, though it would later resurface in *Doomwatch* (1970–1972). Webber put forward 'the idea that great scientists of the past might continue in some form of existence and could be contacted to discover further advances they had made'. This, too, was turned down.[13]

The shape of the series emerged from several meetings and discussions in the early spring of 1963. There were to be four characters: a 'with-it girl of 15' called Bridget or Biddy and a schoolteacher called Lola McGovern were to be the 'loyalty' characters for female viewers, while for male viewers there was another teacher, Cliff. Schoolmasters across the country would no doubt have been delighted to hear they would be represented by a character described as 'physically perfect, strong and courageous, a gorgeous dish'. The last principal character was a mysterious figure known as 'Doctor Who':

> A frail old man lost in space and time. They give him this name because they don't know who he is. He seems not to remember where he has come from; he is suspicious and capable of sudden malignance; he seems to have some unidentified enemy; he is searching for something as well as fleeing from something. He has a 'machine' which enables them to travel together through time, through space, and through matter.[14]

The mystery of 'Doctor Who' was such that the writers themselves could not decide who he was or where he came from. One suggestion was that he came from the future in a stolen time machine and 'is thus an extension of the scientist who has opted out' ('Don't like this,' someone, probably Newman, has written in the margin); another was that he was pursued by the authorities of his own time who 'are seriously concerned to prevent his monkeying with time, because his secret intention, when he finds his ideal past, is to destroy or nullify the future' (the marginal comment here is 'nuts!'). While the character of 'Doctor Who' still had to be refined, the other ingredients of the format – his 'unreliable' and 'faulty' time-and-space travel machine and his three travelling companions – had now taken firm shape.

Moreover, it was agreed that the series, now entitled *Doctor Who*, was to have an educational as well as simply an entertainment remit. One discussion document states:

> The series is neither fantasy nor space travel nor science fiction. The basic premise is that four characters are projected into real environments based

> on the best factual information of situations in time and space and in any material state we can realise in practical terms. Using unusual, exciting backgrounds or ordinary backgrounds seen unusually, each story will have a strong informational core based on fact.[15]

To this extent the two schoolteachers became a history teacher (now called Barbara Wright) and a science teacher (Ian Chesterton) to enable them to explain the different environments in which they found themselves. A theme that persisted from *Guardians of Time* was that, if the characters travelled back to periods of the Earth's past, they were not allowed to tinker with history: 'It is also emphasised that the four characters cannot make history. Advice must not be proffered to Nelson on his battle tactics when approaching the Nile nor must bon mots be put into the mouth of Oscar Wilde.' As we will see, this rule against interfering with the past was to be honoured more in the breach than in the observance.

By April 1963 it had been agreed that the new serial would run for 52 weeks, starting on 27 July, and that it would be budgeted at £2,300 per episode with an additional £500 for building a space/time machine that would be used throughout all the episodes.[16] At this stage there is still no evidence that Newman himself was closely involved in the development of the series. He participated in discussions with Wilson and Webber in May 1963, but his first significant intervention came in a memorandum of 10 June when he rejected their proposal for the first story, entitled 'The Giants', in which the four travellers would be accidentally miniaturised: he found the four-episode story 'extremely thin on incident and character' and felt that it was 'hardly practical for live television'.[17] An issue that was to dog *Doctor Who* throughout its twenty-six years of regular transmission on the BBC was already becoming apparent: that the budget allocated was inadequate to meet its needs for sets and special effects. Wilson chafed at having to work within the 'normal Saturday afternoon series level', though he felt, nevertheless, that 'what we have here is something very much better both in content and production value than we could normally expect for this kind of money and effort'.[18]

There is evidence, even at this early stage, of much unease about *Doctor Who* within the BBC. The launch of the series was delayed several times – in the event the first episode was not transmitted until 23 No-

vember – due to a series of disputes over resources and scripts that Newman, in one memorandum, referred to as the 'Dr Who hassle'. There
was a body of opinion within the technical departments of the BBC
that the proposed series was far too ambitious for the corporation. The
Head of Television Design complained that 'to embark on a series of
this kind and length in these circumstances will undoubtedly put this
Department in an untenable situation and, as a natural corollary, will
throw Scenic Servicing Department for a complete "burton". This is the
kind of crazy enterprise which both Departments can well do without.'[19]
The Scenic Servicing Department similarly urged that 'you should think
twice before proceeding with a weekly series of this nature.'[20] Newman
professed himself 'absolutely flabbergasted' when told by Joanna Spicer,
the Assistant Controller of Television, that *Doctor Who* had not gone
through the proper approvals process.[21] An indication of the low cultural value attached to *Doctor Who* was that, for a programme requiring the
extensive use of visual effects, it was allocated initially to the notoriously
poorly equipped Studio D at Lime Grove (bought by the BBC from the
Rank Organisation in 1949). Story editor David Whitaker pleaded for
the 'eventual transfer from "D" to a studio capable of handling the visual
effects which are, after all, an integral part of this project'.[22] The shortcomings of the studio pushed up the budget, which by the autumn of
1963 had risen to £4,000 per episode. This almost resulted in the abor-
tion of the series. 'Such a costly serial is not one that I can afford space
for in this financial year,' Donald Baverstock told Wilson. 'You should
not therefore proceed any further with the production of more than 4
episodes.'[23] Further evidence that Baverstock himself was not favourably
disposed towards the series is revealed in a memorandum from Wilson
two weeks before the first episode was broadcast in which he professed
himself 'unhappy' when told 'that the proposal to give "Dr Who" the
front page of the "Radio Times" had now been abandoned. It was particularly distressing to hear that one reason given was lack of confidence
in the programme at Controller level.'[24] It would not be the last time that
Doctor Who came under threat from a Controller of BBC1.

The various problems that beset *Doctor Who* during its pre-production
period were in large measure due to the fact that nothing quite like it
had been attempted before. Unlike the *Quatermass* and *Andromeda*
serials, which ran for only six or seven weeks, *Doctor Who* was planned
to run throughout the year. David Whitaker, in line with directives from

both Wilson and Newman, intended that the series would alternate both historical and futuristic stories. On 31 July he reported that '[a] pattern is beginning to emerge for this series of serials' and averred that his aim was 'to avoid possible future duplication of periods of history or environments by Saturday evening films, US or foreign television shows and so on, securing for *Doctor Who* an additional strength in its constantly varying locales, costume and motivations'.[25] The content of the first season, however, did not take shape until very late in the day, with two of the scripted serials abandoned and a two-episode 'filler' story concocted in response to the second serial going over budget.[26]

The appointment of Verity Lambert as producer of *Doctor Who* – at the time the only female television drama producer at the BBC – has sometimes been claimed as a progressive move by Newman to promote the place of women within the corporation. Equally, it may be that the appointment of a relatively inexperienced new producer – Lambert had worked for a short while in New York and had been a production assistant at ABC when Newman headed the Drama Department there – might be taken as a sign that *Doctor Who* was not regarded as being particularly important. Whatever the reason for her appointment, however, it is clear that Lambert had definite ideas about the sort of programme that *Doctor Who* should be. She was adamant that it was not just a children's programme:

> I have strong views on the level of intelligence we should be aiming at ... *Dr Who* goes out at a time when there is a large child audience but it is intended more as a story for the whole family. And anyway children today are very sophisticated and I don't allow scripts which seem to talk down to them.[27]

There is good reason to believe, notwithstanding the collaborative nature of television production, that Lambert had a decisive influence on the early history of *Doctor Who*.

It was Lambert, for example, who cast William Hartnell in the title role, which did much to set the tone of *Doctor Who*. Hartnell was a veteran character actor of British stage and screen who hitherto had usually been cast either as nasty underworld types (memorably so as Pinkie Brown's henchman Dallow in *Brighton Rock*) or as tough, no-nonsense NCOs (*The Way Ahead*, *Yangtze Incident*, *Private's Progress*,

Carry On Sergeant). He was already familiar to television audiences as Sergeant-Major Bullimore in Granada's *The Army Game* (1957–1961). Hartnell played the Doctor as a curmudgeonly, cantankerous eccentric, impatient and prone to fits of temper but also possessing a mischievous and impish sense of humour. Hartnell was 55 when he began playing the Doctor, but his Edwardian-styled costume and his highly mannered, absent-minded style of acting (due, in some measure, to his difficulty in remembering his lines), along with a long white wig, made him appear older. It was due in large measure to Hartnell's central performance that *Doctor Who* would appeal to viewers of different ages: while, for young children, he became an idealised 'grandfather' figure, he also appealed to adolescents as a defiantly anti-establishment character. The second male lead, Ian Chesterton, went to actor William Russell, who had a suitably heroic pedigree from having starred in the ATV swashbuckling series *The Adventures of Sir Lancelot* (1956–1957). A running joke of early episodes of *Doctor Who* – that the Doctor kept forgetting Chesterton's surname and would refer to him as 'Chesterfield', 'Chesterman' and other variations – was incorporated from rehearsals when Hartnell could never pronounce the name correctly.

While the Doctor and Chesterton provided identification figures for male viewers, the two female companions represented contrasting types of femininity. Barbara Wright (played by Jacqueline Hill) is very much the 'mature' woman envisaged by the original breakdown of loyalty characters: sensible, level-headed and practical. Barbara describes herself as 'a very unwilling adventurer' and clashes with the Doctor over his inability to return her home. Barbara's assertiveness represents a challenge to the authority of the Doctor, who, initially at least, seems something of an elderly misogynist. In contrast, Susan (Carole Ann Ford) – now referred to as the Doctor's 'granddaughter' in order to alleviate any concerns viewers might have entertained about the propriety of their relationship – is the 'immature' female prone to getting into trouble. Susan is a precocious teenager intended as a point of identification for girls of a similar age (she is introduced listening to pop music on a transistor radio), though her advanced scientific knowledge also marks her difference from her contemporaries. The case of Susan provides the first example of the limitations on characterisation imposed by the *Doctor Who* formula: she was required to fulfil the role of 'screamer' and often had little to do beyond looking pretty and frightened. Ford became the first *Doctor Who* 'regular' to leave the series, after 51 episodes, complaining that her character had not been allowed to develop.

The first episode of *Doctor Who*, 'An Unearthly Child', established the characters and their relationships to each other. The two schoolteachers are curious about one of their pupils at Coal Hill School: Susan Foreman is exceptionally knowledgeable about science but seems ignorant of everyday matters such as how many shillings there are to a pound ('She said she thought we were on the decimal system'). The teachers follow Susan home, which appears to be in a junkyard, where they observe a mysterious old man about to enter a police box from inside which they hear Susan's voice. Believing the old man to have imprisoned his granddaughter in the police box, the two force their way inside, only to discover that it contains a technologically highly advanced control console and, moreover, appears bigger on the inside than on the outside. Susan explains that the police box is in fact a space/time machine known as TARDIS ('I made [it] up from the initials: Time And Relative Dimension In Space'). The Doctor reveals that he and Susan are 'wanderers in the fourth dimension' and have become 'exiles … cut off from our own planet without friends or protection'. As the Doctor and Susan debate whether Ian and Barbara will reveal their secret to the world, Ian looks for the switch to open the doors but receives an electric shock. The TARDIS is set in motion when Susan tries to prevent the Doctor from operating the controls and its occupants are temporarily disoriented. The last shot is an exterior of the police box perched in a barren, inhospitable landscape as a menacing shadow falls across it.

There were, in fact, two versions of 'An Unearthly Child'. The first, recorded on 27 September, was not used. It was not unknown for two versions of a pilot episode to be shot and even before the first recording Lambert had indicated that it 'may be re-recorded at a later date'.[28] The second version was recorded on 18 October. There are several subtle, but important, differences between the two versions, especially regarding the characterisations of Susan and the Doctor. The first version implies that they come from the distant future ('I was born in the forty-ninth century,' Susan remarks) and includes a slightly different explanation of the origins of the mysterious pair ('We are not of this race, we are not of this Earth. We are wanderers in the fourth dimensions of space and time, cut of from our own planet and our own people by aeons and universes far beyond the reach of your most advanced sciences').

The most significant difference, however, is the characterisation of the Doctor himself. In the first version he is much more abrasive, turning angrily on Susan for allowing herself to be followed home. In this version the Doctor deliberately electrocutes Ian when the latter tries to interfere with the control panel and the TARDIS is set in motion following a physical struggle between Ian and the Doctor. David Whitaker felt that the characterisation of the Doctor was too aggressive and that 'he should be more like the old Professor that Frank Morgan played in *The Wizard of Oz*, only a little more authentic'.[29] In the second version, therefore, Hartnell portrays a rather less abrasive version of the Doctor, who is more amused than angered by the intrusion of the two teachers. He is much warmer towards Susan (calling her 'My dear child' rather than 'You stupid child'), he does not deliberately electrocute Ian and there is no physical struggle between them.

The second version of 'An Unearthly Child' was broadcast at 5.15 pm on Saturday 23 November. It was an inauspicious start: the assassination of US President John F. Kennedy the previous day inevitably overshadowed the launch of a new television drama series. Public reaction was muted. There were short, though favourable, notices in the *Daily Mail* ('must have delighted the hearts of the *Telegoons* who followed') and, of all places, the *Daily Worker* ('a very satisfying "cliff-hanger"').[30] The first episode was watched by an estimated 9.1 per cent of the viewing audience, or approximately 4.4 million viewers. The BBC's Audience Research Department calculated that it achieved a higher-than-average reaction index of 63 (though this declined over later episodes) and found that viewers were favourably disposed towards it overall. One respondent described it as 'a cross between [H.G.] Wells's *The Time Machine* and a space-age *Old Curiosity Shop*'. The viewing sample particularly praised the use of visual and sound effects in helping to create an 'out of this world atmosphere'.[31] The sound effects, including the eerie theme music and the 'wheezing' dematerialisation noise of the TARDIS, were created by the BBC's Radiophonic Workshop. 'An Unearthly Child' was repeated the following week, immediately before the second episode ('The Cave of Skulls'), by which time the audience had risen to 6.4 million. The average audience for the first four-episode serial was 6 million (12.3 per cent of potential viewers) – a respectable, if far from spectacular, figure.

The first full serial – variously referred to as '100,000 BC' and 'The Tribe of Gum' – has been so completely overshadowed in the popular historiography of *Doctor Who* that some accounts mistakenly cite the next serial, 'The Daleks', as being the first. To a large extent the 'writing out' of the serial from *Doctor Who* history was due to David Whitaker, who, when writing the first spin-off novelisation, omitted the first adventure in its entirety and proceeded directly from Ian and Barbara's entrance into the TARDIS (and that in a different version to 'An Unearthly Child') to the Dalek story.[32] In the days before home video, and until the first serial was repeated on BBC2 as part of the season 'The Five Faces of Doctor Who' in 1981, the Target novelisations were the closest that fans had to the original programmes. Yet there are features in the first *Doctor Who* serial that are unique to that adventure and therefore occupy a significant place in the series' internal history. It is a narrative of displacement in which the four time travellers find themselves pitched into a desperate struggle for survival during the Stone Age. It dramatises conflict between savagery and civilisation in which neither the travellers nor the primitives can comprehend the values of the others: the people of the tribe do not understand why the strangers stop to help a wounded man, while Ian is furious when the tribal leader Za, whom they have helped, refuses to release them when they have shown him how to make the fire which he needs to assert his authority over the tribe. In its representation of the violent contest between dominant males, culminating in a fight to the death between Za and his rival Kal, the story anticipates Hammer's prehistoric epic *One Million Years BC* (dir. Don Chaffey, 1966) by a full three years. It is probably the most brutal of all *Doctor Who* adventures and also shows the character of the Doctor himself in the least sympathetic light. At one point in the third episode ('The Forest of Fear') he appears to be contemplating finishing off the wounded Za with a sharp stone so as not to impede their escape. This is more in line with the Doctor of the original, untransmitted pilot episode rather than the Doctor of the first episode as broadcast, suggesting that the changes in his manner and behaviour were not consistently applied in the following episodes.

It was the second story, 'The Daleks', that firmly established the place of *Doctor Who* in the public's imagination. There was a significant increase in the audience during the course of this serial, rising from 6.9 million for the first episode ('The Dead Planet') to 10.4 million for the last ('The Rescue'). Audience Research also found that viewers' appreciation increased, with the reaction index rising from 59 for the first episode to 65 for the last.[33] It was now apparent that the BBC had a significant popular success on its hands. It was the success of 'The Daleks' that convinced Baverstock to allow *Doctor Who* to continue: on 31 December, he authorised the series to run for 36 weeks (later extended to 42).[34]

There is a certain irony in the fact that the Daleks themselves exemplified precisely the sort of 'bug-eyed monsters' that the BBC had been so concerned to avoid. Newman later professed himself 'livid with anger' when he saw them. Yet, as an early synopsis suggests, it was conceived as a story with wider allegorical overtones:

> The Travellers ... find themselves in a world ruined by a 'Neutron' bomb, a destroyer of human tissue. Two races inhabit this world, the first living in an underground city, protected by anti-radiation suits and the second living miserably in the petrified forests among lifeless plants and crystallised flowers, protected by an anti-radiation drug and existing on rapidly diminishing stores of food. The race living in the underground city are preparing to emerge to rebuild the world, since radiation is diminishing and the Travellers find that they are forced to involve themselves in the struggle between the two opposing sides, the beauty and grace of one unevenly matched against the brilliant intelligence but malignant evil of the other.[35]

To this extent 'The Daleks' belongs to a lineage of apocalyptic fantasy in which civilisation is destroyed by atomic war and the survivors must contend with radiation pollution. This was a real anxiety at the height of the Cold War in the 1950s and 1960s, informing the work of writers such as Nevil Shute (*On the Beach*), John Wyndham (*The Chrysalids*) and Poul Anderson (*Twilight World*). The SF B-movie *The Day the World Ended* (dir. Roger Corman, 1955) to some extent anticipated 'The Daleks' in its narrative of a small group of survivors in the aftermath of a nuclear holocaust threatened by radiation-generated monsters. Films such as this may have been derided for their risible scenarios, but nuclear anxieties were also evident in more serious fare, such as the taut thriller *The Day the Earth Caught Fire* (dir. Val Guest, 1961) and the harrowing docudrama *The War Game* (dir. Peter Watkins, 1965) – the latter commissioned by the BBC but not televised on the grounds that it was 'too horrifying for the medium of broadcasting'.[36]

'The Daleks', indeed, is an allegorical narrative that works on several different levels. It is, for one thing, an allegory of a nuclear holocaust: the planet Skaro has been devastated by a neutron war that has not only destroyed most living matter but has also left the survivors uncertain about who started it in the first place. Two races have survived: the Daleks, hideous mutations encased in mechanical transport machines, are technologically advanced but entirely malevolent and bent on conquering the planet for themselves, whereas the Thals, a humanoid race, are a tribe of hunter-gatherers who live in the petrified forest and wish to co-exist with the Daleks in peace. This idea is a familiar feature of British SF and one does not have to look far for antecedents, such as *The Time Machine*, which posits the Earth of the future inhabited by the hideous, subterranean Morlocks and the beautiful, gentle, surface-dwelling Eloi (H.G. Wells's novel had been filmed by George Pal in 1960) or the comic strip *Dan Dare – Pilot of the Future* in the boys' paper *Eagle*, with its two societies on Venus, the monstrous, totalitarian Treens of the northern hemisphere and the peaceful, democratic Therons in the southern hemisphere. Indeed, there are sufficient similarities, besides their names, between the Therons and the Thals (both are tall, beautiful and blonde), and between the Treens and the Daleks (malevolent, dehumanised, technocratic), to suggest that Terry Nation may have been influenced, whether consciously or not, by *Dan Dare*. The Daleks represent an extreme form of technocracy: they live in an ant-like colony with a structured, hierarchical order, they are entirely rational and they have lost all conscience or sense of morality. Their hatred of the Thals can readily be interpreted as an allegory of racial intolerance in so far as they regard the Thals as mutations. The Daleks have 'a dislike for the unlike', as Ian explains to the Thals: 'They're afraid of you because you're different from them.' The Daleks plan to destroy the Thals by polluting the atmosphere of the planet with radiation, having discovered that in their protective casings they have not only become immune to its effects but in fact have become dependent upon it for their own survival. It has often been suggested, moreover, that the aim of the Daleks to 'exterminate' the Thals is an allegory of the Holocaust: the Daleks/Nazis are the ruthless automatons intent on committing mass genocide, while the Thals/Jews are the nomadic wanderers cast out into the wilderness. It is unclear whether this was in fact Nation's intent, though he later averred that it was and he made later Dalek stories much more explicit in this regard.[37]

Why, then, given their utter disregard for humanity and their total lack of compassion, were the Daleks so much liked by children? There is ample evidence of their popularity, not only in the sale of Dalek toys but also in the letters received by the BBC: 'My small son Phillip aged 4 yrs simply loves those Daleks which have been appearing on the BBC serial "Dr Who".' There were requests from children for pictures of the Daleks and even for them to attend birthday parties.[38] There are various explanations for the popularity of the Daleks, from the psychological (that the temper tantrums of the Daleks represented an essentially childlike mentality) to the practical (that they were ideal for imitating in the playground). Whatever the reason, it seems that many children identified with the Daleks rather than being horrified by them. Huw Wheldon, who succeeded Baverstock as Controller of Programmes, attested to their popularity when he revealed: 'I've got two little kids and they put waste paper baskets on their heads and run around yelling "Exterminate! Exterminate!"'[39]

This was perhaps not the reaction Nation had expected when he described the Daleks as 'hideous, machine-like creatures [with] no human features. A lens of a flexible shaft that acts as an eye. Arms with mechanical grips for hands.' The actual 'look' of the Daleks was the work of designer Raymond Cusick, who reportedly based their appearance on 'a troupe of Russian dancers then playing in London who wore long dresses and had a rolling gait which gave the impression that they had no legs'.[40] The success of the Daleks in visual terms was quite simply that, unlike so many later *Doctor Who* creatures, they did not look like actors wearing a baggy rubber monster suit. Their appearance and their silent movement was both menacing and plausible. It later became something of a standing joke that the Daleks' plans for conquest of the universe would be seriously hampered by their inability to climb stairs.[41] Yet this was not really an issue in the first story, which had the Daleks confined to a city with smooth, polished metallic surfaces and equipped with lifts, where their movement was powered by static electricity. The Daleks' city is an example of isomorphic design where the spaces and perspectives are functional for the Dalek machines but are cramped for the actors playing the humanoid characters, who have to bend their heads to pass along the low-ceilinged corridors. Cusick based his design of the city on the SF film *Things to Come* (dir. William Cameron Menzies, 1936), albeit conceived on a smaller scale and with due regard for budgetary limitations.[42] It was only in later stories, when the Daleks were encountered outside their original habitat, that the problem of their motion became dramatically limiting.

'The Daleks' is also important in the internal history of *Doctor Who* for other reasons besides the introduction of the Doctor's most implacable foes. It is during the course of this adventure that the character of the Doctor himself undergoes significant development. In the first episode it is the Doctor's scientific curiosity that endangers the lives of his companions: determined to explore the city, against the wishes of the others, he deliberately sabotages the TARDIS by removing a vital part (a fluid link containing mercury) and claims that he needs to go into the city to find a replacement. The Thals help the travellers by leaving drugs that counter the effect of radiation, but, having escaped from the city after capture by the Daleks, the Doctor sees no reason to help the Thals and is quite prepared to leave them to their fate at the hands of the Daleks ('The Thals are no concern of ours. We cannot jeopardise our lives and get involved in an affair which is none of our business.'). It is only when he realises that the fluid link has been left behind in the Dalek city that the Doctor decides to 'get involved', and this is because he now needs the Thals' assistance rather than for any altruistic reason. The Doctor and Ian have to persuade the Thals to mount an attack on the Dalek city ('What argument can you use to get a man to sacrifice himself for you?' Ian asks) and to this extent the narrative rehearses the debate around pacifism ('Pacifism only works when everyone feels the same') that, in the context of the early 1960s, has implicit Cold War undertones. Again there are similarities with *Dan Dare*, where Dan had appealed to the initially reluctant Therons to fight the Treens. It is only towards the end of the story that the Doctor expresses his horror at the sheer malevolence of the Daleks ('This senseless, evil killing!') and displays the sense of moral outrage that became integral to the character's psychological make-up.

The average audience for the first season of *Doctor Who* was 8.1 million per episode, with the share achieved by 'The Daleks' maintained throughout the first four months of 1964 before falling away during the summer. This probably reflects the usual seasonal fluctuation in viewing patterns rather than any decline in the popularity of the series itself. The qualitative evidence suggests that *Doctor Who* was very well-liked by its aficionados. 'I have seen every episode of "Dr Who" and I must say it is one of the best programmes for us younger viewers that has been on television,' wrote one highly articulate young correspondent. Particularly interesting, given the series' educational remit, is the testimony of a special needs teacher: 'Your current serial "Dr Who" is providing considerable enjoyment & interest to my class of 17 mentally retarded children. In fact, it has been the first real source of enthusiasm for work, for a long time.'[43] When it returned later in the year, after a six-week autumn break, the second season of *Doctor Who* achieved a more consistent audience share, averaging 10.5 million per episode with less evident seasonal fluctuation. Critics were now taking notice. 'I overcame my allergy to science fiction to watch the new *Dr Who* series,' reported T.C. Worseley in the *Financial Times*, while Mary Crozier in *The Guardian* felt that '*Dr Who* deserves to be popular' and 'represents a real effort of the imagination'. Not all their colleagues were so taken with it, however. Peter Black in the *Daily Mail* felt that the main protagonists 'are the dullest quartet in fiction', and John Holmstrom in the *New Statesman* complained about 'the wooden charmlessness of the adventurers, both as written and performed, the lamentably unchilling plastic monsters or (in the historical episodes) the pasteboard Romans, Saracens or French Revolutionaries'.[44]

It has sometimes been suggested that the historical episodes of *Doctor Who* were less popular than the science fiction-oriented storylines. One commentator, for example, writes of audience ratings 'taking a nosedive whenever it returned to earthbound costume drama'.[45] This verdict is not, however, borne out by the evidence: the audience share for the historical serials is very much in line with that for the science fiction serials.[46] The fact that historical narratives constituted a third of all *Doctor Who* stories during its first three seasons, with nine of the 26 serials set in either the historical or a mythical past, would hardly seem to suggest that the genre was less popular. The qualitative evidence, moreover, suggests that the historical stories were appreciated by viewers. Donald Wilson, writing in response to one correspondent who suggested that 'children are not interested in something attempting to be historical,' claimed: 'We find that there is very little difference in their letters and in our audience surveys, and perhaps it is that the past subjects do have some bearing on lessons that the children are having to do.' In a revealing aside, however, he added that 'we only regard the historical stories as necessary make-weights between the futuristic science fiction ones.'[47] What complaints there were about the historical stories tended to focus on examples of historical detail. Two 'graduate archeologists' [sic] complained of the 'completely unnecessary vagueness and numerous archeological howlers' in the first story. And the honorary secretary of the Napoleon I Society took issue with the liberties taken in Dennis Spooner's script for 'The Reign of Terror': 'That which children see on television will stick in their minds for many years despite the lectures of teachers and the lessons learnt from the text books. The BBC's action in this case is deeply to be regretted.'[48]

Spooner, who succeeded Whitaker as story editor during the second season of *Doctor Who*, remarked: 'Writers have to be divided into those who can cope with trips back into the past and those who can write adventures set in the future. Very few can do both.'[49] The most prolific writer of historical *Doctor Who*, with three serials in total ('Marco Polo', 'The Aztecs', 'The Massacre'), was John Lucarotti, whose scripts were characterised by their attention to detail and moral seriousness. Other writers, including Spooner himself ('The Romans', 'The Time Meddler') and Donald Cotton ('The Myth Makers', 'The Gunfighters'), were less concerned with authenticity and instead deployed mythic aspects of the past, resulting in a more flexible interpretation of history. Terry Nation, regarded as an SF specialist, also wrote an aborted serial set during the Indian Mutiny of 1857, 'The Red Fort', which was abandoned at a cost of £1,834, despite having 'exceeded expectations in quality of writing'.[50] Historical *Doctor Who* tended to focus on periods of the past that were taught in schools and would, therefore, be familiar to children, but the series did not exclusively privilege British history.[51]

The educational, instructional remit of *Doctor Who* is very apparent in such stories as Lucarotti's 'Marco Polo' (#4) and Whitaker's 'The Crusade' (#14). In 'Marco Polo', Lucarotti uses the *Doctor Who* formula to provide viewers with a history lesson: the TARDIS materialises in the Himalayas in 1289, where the travellers meet Marco Polo and join him on his trek across the Gobi Desert to the court of Kublai Khan. Polo plans to make the Khan a gift of the Doctor's 'unusual caravan' in order to win his release from the Khan's service. The narrative takes place over a period of several months and employs various authenticating devices, such as inserts of a map showing the route and voiceovers by Polo as he records the journey in his journal. The characterisation of Polo (Mark Eden) as a civilised European who befriends the Doctor and his companions adds a note of psychological realism. The story ends with the Doctor playing backgammon with Kublai Khan for ownership of the TARDIS, and Polo himself is left wondering who the mysterious travellers were. 'The Crusade' follows a similar pattern as the TARDIS materialises in the Holy Land in the twelfth century and the time travellers meet Richard the Lionheart. Here the adventure narrative – Ian, knighted by Richard, has to rescue Barbara, kidnapped by the Saracen warlord El Akir to add to his harem – is secondary to Whitaker's historically revisionist exploration of the character of Richard (Julian Glover). In contrast to the warmonger of popular historiography, Richard is characterised as a war-weary warrior ('All wise men look for peace') who is sickened by the brutality of warfare ('This blood-letting must stop!'). To this end he plans to make peace with Saladin through a marriage alliance between Saladin's brother Saphadin and his own sister, Princess Joanna. It is only when he realises that Joanna is an unwilling partner in the proposed marriage that Richard accepts he must continue the war. The time travellers leave as Richard prepares to march on Jerusalem ('Even now his army marches out on a campaign they can never win'), with the Doctor reminding his companions that they were right not to tell Richard he would never take the city ('No, child. History must run its course.').

The moral imperative of not interfering with the past or altering the course of history is a recurring theme of Lucarotti's *Doctor Who* scripts. In 'The Aztecs' (#6), for example, the TARDIS lands in Mexico a century before the arrival of the Conquistadors, where Barbara is mistaken for the reincarnation of high priestess Yetaxa. Horrified by the Aztecs' custom of human sacrifice, Barbara resolves to end the practice, despite the Doctor's protests:

The Doctor: There is to be a human sacrifice today at the rain ceremony … And you must not interfere. Do you understand?

Barbara: I can't just sit by and watch.

The Doctor: No, Barbara. Ian agrees with me. He's got to escort the victim to the altar.

Barbara: He has to [do] what?

The Doctor: Yes, they've made him a warrior. And he's promised me not to interfere with the sacrifice.

Barbara: Well, they've made me a goddess. And I forbid it!

The Doctor: Barbara, no!

Barbara: There'll be no sacrifice this afternoon, Doctor, or ever again.
                 The reincarnation of Yetaxa will prove to the people that you
                 don't need to sacrifice a human being to make it rain.

The Doctor: Barbara, no!

Barbara: It's no good, Doctor. My mind's made up. This is the beginning
                 of the end of the sun god.

The Doctor: What are you talking about?

Barbara: Oh, don't you see? If I could start the destruction of everything
                 that's evil here, then everything that is good would survive
                 when Cortez lands.

The Doctor: But you can't rewrite history, not one line ... Barbara, one
                 last appeal. What you are trying to do is utterly impossible. I
                 know, believe me, I know.

Barbara: Not Barbara. Yetaxa.

Ignoring the Doctor's warning, Barbara orders the sacrifice to halt, only
to find that she has offended the victim ('You have denied me honour!')
who jumps to his death anyway. She is left dismayed that she was unable
to bring about any change for the better ('What is the point of travelling
in time and space? You can't change anything – nothing'). In this sense
'The Aztecs' is a morality tale that asserts the need to understand the past
on its own terms. Barbara's twentieth-century European humanism is as
alien to the civilisation of the Aztecs as their customs are horrifying to
her modern sensibilities.

The doctrine of non-interference in the past is asserted again in 'The
Massacre' (#22), set in Paris at the time of the Catholic plot to murder
Huguenots on St Bartholomew's Eve (23 August 1572). The Doctor
chooses not to warn Anne Chaplet, a Huguenot servant girl who has
helped them, about the impending massacre, explaining to his outraged

companion Steven (Peter Purves) that it is not for him to interfere with the course of history:

> My dear Steven, history sometimes gives us a terrible shock, and that is because we don't quite fully understand. Why should we? After all, we're all too small to realise its final pattern. Therefore, don't try and judge it from where you stand. I was right to do as I did. Yes, that I firmly believe.

On this occasion the script offers a somewhat contrived solution to the moral dilemma: in a coda the TARDIS lands in the present where the Doctor and Steven meet Dorothea ('Dodo') Chaplet, whom, it is implied, is Anne's descendant.

By the third season of *Doctor Who*, however, the morality tale of 'The Massacre' was out of step with the trajectory the series' historical stories were taking. Dennis Spooner was largely responsible for this shift of direction. In his second-season finale 'The Time Meddler' (#17), for example, the TARDIS lands on the coast of north-eastern England in 1066 where Steven and Vicki (Maureen O'Brien) are surprised to discover a wristwatch and the Doctor finds that the sound of chanting monks from a monastery comes from a gramophone. It transpires that the mysterious 'Monk' who lives in the monastery is another time traveller from the same (unnamed) planet as the Doctor – he even has his own TARDIS (a superior 'Mark Four') – and his favourite pastime is interfering with the Earth's past ('Do you really think the Ancient Britons could have built Stonehenge without the aid of my anti-gravitational lift?'). The Monk has hatched 'a master plan to end all master plans': to avert Harold Godwinsson's defeat at the Battle of Hastings by destroying the Viking invasion fleet of Harald Hardrada with an atomic cannon, thus leaving the Saxon army fresh to face the Normans without first having to fight the Battle of Stamford Bridge. It is difficult not to be sympathetic with the Monk's aims. He tells the Doctor:

> I want to improve things ... King Harold – I know he'd be a good king. There wouldn't be all those wars in Europe – those claims over France went on for years and years. With peace, the people would be able to better themselves. A few hints and tips from me, they'd be able to have jet airliners by 1320!

It should be clear from this that Spooner was not treating the subject with anything like the moral seriousness of Lucarotti. The Meddling Monk himself (a superbly comic performance by future 'Carry On' regular Peter Butterworth) is a mischief-maker rather than a diabolical villain and his response to the Doctor's familiar edict of non-interference is sublime:

> *The Doctor*:   You know as well as I do the golden rule about space and time travelling. Never, never interfere with the course of history.

> *The Monk*:   And who says so? Doctor, it's more fun my way.

In the event the Doctor foils the Monk's plan and leaves him stranded in 1066 by removing the dimensional control of his TARDIS.

That Spooner wanted to have 'more fun' in his treatment of history had already been demonstrated in 'The Romans' (#12). This serial was written and played as a comedy with scant regard for historical authenticity. Relaxing in a villa near Rome during the first century AD, Ian and Barbara are kidnapped by slave traders, while the Doctor is mistaken for the famous lyre player, Maximus Pettulian, and becomes involved in intrigues at court. 'The Romans' is a parody of biblical epics such as *The Sign of the Cross* (dir. Cecil B. De Mille, 1932) and *Quo Vadis?* (dir. Mervyn le Roy, 1951), while its characterisation of a comic Emperor Nero (Derek Francis), who chases Barbara around the palace corridors, has affinities with the lecherous historical characters who populated the costumed 'Carry On' romps such as *Carry On Cleo* (dir. Gerald Thomas, 1964). It is implied that the Doctor gives Nero the idea of burning Rome when he sets fire to Nero's plans for the new Rome by refracting sunlight through his spectacles. That the Ancient World lent itself to a rather looser interpretation of the past was illustrated again in Donald Cotton's 'The Myth Makers' (#20). Here the viewer's pleasure arises from the script's knowing and playful deconstruction of the classics. The TARDIS materialises on the Plain of Troy just as Achilles and Hector are engaged in single combat; the Doctor's appearance distracts Hector, who is slain by Achilles. The important point about 'The Myth Makers' is that it is set in a mythical rather than a historical past and so is unconstrained by recorded events. It offers an extremely irreverent interpretation of the Trojan War where Menelaus is somewhat less than dismayed by the abduction of Helen ('I was heartily glad to see the back of her') and where Paris is contemptuous of Cassandra's prophetic dream about a giant horse ('Yes, well, I hardly think we need trouble to interpret that one'). Achilles believes the Doctor is none other than Zeus himself, but Agamemnon and Odysseus are sceptical. They charge him with devising the means to end their siege of Troy. Contrary to expectations, the Doctor initially dismisses the idea of a wooden horse as being too far-fetched ('I couldn't possibly suggest that. The whole story is obviously absurd. Probably invented by Homer as some good dramatic device'), but when he is unable to think of any other solution he not only designs the Trojan Horse but actually travels inside it to rejoin his companions in the city. Vicki, meanwhile, has fallen in love with a Trojan prince, Troilus. King Priam, thinking Vicki an unsuitable name for a girl, calls her Cressida instead. In this adventure, therefore, the time travellers have not only influenced the course of history, but have themselves become part of it.

Cotton's parodic approach to history was demonstrated again in 'The Gunfighters' (#25), a delirious spoof Western informed not by the historical reality of the American West but by the conventions of the genre familiar to British audiences through imported television series such as *Gunsmoke*, *Cheyenne*, *The Life and Legend of Wyatt Earp* and *Tales of Wells Fargo*. 'The Gunfighters' belongs to the little-regarded genre of the British comedy Western, including *The Sheriff of Fractured Jaw* (dir. Raoul Walsh, 1958) and *Carry On Cowboy* (dir. Gerald Thomas, 1965), representing the Wild West as a place of saloons, gunfights, lynch mobs and bad accents. This was a conscious production decision: new producer Innes Lloyd felt 'that it would be absurd to try and make a traditional western – I would suggest that the approach might be more on the lines of "Cat Ballou" – tongue in cheek'.[52] The TARDIS arrives in Tombstone in 1881 and the Doctor, suffering from toothache, has a molar extracted by Doc Holliday. The Doctor becomes embroiled in the struggle for control of Tombstone between the Earps and the Clantons, and, contrary to his usual mantra of non-interference, tries to prevent the famous gunfight at the O.K. Corral ('I have come along to call off your boys from embarking on this ridiculous duel,' he tells Pa Clanton). In the event the Doctor and his companions are spectators to the gunfight.

A myth has grown that 'The Gunfighters' had the lowest-ever viewing figures for the series.[53] In fact its average audience of 6.25 million was higher than the next two adventures ('The Savages' and 'The War Machines'), reflecting a general decline in the *Doctor Who* audience towards the end of the third season. Its qualitative reception, however, was poor, recording a low reaction index (30) and receiving a 'critical barrage from viewers in the sample'.[54] Newman thought that 'it was a very sad serial despite the fact that it was quite well acted and certainly well shot' and felt that the whole comedy approach to the story was 'misconceived':

> Somehow or other Dr Who audiences, as proven from many past successes, always want to believe in the particular life-and-death situation that Dr Who and his companions find themselves in. The micky-taking aspects of this particular one I think alienated all except the most sophisticated – and I'm not even sure about the latter.[55]

The Audience Research Report on 'The Gunfighters' suggested that 'viewers on the whole seemed pretty disgusted with a story that was not in the science-fiction genre they associate with *Dr Who*.' This is more revealing of the popular perception of *Doctor Who* than its actual content, for SF stories outnumbered historical stories by a ratio of only three-to-two during the early years of the series. Nor was the response to the SF stories consistent. This is exemplified by 'The Web Planet', which achieved the highest audience for any *Doctor Who* story during the 1960s (an average of 12.5 million), but was far less appreciated than many others with a low reaction index of 42 (the season's average was 55). It 'appeared that many viewers had found this last set of adventures centring round the Web Planet something of a disappointment, less arresting and entertaining than other Dr Who stories they had seen'.[56]

It is difficult to generalise about the science fiction content of *Doctor Who* during its early years, for, unlike later periods when distinct production trends emerged, the range of SF narratives and themes during the formative years of the series was, to say the least, eclectic. This may have been a legacy of the programme's origins in the Script Department's survey of the field of SF literature. David Whitaker was interested in establishing links with the wider SF community and in September 1964 he approached the agents of several authors, including

John Wyndham, John Brunner and Charles Eric Maine, to enquire whether they would be interested in writing for *Doctor Who*.[57] Although in the event this did not materialise, there is reason to believe that the production team did keep abreast of the literary form of the genre. Amongst the SF themes and templates that featured in early *Doctor Who*, for example, were those of 'first contact' with an alien race ('The Sensorites'), the time-distortion paradox ('The Space Museum') and the narrative of planetary extinction and journey to colonise another world ('The Ark'). This diversity of content demonstrates the desire of the early *Doctor Who* production team to explore a range of narrative possibilities within the genre.

It would probably be more accurate to describe *Doctor Who* as science fantasy rather than pure science fiction, in that its plots did go beyond the limit of what was scientifically or technologically plausible. 'The Keys of Marinus' (#5) – one of only two non-Dalek *Doctor Who* scripts by Terry Nation – is the series' earliest, and arguably its best, excursion into the sub-genre known as planetary romance. This template typically 'involves characters in hectic adventures on another planet. It often features a long journey through a number of gaudily exotic environments, where many strange creatures and peculiar societies are to be found.'[58] The TARDIS lands on the planet of Marinus, where a pyramid stands on an island of glass surrounded by a sea of acid. The Doctor and his companions meet the Keeper of the Conscience of Marinus, who explains that the Conscience was a machine that became so powerful it could control the minds of men. The machine has long been disabled, but the Voords, who want to use its power for their own ends, now seek to reactivate it. The Keeper sends the Doctor and his companions to find four 'micro circuits' that he has hidden all over Marinus. 'The Keys of Marinus' is an example of the picaresque in which each episode is not only relatively self-contained but also takes place in a different planetary environment: the city of Morphoton where 'people are perhaps the most contented in the universe' but where external appearances prove deceptive; a living jungle that attacks the travellers; a freezing tundra where the key is in an ice cave protected by mysterious guardians; and the petty bureaucratic city-state of Millennius, where Ian finds himself on trial for the theft of the key. Its resolution provides the first statement of what would become a recurring theme of *Doctor Who* and what, moreover, has always been an important motif of SF: the superiority of man over machine. As the

Doctor tells the Keeper's daughter Sabetha: 'I don't believe that man was made to be controlled by machines. Machines can make laws, but they cannot preserve justice. Only human beings can do that.'

'The Web Planet' (#13), despite its relatively lukewarm reception, is another good example of the ambition of *Doctor Who* during its formative years. Written by Bill Strutton, this was nothing less than an attempt to create an entirely alien world. The official synopsis described it thus: 'This story is about a planet in another galaxy where evolution has taken a different form in that insects have become dominant races.'[59] The evolutionary theme had long been a feature of literary SF and had recently found expression in Pierre Boulle's 1963 novel *Monkey Planet*, later filmed as *Planet of the Apes* (dir. Franklin Schaffner, 1968). 'The Web Planet' is set on Vortis, a planet inhabited by two antagonistic species: the Zarbi, a race of giant telepathic ants, and the butterfly-like Menoptera. The Menoptera are trying to reclaim the planet from the Zarbi, who once co-existed peacefully but then came under the influence of the 'dark power' of the Animus, which has made them hostile. What is particularly innovative about 'The Web Planet' is its attempt to visualise Vortis as an entirely alien environment by using disorienting lenses that are supposed to create an impression of the rarefied atmosphere of the planet. This also made it an expensive serial to produce. Spooner later revealed that 'we decided not to do anything like that again. Not because of the story content, but because of the sheer cost and technical problems involved.'[60]

A recurring tendency of *Doctor Who* from the outset has been the use of SF apparatus in support of morality tales. 'Galaxy Four' (#18) is an early example of this trend. Landing on a barren planet only days before its destruction, the Doctor and his companions encounter members of two species marooned there: the all-female, statuesque, blonde Drahvins and the hideously ugly, ammonia-breathing, slug-like Rills. They are initially 'rescued' by Drahvins, who claim the Rills seek to destroy them, but it transpires that the Drahvins are emotionless clones who are in fact the aggressors, whereas the Rills are an intelligent and peaceful race who have been using their scientific knowledge to repair their ship, which the Drahvins covet for themselves. 'The Savages' (#26) is another example of a morality play, this time with an obvious generic reference point. The TARDIS lands on a planet in the distant future inhabited by two tribes, the advanced, cultured Elders and the primitive, cave-dwelling Savages.

The Elders have developed a process of transference and periodically round up groups of Savages in order to drain their 'life force' and thus enhance their own mental and physical abilities. An exchange between the Doctor and Jano, one of the Elders' leaders, not only rehearses the moral issues but also makes the political allegory quite explicit:

> *Jano*:   I am sorry you take this attitude, Doctor. It is most unscientific. You are standing in the way of human progress.
>
> *The Doctor*: Human progress, sir! How dare you call your treatment of these people progress!?
>
> *Jano*:   They are hardly people, Doctor. They are not like us.
>
> *The Doctor*: I fail to see the difference.
>
> *Jano*:   Do you not realise that all progress is based on exploitation?
>
> *The Doctor*: Exploitation, indeed! This, sir, is protracted murder!

It will probably be clear that this is a thinly veiled reworking of *The Time Machine*, in which the Morlocks had represented the oppressed proletariat and the Eloi the effete ruling classes. In contrast to Wells's moral pessimism, however, 'The Savages' provides a more affirmative outcome, in which Jano, attempting to drain the Doctor's life force, becomes imbued with his libertarian and humanistic values: 'You wanted my intellect. You got it. And along with it you received a little conscience.'

The narrative of displacement was another recurring motif of early *Doctor Who*, consistent with the original intent of placing the protagonists against unusual backgrounds. A number of stories use the device of taking the TARDIS crew out of the 'known' universe and plunging them into an entirely unfamiliar environment. The second-season opener 'Planet of Giants' (#9) fulfilled the long-held ambition of producing a miniaturisation story, though its original four episodes were compressed into three when it was decided that the story was too thin to sustain the length. A dimensional anomaly causes the TARDIS to shrink in size so that its crew are only one inch tall. An ordinary back garden thus becomes a series of deadly hazards as they encounter giant insects and are terrorised by a pet cat. 'Planet of Giants' is another example of a *Doctor Who* story with a specific generic reference point, in this instance the classic genre film *The Incredible Shrinking Man* (dir. Jack Arnold, 1957). A more original variation on the displacement narrative was 'The Celestial Toymaker' (#24), demonstrating yet again the scope and ambition of early *Doctor Who* in that it represents an excursion into pure fantasy rather than science fiction proper. The TARDIS materialises in the Celestial Toyroom where its crew meet the Toymaker (Michael Gough) – an old enemy of the Doctor – who forces them to play a series of games for his amusement. The Toymaker is an immortal whose apparently innocuous games (not unlike the mock-tournament game show *It's A Knockout*) have far-reaching consequences: if the travellers lose they are destined to be trapped in his domain forever. The notion of a realm of the fantastic would later be explored, to even better effect, in the Second Doctor adventure 'The Mind Robber'.

Yet for all the inventiveness and diversity of its storylines, the success of *Doctor Who* was sealed by the popularity of its first alien monsters. Ever since the end of 'The Daleks' there had been speculation that the barking pepper pots would return to terrorise the universe again. In February 1964, in response to an enquiry about merchandising and exploitation opportunities, Donald Wilson said: 'We have in mind, of course, to try and resurrect the Daleks but with the writing we at present have in hand it is hardly likely to happen until well on in the summer.'[61] In the event their return was cannily timed to conclude on Boxing Day 1964 when 12.5 million viewers tuned in for 'Flashpoint', the final episode of 'The Dalek Invasion of Earth' (#10). This was a landmark *Doctor Who* story in many respects: it marked the first extensive use of location filming, the series' first *Radio Times* cover, the first example of the alien invasion narrative that was to become such a regular motif of the series and the first occasion that one of the Doctor's companions (Susan) departed at the end of the adventure. The TARDIS arrives in a derelict and deserted London of the twenty-second century, where the sight of a Dalek emerging from the River Thames provides the shocking revelation that the Earth has been attacked and conquered. 'The Dalek Invasion of Earth' follows the *War of the Worlds* template of an alien invasion of Earth centred on the south of England in which the invaders, possessing superior technology, seek to subjugate all human beings and exploit the planet for their own ends. Its 'alternative history' of Britain invaded but resisting the aggressor has been interpreted as an allegory of the Second World War and the narrative of resistance to tyranny.[62] Shots of Dalek patrols against familiar landmarks such as Trafalgar Square, Westminster Bridge and the Cenotaph in Whitehall remind audiences of how close Britain came to invasion only 24 years earlier. In this sense the serial brings to mind another example of alternative history: the docudrama *It Happened Here* (dirs. Kevin Brownlow & Andrew Mollo, 1963) with its shots of German soldiers goose-stepping along Whitehall. 'The Dalek Invasion of Earth' dares to consider what might have happened to Britain if the country had been invaded and posits some disturbing answers: as well as heroic resistance fighters there are black marketeers (represented by the character of Ashton who provides food for slave workers at an extortionate cost) and collaborators (the two women who betray Barbara to the Daleks in return for food). The Dalek/Nazi parallels, implicit in the first story, become more explicit. The Daleks use radio propaganda broadcasts and round up people for slave labour – both tactics employed by the Nazis in the occupied countries – and their rhetoric is all about surrender and subjugation ('Resistance is useless'). There are clear fascist overtones in the Dalek Supreme's order to 'arrange for the extermination of all human beings', and one Dalek voice can even be heard to use the phrase 'the final solution'.

The allegory of 'The Dalek Invasion of Earth', so obvious in hindsight, would seem to have passed contemporaries by. The serial did attract comment, however, for its horrific content. One concerned mother wrote to complain:

> I found the beginning of the series so horrifying as to compare with the 'Quatermass' series of some years ago where at least it was for adults and a previous warning was given ... Children are impressionable enough these days and I did think with all the publicity now given to the barring of horror comics, films and TV plays that a more thoughtful and considerate approach should be given to children.[63]

This was an early instance of a familiar charge that would be levelled against *Doctor Who* throughout its history. On this occasion, however, the charge was rebutted by another parent:

> I read in yesterday's newspaper that you are considering censoring the *Dr*

Who programme as it is too violent for children. May I please implore you not to do so. I have three children aged 13-yrs, 10-yrs and 8-yrs. They each dash home from shopping on a Saturday in order not to miss this programme and before they used to sit patiently waiting for something gruesome to happen. At least they are contented ... My youngest son is pleading for a Dalek outfit for a Christmas present.[64]

The wave of 'Dalekmania' sparked by 'The Dalek Invasion of Earth' – exemplified by Dalek toys, Dalek comics, even Dalek confectionery – lends further credence to the view that children were fascinated rather than repelled by the creatures. Further Dalek serials were bound to follow, and did, with increasing frequency. 'The Chase' (#16) largely eschewed the allegorical overtones of 'The Dalek Invasion of Earth' in favour of an adventure narrative as the Daleks, having built their own time machine, pursue the TARDIS 'through all eternity' in an attempt to exterminate their 'greatest enemies'. Like 'The Keys of Marinus', the narrative spans a variety of different environments, both extraterrestrial (the desert world of Aridius, the jungle planet of Mechanus) and Earthbound. Responding, perhaps, to the charge that the previous story had been too horrific, 'The Chase' inclines more towards comedy. Thus there are scenes in which the Daleks are perplexed by a hillbilly American tourist on top of the Empire State Building and where they are confronted by fairground robots of Frankenstein's Monster and Count Dracula. The irreverent attitude towards history that was increasingly affecting the series is exemplified again by a sequence in which the Daleks' appearance on a nineteenth-century sailing ship causes the terrified crew to leap overboard: the camera tracks around the deserted ship and picks out the name of the *Mary Celeste*. *Sunday Telegraph* critic Philip Purser, however, was unimpressed: 'The Daleks, recalled with increasing frequency and increasing desperation, are fast losing their ancient menace; one of them has acquired a South London accent and another is undoubtedly queer.'[65]

The aim of 'The Daleks' Master Plan' (#21), according to director Douglas Camfield, was 'to give back the Daleks their former menace'.[66] This fourth Dalek serial had a troubled production history. It was expanded from six episodes to twelve on the instructions of Huw Wheldon, allegedly because his mother was a fan of the Daleks. 'The Daleks' Master Plan' was nothing if not ambitious: an epic adventure in which the Daleks have built an alliance of different races greedy for power to support their bid for conquest of the galaxy. It represents the series' first excursion into pure space opera, positing that, by *c.* AD 4000, the Earth has become the centre of a galactic federation protected by the Space Security Service and governed by the Guardian of the Solar System (who, it transpires, is in league with the Daleks because he covets even greater power than that bestowed upon an elected ruler). The Doctor steals a vital component from the Daleks' supreme weapon, the Time Destructor, and much of the serial replays 'The Chase' as a Dalek task force pursues him through time and space to recover it. Yet for all its epic qualities, 'The Daleks' Master Plan' is ultimately somewhat unsatisfactory. It is an uneven adventure split uncomfortably in style between the comedy elements of 'The Chase' and the more serious content of 'The Dalek Invasion of Earth'. Thus, on the one hand, there are comedy incidents, including a chase through a 1920s Hollywood film studio, a stop-off at a Lord's Test Match between England and Australia and a reappearance by the Meddling Monk. On the other hand, however, there are moments of tragedy with the death of two companions, the Trojan slave girl Katarina who had joined the TARDIS crew at the end of 'The Myth Makers' and Space Security agent Sara Kingdom who dies horribly from rapid ageing when the Time Destructor is finally activated. Some viewers found her death 'a bit too nasty'.[67] The unevenness of 'The Daleks' Master Plan' can be attributed to the fact that writing chores were divided between Terry Nation and Dennis Spooner, with Spooner completing the story when Nation's duties as script editor of the ITC action-adventure series *The Baron* (1965–1966) took him away from *Doctor Who*.

'The Daleks' Master Plan' maintained a consistent audience of around 9.4 million (its lowest share came on Christmas Day), though the qualitative evidence suggests that viewers found it a strain to stay with the serial to the end. There were complaints that 'this particular story is running out of good, solid ideas' and that 'it is becoming confusingly meandering in plot'. A quarter of the viewing sample were 'tiring of this particular story and the ubiquitous Daleks'.[68] It had also placed considerable strain on resources. Early in its run the Head of Design complained that the serial 'is proving a near disaster' as the schedule meant the director had little time to consult the designers over future episodes: 'I understand that the Director is doing all possible to meet his dates but that his commitment to twelve consecutive episodes has made this virtually impossible.'[69] For all the problems, however, the production team was evidently satisfied with the result. Producer John Wiles felt that 'in spite of immense difficulties, the 12-part Dalek Serial was mounted and presented with a certain amount of gloss'; and Newman told Camfield that 'you have done a splendid job.'[70]

It may have been that the decision to mount an epic Dalek serial had been influenced by the appearance of the Daleks in the cinema. The popular success of the Daleks led to two spin-off feature films: *Dr. Who and the Daleks* (dir. Gordon Flemyng, 1965) and *Daleks' Invasion Earth 2150 A.D.* (dir. Gordon Flemyng, 1966). These were produced separately from and independently of the television series, with an entirely different cast and crew. Both were produced by Amicus Films, a production company set up by two Americans, Milton Subotsky and Max J. Rosenberg, specialising in horror and exploitation films but also, like its erstwhile rival Hammer, turning out films for family audiences during school holidays. In partnership with film financier Joe Vegoda, whose company Aaru co-financed the two films, Subotsky and Rosenberg produced the films at Shepperton Studios and released them during the summer holiday periods: *Dr. Who and the Daleks* opened in London on 24 June 1965, *Daleks' Invasion Earth 2150 A.D.* on 22 July 1966.[71]

The Dalek films have generally been dismissed as inferior versions of the television series. This has ever been the fate of television spin-off films: in adaptation for the cinema they tend to lose the characteristics that had made them distinctive and successful in the first place. Yet this charge is not entirely fair, either in respect of the television spin-off as a genre or, specifically, in the case of the Dalek films. In terms of their production values, the Dalek films provided two things that television did not: Technicolor and widescreen. These points were emphasised in the voiceover for the cinema trailer for *Dr. Who and the Daleks*: 'Now you can see them on the big screen in colour. Closer than ever before. So close you can feel their fire. So thrilling you must be there.' It was evident from the promotion of the films, moreover, that the Daleks themselves, rather than the character of 'Dr. Who', were the main selling points. Indeed, the name 'Dr. Who' was omitted entirely from the title of the second film. That the films were intended for children, rather than for the wider audience of the BBC series, is evident in the changes to content and characterisation made by Subotsky in adapting Nation's television scripts. Thus the moral debates are largely absent, a new element of slapstick comedy is introduced and the Daleks themselves seem rather less frightening than they had on the small screen. Their weapons, for example, shoot compressed gas that looks more like fire-extinguisher foam than the 'fire' described in the trailer.

The most significant changes are in the characterisations. 'Dr. Who', played in both films by Peter Cushing, is not the cantankerous other-worldly Doctor of 'An Unearthly Child', but a loveable old Mr Chips who 'actively invites identification from the child audience'.[72] In *Dr. Who and the Daleks* he is introduced reading the *Eagle*, a point of reference that establishes the juvenile, comic-strip nature of the film. In this version he is not a mysterious traveller in the fourth dimension but an eccentric scientist whose latest invention is the time machine TARDIS. While the exterior of the TARDIS still resembles a police box, its interior, in contrast to the smooth, clean, futuristic design of the television series, is a mess of untidy wires and levers that more closely resembles Wells's *The Time Machine*. The character of Susan is no unearthly child but a real granddaughter who, significantly, is somewhat younger than her television equivalent (Roberta Tovey, who played Susan in both films, was 12 at the time of the first but plays Susan as an eight-year-old). This is the clearest indication that the films were targeted at a younger audience because, as the BBC's concept of 'loyalty characters' had asserted, children tend not to identify with characters younger than themselves. And, in contrast to the two schoolteachers Ian and Barbara, whose role in the series had been a sure indication of its educational intent and didactic purpose, the characters in the films are recast as 'comic relief' and 'glamour' roles respectively. In *Dr. Who and the Daleks* Barbara (Jennie Linden) is Susan's elder sister and Ian (Roy Castle) is her boyfriend, who accidentally sets the TARDIS in flight when he stumbles against the controls. In *Daleks' Invasion Earth 2150 A.D.*, their parts are taken by the Doctor's niece Louise (Jill Curzon) and Tom Campbell (Bernard Cribbins), a policeman who stumbles into the TARDIS believing it to be a real police box. Castle and Cribbins are both comedy performers whose good-natured if ultimately rather tedious clowning injects an element of broad slapstick into the films that had never been present in the television series. Neither Linden nor Curzon has much to do other than look pretty and scream, though the casting of contemporary young women, rather than teenagers or the more mature woman personified by Jacqueline Hill's Barbara, might have influenced the future casting of the Doctor's television companions.

Although they are usually regarded as a pair, there are in fact significant differences between the two films, especially in terms of their visual style. *Dr. Who and the Daleks* is entirely studio-bound and its set design is more overtly fantastic. The petrified forest of Skaro is less frightening in colour than it had been in monochrome: more *Magic Roundabout* than Brothers Grimm. It brings to mind the fantastic worlds of children's fiction (Wonderland, Narnia, Oz) and to this extent renders Susan's excursion there safe: nothing really bad could happen to her in this magical kingdom. The Daleks, now colour-coded according to function, are also less frightening in bright primary colours, looking more like the toy Daleks flooding the toyshops in 1965 than the sinister silver-grey creatures of the television series. In contrast, *Daleks' Invasion Earth 2150 A.D.* makes extensive use of locations (the Dalek rising from the Thames, for example, is impressively staged) and has a more realistic visual style appropriate to its Earthbound location. Critics, however, remarked that the sets and costumes appeared to be very much of their time. '[If] this is what London will look like in 2150AD,' wrote one reviewer, 'I can only say that it looks very old-fashioned: positively 1966 ...'[73]

Dr. Who and the Daleks, dismissed as juvenile nonsense by most film critics, was nevertheless a popular success that made it into the top ten box-office attractions in Britain in 1965. It probably benefited from its summer release, which coincided with transmission of 'The Chase' on television. *Daleks' Invasion Earth 2150 A.D.*, although reckoned by most aficionados to be the better of the two films, was, however, less successful at the box office. This would suggest, if it suggests anything all, that the height of 'Dalekmania' had passed by the summer of 1966. Like all popular cultural phenomena, it was a historically specific and short-lived craze. In 1966, 'Dalekmania' gave way to 'Batmania' following the success of the colourful American comic-strip series *Batman*. Subotsky and Rosenberg did not take up their option for a third film. The two Dalek films may have lacked the narrative complexity of the television series, but they were significant in one very important respect: they had suggested, for the first time, that there might conceivably be another 'Doctor Who'.

2

Monsters, Inc.

1966–1969

There is evil here and we must stay. There are some corners of the universe which have bred the most terrible things. Things which act against everything that we believe in. They must be fought.

The Doctor (Patrick Troughton) in 'The Moonbase'

On 29 October 1966, a few minutes into the final episode of 'The Tenth Planet' (#29), during which he encountered for the first time a deadly new enemy called the Cybermen, a frail and weary Doctor remarked that 'this old body of mine is wearing a bit thin'. With the Cybermen foiled in their attempt to conquer the Earth, for the time being at least, the Doctor staggered back to the TARDIS where, before the astonished eyes of his companions Ben and Polly, he collapsed to the floor and underwent some form of metaphysical change to the extent that his facial appearance was completely transformed. The last episode of 'The Tenth Planet' is one of those missing from the archives, though the transformation sequence – achieved by a slow mix and dissolve from a close-up of William Hartnell's face to a close-up of the new 'Doctor Who', Patrick Troughton – has survived. In hindsight the notion of the Doctor's 'renewal' (only later did the process come to be known as 'regeneration') would seem to have been an inspired narrative strategy that guaranteed the longevity of the series, but in the autumn of 1966 it was a hastily devised solution to a very immediate problem.

Doctor Who was not, as some commentators have averred, the first television drama series to change its leading actor. The American comedy-

Western series *Maverick* (1959–1962), for example, had responded to the departure of its original star James Garner (Bret Maverick) by bringing in unlikely casting Roger Moore as English cousin Beauregard Maverick, though this proved only a temporary extension to the life of the series. In the case of *Doctor Who*, the change was forced upon the production team not by a contract dispute, as in Garner's case, but by the deteriorating health of William Hartnell. Hartnell had never enjoyed robust health at the best of times, and by 1966 the strain of the hectic rehearsal and recording schedule of *Doctor Who* was taking its toll. He was increasingly exhibiting symptoms of what would later be diagnosed as arteriosclerosis, which made it difficult to remember his lines. It was during the annual recording break in 1966 that it was agreed, by mutual consent, that Hartnell would leave the series. Consistent with *Doctor Who*'s production practice at the time, the first serial of the fourth season ('The Smugglers') had been recorded before the break, so Hartnell would return for one more story. As it happened, bronchitis forced him to miss the third episode of 'The Tenth Planet' and he was present only for part of the fourth. The director Derek Martinus assured Hartnell that 'Gerry [Davis, script editor and writer] has been very clever and has managed to write around you'.[1]

Much consideration was given to the character of the new 'Doctor Who'. Crucially, it was agreed that the replacement should be as different from Hartnell as possible. It was this decision that probably ensured the continuation of the series: to have cast an actor in similar mould would almost certainly have brought unfavourable comparisons with his predecessor. It was suggested that the new Doctor should have the 'strong, piercing eyes of the explorer or Sea Captain. His hair is wild and his clothes look rather the worse for wear (this is a legacy from the metaphysical change which took place in the Tardis).' It seems that the production team looked to another famous fictional character for inspiration: it was suggested that the new Doctor would exhibit 'the sardonic humour of Sherlock Holmes' – Douglas Wilmer had recently played the Great Detective in a BBC series of 1965 – and that 'we will introduce a love of disguises which will help and sometimes disconcert his friends.'[2]

Several actors were reportedly approached, including Ron Moody, Michael Hordern, Patrick Wymark and Trevor Howard, though in the event the role went to Patrick Troughton. According to Sydney Newman:

'Our problem in choosing the new Dr Who was very difficult because we have decided to make considerable changes in the personality of the character. We believe that we have found exactly the man we wanted.'[3] Troughton, 46 when he took over from Hartnell, was a marvellously craggy-faced character actor who had been in British films since the late 1940s and had played a memorable Quilp in a television production of *The Old Curiosity Shop* in 1962. The writers' guide described the new Doctor thus:

> The new Doctor is younger than the former (Hartnell) characterisation. He is more of an enigma, using humour to gain his ends rather than direct confrontation. His clowning tends to make his enemies underrate him and his obsession with apparent trivialities, clothes, novelties of all kinds, etc., is usually a device merely to give him time to examine a newly-discovered clue.[4]

The idea of the Doctor using disguises ('His disguise is that of a Scarlet Pimpernel and used for the same purpose') did not persist beyond his first few stories, but his shabby appearance did. With his baggy trousers and oversized, long-sleeved morning coat, Troughton's Doctor has been described as a 'cosmic hobo'. One critic described him as 'a clown looking and acting like one of the Marx Brothers. Instead of modifying nonsense, his interpretation of the part only heightens it.'[5] Yet Troughton's clowning and apparent timidity ('When I say run – run!' became his catchphrase) belie the deep intelligence and keen powers of observation of his Doctor. Outwardly he is unassuming, more affable than his predecessor and patient when explaining things to his companions, but he possesses the same insatiable curiosity, scientific prowess and moral sense of the First Doctor. Troughton's Doctor, more so than Hartnell's, is associated with certain props, such as his recorder (which he plays, badly, to relieve stressful situations) and the famous sonic screwdriver. This device (introduced in 'Fury from the Deep') represents a change in policy by the *Doctor Who* production team towards 'magical' gadgets – an early production document declared, 'If the Doctor had a rolled umbrella, it would not be of the James Bond variety'[6] – and it would become a reliable, if monotonous, means of getting the Doctor out of trouble for many years to come.

For all that the 'renewal' of the Doctor was an improvised response to an immediate circumstance, however, there is reason to believe that some sort of change of format would sooner or later have become necessary. Stewart Lane, television critic of the *Daily Worker*, averred that in its third year the series 'is definitely showing signs of age, and my spies have it that even the youngsters are getting tired of it'.[7] The quantitative evidence bears out the view that *Doctor Who*'s popularity had been declining for some time. There was a significant diminution of its audience during its third season in 1965–1966, which began with over 9 million viewers ('Galaxy 4') but ended with only 5.2 million ('The War Machines'). Moreover, the series' return in September 1966 after its annual break did not, as previously, lure back those viewers lost during the summer but confirmed that the overall trend was one of decline: the fourth-season opener 'The Smugglers' attracted an average of only 4.5 million, the lowest audience for *Doctor Who* since the series began.

Obvious reasons for the diminishing popularity of *Doctor Who* in the mid 1960s are not immediately apparent. The qualitative evidence suggests that audiences found the content of the third season of variable quality, including some of the most innovative stories to date (such as 'The Celestial Toymaker') but also some of the least popular ('The Gunfighters', for example). This may be explained by a lack of stability at the level of production. Unlike the first two seasons, when there had been the same producer (Lambert) throughout and, but for the last story of the second season, two story editors (Whitaker for the first season, Spooner for most of the second), the third season saw no fewer than three different producers (Lambert, John Wiles and Innes Lloyd) and two story editors (Donald Tosh and Gerry Davis). There was also, for the first time, direct competition for *Doctor Who* on the ITV network, where most regions were screening the imported American SF series *Lost in Space*, which, although not attracting as large a following as *Doctor Who* (it never achieved more than an 11 per cent share compared to *Doctor Who*'s third-season average of 15.2 per cent) would, nevertheless, have been competing for the same audience of genre fans.

How far did the new 'Doctor Who' turn around the fortunes of the programme? Lloyd and Davis played safe with Patrick Troughton's first adventure by bringing back the Doctor's most popular adversaries, resulting in an average audience of 7.8 million for 'The Power of the Daleks'. An average of 7.4 million was maintained for the rest of the season, suggesting that audiences had accepted the change of star. This was maintained into the fifth season in 1967–1968 – popularly known as the 'season of the monsters' – which averaged 7.2 million. The fourth and fifth seasons of *Doctor Who*, therefore, saw a more consistent audience for the series. While it did not again reach the heights of 'The Dalek Invasion of Earth' or 'The Web Planet', it was, nevertheless, not subject to the sort of fluctuation that had characterised the third season. Although this period witnessed a high turnover of story editors (Davis, Victor Pemberton, Peter Bryant and Derrick Sherwin), this does not seem to have adversely affected the series. In large measure this was because Innes Lloyd, in particular, had now stamped his authority on *Doctor Who* to such an extent that the style and content remained relatively unaffected when he left at the end of 1967. It was during Lloyd's tenure that the alien invasion or intrusion narrative – often set in an isolated base or outpost that also imposed a more uniform visual style on the series by dint of its enclosed, budget-conscious sets – came to the fore. The diversity of SF templates that had characterised the early seasons of *Doctor Who* was no longer apparent. Instead it would be the 'Threat and Disaster' template that would most determine the series' content in the years to come.

One of the reasons why the Troughton 'era' is so fondly remembered by *Doctor Who* aficionados is that it was during his time that most of the key monsters were established. It is a singular fact that Hartnell's Doctor had faced only one recurring foe (the Daleks), whereas Troughton's Doctor seemed forever to be running into Cybermen (four times), Ice Warriors (twice) and Yeti (twice), as well as a further two encounters with the Daleks. This greater emphasis on monsters was part of the new production policy initiated by Innes Lloyd, largely with a view to finding enemies for the Doctor to match the popularity of the Daleks.

This became necessary when Terry Nation, who owned part copyright in the Daleks, decided to try to market them (albeit unsuccessfully) in the USA. The writing of the two Dalek stories for the fourth season was delegated to former story editor David Whitaker. 'The Evil of the Daleks' (#36) was intended to be the final Dalek story: its last episode featured a revolt by Daleks against the authority of the Emperor Dalek. This is engineered by the Doctor, who, captured by the Daleks and taken back to Skaro, has been forced to undertake a series of experiments in order to isolate the reasons why the Daleks have always been defeated. The aim of the Emperor is to isolate 'the Dalek factor' (obedience, ruthlessness, aggression) and to use the TARDIS to 'spread it to the entire history of

Earth'. However, the Doctor contrives to instil enough Daleks with 'the human factor' (compassion, tolerance, conscience) that they question their orders and turn on the Emperor. The Daleks destroy themselves in a civil war and the Doctor remarks that 'I think we have seen the end of the Daleks forever!'

'The Evil of the Daleks' had a lower audience share than the previous Dalek serials, averaging only 6.4 million, though Audience Research found that children 'still adored the Daleks, and were devastated by the suggestion that these amusing and fantastic creatures had been finally and irrevocably wiped out'.[8] The search to find a replacement for the Daleks had begun early in Lloyd's tenure before the introduction of the new Doctor. Following 'The War Machines', for example, Lloyd had told designer Raymond London: 'I believe that the War Machines can well rank as future Daleks.'[9] The Daleks were still the yardstick for new *Doctor Who* monsters some two years after their farewell appearance. In 1969, for example, Audience Research reported: 'The Ice Warriors had a similar appeal, some noted, to the very popular Daleks.'[10] The return of popular monsters was indicative of the direction *Doctor Who* was taking in the later 1960s.

The change of direction for *Doctor Who* instigated in large measure by Lloyd had several important consequences for the series. A major casualty of the shift was the historical narrative, which was a conscious production decision. Lloyd had already signalled that he was no fan of historical stories in his response to 'The Gunfighters': '[It] has been proved before that if you put him [the Doctor] next to historical characters, even though we felt that these were more exciting than others we have done, it does in some way diminish the feeling the audience has of him as a Science Fiction figure.'[11] This seems also to have been the popular view of the series. Audiences found 'the science fiction sequences in the "Dr Who" series generally more thrilling than when Tardis travels backwards rather than forwards in time'.[12] Critic Francis Hope concurred: 'Science-fiction plays on our terror of a future out of control … A Dalek in a Victorian antique-dealer's study is merely a comic anachronism; a Dalek next week or next decade is on the margin of being a terrifying possibility.'[13]

'The Highlanders' (#31) marked the last appearance for over 15 years of the traditional *Doctor Who* historical narrative (one with no alien presence other than the Doctor and no SF content other than the

TARDIS). This story, by Elwyn Jones and Gerry Davis, represented a compromise between the competing modes of didactic history and genre spoof that had characterised the historical stories during Hartnell's reign. The TARDIS arrives in Scotland in the aftermath of the defeat of Bonnie Prince Charlie and his supporters at Culloden Moor in 1746. The generic reference point for 'The Highlanders' would seem to have been the historical romances of Sir Walter Scott and Robert Louis Stevenson: it is an adventure yarn in which the Doctor and his companions come to the assistance of members of the Clan McLaren as they flee from murderous redcoats and are captured by the villainous Solicitor Grey, who intends to transport them as slaves to the West Indies. It is during this adventure, his second, that Troughton's Doctor comes into his own, his 'Scarlet Pimpernel' traits evident in his impersonation of a 'German' doctor and in disguising himself as an old crone to escape his pursuers. Yet 'The Highlanders' does not shy away from the more uncomfortable realities of the past. It acknowledges the brutality of the English-Hanoverian army in suppressing the rebels ('The English troops are butchering all the wounded and hanging all their prisoners'), while at the same time distancing itself from mythologising the cause of the Young Pretender ('He was the first to leave the field,' one of the prince's supporters remarks bitterly). In this context it is worth noting that the BBC Documentary Department had recently produced *Culloden* (dir. Peter Watkins, 1964), a documentary-style reconstruction of the battle and its aftermath, that had portrayed Bonnie Prince Charlie as a drunkard and had presented in graphic detail the brutal pacification of the Highlands by the Duke of Cumberland's army.[14] That apart, the main significance of 'The Highlanders' for the internal history of *Doctor Who* lay in the introduction of Jamie Macrimmon (Frazer Hines), whose character was so popular that he became a constant travelling companion for the rest of the Troughton period.

The role of the Doctor's companions provides another example of how the series was changing. The original 'loyalty' characters had left during the second season, though their initial successors had been like-for-like replacements. Thus the replacement for William Russell had been Peter Purves, whose character of astronaut Steven Taylor fulfilled much the same action-man role, while the role of the teenager was filled, following Carole Ann Ford's departure at the end of 'The Dalek Invasion of Earth', first by Maureen O'Brien (Vicki) and then by Jackie Lane (Dodo). None of these actors remained in the series long enough for their characters to develop. There seems to have been a conscious decision to present the two girls as rather androgynous, sexless characters: in 'The Crusade' the Doctor had even disguised Vicki as a page boy in order to protect her from unwanted male attention. From the end of the third season, however – again coinciding with Lloyd's tenure as producer – there was a perceptible shift towards making the companions more contemporary. This was largely in response to changes in the programme's audience: research had found that during the third season nearly two-thirds of regular *Doctor Who* viewers were over fifteen.[15] The concluding third-season adventure 'The War Machines' introduced two new companions who, for the first time, represented young adults rather than either teenagers or mature males, in the form of Cockney sailor Ben Jackson (Michael Craze) and cocktail waitress Polly (Anneke Wills). Ben and Polly continued travelling with the new Doctor – a theme of the first episode of 'The Power of the Daleks' is that Ben is initially distrustful of this Doctor whom he believes to be an impostor – though the arrival of Jamie rendered the second male companion redundant. Ben and Polly left together at the end of 'The Faceless Ones'. That Jamie lasted longer than any previous companion was due in large measure to Frazer Hines's engaging performance as the simple, superstitious Scot who is 'constantly amazed and perplexed that he is wandering through Space and Time'.[16] In many respects Jamie is the ideal male companion for *Doctor Who*: his naive, childlike curiosity made him a point of identification for younger viewers (he regards the Doctor as 'a strange, lovable, wee chap ... He is obviously some sort of genial Wizard or Magician'), while his physical courage and acts of derring-do would appeal to adolescent males. There is, alas, no evidence in the audience research to suggest what effect the weekly sight of Hines's knees might have had on female viewers.

As far as the casting and characterisation of the female companions is concerned, however, *Doctor Who* cannot escape the charge levelled at many products of popular culture that it is cut to the cloth of male desire. Anneke Wills's Polly was the first female companion to exhibit any degree of sex appeal: Polly represented that archetypal sixties construction of femininity, the 'dolly bird', whose trendy clothes (mini-dresses and boyish caps) placed her firmly within contemporary fashion, while the 'look' of the svelte, blonde, pretty Wills was similar to such sixties icons as actress Julie Christie and model Jean Shrimpton.

However, in contrast to the thoroughly emancipated heroines of the ABC secret agent adventure series *The Avengers* (1961–1969) – Honor Blackman's Cathy Gale and Diana Rigg's Emma Peel – Polly was a rather more conventional screaming heroine who usually needed rescuing. Ann Lawrence of the *Morning Star* was even moved to complain: 'I wish we could have a little less screaming from Anneke Wills as Polly … Isn't it possible to allow her a slightly more intelligent reaction to sudden shock?'[17] Much the same criticism was made of Juliet Harmer, heroine of the BBC's *Avengers* clone *Adam Adamant Lives!* (1966–1967) – one critic described her as 'a breathless blonde dolly'[18] – and it is interesting to note that while the corporation was adept at devising eccentric male protagonists it struggled, in the mid 1960s, to come to terms with the sort of progressive female role that characterised *The Avengers*. Following the departure of Ben and Polly, the Doctor and Jamie were careful to collect only young, pretty female companions. These represented contrasting types of femininity: Victoria Waterfield (Deborah Watling), whom the Doctor takes under his wing after her father is killed by the Daleks, was a naive, demure young woman from Victorian England, whereas her successor, shapely twenty-first-century astrophysicist Zoë Heriot (Wendy Padbury), was intelligent, assertive and supposed to represent an intellectual challenge to the Doctor. By now it was clear from their costumes that the female companions were there to provide an element of glamour: Watling's long Victorian skirts quickly became shorter (she even remarks upon this herself in 'The Tomb of the Cybermen'), while Padbury modelled a range of sub-*Avengers* fashions including a PVC mini-skirt ('The Krotons') and a remarkable figure-hugging lamé costume ('The Mind Robber') whose entire *raison d'être* seems to have been to allow the camera to linger on her *derrière*. Following the sober attire of the original companions Ian and Barbara (both respectable schoolteachers, after all), it would seem that costume design in *Doctor Who* was making a conscious attempt to catch up with the fashions and youth-oriented culture of 'Swinging London'.

If the casting of physically attractive female companions exemplified a new direction for *Doctor Who*, however, it did not attract as much attention at the time as another trend that was not to the liking of various commentators – the increasingly horrific and violent content of the series. As a programme whose audience included a significant percentage of younger children, *Doctor Who* was always vulnerable to charges of being unsuitable for such viewers. There had been occasional letters of complaint from concerned parents almost from the start of the series, but it was during the Troughton period, with its greater emphasis on monsters, that the cause was taken up by the press. Francis Hope complained that *Doctor Who*

> is just too frightening for some real children. I know of one four-year-old who stood rigid with terror in front of the soft-whispering Ice Warriors, inviting his mother to come and hold his hand in case she was frightened, but I know many more households where the programme's name is forbidden in case the older children acquire a taste for it and the younger ones refuse to be excluded.[19]

Complaints about the level of violence in *Doctor Who* reached a crescendo over 'The Tomb of the Cybermen' (#37), which was debated on the BBC's viewers' discussion programme *Talkback* in October 1967. Kit Pedler, co-writer of 'The Tomb of the Cybermen', responded to the criticisms with an assurance that 'the production team and the writers on this programme take very particular care to ensure that the material transmitted is in no way injurious to the psychology of children.' He went on:

> Of course the programme sets out to frighten, but to frighten in a way that allows the child to react successfully without itself becoming essentially involved. The BBC would certainly not allow any sadistic or referable human cruelty to appear on the programme and all the 'villains' in the stories are carefully designed to be non-human.[20]

The argument that the horror of *Doctor Who* was 'safe' because it was presented in a context of outright fantasy was also put forward by Julian Critchley in *The Times*, who called it 'the most successful of children's programmes ... Doctor Who's infallibility is a device that allows even a nervous child to believe that in spite of the most alarming experiences all will be well in the end. It is reality, or what passes for it, that children find truly terrifying.'[21]

Evidence from Audience Research regarding the effects of *Doctor Who* on children is mixed: undoubtedly the youngest children did find it frightening, though at the same time, as one parent put it, 'my kids thrived on the horror.'[22] In this sense *Doctor Who* was rather like a fairy tale or a story such as *The Wizard of Oz*: part of its appeal was the sensation of being frightened. The standard defence of the *Doctor Who* production team has always been that children are capable of differentiating between fantasy and reality, and that as long as the frightening content is contained within an obviously fantastic context then it is not harmful. There were occasions, however, on which they transgressed the boundary of acceptable horror. One particularly notorious instance was the cliff-hanger ending of the first episode of 'The Underwater Menace' (#32). The Doctor and his companions have arrived in Atlantis where they discover the Atlanteans have created a species of 'fish people' by operating on shipwrecked humans and inserting plastic gills so they can breathe underwater. The first episode ends with a terrified, screaming Polly being dragged into an operating theatre and forcibly restrained as the Atlanteans prepare to operate on her. An organisation calling itself the National Association for the Welfare of Children in Hospital (NAWCH) complained that the scene would be distressing

> [for] about 5,000 children [who] will have some sort of operation during the course of this week – more than half of them for the removal of tonsils and adenoids ... We realise that thrillers have to be made frightening and exciting; but is it fair to do this by playing on a situation which children are going to need all their courage to face in real life?[23]

Lloyd was measured in his response: he averred that 'the last thing any programme such as ours wishes to do is to cause fear which can be carried into ordinary life, especially where children are concerned', though claimed that *Doctor Who* 'is, I believe, accepted by children as a fantasy, which bears little relation to their everyday existence' and suggested that the 'many fantastic situations' in the episode 'would dissipate any reality which they felt about the operation scene at the end'. Without actually conceding the point, nevertheless, he concluded: 'We are, naturally, most concerned if the effect does frighten children who are faced with an operation, and certainly in future scripts we will pay particular attention to the points you have raised.'[24]

At the same time as highlighting its 'many fantastic situations', however, Lloyd was attempting to push *Doctor Who* in a more realistic direction. Another consequence of his new production policy was a trend away from outright fantasy and towards more serious SF themes concerned with mapping the possible course of scientific and technological progress. The time-travel premise of *Doctor Who* could never be described as 'hard' SF, of course, but, particularly during Gerry Davis's stint as story editor, there was a concern to represent more plausible futuristic scenarios. A good example of this is 'The Moonbase' (#33), in which the Cybermen attempt to take over a weather-control station on the moon. The suggestion that there would be lunar colonies by 2070 was a not entirely far-fetched scenario in the mid 1960s at the time of the American 'Apollo' space programme. Scenes on the lunar surface are realised with a degree of visual authenticity by director Morris Barry, using slow-motion to create the sort of movement that anticipates television pictures of astronauts walking on the moon only a few years later. Ann Lawrence approved of the more realistic treatment: 'Written by Kit Pedler, himself a scientist and research worker, the present adventure of the crew of the Tardis has a better-balanced mixture of science and fiction.'[25] It would seem that viewers agreed:

> This particular *Dr Who* adventure, 'The Moonbase', seems on the whole to have kept many in the sample fairly happily entertained. They often took it with a large grain of salt, but, even so, enjoyed a situation that, as a Fitter pointed out, reflects 'the dream of many to reach the moon'. The idea of being able to control the Earth's weather from a moon station was original too, as other viewers maintained, and the story won approval from another group because it was real science-fiction, at least in reference to the electronic technicalities with which Hobson, Dr Who and the rest of the team were concerned.[26]

Much the same story was reworked in 'The Seeds of Death' (#48), in which the Ice Warriors, this time, take control of a lunar station as the first step in their planned invasion of Earth. On this occasion, audiences 'appreciated an imaginative science fiction script with an ingenious but not too far-fetched plot'. One respondent said: 'The fact that some of the incidents *could* just happen in the future, i.e. the station to control weather, added to my enjoyment.'[27] Stuart Hood admired 'The Space Pirates' (#49), which attempted to present a realistic view of space travel and whose transmission coincided with the Apollo 9 mission. Hood noted 'the extent to which the inventors of the series have kept pace with the observed (and televised) advances of modern technology'. 'It is one of the great strengths of *Dr Who*,' he added, 'that, while it refers back to archetypal situations involving extreme danger and survival from it, it also aims at credibility in detail.'[28]

The attempt to relate *Doctor Who* to the themes of hard SF was due in large measure to the influence of Dr Christopher Magnus Howard ('Kit') Pedler, who became an unofficial scientific adviser to the series during Davis's time as story editor following appearances on the popular science series *Horizon*. Pedler, an ophthalmologist and a leading authority on electron-microscopy, contributed ideas for several *Doctor Who* stories in the mid 1960s. The first serial he devised, though actually written by Ian Stuart Black, was 'The War Machines' (#27), which is concerned with a theme that had become topical in the 1960s: the policing of technological progress. The Doctor (here in his William Hartnell incarnation) arrives back in contemporary London where he is disturbed by the atmosphere around the Post Office Tower (recently opened in 1966) and suspects that something is amiss. It transpires that a super-computer known as WOTAN (World Operating Thought ANalogue), designed by members of the Royal Scientific Club, is based in the Tower. WOTAN is logical and supremely powerful: it concludes that 'the world cannot progress further with mankind running it' and proceeds to brainwash its operators into building an army of tank-like war robots that it unleashes against London. The notion that technology, left unchecked, represents a real threat to mankind's future is made chillingly clear when the brainwashed Major Green declares to Ben: 'You are the enemy of mechanised evolution. Nothing must be allowed to prevent the machines from taking over. They are the next stage in the growth of life on Earth. All obstacles will be swept aside – including you.' In this regard 'The War Machines' can be located within a lineage of warning narratives about technology running amok and turning on mankind. Its omnipotent, malevolent super-computer anticipates SF films such as *2001: A Space Odyssey* (dir. Stanley Kubrick, 1968), *Colossus – The Forbin Project* (dir. Joseph Sargent, 1969) and *Demon Seed* (dir. Donald Cammell, 1977), as well as several episodes of *Star Trek* ('The Changeling' and 'The Ultimate Computer', both 1967), while the confrontation between man and intelligent machines would form the basis of the SF classic *The Terminator* (dir. James Cameron, 1984): in this particular instance *Doctor Who* was ahead of the field of topical SF. 'The War Machines' is important for other reasons, too. Like 'The Dalek Invasion of Earth', it refers explicitly to the historical experience of the Second World War as the war machines bring their devastation to London: 'The city of London has responded with characteristic calm to the emergency,' declares newsreader Kenneth Kendall, whose appearance as himself represents, in its way, a sort of authenticating device. When the army is called in to fight the war machines, furthermore, it anticipates the later UNIT stories in which the enemy threat is defeated by a combination of British military force and the Doctor's scientific knowledge: he neutralises the machines with a magnetic field and reprograms them to attack and destroy WOTAN. On this occasion, however, viewers were less than impressed: the story 'held little or no appeal for about half the sample' who, it seems, found the premise 'preposterous' and 'too absurdly fantastic to accept'.[29]

Pedler's most significant contribution to *Doctor Who*, however, was in the creation of the Cybermen, who came to rank second only to the Daleks in the series' gallery of monsters. Pedler was fascinated by the notion of what might happen to human beings if they were able to replace limbs and organs with artificial parts: he had a phobia of 'dehumanised medicine' and 'conceived the idea of someone with so many mechanical replacements that he didn't know whether he was human or machine'.[30] The Cybermen had both cultural and scientific ancestry. The notion of replacing body parts had informed Mary Shelley's *Frankenstein*, first published in 1818, while various types of robots and androids had been a staple of SF cinema since *Metropolis* (dir. Fritz Lang, 1926). The silver, metallic, humanoid-shaped appearance of the Cybermen is visually reminiscent of the giant robot Gort in the SF classic *The Day the Earth Stood Still* (dir. Robert Wise, 1951), whose body, like the Cybermen, was impregnable to small arms and who was armed with a built-in disintegrator ray. The Cybermen, however, were not mechanically constructed robots but rather cyborgs (cybernetic organisms) who had replaced their flesh-and-blood bodies with mechanical parts. The science informing this idea was not entirely implausible: prosthetics and plastic surgery had made significant advances during the Second World War; the 1960s saw the development of the first implantable heart pacemakers; and organ replacement surgery became a reality when the pioneering surgeon Dr Christiaan Barnard performed the first heart transplant in 1967. It was the ethical and philosophical issues arising from the theoretical possibilities of cybernetics and bio-mechanics that informed the creation of the Cybermen.

The Cybermen represented the nightmarish possibilities of 'dehumanised medicine': physical augmentation taken to its extreme. Once they had been humanoid, inhabitants of the Earth's 'twin planet' of Mondas but, seeing their race dying from disease, they had replaced their limbs and organs with artificial parts to the extent that they had become more machine than man. The Cybermen regard themselves as superior to human beings because during the process of augmentation 'certain weaknesses have been removed … You call them emotions.' Consequently the Cybermen themselves have become a race of unfeeling automatons who 'are equipped to survive … Anything else is of no importance.' The difference between human beings and the Cybermen is first rehearsed in 'The Tenth Planet' in which a party of Cybermen attack a space-tracking station at the South Pole in December 1986. They intend to drain the Earth of its energy and to turn its inhabitants into Cybermen:

> *Krail*
> *(Cyberman)*: You must come and live with us.
>
> *Polly*: We cannot live with you. You're different. You've got no feelings.
>
> *Krail*: Fee-lings. I do not understand that word.
>
> *The Doctor*: Emotions. Love, pride, hate, fear. Have you no emotions, sir?
>
> *Krail*: Come to Mondas and you will have no need of emotions. You will become like us.
>
> *Polly*: Like you?
>
> *Krail*: We have freedom from disease, protection against heat and cold, true mastery. Do you prefer to die in misery?

The Cybermen are physically stronger than humans and are more technologically advanced, though it turns out (in this first story at least) that they are vulnerable to radiation. The only solution to their threat is to destroy their planet with a super-nuke known as the Z-Bomb. The Earth is saved by using a weapon of immense destructive power: an affirmation, perhaps, of the nuclear deterrent, but also, only two decades after Hiroshima and Nagasaki, a reminder of the technological monster unleashed by the atomic bomb.

The Cybermen were popular enough with viewers to warrant their quick return. 'I am exceedingly keen to get the maximum screen promotion for this programme as our audience figures begin to show a marked upward trend, which, obviously, we want to maintain,' Lloyd remarked a fortnight before broadcast of the first episode of 'The Moonbase'.[31] The return of the Cybermen brought a higher reaction index (58 for the last episode) than the preceding serial 'The Underwater Menace' (a highest index of 48) and ensured that they would become recurring adversaries. Although Pedler was credited as co-writer (sometimes even as sole writer) of the Cyberman serials, the actual scripts were mostly written by Davis and, later, by Whitaker and Sherwin. Later Cyberman stories were criticised for being narratively similar – 'The Tenth Planet', 'The Moonbase' and 'The Wheel in Space' all adhered to the same basic formula as the Cybermen attempt to take over an isolated outpost as a prelude to an invasion of the Earth – but the Cybermen themselves would remain an audience-pleasing adversary. The design of the Cyber costumes was modified over the subsequent serials – later-generation Cybermen were more streamlined than the cloth-faced, lumbering giants carrying hairdryers on their heads who appeared in 'The Tenth Planet' – and what was initially a way of making the suits more actor-friendly also became a means of showing the evolution of the Cyber race as they shed their remaining human parts and became increasingly robotic in appearance. They seem to have been more frightening for children than the Daleks. Ann Lawrence, for example, wrote that the Cybermen 'gave my daughter nightmares. When I asked her why she was frightened of the Cybermen but not of the Daleks, she replied that the Cybermen looked like terrible human beings, whereas the Daleks were just Daleks.'[32]

'The Tomb of the Cybermen' – regarded by many aficionados as one of the very best of all *Doctor Who* stories – not only differed from the usual Cyberman formula but also marked one of the first occasions when the series referred to its own mythology in an overtly self-conscious way. It takes place on an unnamed planet at some time in the future where an archaeological expedition from Earth has found the entrance to the lost city of Telos, believed to contain 'the last remnants of the Cybermen' who are now thought to be extinct ('They've been dead for the last five hundred years'). Entering the city, the expedition finds Cybermen frozen in cryogenic preservation chambers. They are revived by expedition member Klieg, a megalomaniac who seeks the knowledge and strength of the Cybermen to aid his own quest for power ('You see, Doctor, yours is the privilege to witness for the first time the union between their mass power and my absolute intelligence'). With its narrative of avaricious archaeologists opening a sealed tomb and reawakening the sleeping monster that lies within, 'The Tomb of the Cybermen' has drawn comparisons with the horror genre of Mummy films, exemplified by Universal Studios in the 1940s and by Hammer Films in the 1960s. Here, however, it is not an ancient supernatural curse that is awakened, but a futuristic technological menace. It transpires that the Cybermen have set a trap for the expedition, whom they plan to turn into 'the first of a new race of Cybermen'. The response of the Cyber Controller to Jamie's protest is chilling indeed:

Jamie:	A new race of Cybermen? But we're human! We're not like you!
Cyber Controller:	You – will – be.

The sequence of the Cybermen emerging from their cryogenic preservation units is one of the most memorable moments in the series' history: it might be interpreted as a symbolic 'birth' as they break through the protective membranes that seal them inside the womb. If this seems a rather fanciful reading, then the climax of the serial includes what seems a very conscious homage to H. Rider Haggard as the character of Toberman – the loyal black servant of the treacherous Kaftan, whose arm has been replaced with a cybernetic limb – dies while holding back the great doors of the tomb to seal the Cybermen inside. His last words ('They shall never pass Toberman') irresistibly bring to mind the death of the great warrior Umslopogaas 'holding the stair' at the end of Haggard's *Allan Quatermain*. It is often said that *Doctor Who* is at its best when such influences are apparent: 'The Tomb of the

Cybermen' illustrates how the series is able simultaneously to draw on themes and motifs from other sources whilst incorporating them within its own mythology.

The Cyberman stories are archetypal of the Troughton period, which was dominated by the 'Threat and Disaster' school of SF and which featured numerous serials set in isolated, confined outposts where a small group of people battle alien invaders: others, in addition to those already mentioned, include 'The Power of the Daleks', 'The Macra Terror', 'The Ice Warriors', 'The Web of Fear', 'Fury from the Deep' and 'The Seeds of Death'. The invasion or intrusion narrative is posited on a threat to the 'known' world from an 'unknown' source: the monster is discovered and goes on the rampage, threatening the whole of humanity, until it is finally destroyed by a combination of scientific knowledge (provided by the Doctor) and human ingenuity. There is much textual evidence to suggest that the intrusion narratives of *Doctor Who* were modelled on specific generic examples: indeed this was clearly a deliberate production strategy. It was to the classic Howard Hawks-produced SF/horror film *The Thing from Another World* (dir. Christian Nyby, 1951), for example, that director Derek Martinus looked when shooting the Brian Hayles-scripted 'The Ice Warriors' (#39). There are too many narrative and visual similarities to be mere coincidence: the isolated scientific base, the discovery of an alien creature encased in ice, the scene of the creature's revival, its apparent invulnerability to weapons, the failed attempt to befriend it and the climactic destruction of the creature in a fiery inferno. Here the 'thing' is Varga and the other world is 'the red planet': it is one of the scientists who dubs the giant, lumbering, scaly-armoured creature an 'Ice Warrior'. Varga (played by Bernard Bresslaw) was 'a long part, involving much more than is usual with a "Who" monster'.[33] His hostility is explained in terms of his realisation of his own difference in a world that is not his: 'They would not help me. They would keep me as a curiosity, and they would leave my warriors for dead. But with my men, I can talk from strength. Then we shall decide whether to go back to our own world or to conquer this.' The conventional interpretation of SF/horror intrusion narratives of this sort is to characterise the monster as a form of 'Other' that represents cultural anxieties around race and immigration. To this extent *Doctor Who* can be seen as responding to social tensions: it was in April 1968 that the controversial right-wing Conservative MP Enoch Powell advocated the repatriation of

Commonwealth immigrants in a speech at Birmingham during which he provocatively quoted a classical reference to the River Tiber 'foaming with much blood'.[34]

The influence of other generic sources is illustrated once again by 'The Abominable Snowmen' (#38), which shares several motifs in common with Hammer's *The Abominable Snowman* (dir. Val Guest, 1957), adapted by *Quatermass* writer Nigel Kneale from his 1955 television play *The Creature*: the bleak Himalayan setting, the explorer searching for the elusive creatures rumoured to roam the mountains, the isolated monastery where the monks guard their secrets from the outside world and the Yeti themselves. In this instance, however, the Yeti turn out not to be indigenous inhabitants but robots who are controlled by the 'Great Intelligence', a formless entity in outer space that intends to take over the world. It is an early example of what would become a regular motif of *Doctor Who*: to explain familiar myths of the Earth's past through an extra-terrestrial presence. (This idea also featured in the SF-secret agent series *The Six Million Dollar Man*, in which the North American equivalent of the Yeti, Big Foot, turns out to be a robot controlled by aliens who have landed on Earth.) The serial was popular enough to warrant a sequel, 'The Web of Fear' (#41), in which the Yeti return to infest the London Underground. Directed by Douglas Camfield, 'The Web of Fear' is one of the classic *Doctor Who* stories, making highly effective use of its enclosed, claustrophobic sets to create an atmosphere of paranoia and terror. It derives its impact from the intrusion of an alien presence into an identifiable setting that would be familiar to many viewers: what was just another monster when seen in the distant Himalayas becomes the stuff of nightmares when brought closer to home. So frightening was this story, indeed, that it has become part of *Doctor Who* folklore that 'The Web of Fear' did for the Piccadilly Line what *Psycho* (dir. Alfred Hitchcock, 1960) had done for motel showers and what *Jaws* (dir. Steven Spielberg, 1975) would do for beach holidays. In locating its horror in the Underground – an idea later used to good effect in the film *Death Line* (dir. Gary Sherman, 1972) – 'The Web of Fear' can also be located within a rich tradition of horrific and thriller narratives in which a 'chaos world' of menace and disorder lurks beneath the surface of everyday normality.

The motif of monsters emerging from the depths is a recurring one throughout the Troughton period. In 'Fury from the Deep' (#42), for example, the threat is represented by living seaweed – 'a parasite that attaches itself to other living things' – that rises from the ocean floor and attacks the crew of a gas refinery. This story is an early example of the environmentalist theme that would come to inform *Doctor Who* during the 1970s. In what seems an ironic riposte to the series' critics, the killer seaweed proves vulnerable to extreme noise and is destroyed by a recording of Victoria's screams. In 'The Macra Terror' (#34) the giant crab-like monsters threatening a human colony seem like an homage to 1950s B-movie creature features such as *Them!* (dir. Gordon Douglas, 1954), *Tarantula* (dir. Jack Arnold, 1955) and *The Black Scorpion* (dir. Edward Ludwig, 1957), though on a deeper level the serial can be interpreted as a dystopian narrative of social control in the tradition of George Orwell's *Nineteen Eighty-Four* (1949). The 'Big Brother' here is the Controller who uses broadcast propaganda to indoctrinate the colony's inhabitants into thinking they are happy when in fact they are being exploited. A scene in which a group of miners sing of how they enjoy their work ('Everyone up, the sun is out … We're the gang that works the hardest, rah rah rah') is reminiscent of the Soviet 'tractor musicals' of the 1930s where happy workers sing about their efforts to improve their work quotas and to extol the Five-Year Plan.

'The Invasion' (#46), very much a prototype for the future trajectory of *Doctor Who* in the 1970s, brings together three separate strands that are all characteristic of this period in the series' history. The first is the intrusion of an alien invader (revealed at the end of the fourth episode to be none other than the Cybermen) into familiar London settings. The serial includes a signature *Doctor Who* image as the Cybermen march down the steps in front of St Paul's Cathedral: a sequence that manages simultaneously to be both entirely incongruous yet resonates with historic meaning (the landmark that the *Luftwaffe* could not destroy). The second strand is the theme of technological paranoia. Here the Cybermen have made an alliance with industrialist Tobias Vaughn, whose International Electromatics Corporation has inserted micro-circuits capable of controlling human minds in everyday electrical devices. The megalomaniac Vaughn is a first cousin of the crazed automation experts who populated *The Avengers*: 'Uniformity, duplication. My whole empire is based on that principle. The very model of business efficiency.' Vaughn desires to control the world and plans to use the Cybermen as a means to an end, forcing the captive Professor Watkins to build a device to control them by inducing fear – an emotional reaction unknown to the Cybermen. The third strand is that the invasion is defeated by a combination of the Doctor's scientific knowledge and British military force. 'The Invasion' is significant in the internal history of *Doctor Who* in that it introduces UNIT (United Nations Intelligence Taskforce), a top-secret paramilitary organisation created specifically to deal with such occurrences. The British section of UNIT is led by Brigadier Lethbridge-Stewart (Nicholas Courtney) who had first appeared, as a colonel, in 'The Web of Fear' and whose sangfroid in the face of alien invaders would secure him a regular supporting role in the series during the 1970s. As the last episode of 'The Invasion' includes a prominent credit acknowledging the assistance of the Ministry of Defence it would seem that the story enjoyed a level of official support. The serial asserts Britain's ability to defend herself: it is a British missile battery that destroys the Cyber fleet and British troops who battle the Cybermen on the ground. To this extent it belongs squarely in the tradition of using SF as a form of Cold War propaganda.

'The Invasion' is yet another example of the 'Threat and Disaster' type of narrative that predominated in *Doctor Who* during the late 1960s. There were some complaints from viewers, however, that the series 'had become too familiar and repetitive ... New ideas and themes were required'.[35] The production team was sensitive to such criticism. There was an attempt during the sixth season in 1968–1969 – produced by Peter Bryant and then Derrick Sherwin, with Sherwin and Terrance Dicks as story editors – to reintroduce a greater level of narrative variation in line with earlier seasons. 'The Dominators' (#44), for example, overlaid its familiar narrative of resistance to totalitarianism with an allegorical dimension that was explicitly anti-pacifist. The cruel Dominators ('masters of the ten galaxies') and their deadly robotic servants the Quarks invade the peaceful planet of Dulkis ('a society of total pacifists') in order to exploit its natural resources for their war effort. The Dulcians, who have rejected war and violence, are unwilling to resist and unable to comprehend that the Dominators are not reasonable like themselves ('For centuries we have lived in peace. We have proved that universal gentleness will cause aggression to die'). The message is unequivocal: pacifism is not a practical answer to aggressors and resistance is preferable to oppression ('All submission leads to slavery. We must fight!').

Another attempt to vary the content, 'The Krotons' (#47), was the first *Doctor Who* script by one of the series' most prolific writers, Robert Holmes, who felt that it 'gets away from the usual pattern up to now – in part at any rate – so that Dr Who & Co. have only themselves to worry about'.[36] The Doctor and his companions arrive on a planet where a peaceful race known as the Gonds live in thrall to the Krotons, crystalline beings whose spaceship landed there many centuries ago. The Krotons control the education of the Gonds through special machines in a Hall of Knowledge and every generation the most promising students are selected to become 'companions' of the Krotons. The Doctor discovers that the Krotons feed off the mental energy of the Gonds, and that they are attempting to revive their dormant fellows. Although handicapped by its less-than-terrifying monsters (the Krotons themselves look like large egg boxes and one of them speaks with a pronounced Brummie accent), the idea behind 'The Krotons' is quite imaginative and certainly different from other *Doctor Who* stories of the time. It has a number of similarities to a 1967 *Star Trek* episode, 'The Apple', in which a living computer ensures that the people who maintain it live in complete ignorance of scientific and technological progress: here the arrival of Captain Kirk and his associates is an allegory of the Garden of Eden in which forbidden knowledge is introduced into paradise. 'The Krotons' achieved a higher audience share than 'The Invasion' and qualitative responses described it as an 'excellent science fiction story'.[37]

The most unusual and radical departure from the usual 'Threat and Disaster' formula, however, was 'The Mind Robber' (#45), an excursion into pure fantasy that ranks as one of the most original of all *Doctor Who* stories. To escape a volcanic eruption at the end of the previous story ('The Dominators') the Doctor has to resort to using an emergency unit that 'takes the TARDIS out of the time-space dimension – out of reality'. This is another narrative of displacement in which the protagonists find themselves in an entirely unreal environment: the Land of Fiction, populated by characters from literature and folklore, including Gulliver (who speaks only the words written for him by Swift), Rapunzel, the Medusa and the Karkus (a superhero whom Zoë recognises from a twenty-first-century comic strip). 'I think we may be in a place where nothing is impossible,' the Doctor remarks; the story delights in devising bizarre situations such as Jamie and Zoë being crushed in the pages of a giant book or facing a unicorn that seems about to trample them to death until the Doctor convinces them that it is not real. The Land of Fiction is the creation of 'The Master', who, it transpires, is a writer of adventure stories who 'left England in the summer of 1926' and has now become 'virtually a prisoner' in that he is connected to a machine and forced to invent stories for its amusement. The Doctor is forced to engage in a battle of wits against the machine by devising a story of his own, knowing that if he inadvertently writes something about himself and his companions he will turn them into fictional characters who will no longer exist in reality.

There are various ways of reading 'The Mind Robber'. One is to relate its narrative invention to the crises affecting its production: an extra episode had to be added when another episode fell through and the second episode had to be rewritten when Frazer Hines contracted chickenpox and could not appear that week (he was replaced by another actor, with Jamie's new appearance explained when the Doctor incorrectly pieces together a jigsaw of his face). Another reading is to interpret it all as the Doctor's dream: the textual evidence for this are the narrative *non-sequiturs* and the fact that the next serial ('The Invasion') opens with the Doctor sitting in the same position as he was before the 'explosion' of the TARDIS. Yet another interpretation would be to see 'The Mind Robber' as *Doctor Who*'s version of a hallucinogenic or psychedelic 'trip' of a sort that characterised late 1960s films such as *2001: A Space Odyssey*. An indication that the serial might even have been written under the influence of soft drugs is to be found in a letter from story editor Derrick Sherwin to writer Peter Ling: 'Leave the pure SF and monster bits to those with un-original minds!! I shall still be around to discuss ideas if you feel you want to confer with an almost permanently stoned associate!'[38] The response to 'The Mind Robber', however, was mixed. About a third of viewers thought it 'an enjoyable fantasy' that was 'clever and original', but otherwise 'this episode only served to confirm the growing feeling that the element of fantasy in *Dr Who* was getting out of hand', while some respondents felt that 'it had now deteriorated into ridiculous rubbish which could no longer be dignified by the term Science Fiction'. It was also thought to be 'far too complicated for younger viewers – who were, after all, its main audience'.[39]

Despite the attempts to introduce changes to its format, both the quantitative and the qualitative evidence indicate that, once again, the popularity of *Doctor Who* was waning. The average audience throughout the sixth season was 6.7 million, but there was a haemorrhaging of viewers towards the end with a low of 3.5 million for the eighth episode of the seemingly interminable 'The War Games'. This sort of fluctuation is indicative of the inconsistent quality of the sixth season in comparison to its predecessors, for there was no regular competition on the ITV network where *Land of the Giants*, *Voyage to the Bottom of the Sea* and *Tarzan* were screened in different regions. Audience Research, moreover, found that there was 'no more than moderate interest' in the series amongst its regular viewers. 'Some of the sample,' it was reported, 'who had enjoyed *Dr Who* "in the old days", felt that the stories were getting further and further away from the original intention'.[40]

The declining popularity of *Doctor Who* in 1969 inevitably fuelled speculation about the future of the series. There had been significant institutional changes within the BBC since the series started. Most of those involved with the early history of *Doctor Who* had moved on: Newman had left the corporation in 1967, Lambert joined London Weekend Television shortly afterwards, and Lloyd and Donald Wilson had moved on to other projects. The sixth season was beset by problems: one serial was scrapped during pre-production and a hurried replacement had to be commissioned. At the same time as viewers were leaving, moreover, costs were rising. The fifth season had overspent considerably, and, while the sixth season came in slightly under budget, this was achieved by recourse to longer serials that reduced expenditure on set design by spreading it over more episodes.[41] Furthermore, like William Hartnell before him, Patrick Troughton was feeling the strain of playing 'Doctor Who' for almost three continuous years and had decided to call time. Thus it was that a great deal of uncertainty hung over the series as Terrance Dicks and Malcolm Hulke wrote 'The War Games' (#50), a ten-part serial designed to resolve the various loose ends in case it turned out to be the last ever *Doctor Who*. As it happened the series was renewed, though this decision was not confirmed until after 'The War Games' had been recorded.

'The War Games' exemplifies Tulloch and Alvarado's notion of *Doctor Who* as an 'unfolding text': its significance for the internal history of the series is that it reveals the mystery of 'who' the Doctor really is. In fact it is really two stories in one, a narrative device that would become increasingly familiar in the 1970s. The TARDIS lands on a planet divided into zones each resembling major wars from the Earth's past

(First World War, the Crimea, American Civil War, Napoleonic Wars and others) where thousands of brainwashed soldiers are fighting under the command of alien officers. They have been lifted from their own time zones and are now unwitting participants in an experiment to find 'the most disciplined and courageous fighters'. The technology to do this is provided by the War Chief, who controls a time machine similar to the TARDIS, and who, it turns out, belongs to the same race as the Doctor himself – the Time Lords. The purpose, he tells the Doctor, is 'to conquer the entire galaxy. We are going to bring a new order to the galaxy – a united galactic empire'. 'The War Games' was criticised for its 'uncalled-for degree of violence'. 'Bearing in mind that *Dr Who* is compulsive viewing for a very large number of young children,' complained Ann Lawrence, 'and often very young ones at that, this wholesale killing of people is unsuitable, to say the least.'[42]

It is in the last two episodes of 'The War Games' that the second story emerges, and it represents arguably the most significant turning point in the developing narrative of *Doctor Who*. Realising that he is unable to return all the thousands of combatants to their own times, the Doctor sends a message to the Time Lords requesting their assistance. This is duly given – the powerful Time Lords intervene to end the war games – but the Doctor finds himself called before a tribunal of his own people and put on trial for his misdemeanours. The Time Lords have a strict doctrine of non-interference in the affairs of other planets which the Doctor has broken on many occasions. The Doctor's defence is that he has intervened to help in the struggle against evil forces throughout the universe. The trial rehearses debates around insularity versus intervention and law versus conscience that have both universal and specific historical resonances. The Doctor's argument is a moralistic one: that those with the power to do so should stand against the forces of evil. He shows the tribunal mental images of the monsters he has encountered and tells them: 'All these evils I have fought, while you have done nothing but observe. True, I am guilty of interference – just as you are guilty of failing to use your great powers to help those in need.' In the context of twentieth-century Britain, pro-interventionist narratives have invariably been directed towards the USA. In this regard, 'The War Games' might be seen as another of *Doctor Who*'s allegories of the events of the Second World War. It also has possible Cold War overtones: the Time Lords might be seen as a sort of outer-space United Nations who are the last court of appeal for disputes. The United Nations had intervened in the Korean War (1950–1953) and in the Congo during the early 1960s, but it had failed to mount successful opposition to Soviet military intervention in Hungary (1956) or Czechoslovakia (1968).

The outcome of the Doctor's trial is that the Time Lords accept there are occasions when intervention may be justified and decree that his punishment for the transgression of their laws will be his exile to Earth in the twentieth century ('We have noted your particular interest in the planet Earth. The frequency of your visits must have given you special knowledge of that world and its problems'). The Doctor's companions are returned to their own times, his TARDIS is immobilised and the Doctor is forced to change his appearance again. 'The War Games' marks a point of natural closure for *Doctor Who* on several levels: narrative, cultural and institutional. It was signalling that when it returned (after a hitherto unprecedented six-month gap) it would be in a new format and would feature a new 'Doctor Who'. There would be a new production team, with incumbent producer Sherwin supervising only the first serial of the next season, and it would also be in colour, consistent with the introduction of colour broadcasting on BBC1 from November 1969. That *Doctor Who* would survive into the 1970s, especially given its diminishing audience towards the end of its sixth season, was probably due in some measure to external factors. The last episode of 'The War Games' was broadcast on 21 June 1969. A month later, on 21 July, television broadcast images of Apollo 11 astronauts Neil Armstrong and Buzz Aldrin on the surface of the Moon. The Apollo 11 mission represents, symbolically, the moment when science fact overtook science fiction. The 'dream' of reaching the Moon mentioned by one viewer only two years before had become reality. This influenced the trajectory of the SF genre in various ways, the most significant of which was a shift back to more plausible and realistic scenarios. Man had reached the Moon, but *Doctor Who* was about to come back down to Earth.

3

Earthbound

1970–1974

I had a great belief that it was much more frightening to stay on Earth – that all the threats should come to Earth, rather than us going off to other planets. There's nothing more alarming than coming home and finding a Yeti sitting on your loo in Tooting Bec.

Jon Pertwee (Third Doctor)
speaking on *Doctor Who: 30 Years in the TARDIS*

As it moved into the 1970s, *Doctor Who* again underwent changes in both its format and its style. In the series' internal history this was the time of the Doctor's 'exile' on Earth, during which he became the unofficial scientific adviser to UNIT, the special military organisation formed to combat the ever more frequent alien invasions that occurred during these years. The decision to maroon the Doctor on Earth has usually been seen as a cost-cutting exercise to reduce expenditure on extraterrestrial sets, though any saving in this regard was offset by the increased cost of making the series in colour. In real terms the budget for *Doctor Who* actually increased in the early and mid 1970s. Where production economies were evident, however, was in the reduction of the number of episodes: each season now ran for only half the year, 25 or 26 weeks, rather than the 40-plus weeks that had hitherto been the case. Furthermore, it was a new Doctor who fell out of the TARDIS in the first episode of 'Spearhead from Space' in the form of Jon Pertwee, whose casting had been announced at the end of the previous season.

Following the troubled sixth season in 1968–1969, the early 1970s was a time of greater stability for the series with one producer (Barry Letts) and one script editor (Terrance Dicks) at the helm throughout the next five years and a regular production base at Television Centre, with Ealing Studios used for some film sequences. (An exception is 'Spearhead from Space', which was largely shot on 16-millimetre film at the BBC Training Centre at Wood Norton when a technicians' strike made Television Centre unavailable.) The broadcast schedule was changed so that each season of *Doctor Who* would start just before or after the New Year and would run for six months. These were years during which the popularity of the series showed a marked upward trend with average audiences of 7 million in 1970, 7.8 million in 1971, 8.3 million in 1972, 8.9 million in 1973 and 8.8 million in 1974. There are various reasons for the renewed popularity of *Doctor Who*: shorter seasons meant less viewer 'fatigue' as they went on, while the switch to colour enabled the series to hold its own against glossy ITV competition such as Gerry Anderson's *UFO* and American imports such as *Bonanza*, *Tarzan* and repeats of *The Man From U.N.C.L.E.* shown against *Doctor Who* in different regions. Letts and Dicks ensured that the launch of each new season was marked by a special event that would attract interest: the introduction of the new Doctor ('Spearhead from Space'), the arrival of a new arch-villain with the Master ('Terror of the Autons'), the return after a five-year absence of the Doctor's oldest foes ('Day of the Daleks') and the tenth-anniversary special that contrived to unite all three incarnations of the Time Lord ('The Three Doctors').

Stylistically this was a very different *Doctor Who* to what it had been during the 1960s. There was a shift away from the closed, claustrophobic sets of the Troughton episodes and towards more extensive use of outdoor locations: the differences in grain between exteriors shot on film and videotaped studio interiors is much less stark in colour than in monochrome. Colour also allowed the series' designers to explore new avenues in realising the alien menaces. In this regard it is significant that robotic villains with a silver metallic appearance suited to black and white became less prominent after 1970 (the Cybermen, the most prolific villains of the late 1960s, were now conspicuous by their absence) and that organic monsters (Silurians, Sea Devils, Axons, Ogrons, Draconians, Ice Warriors) predominated now their costumes could be more effectively realised. *Doctor Who* conformed to the pulp

SF tradition that green is the preferred colour for monsters (Sea Devils and Ice Warriors, for example), though the Axons are golden and the Ogrons black. Perhaps the most significant consequence of colour, however, was the greater opportunities it allowed for the realisation of visual effects. *Doctor Who* now made extensive use of a technical process called Colour Separation Overlay (CSO) – often referred to as 'blue screen' – which allows images from two cameras to be mixed by shooting backgrounds on one and actors against a neutral (usually blue) background on another. This process was to be the mainstay of *Doctor Who*'s visual effects throughout the 1970s until it was superseded by digital technology in the 1980s.

The changes to the style and content of *Doctor Who* were largely in response to the changing nature of its audience. The new production team regarded their audience as being more 'adult' than it had been when the series began in the 1960s (many had grown up with it) and consequently adopted a more 'realistic' approach to content and characterisation. Dicks averred that 'one of the big shifts in policy we've tried to make on "Who" is the development of more adult realistic characters and of a strong human interest theme running through every story, as well as the very necessary fights, action, monsters etc.'[1] Dicks wanted to orient the series towards a more hard-edged style of SF and to distance it from the outright fantasy represented by stories such as 'The Mind Robber'. He was sceptical, for example, about the first draft of 'The Three Doctors' by Bob Baker and Dave Martin: 'Bitter experience has taught us that stories set in dreamland, fairyland, limbo or any other metaphysical setting simply don't grab our audience, because the "It's only a sort of dream" makes them lose interest. Everything must be physically real, a real planet with real dangers and monsters.'[2] This approach seems to have been welcomed. Stewart Lane noted with approval: 'No longer labelled "For children" – though I'll bet plenty enough will still watch it – and with previously "compulsory" adolescent characters in the cast eliminated, this Saturday afternoon BBC-1 series has had a shot in the arm with the advent of Jon Pertwee in the role of Dr Who.'[3]

It had been expected that Pertwee, known principally as a comedy actor from his role in the radio series *The Navy Lark* (on air since 1959) where his talent for mimicry earned him the sobriquet of 'Man of a Thousand Voices', would bring his comic skills to *Doctor Who*. Yet in fact Pertwee 'accepted the part after being assured that I could play the character straight. As I see it, this is the only way Dr Who can be played by any actor.'[4] This was very much in contrast to his predecessor Patrick Troughton: one a character actor who played the Doctor as a clown, the other a clown who played him as a strongly heroic role. Pertwee, in his early fifties, tall and with striking white hair (his successor Tom Baker once described him as looking like 'a tall light bulb') brought a tremendous physical authority to the part. He was much more of an action-man than either of his predecessors: skilled in the martial art of 'Venusian aikido' and with a predilection for electronic gadgets and fast motor vehicles (motorcycle, wetbike, autogiro), his Doctor invokes comparisons with James Bond. Britton and Barker write that Pertwee 'played the Doctor as an implacable ultra-English hero in the Bulldog Drummond mold'.[5] There is also more than a suggestion of Sherlock Holmes in his characterisation: he is often seen tinkering in his laboratory (a recurring theme of his early stories was the Doctor's attempts to repair the disabled TARDIS), he is impatient with those whose intellect does not match his own, he treats authority figures with contempt, and his eccentricities are tolerated by his nominal employers who call him in to solve problems that defy conventional explanation. The device of having the Doctor acting as a quasi-official scientific consultant also recalls the *Quatermass* serials. In the seventh and eighth seasons, especially, there is a strong element of 'Quatermassery' in the narratives of alien infiltrations ('Spearhead from Space', 'Terror of the Autons', 'The Claws of Axos'), missing astronauts ('The Ambassadors of Death'), top-secret research projects ('Doctor Who and the Silurians', 'Inferno') and the awakening of elemental psycho-kinetic forces ('The Dæmons').

It is often argued that characters in popular drama series are archetypes who represent social and cultural values. In *The Avengers*, for example, the character of John Steed stands for tradition (exemplified in his gentlemanly manners, elegantly tailored suits and his vintage Bentley) while his female partners represent modernity (progressive young women who wear contemporary fashions and drive sports cars). In this respect Pertwee's characterisation of the Doctor is a mixture of tradition and modernity. This is exemplified in his choice of vehicles: the Doctor drives a vintage Edwardian roadster (known affectionately as 'Bessie') but in his last season also builds a sleek, futuristic 'Whomobile' capable of taking to the sky. With his flamboyant dress style – Pertwee favoured ruffled shirts, coloured velvet jackets and flowing cloaks – the

Third Doctor was the first who was 'bang up-to-date in fashion terms'.[6] Like Peter Wyngarde's Jason King in the ITC series of the early 1970s he is an elegant dandy whose apparel exemplifies the 'peacock revolution' in men's fashions during the 1960s. One critic described him appropriately as 'a dignified, dandified technocrat'.[7] This Doctor is both trendy and patrician: thus he appeals to both youthful and more mature viewers.

Pertwee's natural authority made him the first single-companion Doctor, and, as he possessed both the heroic and the fashion credentials to make redundant the role of a younger male companion, his sidekicks were always female. Here, the gender politics of *Doctor Who* again demonstrate the limitations of the format as far as the characterisation of the female companion is concerned. Pertwee's first companion was Liz Shaw (Caroline John), who, as a Cambridge University research scientist attached to UNIT, was rational, sceptical and very far from the screaming bimbo stereotype of some of her predecessors. However, her obvious intelligence proved ill-suited to the main narrative function of the assistant in *Doctor Who*: to ask the questions that allow the Doctor to show off his superior knowledge and intellectual prowess. For this reason – and also because the character was thought not to appeal to younger viewers – she was written out after one season. Her replacement reverted to the screaming bimbo type in the form of Jo Grant (Katy Manning), a well-meaning but rather accident-prone dolly bird whose uncle at the United Nations has pulled strings to find her a job on the UNIT staff. That the series' writers were fully aware of the narrative role assigned to the assistant is evident in the Brigadier's remark (in 'Terror of the Autons') that what the Doctor really needs is 'someone to pass your test tubes and tell you how brilliant you are'. The combination of Manning's engaging personality and 'kooky' sex appeal (highlighted by dressing her in mini-skirts and PVC boots) made her one of the most popular companions, to the extent that she stayed for three seasons. (She also acquired an extra-diegetic significance in the popular history of *Doctor Who* when she posed, topless, with a Dalek for a top-shelf men's magazine.) Her replacement, in Pertwee's last season, returned again to the intelligent, assertive woman with the character of investigative journalist Sarah Jane Smith (Elisabeth Sladen). Sarah Jane would prove to be another very popular companion, not least because her intelligence is expressed in terms of her inquisitiveness rather than knowledge: she is neither 'brainy' like Liz, nor is she a hapless innocent like Jo. Her passionate defence of women's rights – 'The Time Warrior' and 'The Monster of Peladon' both allow her space to make an explicitly pro-feminist statement – is usually seen as *Doctor Who*'s attempt to come to terms with the rise of 'Women's Lib' in the 1970s.[8] Sladen's clothes eschewed the mini-skirted, Chelsea Road style of her predecessor in favour of more 'masculine' attire (trouser suits or a brown leather jacket) in order to assert the character's feminist credentials.

The introduction of stronger female roles is clearly something that Dicks encouraged. There had occasionally been significant supporting parts for women in *Doctor Who* (Sara Kingdom in 'The Daleks' Master Plan', for instance), but this became more common in the 1970s. In 'Planet of the Daleks', for example, Dicks asked Terry Nation to develop the part of a female Thal in order to give her a more active role rather than being there solely for her sex appeal: 'What about Rebec? What has she got to offer us, apart, of course, from the big boobs? One thing could be that she is a lady of strong character and immediately clashes with Taron about the conduct of the expedition. She might be his equal or superior in rank.'[9] And in 'Death to the Daleks' the part of Earth Space Corps marine Jill Tarrant was conceived as 'an Israeli Girl-soldier type – not dolly, but sexy, although a little butch'.[10]

The space provided by the absence of a male companion was filled by fleshing out the supporting roles of members of UNIT – the unflappable Brigadier Lethbridge-Stewart, his easy-going second-in-command Captain Mike Yates (Richard Franklin) and the dependable Sergeant Benton (John Levene) – and by the introduction of a recurring foe for the Doctor. The Master, played with suave menace by Roger Delgado, is a renegade Time Lord who acts as a front man for the various alien species attempting to invade the Earth. The writers' guide described the Master as 'sinister, polished, charming. A manipulator of evil ends with a vested interest in chaos and misrule, which he turns to his own profit … A long standing and implacable enemy of the Doctor, he is the force of evil bound to oppose the Doctor's force of good.'[11] Like the Doctor, the Master is an amalgamation of various (villainous) archetypes: his pointed black beard and 'hypnotic' eyes hark back to the villains of Victorian melodrama, while the high-buttoned Nehru suit has been the dress code of choice for fashion-conscious super-villains such as Ernst Stavro Blofeld (from the Bond films) and the Hood (arch-enemy of International Rescue in *Thunderbirds*). Most of all, the Master is the Professor Moriarty figure to the Doctor's Sherlock Holmes: the two antagonists respect each other's intelligence and each professes a grudging admiration for the other. It had been planned to conclude Pertwee's last season with a battle to the death between the Doctor and the Master entitled 'The Final Game' – the title suggests an homage to the deadly encounter between Holmes and Moriarty at the Reichenbach Falls in 'The Final Problem' – though tragically Delgado died in a car accident whilst being driven to a film location in Turkey in 1973 and the character was dropped from the remainder of Pertwee's stories.

The narrative formula of *Doctor Who* in the early 1970s has been criticised by some aficionados for turning the Doctor into an 'establishment' character. Hartnell and Troughton were both outsiders with a defiantly anti-authoritarian streak, but Pertwee turned the Doctor in some people's eyes into an authority figure who was closely associated with the military. This criticism is largely unfair. The Doctor's relationship with the establishment is constantly problematised and he is often in conflict with both the military and the civilian authorities. In 'Doctor Who and the Silurians', for example, he deplores the Brigadier's decision to respond to the unknown with a display of armed force: 'That's typical of the military mind, isn't it? Present them with a new problem and they start shooting at it!' Indeed, his relationship with the Brigadier is edgy at first – in 'Spearhead from Space' the Brigadier does not initially believe that the Doctor is the same person he met during the Yeti and Cybermen emergencies – and it takes a while for a genuine friendship to develop. Politicians and civil servants fare no better: the ubiquitous men from the ministry are invariably characterised as pompous, interfering and incompetent. Furthermore, a recurring theme is that establishment characters (government ministers, generals) are not to be trusted. Several stories, including 'The Ambassadors of Death' and 'Invasion of the Dinosaurs', feature conspiracies in high places. The conspiracy thriller was voguish in the 1970s, exemplified by films such as *The Parallax View* (dir. Alan J. Pakula, 1974) and *The Internecine Project* (dir. Ken Hughes, 1974), a trend that is usually related to the Watergate scandal that brought about the downfall of US President Richard Nixon. Britain had its own share of political scandals during these years, the most serious being the resignation of Home Secretary Reginald Maudling in 1972 over allegations of corruption. The Doctor is so frequently in conflict with authority, indeed, that it is entirely misleading to regard him as an 'establishment' figure. Rather, like Professor Quatermass, he is something of a loose cannon: his scientific knowledge makes him useful to the authorities, but he is distrustful of them, as they are of him.

It could be argued, indeed, that it was during the early 1970s that *Doctor Who* was at its most critical of British society. Asa Briggs suggests that during these years it 'presented a social landscape in which there were often alarming contrasts of class and power'.[12] Internal evidence would indicate that the stories are set approximately a decade in the future, but it is an uncomfortably sinister projection of the sort of society that Britain might become. This is a Britain that seems full of 'restricted areas': atomic research centres, monitoring stations, biochemical plants and all manner of secret military installations. To this extent *Doctor Who* recalls *Quatermass II* in its representation of a secret state that has become part of the British landscape. With its recurring themes of conspiracy and cover-up, this period of *Doctor Who* is the most paranoid in the series' history, anticipating *The X-Files* (1993–2002) by a full two decades. Moreover, there is an acute sense of Britain's increased insecurity and vulnerability. This is evident not only in the frequency with which the country is invaded, but also by the reliance on outside help to combat the invaders. UNIT, significantly, is an international organisation (several times the Brigadier's men come into conflict with the regular army, as in 'Spearhead from Space', 'The Claws of Axos' and 'Invasion of the Dinosaurs'), and in any event the military solution on its own is usually ineffective. A recognition of the decline of British power informs 'The Claws of Axos' (#57) in which the ostensibly friendly Axons offer a mineral that they claim will solve all the world's food and energy shortages. Their secret plan to drain the Earth of its energy is nearly foiled, however, when a career-minded civil servant attempts to secure sole use of the Axonite for the British government.

Another criticism sometimes levelled against the series is that all the Pertwee stories are the same: the Doctor and UNIT defeat an attempt to invade the Earth by an alien power. Matthew Coady in the *Daily Mirror*, for example, complained that the series was ignoring the 'limitless freedoms offered by science fiction' and had turned into 'an indifferent, gadgetry-packed galactic version of the adventures of Sexton Blake'.[13] The UNIT/invasion narrative predominated throughout the first two Pertwee seasons but became less frequent during the remaining three, in which UNIT stories alternated with adventures in space and time as the Doctor regained use of his TARDIS. In total, 13 of the 24 Pertwee serials are UNIT narratives, while UNIT features tangentially in another two and nine have no UNIT involvement at all.[14] Like Innes Lloyd's period in charge during the mid 1960s, and like the Philip Hinchcliffe-Robert Holmes regime that would succeed it, the Letts-Dicks-Pertwee era is associated with a particular type of story that set the tone for that period of *Doctor Who*. To regard all episodes as being the same, however, is unfair. Even in the UNIT stories that predominate, different narrative patterns and structures emerge.

The classic examples of the UNIT/invasion narrative are 'Spearhead from Space' (#51) and its sequel 'Terror of the Autons' (#55), both written by Robert Holmes. 'Spearhead from Space' begins with a clear homage to *Quatermass II* as a radar station tracks a shower of meteorites that land in formation in Essex. And it borrows its main plot elements from the same source: the meteorites are in fact capsules which contain part of an alien entity whose aim is to take over the world by stealth through the substitution of key political and military personnel. In this instance the invader is the Nestene Consciousness and their instruments are the Autons, deadly man-shaped plastic robots with built-in disintegrator guns. The blank-faced, boiler-suited Autons are visually reminiscent of the Cybernauts in *The Avengers* and the last episode of the serial includes a famous sequence as a line of shop-window mannequins suddenly come to life and attack people in the street. The motif of replacing politicians and generals with living dummies harks back to the 'takeover' narratives of films like *Invasion of the Body Snatchers* (dir. Don Siegel, 1956). It was, wrote Coady, 'this use of everyday reality which gave the notion that the dummies were waiting to take over the horrific turn of the screw'.[15] The 'horrific turn' is even more evident in 'Terror of the Autons'. Here, the second Nestene invasion of the Earth is engineered by the Master, who steals the last remaining Nestene energy unit from the National Space Museum. On this occasion the Autons are capable of taking the form of any object made from plastic and the serial is chiefly notable for its many ingenious plastic-related killings: suffocation by plastic chair, murder by plastic troll-doll, attempted strangulation by plastic telephone flex, death by killer plastic daffodil. The killer doll is explicitly coded as horrific through its fangs and repulsive face ('It wasn't intended for children, naturally,' a character remarks in order to make the point), but this was not sufficient to appease the series' critics.

'Terror of the Autons' was severely criticised for having transgressed the boundaries of acceptable horror. Critics attacked the serial using the same arguments that the BBC had used previously to defend it: that children could accept fantasy horror when it was something that was obviously unreal but that realistic horror in an everyday situation was too disturbing for early-evening viewing. Sylvia Clayton in the *Daily Telegraph*, for example, argued that 'plastic monsters come from within the range of a child's domestic scene' and averred that 'small children of my acquaintance have found these devices terrifying in a way fantasy figures such as the Daleks and the Cybermen were not.' *The Sun* concurred: 'While he fights Daleks and so forth, few children can be genuinely upset. It was when policemen turned out to be faceless monsters that children got worried and their parents disturbed.'[16] It was partly in response to criticisms such as these that Letts and Dicks decided to reintroduce outer-space adventures, even if only occasionally at first, from the eighth season – a decision which, according to *The Sun*, came 'to the relief of parents all over the country'. They were cautious thereafter not to transgress again. 'In the present climate of opinion we have to be very careful about violence, massacres and gloom,' Dicks told Terry Nation.[17] It is evident, therefore, that the production team were sensitive to criticism and that the horrific aspects of *Doctor Who* were consciously toned down in response to public pressure.

The Auton serials exemplify a straightforward type of invasion narrative in which an implacable threat attempts to bring about 'the destruction of humanity' (as the Master puts it matter-of-factly). Yet not all the invasion stories took this form. 'The Ambassadors of Death' (#53) illustrates that even in the first Earthbound season there would be a considered attempt to vary the formula and explore the possibilities of this type of narrative. The initial point of reference here would seem to have been *The Quatermass Experiment* in which astronauts returning from contact with an alien life form bring terror back to the Earth, though it also shares elements with *Captain Scarlet and the Mysterons* (1967–1968) in which the war between Earth's 'Spectrum' agents and the Mysterons was triggered accidentally by a space probe landing on Mars. Contact has been lost with the crew of Mars Probe 7 and with the recovery vehicle sent to investigate its disappearance. The Doctor realises that a strange sound transmitted from space is a form of message, but when the capsule is recovered the space-suited figures who emerge are not the missing astronauts. They are captured by a group led by General Carrington, who fears 'an alien invasion with the collaboration of a foreign power'. The Doctor pilots another recovery vehicle and makes contact with the alien mother ship where he discovers the three Earth astronauts alive and well but their alien hosts upset by the treatment of their 'ambassadors'. General Carrington, himself a former astronaut, has gone insane, believing it his 'moral duty' to 'alert the world to the menace of alien invasion'. Carrington's paranoia arises from a previous expedition to Mars that he commanded, when his fellow astronauts were killed (accidentally as it turns out) by the aliens who do not realise their touch is fatal to human beings. He uses the ambassadors (a life form dependent on radiation) to attack a number of strategic installations in order to create the impression they are hostile and plans to make a television broadcast urging the world's powers to retaliate.

The production history of 'The Ambassadors of Death' demonstrates how the style and ethos of *Doctor Who* had changed. It was conceived by former editor David Whitaker, but his scripts 'didn't quite work', according to Derrick Sherwin, who told him that 'we are approaching the series from a much more realistic point of view; in other words the style is somewhat more sophisticated than we have previously used in other serials.'[18] In the event the scripts were extensively rewritten by Malcolm Hulke, though Whitaker retained his on-screen credit. Evidence that the revised serial was deemed a significant success is to be found in Dicks's claim that it was 'one of our most popular serials last year. Viewing figures reached nine million at one point and part of the first episode was shown to an international drama conference, to great acclaim!'[19] 'The Ambassadors of Death' again demonstrates the flexibility of the *Doctor Who* format, but at the same time it was bound by the extent of its difference to be a one-off: an SF adventure series requires its quota of 'Threat and Disaster' narratives in order to provide the norm against which different stories can be set.

Not all invaders are necessarily extraterrestrial in origin. Both 'Doctor Who and the Silurians' (#52) and 'The Sea Devils' (#62) by Malcolm Hulke are posited on the notion that other inhabitants of the Earth may attempt to claim (or reclaim) it for themselves. In 'Doctor Who and the Silurians', disturbances at an atomic research centre built into a series of caves in Derbyshire lead to the discovery of a subterranean reptilian race. The Silurians are the survivors of an intelligent species who inhabited the Earth 200 million years ago 'before the great continental drift'. They predicted a cosmic disaster when another planet seemed about to crash into the Earth (in fact it was caught in the Earth's gravity and became the Moon) and so used their advanced scientific knowledge to devise hibernation units for their people. The Silurians have now been awakened from their hibernation by the building of the atomic research centre and intend to reclaim a planet which they regard as being rightfully theirs ('This is our planet. We were here before man'). Attempting, for once, not to represent the alien species as a single, undifferentiated mass, Hulke is at pains to show differences of opinion amongst the Silurians between those who do not want to destroy the human race ('These strange apes have developed some kind of civilisation') and a more belligerent faction who argue for its annihilation ('The apes have become dangerous. They must be destroyed'). The Doctor attempts to mediate in the dispute by acting as an honest broker between the Silurians and the humans but his efforts are foiled by belligerence on both sides. The Silurians attempt to wipe out the human race with a deadly bacteria; the Brigadier retaliates by blowing up the Silurian caves. The Doctor is disgusted at the outcome: 'That's murder! They were intelligent alien beings – a whole race of them. And he's just wiped them out!'

The theme is rehearsed again in 'The Sea Devils'. A series of unexplained attacks on shipping in the English Channel leads to the discovery of another colony of reptiles – 'a different species, completely adapted to life underwater'. This species also intend to recolonise the world for themselves ('This is our planet. My people ruled the Earth when man was only an ape … We shall destroy man and reclaim the planet'). Again the Doctor attempts to mediate, but is foiled in this instance by the Master, who, from his island prison, has secretly made contact with the Sea Devils. The outcome is the same: the Sea Devils, repulsed in their attack on a naval base, are destroyed by depth charges. Cull suggests that these two stories 'reflected contemporary issues then coming to a head in the Middle East and Northern Ireland'.[20] In this reading, the belligerent factions amongst the Silurians and Sea Devils stand for the PLO and the IRA: groups claiming to represent those dispossessed and displaced inhabitants who resort to violence to assert their territorial claims. The theme of who 'owns' the planet also has a more universal resonance, of course, and to this extent the stories bring to mind the place of displaced indigenous populations such as the Native Americans or the Aboriginal population of Australia.

Three of the UNIT stories in particular are important not only for their variation from the familiar invasion pattern but also because they provide examples of different SF themes. 'Inferno' (#54) is the only instance in televised *Doctor Who* of the idea of parallel or alternate worlds, a motif that has informed a whole sub-genre of literary SF and was a favourite device of *Star Trek*. In 'Inferno', UNIT is responsible for the security of an experimental project to provide a new source of energy by drilling through the Earth's crust. The Doctor, working in a hut on the edge of the compound, is attempting to find a new power source for the TARDIS by tapping into the excess energy generated from the drilling. A power surge causes the Doctor to be transported into 'a parallel space-time continuum'. He finds himself in an alternate Britain that has become a fascist police state: UNIT has become the RSF (Republican Security Force) and the Brigadier has become the sinister, eye-patched Brigade Leader. 'Inferno' imagines a totalitarian Britain just as nightmarish as Orwell's (referred to in the ubiquitous posters declaring 'Unity Is Strength') in which 'the Party' rules through terror and where order is maintained by a thuggish military regime. Two particular points are significant. The first is that, unlike *Nineteen Eighty-Four*, there is a suggestion here that resistance to the regime is not entirely futile: the Doctor is able to convince the more rationally minded that he is not a saboteur and that he has indeed come from a parallel dimension. The second, relevant to the SF genre as well as to theories of historical determinism, is the assertion that it is possible to change the course of events. In the parallel dimension the Doctor witnesses the end of the world (literally) when the drill penetrates the Earth's crust and causes catastrophic disaster in the form of massive volcanic eruptions and lava flows. Escaping back to the 'real' world, however, he is able to prevent the same outcome. Thus what happens in one universe is not necessarily repeated in others. The Doctor realises that there is 'an infinity of universes – *ergo* an infinite number of choices – so free will is not an illusion after all – the pattern can be changed.' 'Inferno' therefore posits an idea of history that allows for the role of individual agency rather than an entirely deterministic or structural explanation in which events are brought about by impersonal forces outside people's control. On this occasion the writer, Don Houghton, was clearly happy with the result, complimenting director Douglas Camfield 'for the wonderful job you did on "Inferno". It's not often these days that a writer can see his work interpreted with such care and imagination.'[21]

'Day of the Daleks' (#60) is another multi-layered example of an SF template that here receives its most complex and thoughtful variation in the series: the time-loop paradox. With the world on the brink of a third world war, UNIT is responsible for protecting diplomat Sir Reginald Styles, whose effort to bring together world leaders for a summit conference is the last hope for preventing global catastrophe. The Doctor is called in when a 'ghost' attacks Styles at the country house where the peace conference is to be held. It turns out that the 'ghosts' are guerrilla fighters from the future who have travelled back in time in order to assassinate Styles but have 'vanished' back into their own time before completing their mission. The Doctor follows the guerrillas in time to the twenty-second century, where he discovers the Earth (once again) under the control of the Daleks and their ape-like servants the Ogrons. The guerrillas explain that, according to their history, Styles caused the wars that led to the devastation of the planet and the death of seven-eighths of its population, leaving it vulnerable to invasion by the Daleks. The Doctor realises, however, that it was not Styles who blew up the peace conference, but the guerrillas themselves. As he explains to them: 'You're trapped in a temporal paradox. Styles didn't cause that explosion and start those wars. You did it yourselves!' Quite apart from the philosophical issues arising from this convoluted narrative, however, 'Day of the Daleks' is interesting for other reasons. It again exemplifies a sort of alternative history that imagines Britain under occupation. References to the Nazis and the Holocaust are even more explicit than in 'The Dalek Invasion of Earth' – the Daleks run the planet as a giant labour camp, working the surviving inhabitants to death – and the Doctor even invokes a specific historical analogy when he describes the Controller (a human security officer working for the Daleks) as 'a quisling'. The Controller's rebuttal of this charge recalls the defence of those accused of collaboration in occupied countries during the Second World War: 'They [the Daleks] chose a few humans to help them get things going again, to organise the remaining population ... We have helped make things better for the others. We have gained concessions. I have saved lives.' Again the outcome is optimistic and morally affirmative: the Controller dies a redemptive death by assisting the Doctor's escape, and the Doctor engineers events so that it is the Dalek invasion force, rather than the peace conference delegates, who are blown up in the twentieth century.

'The Dæmons' (#59) is another example of how *Doctor Who*, at its very best, is able to combine themes and motifs from different genres. In this serial the Doctor investigates the unusual events that have attended the excavation of an ancient burial site near the village of Devil's End. The culprit is the Master, who, disguised as the local vicar, has been dabbling in black magic. The Doctor is dismissive of any supernatural explanation, asserting the credo of scientific rationalism: 'Everything that happens in life has to have a scientific explanation – if you know where to look for it.' Of course he is proved correct: it transpires that the 'devil' conjured up by the Master is in fact Azal, 'last of the Dæmons', and the burial site is a spaceship that landed on Earth thousands of years ago. Azal is a towering, horned apparition whose corporeal appearance, glimpsed occasionally over the centuries, has been taken for the Devil. The most direct reference point for 'The Dæmons' is *Quatermass and the Pit*, which had similarly attempted to explain the occult through a discourse of scientific rationalism by attributing the appearance of the Devil to the inherited 'race memory' of the Martians who landed on the Earth millions of years ago. The suggestion that the Earth is a giant laboratory experiment in which alien visitors have determined the course of scientific development (the Renaissance and the Industrial Revolution are both attributed to the intervention of the Dæmons) would inform future *Doctor Who* script editor Douglas Adams in his radio and television serial *The Hitchhiker's Guide to the Galaxy* (1978, 1981), while the motif of paganism and occult practices in a remote rural community anticipates the cult British horror film *The Wicker Man* (dir. Robin Hardy, 1973).

Elsewhere, *Doctor Who* continued to be informed by contemporary issues. The most obvious manifestation of the series' responsiveness to the topical issues of the day is the emergence of the eco-catastrophe narrative in such stories as Robert Sloman's 'The Green Death' (#69) and Malcolm Hulke's 'Invasion of the Dinosaurs' (#71). The early 1970s witnessed a growing public awareness of ecological and environmental problems, fuelled by pressure groups such as the Friends of the Earth (founded in 1969) and Greenpeace (formed in 1971). The permeation of these concerns into popular culture was reflected in a variety of forms, ranging from the gentle humour of the BBC's 'self-sufficiency' sitcom *The Good Life* (1975–1978) to the dystopian vision of *Soylent Green* (dir. Richard Fleischer, 1973). 'The Green Death' is perhaps the most politically radical of all *Doctor Who* stories. The Doctor is called in to investigate a mysterious death in a disused mine in South Wales ('It's exactly your cup of tea. The fellow's bright green, apparently, and dead!') and discovers that the cause is toxic waste pumped into the mine from a nearby chemical factory. Industrial pollution has not only created a deadly green sludge that kills anyone who comes into contact with it but has also caused 'atavistic mutation' in the form of aggressive giant maggots. Sloman establishes an ideological opposition between the forces of corporate capitalism (represented by Global Chemicals whose motto is 'efficiency, productivity and profit') and the environmentalist lobby (represented by the young 'Professor' Clifford Jones, who longs to escape from 'the plastic-stinking petrol rat trap' and advocates alternative sources of energy). The narrative sides unequivocally with the environmentalists, revealing Global Chemicals to be run by a megalomaniac super-computer known as 'Boss'. 'The Green Death' therefore equates big business with technocracy and corporate fascism, whereas environmentalism is associated with individual freedom and entrepreneurial enterprise (the Professor and his colleagues in 'the nut hutch' have grown a 'high-protein fungus' to be used as a meat substitute). That we are clearly meant to admire Professor Jones is illustrated when Jo leaves UNIT to marry him, telling the Doctor that 'he reminds me of a sort of younger you'. One critic noted the 'trendy ecological theme' and praised 'the complete conviction of all concerned'.[22]

The soap-box radicalism of 'The Green Death' illustrates that *Doctor Who* is not as hidebound by social and political conservatism as some commentators would believe. It is the flexibility of its format that allows different writers to engage with topical issues in such a direct way. 'Invasion of the Dinosaurs', for example, is informed by much the same idea as 'The Green Death'. Arriving back in London after 'a little jaunt' in the TARDIS, the Doctor and Sarah Jane Smith find the streets eerily deserted and the capital subject to martial law. London has been evacuated (yet another incident recalling the Second World War) due to the unexplained appearance of prehistoric dinosaurs in the streets. The Doctor soon deduces that the dinosaurs are being transported from their own time to the present and their appearance is meant to clear London for a more sinister purpose. A group of radical environmentalists have devised 'Operation Golden Age': they plan to use a time machine to 'roll back time' in order to return the Earth to 'an earlier, purer age' before it was corrupted by technology, industry and pollution. This will have the effect, however, that all except a select group of people will cease to exist. The Doctor is sympathetic to their aims but cannot accept their method, urging them instead to 'take the world you've got and try to make something of it'. 'Invasion of the Dinosaurs' is often derided for its unconvincing puppet dinosaurs, but this is to ignore the underlying radicalism of its narrative. For one thing, the conspiracy extends to the lower echelons of government, masterminded by a charming but duplicitous minister, Grover, and is supported by members of the army, including Captain Yates, who has turned politically 'green' after his experiences in South Wales. Furthermore, while the attempt to roll back time is thwarted, the story ends with the Doctor suggesting they were right about the problem if not the solution: 'Of course he was mad. But at least he realised the dangers that this planet of yours is in, Brigadier. The danger of it becoming one vast garbage dump inhabited only by rats … It's not the oil and the filth and the poisonous chemicals that are the real cause of pollution, Brigadier. It's simply greed.'

'Invasion of the Dinosaurs' had started from an entirely different premise. Hulke had proposed a story entitled 'Bridgehead from Space' in which aliens have taken over London, unleashing monsters to patrol the streets. The government has conceded defeat and 'a sort of Vichy government has been set up in Harrogate.' It was to have been an explicitly allegorical story: 'Churchill vs. the appeasement policy'.[23] Hulke even suggested a scene in which the prime minister returned from a meeting with the aliens and announced to waiting reporters that he had secured a deal with them whilst waving a piece of computer paper in the air. This synopsis was left undeveloped, probably on the grounds that it was too similar to 'Day of the Daleks', though a few remnants of the original idea remain in 'Invasion of the Dinosaurs': monsters in the streets of London and the evacuation of the government to Harrogate.

Allegory is a recurring narrative strategy in *Doctor Who* during the early 1970s. This would suggest that the Letts-Dicks regime was particularly receptive to the notion of using the series to respond to wider social and political issues. Particular stories can be seen as commentaries on various aspects of Britain's historical experience, including decolonisation ('The

Mutants'), entrance into the Common Market ('The Curse of Peladon') and industrial relations during the Heath government ('The Monster of Peladon'). 'The Mutants' (#63), by Bob Baker and Dave Martin, posits that a thousand years in the future the Earth has become the centre of a vast interstellar empire. Explicit parallels are invoked between Earth's empire of the distant future and the British Empire. Historians would have understood the Doctor's reference to Gibbon, whose *Decline and Fall of the Roman Empire* was itself partly an allegory. The story is set on the planet of Solos, an Earth colony for 500 years, now on the verge of achieving its independence. The Marshal, governor of Solos, is opposed to granting independence to the Solonians, but is overruled by the more pragmatic Administrator:

Marshal: Give them independence and they'll starve out of total incompetence.

Administrator: Nevertheless, they shall have their independence – whether they're ready for it or not.

Marshal: When you summoned this conference, Administrator, I assumed you'd follow your usual line ... Fob them off with promises, a few minor concessions. It's always worked before.

Administrator: This time I'm conceding all Ky's demands. We have no choice. We must return to Earth.

It is impossible not to see this dialogue as a commentary on Britain's retreat from empire: the preceding decade had seen many British colonies granted their independence. The arguments it rehearses for and against decolonisation are precisely those that had prevailed in Britain in the aftermath of Suez: the view that native populations (especially in Africa) were not ready for self-government was overcome by the pragmatism of those politicians (Harold Macmillan and Iain Macleod foremost amongst them) who accepted the necessity of withdrawal. 'The Mutants' is an explicitly anti-imperialist narrative, portraying the Marshal as a brutal dictator and the Solonian leader Ky as a freedom fighter with a Marxist view of colonialism: 'Once we were farmers and hunters. The land was green, the rivers ran clear, the air was sweet to breathe. Then the Overlords came, bringing poison with them, calling it progress. We toiled in their mines, we became slaves – worse than slaves.' There is a direct parallel in the way in which the Doctor realises the way to smooth the transition to independence is for the former colonial authorities to work with Ky, recalling how the British government had worked with various nationalist leaders whom it had previously jailed: Archbishop Makarios of Cyprus, Jomo Kenyatta of Kenya and Kenneth Kaunda of Zambia.

'The Curse of Peladon' (#61), by Brian Hayles, revolves around a planet applying for membership of the Galactic Federation (described in Hayles's treatment as 'a kind of U.N. of all intelligent races'). Peladon is a feudal society that is just starting to modernise: the young King wants to join the Federation, but he is opposed by his High Priest, Hepesh, who fears that Peladon will lose its independence and wishes to maintain the traditional ways of life. Hepesh argues that the Federation will 'exploit us for our minerals, enslave us with their machines, corrupt us with their technology'. Hepesh is characterised in no uncertain terms as a reactionary who would return Peladon to the dark ages. In contrast it is the wise counsel of the Doctor (mistaken upon his arrival for the Federation's chairman delegate from Earth) that persuades the King that joining the Federation will be a progressive move to bring economic benefits to the planet and help improve the condition of his people. The debates rehearsed for and against joining the Federation echo directly those for and against British membership of the European Economic Community (EEC) or Common Market, with the Doctor cast in the unlikely role of Prime Minister Edward Heath. Heath was a committed pro-European who had been chief negotiator when the Macmillan government applied to join the EEC in the early 1960s and who successfully negotiated Britain's entry a decade later. There are further parallels. Federation law 'allows only unanimous decisions' and any member can veto Peladon's application; the right of veto had twice been used by the French in the 1960s to exclude Britain from the EEC. In advocating membership, moreover, the Doctor has to overcome his hostility towards an old enemy as the Martian delegation is led by the Ice Lord Izlyr, who asserts that his people have now renounced wars of territorial conquest in favour of co-operation with their neighbours.

This interpretation of 'The Curse of Peladon' might be regarded as somewhat fanciful were it not for the timing of the story: its first episode was broadcast on 29 January 1972, one week after signature of the treaty of accession in Brussels (22 January) that enabled Britain's entry into the EEC some eleven months later. The BBC Archives, furthermore, reveal that 'The Curse of Peladon' combined elements from two story ideas submitted by Hayles in 1971. 'Doctor Who and the Shape of Terror' featured a space ship crew stranded on a barren planet who fall prey to a protoplasm monster known as the Energid. Dicks felt that it was too close to 'Colony in Space' ('barren planet, rich mineral deposits, baddy security forces') and thought that the Energid was 'not a sufficiently personalised menace'. However, he liked the basic situation, telling Hayles: 'Start again with "10 Little Niggers" basis.'[24] Hayles's other synopsis, 'Doctor Who and the Brain-Dead', had the Ice Warriors attempting to take over the Earth using a weapon that turns people into zombies. It would begin with the sabotage of 'the European com-sat' base: the suspected saboteurs are a group known as the Isolationists – 'known to be actively attempting to undermine European scientific co-operation on the grounds of conservation' – though the real culprits are 'professional agitators' in league with the Ice Warriors.[25] It would seem, therefore, that Hayles had a 'European' theme in mind from the start. The conservation theme was carried forward into 'Invasion of the Dinosaurs'.

'The Monster of Peladon' (#73) is even more explicitly allegorical. Returning to Peladon 50 years after his first visit, the Doctor finds the planet in a state of civil unrest. The Federation, embroiled in a war against the forces of Galaxy Five, is dependent on the mineral trisilicate. Peladon is rich in the mineral, but the miners are reluctant to embrace the modern technologies and working methods that the Federation's engineers want them to use. The miners' leader Gebek argues that the miners are suffering severe privations ('We earn barely enough to feed our families'), but Chancellor Ortron advises Queen Thalira not to give in to their demands ('This is what comes of softness with the common people'). Clearly this is a commentary on the miners' strikes of 1972 and 1974, the first of which, especially, had been exceptionally bitter and was marked by increased militancy on the part of the National Union of Mineworkers (NUM). Production documents leave no doubt that this meaning was intended: Gebek is referred to as a 'Trade Union leader', while Ortron 'is advocating a hard, Fascist line'.[26] The parallels extend even further: Gebek is characterised as a 'moderate' who favours negotiation between the miners and their rulers, but he is challenged by the radical Ettis who advocates armed revolt in order to realise their objectives. This is analogous to the situation in the NUM, whose moderate president Joe Gormley wanted to find a negotiated settlement to the dispute in 1972 but was unable to control militants such as Arthur Scargill, the Yorkshire Marxist whose use of 'flying pickets' provoked violent confrontations between strikers and police. The Doctor seeks to resolve the dispute by allying with Gebek, though it is the arrival of Commander Azaxyr and his Ice Warriors that unites the Peladonians. Hayles described the role of the Ice Warriors on this occasion as 'law and order heavies'.[27] This was analogous to the role of the police in the 1974 strike, who were organised into mobile squads in order to combat the flying pickets. In the final version Azaxyr leads a breakaway faction of Ice Warriors who have deserted the Federation and joined forces with Galaxy Five.

Perhaps the most sophisticated use of allegory in *Doctor Who*, however, in the sense that it is less overt than in the Peladon serials, is Robert Holmes's 'Carnival of Monsters' (#66), a complex, multi-layered narrative that is regarded as one of the best Pertwee stories. On one level it is a comedy about a travelling showman who possesses a miniscope, a sort of peep-show device that contains miniaturised specimens of different races. The showman Vorg asserts that the fierce Drashigs are 'great favourites with the children', echoing the view of the *Doctor Who* production team that children were fascinated by the monsters. On a more sophisticated level the story can be seen as a commentary on the nature of entertainment. Vorg regards the miniscope as a form of escapism and disavows any suggestion of concealed meaning ('Our purpose is to amuse, simply to amuse. Nothing serious, nothing political'); the Doctor, however, is morally outraged by the 'shameful business' of collecting intelligent species who live in an artificial environment unaware that they have become exhibits in a peep show. And on yet another level it is a satire of bureaucracy and petty officialdom. Vorg has arrived on the planet Inter Minor which has only recently emerged from self-imposed isolation and which is inhabited by humourless petty officials ('Amusement is prohibited. It is pointless'). The ambitious Commissioner Kalik plots a *coup d'état* against the government by releasing the Drashigs (they grow to full size once outside the miniscope's force field) and blaming the ensuing chaos on the lifting of the immigration ban. The theme of immigration was topical in the wake of the Commonwealth

Immigration Acts of 1968 and 1971 which had restricted the rights of people from the former colonies to settle in Britain.

The satirical edge of 'Carnival of Monsters' is indicative of the increasing intellectual sophistication and narrative maturity of *Doctor Who* as it passed its tenth anniversary. Baker and Martin conceived of 'The Three Doctors' (#65) as an homage to *The Seventh Seal* (dir. Ingmar Bergman, 1957), starting 'with a Game of Chess: the cowled figure of Death with his chalkwhite face and skeletal hands is playing the High King – or President – of the Time Lords. The odd thing about the game is that Time Lord has *three* White Kings …'[28] This idea did not impress Dicks, however, who, with the controversy over 'Terror of the Autons' still a recent memory, expressed concern over the imagery: 'I'm afraid the general feel of the piece is more suited to Hammer than to us … The whole atmosphere of mass suicides, corpse filled morgues, lumbering ghastly zombies and man-eating fungus will give our viewers nightmares and our Head of Department apoplexy.'[29] The story was reworked to turn the 'Death' figure into a renegade Time Lord, Omega, the stellar engineer whose work provided the necessary power source for their experiments in time travel but who was trapped inside a black hole and turned into anti-matter. 'The Three Doctors' is really an extended opportunity for *Doctor Who* to celebrate its anniversary. William Hartnell and Patrick Troughton both reprised their roles, though due to his illness Hartnell's role was limited to a few pre-filmed inserts as the First Doctor mediates between his squabbling second and third incarnations.

Robert Sloman's 'Planet of the Spiders' (#74) makes an entirely fitting conclusion to the Letts-Dicks-Pertwee era of *Doctor Who*. Like 'Carnival of Monsters', it is an example of a sophisticated and multi-layered story that can be appreciated on several different levels. On one level, it is an action-adventure narrative, with most of the second episode, for example, devoted to an extended chase sequence involving the 'Whomobile', 'Bessie', an autogiro, a speedboat and a one-man hovercraft. The chase itself is narratively unnecessary – the villain, Lupton, steals the Doctor's blue crystal from UNIT headquarters and eventually evades his pursuers – and to this extent it exemplifies a tendency towards action as a form of spectacle for its own sake that had become a characteristic of the Pertwee stories. There is a comparison to be made here with the James Bond films, which in the early 1970s, especially, had sacrificed narrative cohesion in favour of elaborately staged action sequences involving spectacular vehicle stunts and chases. On another level, 'Planet of the Spiders' exemplifies a form of psychological horror in that it exploits a relatively common fear (arachnophobia) and magnifies it. Audience Research reported that viewers found 'the giant spiders in this story (perhaps mercifully) less life-like than some monsters the series had created'.[30] It may have been that this was a conscious ploy given the sort of criticism *Doctor Who* had attracted in the past for making its horrors too realistic. On another level entirely, 'Planet of the Spiders' is a metaphorical narrative informed by popular psychiatry and psychoanalysis in which the spiders themselves represent the inner demons of the mind. Sarah Jane (acting independently of the Doctor for once in her role as a journalist) is investigating mysterious goings-on at a meditation centre. While most of the residents are seeking spiritual enlightenment, a group led by the megalomaniac Lupton are motivated by greed and power. Their chanting results in the appearance of a giant spider that attaches itself to Lupton's back. The suggestion that monsters represent the unconscious mind has already been raised by Sarah ('If you do start ferreting about in your subconscious, aren't you going to turn up all sorts of nasties? I mean complexes, phobias and what have you?') and in this regard 'Planet of the Spiders' can be interpreted as a cod-Freudian narrative about monsters from the Id. The 'rational' explanation is that the spiders are from the planet Metebelis Three (a recurring joke of the later Pertwee stories was that he was always trying to visit this fabled 'blue planet') and have come to Earth in search of a crystal now in the possession of the Doctor. Finally, 'Planet of the Spiders' is a powerfully allegorical saga of Good and Evil that rises above the usual comic-strip level by exposing the Doctor's own weakness (his 'greed for knowledge') and phobias ('Not all spiders sit on the back … What is it you most fear?' asks the wise old abbot K'anpo, who turns out to be another Time Lord and the Doctor's old tutor). The Doctor realises that he must return the crystal to the cave of the 'Great One', an enormous, mutated spider, knowing that the radiation there will be too much for his body to withstand. He duly returns the crystal, destroying the Great One and releasing the humanoid inhabitants of Metebelis from the tyranny of the spiders' rule. His body riddled with radiation, the Doctor makes it back to Earth where he regenerates in front of Sarah and the Brigadier ('Here we go again!'). Another era for *Doctor Who* was about to begin.

4

High Gothic

1975–1977

The Earth isn't my home, Sarah. I'm a Time Lord ... I'm not a human being. I walk in eternity ... It means I've lived for something like 750 years ... It's about time I found something better to do than run around after the Brigadier.

The Doctor (Tom Baker) in 'Pyramids of Mars'

The mid 1970s are generally described as the 'Gothic' or the 'horrific' period of *Doctor Who*. Once again the content and style of the series changed with the advent of a new producer (Philip Hinchcliffe), a new script editor (Robert Holmes) and a new Doctor (Tom Baker). For many aficionados this period represents the 'golden age' of *Doctor Who* when it attained the peak of its popularity and acquired a distinctive style based on a pastiche of Gothic horror and classic adventure stories.[1] This was a deliberate production strategy on the part of both Hinchcliffe and, in particular, Holmes, who sought to differentiate the programme as far as possible from the preceding Letts-Dicks-Pertwee era. To this extent the Hinchcliffe-Holmes period exemplifies the processes of change that have been integral to the longevity of *Doctor Who* both as an institutional product (its place within the BBC) and as a cultural text (its relationship to different genres and influences). However, this 'golden age' was not without its problems: it was at the moment of its greatest popularity that *Doctor Who* also came under severe public criticism for having become too frightening and horrific for children.

The quantitative evidence demonstrates clearly that the popular audience for *Doctor Who* had reached a level not seen since the first Dalek invasion of Earth. The twelfth season, broadcast during the spring of 1975 in line with the transmission cycle followed since 1970, had been partly mapped out by Letts and Dicks who, knowing there would be a new 'Doctor Who', played safe by including three favourite monsters (Sontarans, Daleks, Cybermen) and a 'story arc' that linked each serial into the next.[2] This season was truncated to 20 weeks, the shortest yet for *Doctor Who*, with the concluding story, 'Terror of the Zygons', carried over to start the next season at the end of August and thus facilitate the series' return to its traditional autumn start. The average audience for the twelfth season was 10 million per episode, a level not achieved since 1964. Over the next two seasons in 1975–1976 and 1976–1977, *Doctor Who*'s audience averaged 11.5 million, making this the period of highest sustained popularity for the series throughout its history, with individual episodes occasionally surpassing 13 million.[3] As far as the size of its audience was concerned, this was indeed *Doctor Who*'s golden age.

Hinchcliffe and Holmes were keen to move *Doctor Who* even more decisively away from the association of a children's series. When former script editor Gerry Davis returned to write 'Revenge of the Cybermen', for example, Holmes told him 'that you have written it only for children. It's too straightforward (particularly in characterisation) and therefore rather dull … "Doctor Who" has probably changed considerably since your connection with it and, these days, we find our audience is ready to accept quite sophisticated concepts.'[4] Audience Research found that by the mid 1970s 'adults over 15' made up 56 per cent of the *Doctor Who* audience.[5] In response, the series now entered its most 'adult' period in terms of content and style. The Hinchcliffe-Holmes stories are darker than the Letts-Dicks stories, exploring much more morally ambiguous terrain ('Genesis of the Daleks', 'The Deadly Assassin') and becoming more horrific in their imagery ('Pyramids of Mars', 'The Brain of Morbius'). The UNIT stories were phased out ('Robot' and 'Terror of the Zygons' are the last full UNIT serials), and *Doctor Who* once again embraced a range of SF tropes informed by writers such as Isaac Asimov ('The Robots of Death') and John Wyndham ('The Seeds of Doom'). Critics approved of this trend. 'You can't take it seriously, yet of late the series has been offering good sci-fi, or "speculative fiction" as pompous trendies would like us to label it,' remarked Shaun Usher, while Peter Fiddick was 'impressed by its freewheeling inventiveness. It mostly shuns the fake moralising of more portentous space-operas like *Star Trek*, and quite right.'[6]

The defining characteristic of the Hinchcliffe-Holmes regime was the emergence of a distinctively Gothic style. This is evident at the level of both narrative and design. The Gothic novel, usually held to originate with Horace Walpole's *The Castle of Otranto* (1765), is a narrative of terror and suspense, often featuring supernatural elements and set in a bleak, sinister location. During its thirteenth and fourteenth seasons, especially, *Doctor Who* can accurately be described as Gothic: it is a world of darkness (both physical and spiritual), horror and violence. The series is pervaded by a genuine sense of menace and the prevailing mood is one of macabre humour. This atmosphere is enhanced by the series' visual style. Sleek modernist sets are largely absent during this period, while alien worlds are represented as bleak and oppressive environments: claustrophobic jungles ('Planet of Evil'), cobwebbed castles ('The Brain of Morbius') and a world blasted by perpetual sandstorms ('The Robots of Death'). The picturesque English village, in best *Avengers* fashion, turns out to be full of danger and conceals a deadly conspiracy ('The Android Invasion'). In the Earthbound stories, the contemporary landscapes of the Pertwee era are displaced by the period trappings and atmospherics of stories such as 'Pyramids of Mars' and 'The Talons of Weng-Chiang'. The Victorian 'look' even extended to the control room of the TARDIS, which was redesigned for the fourteenth season in a 'retro' style replete with wood panelling and brass fittings.

This Gothic style did not suddenly manifest itself following the arrival of Hinchcliffe and Holmes but rather emerged over a period of time. In this sense, the twelfth season in 1975 represents a transitional period between the Letts-Dicks era and the Hinchcliffe-Holmes era. 'Robot' (#75), for example, belongs in spirit to the Letts-Dicks era, which is hardly surprising given that it was written by Dicks, who 'invented' a tradition that the departing script editor should write the first story for his successor. It is a UNIT story including familiar devices such as the disillusioned scientist advocating 'alternative technology' and the sinister crypto-fascist organisation bent on world domination (in this instance the Scientific Reform Society advocating 'rule by a self-elected elite' in order to create a 'new scientific order'). Overlaid onto this is a pastiche of *King Kong* (dir. Merian C. Cooper, 1933) in which the powerful and apparently indestructible 'K1' robot controlled by the villains develops a touching affection for Sarah Jane Smith.

'The Ark in Space' (#76), on the other hand, which Holmes rewrote from scratch after the original scripts by John Lucarotti did not pass muster, anticipates the more horrific style that would emerge over the next two years. The TARDIS materialises on space station Nerva, carrying in cryogenic suspension the survivors of a cataclysm that has destroyed life on Earth many centuries in the future. It turns out, however, that the station has been infiltrated by the parasitic Wirrn which require human hosts to hatch their larvae. This combination of SF and horror anticipates *Alien* (dir. Ridley Scott, 1979) in its exploration of the anxiety arising from the corruption of the human body by an invasive 'Other'. The motifs of infection and disease are represented visually in the contrast between the sterile, white sets of the space station and the pupating larvae that infest it. The visceral gore (even if the larvae suspiciously resemble green plastic bubble-wrap) indicates the direction the series would take. If these two stories represent the past and future trajectories of *Doctor Who*, then the season's concluding adventure 'Revenge of the Cybermen' (#79) – designed in part to reduce costs by using the space station sets from 'The Ark in Space' – was regarded within the production team as 'the resurrection of a boring monster'.[7] The last group of Cybermen are foiled in their attempt to destroy Voga, the planet of gold, but an indication that *Doctor Who* wanted to distance itself from its past is evident in the Doctor's contempt for the formerly terrifying Cybermen themselves: 'You've no home planet, no influence, nothing. You're just a pathetic bunch of tin soldiers skulking about the galaxy in an ancient spaceship.'

The reinterpretation of *Doctor Who*'s own mythos is most evident in Terry Nation's 'Genesis of the Daleks' (#78), undoubtedly the most significant story of the twelfth season and one that frequently tops fans' polls of favourite *Doctor Who* stories. If, hitherto, *Doctor Who* had been an 'unfolding text' in which new knowledge is gradually revealed, 'Genesis of the Daleks' is the first example of outright revisionism in the series' history in that it offers an entirely different narrative of the origins of the Daleks to that previously suggested.[8] The Doctor returns to Skaro at the moment of the creation of the Daleks, which, it transpires, are the invention of the brilliant but twisted Kaled scientist Davros. The Kaleds are engaged in a centuries-old, attritional war against the Thals. Davros leads a scientific and military elite, set up to design new weapons but now preoccupied with the survival of the Kaled race. The use of chemical weapons is causing genetic mutation in the Kaleds and the 'Mark Three' travel machine has been designed to protect the species into which they will ultimately evolve. Davros, however, has corrupted the mutation in order to create the Daleks, using genetic experimentation to make the creatures entirely ruthless and without conscience. He uses the Daleks to exterminate not only the Thals but also those amongst the Kaleds who oppose him.

It is in 'Genesis of the Daleks' that the allegory between the Daleks and Nazism finds its clearest expression. The Kaleds, with their black uniforms and raised-arm salutes, clearly represent the society of Nazi Germany towards the end of the Second World War: a highly ideological regime engaged in total war and obsessed with 'total extermination of the Thals'. The physical resemblance between the sinister Security Commander Nyder and SS chief Heinrich Himmler is clearly intentional: actor Peter Miles wears SS-style insignia and 'Himmler' spectacles. The motif of a military and scientific elite closeted in an underground bunker while the regular army fights a bloody rearguard action brings to mind the last days of the Third Reich in 1945 when Hitler and his closest allies retreated into the Führer Bunker as the Red Army besieged Berlin. There are clear echoes of Nazi ideology in Davros's rhetoric of power ('Achievement comes through absolute power and power through strength') and in Nyder's statement of racial supremacy ('We must keep the Kaled race pure. Imperfects are rejected'). The revelation that the Daleks are the products of 'perverted science' – a phrase used by Winston Churchill in his 'Finest Hour' speech of 18 June 1940 – further emphasises the meaning overlaid onto the narrative.[9]

Yet 'Genesis of the Daleks' is much more than just an allegory of Nazism. It can also be related to wider scientific, moral and philosophical questions. The competing discourses of 'good' and 'bad' science, for example, rehearse debates around the morality of eugenics. It is significant in this regard that Davros's opponents amongst the scientific elite do not object to the Daleks as such but rather to the way in which he has perverted their development ('The creatures must have a moral sense, a judgement of right and wrong, in fact all the qualities that we believe are essential in ourselves'). Davros, however, believes that the aggression he has introduced into the Daleks is the only way of ensuring their survival ('One race must survive all others and to do this it must dominate ruthlessly'). The resolution of the narrative, furthermore, can be seen as a variation on the Frankenstein story in which the 'bad' scientist is destroyed by the monster he has created. The Daleks, having exterminated all Davros's opponents, reject his authority because 'our programming does not permit us to acknowledge that any creature is superior to the Daleks ... We obey no one. We are the superior beings.' It is Davros's own megalomania, having created the Daleks in his own image and ideology, that causes his own downfall. He begs the Daleks to 'have pity'; the Dalek leader responds that there is no such word in its vocabulary.

Audience Research found that viewers appreciated 'Genesis of the Daleks' as 'more complex than some *Dr Who* adventures ... with underlying questions of conscience'.[10] The Doctor has been sent to Skaro on a special mission for the Time Lords, who 'foresee a time when they [the Daleks] will have destroyed all other life forms and become the dominant creature in the universe' and, ignoring their usual doctrine of non-intervention, have tasked the Doctor with either averting their creation or at least modifying their genetic development 'so that they evolve into less aggressive creatures'. The Doctor has an opportunity to destroy the Daleks when he sets explosive charges in the incubator room containing Dalek embryos, but then he hesitates to set them off. The ensuing scene rehearses a classic moral dilemma:

Sarah: What are you waiting for?

The Doctor: Just touch these two strands together and the Daleks are finished. Have I that right?

Sarah: To destroy the Daleks? You can't doubt it!

The Doctor: Well I do. You see, some things could be better with the Daleks. Many future worlds will become allies just because of their fear of the Daleks.

Sarah: It isn't like that.

The Doctor: But the final responsibility is mine and mine alone. If someone who knew the future pointed a child to you and told you that that child would grow up totally evil, to be a ruthless dictator who would destroy countless millions of lives, could you then kill that child?

Sarah: We are talking about the Daleks, the most evil creatures ever
                  invented. You must destroy them. You must complete your
                  mission for the Time Lords.

The Doctor: Do I have the right? Simply touch one wire against the other
                  and that's it – the Daleks cease to exist. Hundreds of millions
                  of people, thousands of generations, can live without fear, in
                  peace and never even know the word Dalek.

Sarah: Then why not? If it was a disease or a bacteria you were
                  destroying, you wouldn't hesitate.

The Doctor: But if I kill, wipe out a whole intelligent life form, then I
                  become like them. I'd be no better than the Daleks.

There are several fundamental philosophical questions at stake here, including definitions of good and bad actions, whether the end justifies the means, whether the end itself is desirable, and the responsibility of the individual both to society and to his conscience. These questions are too problematic for the Doctor to resolve: when he has the opportunity he cannot bring himself to destroy the Daleks. (Later he returns to the incubator room and blows it up, but it no longer makes a difference as by this time the Dalek production line has been activated and the Doctor knows that he has only delayed rather than destroyed them.) To this end, 'Genesis of the Daleks' concludes with a rare failure for the Doctor – an indication of the series' adult and increasingly dystopian orientation at this time.

The inclusion of a strong Dalek story in the twelfth season, as well as the 'story arc' linking the serials into a continuous narrative thread, was part of the tactic for introducing the new 'Doctor Who'. The various actors considered for the role – including Graham Crowden, Fulton Mackay, Michael Bentine, Richard ('Mr Pastry') Hearne and *Carry On* star Jim Dale – suggest that the producers had no fixed idea about what sort of character Doctor No.4 should be. In the event the role went to Tom Baker, at 41 the youngest 'Doctor Who' to date and the least well-known actor of all those cast. It was his performance as the evil magician Koura in *The Golden Voyage of Sinbad* (dir. Gordon Hessler, 1973) that had persuaded Letts to cast Baker. Tall and broad, with an imposing physical presence, Baker invested the Doctor with a renewed energy and vitality. He had spent several years as a monk in the 1960s and brought an almost religious intensity to the role. As he later confided in his autobiography: 'All that was required of me was to be able to speak gobbledygook with conviction ... It was easy because all my life I had been taught nonsense by priests and teachers on all sorts of subjects.'[11] It is impossible to imagine Jon Pertwee playing the Doctor's 'Have I that right?' dilemma with quite the same conviction and intensity as his successor.

As before, there was a conscious effort to make the new incumbent as different from his predecessor as possible. Baker played the Doctor in a very different style from the suave, patrician Pertwee incarnation. His Doctor is a bohemian intellectual whose non-conformist, anti-authoritarian nature identifies him with the counter-cultural generation of the 1960s now grown to adulthood. It is significant in this regard that a third of *Doctor Who* viewers in the mid 1970s were between the ages of 20 and 50.[12] The most obvious signifier of this Doctor's counter-cultural associations is his fashion sense, which is nothing if not bohemian: knitted waistcoat, red corduroy jacket or beige tweed frock coat, floppy brimmed hat and an absurdly long multicoloured scarf that trails along the floor behind him. Costume designer James Acheson modelled Baker's 'look' on the paintings of Toulouse-Lautrec: to this extent the counter-cultural association of *fin-de-siècle* Montmartre is coded into the Doctor's dress.[13]

That Baker became the longest-serving 'Doctor Who' (he would play the part for 178 episodes over seven years) has tended to obscure the fact that critical and popular responses to his characterisation were initially mixed. In his first adventure, 'Robot', the Fourth Doctor's eccentric behaviour is explained in terms of the effects of his regeneration. Elizabeth Thomas in the *New Statesman* felt that 'the present incumbent of the Doctor's body is beginning to show a nice strain of eccentricity.' After a while, however, Martin Jackson in the *Daily Mail* felt that the new Doctor 'is in danger of becoming a childish prank'.[14] Audience Research found that 'some children obviously thought the new Doctor "silly" ... Others were as yet unsure or, less often, positively attracted to this "crazy but comical" figure'.[15] Baker, for his part, disavowed any comedic intent: 'We are not playing Dr Who for laughs. I was trying to stress his strangeness, that he is not of this world, not human, therefore his reactions would be different from ours'.[16]

The early Baker period maintained continuity with the last Pertwee season through the presence of Elisabeth Sladen as Sarah Jane Smith. Another companion was added in the form of naval surgeon Harry Sullivan (Ian Marter), introduced as a safeguard in case the new Doctor had been an older character less involved in the action. In the event, Harry soon became surplus to requirements. For the concluding episode of 'Revenge of the Cybermen', for example, Hinchcliffe had to ask Davis 'to make the Doctor more obviously active at the climax of the story – perhaps giving him some of Harry's action'.[17] Harry elected to remain on Earth at the end of 'Terror of the Zygons' leaving the Doctor and Sarah to their travels. As the series went on, there were subtle but significant changes in the characterisation of Sarah, whose feminist credentials became less evident as she slipped back into a 'frightened lady' vein of being terrorised by monsters ('The Brain of Morbius') or possessed by aliens ('The Hand of Fear'). Despite the softening of the character, however, the rapport between Baker and Sladen made her one of the most popular companions, and there was genuine sadness amongst fans when she left at the end of 'The Hand of Fear'. Peter Fiddick remarked: 'I have a certain sympathy with the argument that these ladies have served successive Doctors as stereotyped Little Women boosting the Great Male Ego, but Sarah, in both Elizabeth [sic] Sladen's perky performance and the scripts she progressively earned, got a sight nearer to subverting the omnipotence than Robin ever did for Batman.'[18]

The transformation of Sarah from feisty feminist to lady-in-jeopardy was itself largely a consequence of the trend towards more horrific and macabre stories in which, traditionally, the woman's role is to be victimised by the monster. When Sarah wears a long white dress in 'Pyramids of Mars', Doctor Who is making a visual reference to films such as *The Cabinet of Dr Caligari* (dir. Robert Wiene, 1919) and *Frankenstein* (dir. James Whale, 1931) in which the heroine, wearing virginal white, is carried off by the monster. This exemplifies the trend towards pastiche that characterises the Hinchcliffe-Holmes era. Holmes, especially, believed that Doctor Who was at its best when it drew on ideas and imagery from elsewhere. He once remarked: 'All you need is a strong, original idea. It doesn't have to be your own strong, original idea.'[19] In particular, Doctor Who reveals the influence of popular fictions from the nineteenth and early twentieth centuries. Amongst the sources appropriated were *Frankenstein* ('The Brain of Morbius'), *The Strange*

Case of Dr Jekyll and Mr Hyde ('Planet of Evil'), *The Jewel of the Seven Stars* ('Pyramids of Mars') and a heady concoction of Sherlock Holmes and Fu Manchu with a soupçon of *The Phantom of the Opera* ('The Talons of Weng-Chiang'). The influence of motifs from nineteenth-century popular literature can be seen as a conscious attempt to reposition *Doctor Who* in relation to the tradition of 'scientific romance' that preceded science fiction. This strategy serves to locate *Doctor Who* within a distinctively British lineage of imaginative fiction, inspired by writers such as Rider Haggard, Conan Doyle, Bram Stoker, Edgar Wallace and Sax Rohmer, as distinct from the American 'pulp' SF tradition of the later twentieth century.

Pastiche in *Doctor Who* works on two levels, importing both visual/iconographic and structural/ideological references. The highly regarded thirteenth-season adventure 'Pyramids of Mars' (#82) is a good example of these processes. Hinchcliffe and Holmes wanted a serial with an 'Egyptology' theme and commissioned scripts from Lewis Greifer. Greifer's first draft was a contemporary story set largely in the British Museum, but Hinchcliffe felt that 'the Egyptology background is too complex and obscure at the moment'.[20] Holmes was in no doubt what sort of story he wanted: 'Egyptology – to our audience – means stone coffins, mysterious and eerie happenings and, above all, giant mummies wrapped in decaying bandages stalking through studio fog. If this is their expectation I think they are going to feel cheated when it isn't fulfilled.'[21] Holmes did an extensive rewrite of 'Pyramids of Mars', which was credited to a pseudonymous 'Stephen Harris'. Holmes made it a period piece (set in 1911) in order to make full use of the sort of imagery familiar from myriad Universal and Hammer films: linen-suited British archaeologists, sinister fez-wearing Egyptians and killer mummies stalking the woods. In 'Pyramids of Mars' these motifs are woven into a classic *Doctor Who* 'Threat and Disaster' narrative with a 'rational' discursive explanation. Thus the 'mummies' are not the living dead but rather service robots controlled by the powerful alien warlord Sutekh the Destroyer. In making such explicit use of genre iconography, moreover, 'Pyramids of Mars' also positions itself in relation to the pre-existing narrative and structural ideologies of films such as *The Mummy* (dir. Terence Fisher, 1959). Mummy films are usually interpreted in terms of an opposition between imperialism (British) and primitivism (Egyptian) in which the irrational supernatural forces of the latter threaten to undermine the rational social certainties of the former. In 'Pyramids of Mars', this is translated into an opposition between 'all sapient life forms' and the long-extinct Osirans. Centuries ago the Osirans imprisoned their worst criminal, Sutekh, on Earth, but now Sutekh has possessed the mind and body of Egyptologist Marcus Scarman who is building a rocket that will release Sutekh from his imprisonment. It is the horrific visual imagery of the story that remains most vivid, however, not least the robotic mummies which fetishistically kill one victim by crushing him between their protruding, ridged chests.

It was through the intervention of Holmes that 'Pyramids of Mars' was fashioned into a full-blooded Gothic horror. Much the same occurred with 'The Brain of Morbius' (#84). This was originally written by Terrance Dicks, but he felt that Holmes's extensive revisions to the script 'moved a bit further towards horror than I'd care to myself' and asked that his name be removed from the credits. 'I'll leave it to you to design some bland pseudonym,' Dicks concluded amicably.[22] The script was subsequently credited to one 'Robin Bland'. 'The Brain of Morbius' is a pastiche of *Frankenstein* in which mad scientist Solon uses a patchwork of body parts from dead aliens stranded on the planet Karn to create a new body for Morbius, an evil renegade Time Lord whose brain survived his execution and has been kept alive by Solon. The imagery is clearly inspired by Universal and Hammer films: Solon's storm-swept Gothic castle, his crude laboratory with its primitive equipment and the brain of Morbius preserved in a jar all reinforce the story's place in the lineage of horror films. It even adopts the brutish disfigured assistant Condo (whose left hand has been replaced by a sickle) and the climax in which the monster (a massive torso with a giant claw and a goldfish-bowl head) is pursued by a torch-wielding mob from Universal's 1931 *Frankenstein*. 'The Brain of Morbius' once again associates 'bad' science with the monstrous: the Doctor condemns Solon's 'unnatural experiments' and describes Morbius as 'one of the most despicably criminally minded [Time Lords] who ever lived'. It is one of the most violent *Doctor Who* stories in content, including decapitation, strangulation and blood-spattered gunshot wounds amongst its gory highlights. Ironically, it was the pseudonymous Robin Bland to whom one correspondent wrote to complain that *Doctor Who* 'has been changed in a nasty way because it's become more like a horror film that is shown at eleven o'clock at night'.[23]

Holmes's scripts depend upon the audience's knowledge of the generic references for some of their effect. While it might be expected that older viewers would be more likely to recognise the sources, there is evidence that some children also had the cultural competence to decode them. An eleven-year-old girl, for example, wrote to the BBC: 'I think the Doctor Who series are getting far too frightening. The previous adventure about "Morbius" was like a Frankenstein story, and the present one, "The Seeds of Doom", is like "The Day of the Triffids".'[24] In contrast, the scripts of Louis Marks offer a more intellectual approach that is more sophisticated in its use of pastiche but less accessible to children. 'Planet of Evil' (#81), for example, is posited on the notion of a Jekyll-and-Hyde planet at the far edge of the known universe in which an anti-matter creature – seen only in silhouette and visually resembling the 'Id' monster from *Forbidden Planet* (dir. Fred M. Wilcox, 1956) – kills off the members of a scientific expedition. It is an intellectually complex story concerned with themes of the limits and dangers of scientific knowledge: expedition leader Professor Sorensen seeks anti-matter crystals to provide 'a new and inexhaustible supply of energy', but the Doctor warns that he is 'tampering with hideously dangerous forces'. Audience Research reported 'that youngsters had found the story "rather complicated in parts" and were "perplexed by the anti-matter"'.[25] A similar response is evident with Marks's 'The Masque of Mandragora' (#86). Here the medieval Italian setting, a sinister masked brotherhood preparing to sacrifice Sarah on the altar and the masquerade ball visited by Death are clearly influenced by *The Masque of the Red Death* (dir. Roger Corman, 1964). However, Marks is rather less interested in the occult goings-on (explained through the malevolent influence of a non-corporeal alien entity known as the Mandragora Helix) than he is in exploring the intellectual history of Renaissance Italy. The narrative is structured around an opposition between the superstition of the Dark Ages (represented by court astronomer Hieronymous and the sinister Brotherhood of Demnos) and the emergence of scientific reason (exemplified by the idealistic young Duke of San Martino, Giuliano, who believes 'that the world is really a sphere'). Audience Research, however, suggested that the story was too cerebral for younger viewers: 'Not enough action to hold young children. For our five and seven-year-olds we need Daleks and gadgetry.'[26]

In addition to its Gothic narratives and imagery, it was during the

Hinchcliffe-Holmes period that design became integral to the style of *Doctor Who*. Hitherto, with exceptions such as the isomorphic city of 'The Daleks', sets had been largely utilitarian rather than symbolic. Hinchcliffe, however, encouraged designers such as Roger Murray-Leach and Kenneth Sharp to become more ambitious in their use of sets, which, after all, accounted for a significant proportion of the budget for each serial.[27] 'The Robots of Death' (#90) by Chris Boucher, for example, is set on-board a massive commercial sand-mining vehicle where the small human crew is entirely dependent on the servile 'Voc' robots who perform all the menial duties. The plot can be summarised as '*And Then There Were None* Meets *I, Robot*' – a series of grisly murders turn out to have been committed by robots programmed to kill humans – though plot on this occasion is secondary to visual style. Both Sharp's set design and Elizabeth Waller's costumes eschew the standard conventions for representing futuristic environments and robot designs (reflective metal surfaces, clean angles, lots of silver) and instead employ an entirely stylised Art Deco 'look' that has no narrative logic but which imposes a uniform visual logic on the serial. The sets and dressings are sumptuous, the costumes highly extravagant and the face masks of the 'Voc' robots themselves are designed to resemble Greco-Roman sculpture. With their handsomely sculpted faces and quilted body garments, these robots are unlike any others in SF history, their semi-human appearance and soft speaking voices making the threat they represent all the more chilling. Britton and Barker suggest that 'The Robots of Death' is 'one of only two *Doctor Who* episodes where a well-known aesthetic from the history of design was applied wholesale to every aspect of imagery, including make-up'.[28]

The pinnacle of the Hinchcliffe-Holmes period, in terms of both popularity and in its unity of narrative and design, is 'The Deadly Assassin' (#88). This attracted an audience of over 12 million viewers and, like 'Genesis of the Daleks', regularly features in fan polls of favourite *Doctor Who* adventures. The Doctor's only solo outing has him return to his home planet of Gallifrey for the first time since the end of 'The War Games' in a vain attempt to prevent the assassination of the President of the High Council of the Time Lords. Holmes's reference point on this occasion is *The Manchurian Candidate* (dir. John Frankenheimer, 1962) as the Doctor is framed for the assassination of the President and sets out to uncover the truth behind the conspiracy. The assassination has been engineered by the Master, whose body, towards the end of its regenerative cycle, is now a horrific skeleton covered in rotting flesh. Much of the action takes place inside the Matrix, a virtual-reality environment where the Doctor finds himself engaged in a desperate fight for survival against the Master's agent Chancellor Goth. 'The Deadly Assassin' represents two contrasting environments – the 'real' world of Gallifrey and the 'unreal' world of the Matrix – but visualises them entirely against expectations. Thus the 'real' world of Gallifrey is a stylised studio set whereas the 'unreal' dreamscape of the Matrix is shot on location and on film and includes the grittiest and most realistic action scenes ever staged in *Doctor Who* as the Doctor and his antagonist Goth are bruised, bloodied and battered as they fight each other to the point of death.

'The Deadly Assassin' is replete with characteristic Robert Holmes touches, such as references to the CIA (Celestial Intervention Agency) who 'get their fingers into everything' and a marvellous spoof of the BBC's own coverage of state occasions as television presenter Runcible (actor Hugh Walters impersonating David Dimbleby) provides a commentary on the ceremonial process. Most significant, however, is the invention of the society and mythology of the Time Lords. Unlike *Star Trek*, where the Federation represents the acme of liberal and humanitarian values, the supreme civilisation of *Doctor Who* is elitist and hierarchical. The social and political hierarchy of the Time Lords is rather like the England of the Interregnum: a republic that maintains the trappings of aristocracy. It is a technocracy ruled by an elite that breeds megalomaniacs such as Goth ('Wanted power ... wanted to be president') and amoral political pragmatists like Cardinal Borusa who is not averse to a little spin-doctoring in order to preserve the authority of the elite ('We must adjust the truth ... in a way that will maintain public confidence in the Time Lords and their leadership'). The moral corruption of the Time Lords' society is mirrored in the physical corruption of the Master, whose hideously decayed form lurking in the catacomb beneath the Panopticon is, perhaps, an allusion to the Phantom living beneath the Paris Opera House.

It was 'The Deadly Assassin', however, that brought to a head a controversy that had been brewing over the increasingly violent and horrific content of *Doctor Who*. In April 1975, the *Radio Times* had printed a letter complaining about the first episode of 'Genesis of the

Daleks' which began with slow-motion shots of troops being machine-gunned (a direct visual reference to the First World War) and included a scene where the Doctor and his companions stripped gas masks from dead bodies to save themselves from a gas shell. The correspondent felt that these scenes were

> brutal, violent and revolting – totally without plot or point – yet convincingly enough done to be really terrifying for many normal children ... Does the producer of this unpleasant effort really expect a not-too-bright child to know the difference between grim reality on the Falls Road or in Cambodia, and a jolly little Saturday romp with the Doctor?

Hinchcliffe replied that he did believe children were able to distinguish between fantasy and reality, whilst at the same time asserting the doctrine of parental responsibility: 'Though I am sure that most of our audience realise they are watching fiction not fact, of course, ultimately, we have to rely upon parents in the home to decide whether a programme is suitable for their child.' He assured *Radio Times* readers that the production team 'do take great pains to ensure that we never depict any act of violence which could be copied by children' and defended 'Genesis of the Daleks' on the grounds that it 'will be seen to adopt a clearly moral attitude towards senseless warfare'.[29]

While previous *Doctor Who* stories such as 'The Tomb of the Cybermen' and 'Terror of the Autons' had also attracted public censure, it was in the mid 1970s that a campaign against the series was mounted by the unofficial television watchdog that was the National Viewers' and Listeners' Association (NVALA). The NVALA, founded in 1965, had grown out of the 'Clean-Up TV Campaign' led by Mary Whitehouse to oppose what she and her supporters regarded as the decline of Christian morality and the promotion of permissive behaviour by the television industry in general and the BBC in particular. Mrs Whitehouse, whom even her fiercest critics recognise as a woman of high moral principle, was the honorary general-secretary of the NVALA, an organisation that, due to its supporters amongst backbench MPs, enjoyed a higher public profile than its membership probably warranted. By the mid 1970s the NVALA had widened the scope of its activities and was actively engaged in monitoring television output to draw attention to what it regarded as unacceptable levels of violence. In the mid 1970s *Doctor Who* became one of the NVALA's targets: one newspaper reported that Mrs Whitehouse 'believes the Saturday serial is giving nightmares to under-sevens' and claimed that she 'wants to "exterminate" the zany doctor and his unearthly foes'.[30]

To be fair to Whitehouse and the NVALA, there is no evidence that they tried to have *Doctor Who* taken off the air, but they did complain loudly about specific instances of violent content. In one speech, for example, Whitehouse averred: 'Strangulation – by hand, by claw, by obscene vegetable matter – is the latest gimmick, sufficiently close up so that they get the point. And just for a little variety, show the children how the make a Molotov Cocktail.'[31] The most notorious case was the third episode of 'The Deadly Assassin' (broadcast at 6.05 pm on 13 November 1976), which featured a brutal fight between the Doctor and Chancellor Goth in which Goth is set on fire and which ends with Goth attempting to drown the Doctor. The episode's cliffhanger ending was a freeze-frame of Baker's head being held under the water. Whitehouse wrote 'in anger and despair … because at a time when little children would be viewing, you showed violence of a quite unacceptable kind'. Violence 'permeated the programme' and the climax, she felt, 'could only be described as sadistic'.[32] There is probably some justification to her view that the nature of the cliffhanger did contravene the corporation's guidelines ('Young children often regard each instalment as complete in itself and may not be able to see or may even avoid seeing subsequent episodes which could provide the resolution of the situation. For young children even a week may be too long to wait for reassurance that the characters with whom they identify are safe'). Where Whitehouse was mistaken, however, was in her assumption that *Doctor Who* was watched primarily by 'little children'. There is, unfortunately, no breakdown of the audience for 'The Deadly Assassin', though it is reasonable to assume that it would have been similar to 'The Masque of Mandragora', for which there is such evidence. Both serials were part of the same season and were shown in the same post-six o'clock slot between the early evening news and *The Generation Game*. The 'under-sevens' for whom Whitehouse was most concerned comprised only 15 per cent of the viewing sample, with 18 per cent between the ages of eight and eleven and another 11 per cent between twelve and fourteen.[33] To this extent Whitehouse and the NVALA misunderstood the nature of *Doctor Who* as a family rather than a children's programme, the point being that the young children who watched it would, in the majority of cases, be doing so with their parents or other family members. Even so, however, the BBC was sufficiently concerned over the incident that when 'The Deadly Assassin' was repeated the offending sequence was re-edited and the freeze-frame removed, in which form, averred Hinchcliffe, 'it was deemed acceptable ... by the BBC and the British public'.[34]

The most direct evidence of the effect of *Doctor Who* on children came from children themselves. 'The Seeds of Doom' (#85) had also occasioned a complaint from the NVALA, though of rather more value in assessing reaction to the serial are several dozen letters from both parents and children that survive in the BBC Written Archives. 'The Seeds of Doom' attracted controversy both for its violence and for its horrific content, featuring as it did an alien seed-pod that attacks human beings and transforms them into an aggressive vegetable organism called the Krynoid. The evidence is largely inconclusive. The children of All Saints First School, Ilkley, for example, complained that the story was 'too frightening' and that *Doctor Who* was 'changing into a horror film'. Some parents complained that it 'is getting more and more horrific' and that it contained 'an excess of violence merely for the sake of violence'. Against this, however, can be set other young correspondents who felt that it 'is so exciting and one of the best yet'. Some children revelled in the horror: 'I liked the episode very much. I think it was one of the most scariest ones of all, I liked the bit when the plants were taking over, and I also liked the monster' and 'I liked it when Scorbie was pulled under the water when the plant came up and when Chase was killed in the compost machine'.[35]

Hinchcliffe and Holmes had a standard response to the complaints levelled against *Doctor Who*: they would simply disagree with their critics. Thus Hinchcliffe replied to the correspondent complaining of excessive violence in 'The Seeds of Doom' by asserting that while it 'contained several forceful scenes, I don't agree with you that it contained an excess of violence, and certainly not violence for its own sake'.[36] Holmes, similarly, replied to a young critic of 'The Brain of Morbius': 'I think you may be right in feeling that "Doctor Who" is becoming more frightening – we would say more exciting – but I cannot agree that our stories are stupid. In any case your feelings seem not to be generally shared because the programme is now attracting the largest audiences in its history'.[37] The popularity of *Doctor Who* was a factor frequently cited in its defence, the implicit assumption being that it would not attract so many viewers if it was too horrific. Hinchcliffe felt that 'Mrs Whitehouse was making a lot of fuss about nothing' and pointed out, quite reasonably, that 'in the case of very young children it must always be the parents' decision whether a programme is suitable for their own particular child.' He further averred that 'we receive in the office a very large number of letters, essays, pictures, models and even full length stories sent in by young viewers, which vividly illustrate how the programme stimulates them imaginatively and creatively. Often these children are from deprived backgrounds, and in these cases I'm convinced "Doctor Who" has a positive and beneficial influence.'[38]

Towards the end of the Hinchcliffe-Holmes era a rather different sort of controversy arose in respect of the Doctor's new companion. The character of Leela (played by Louise Jameson) again highlights both the possibilities and the limitations of the role of the female companion in *Doctor Who*. Conceived as a more action-oriented heroine to appeal to girl viewers, Leela, introduced in 'The Face of Evil' (#89), is a warrior of the Sevateem tribe who, like the Doctor, has been cast out by her own people. In cultural terms Leela represents an early manifestation of the 'women warriors' of a later generation of US fantasy adventure series such as *Xena: Warrior Princess* (1995–2001) and *Buffy the Vampire Slayer* (1997–2003). There is much anecdotal evidence, certainly, to suggest that girl viewers delighted in Leela's habit of dispatching a succession of monsters with either her trusty hunting knife or a deadly Janis thorn. One (male) critic wrote that Leela was 'a bit of a Woman's Movement sort' and that 'she kills with a knife with the ease of a Royal Marine Commando'.[39] As a role model for girls, however, Leela is extremely problematic: on the one hand she is courageous and self-sufficient, but on the other hand she is primitive, savage and superstitious. The Doctor is outraged when she casually kills an enemy in 'The Face of Evil' ('Who licensed you to slaughter people?') and to this extent the character might be seen as the series' own response to the concerns raised over its violent content.

If the association of Leela's 'independent' femininity with primitivism and savagery is problematic, however, there can be no doubt that the casting and performance of Jameson was intended largely to provide erotic interest for male viewers. In line with the convention for cave-women ever since Raquel Welch donned a fur bikini for *One Million Years BC*, Jameson is clad in a bosom- and thigh-revealing animal skin costume that leaves little to the imagination. There is a tension, therefore, between the characterisation of Leela as a stronger heroine and her visual representation as an object of male fantasy. The subject of Leela's clothes (or, rather, her lack of clothes) quickly became part of the popular discourse of *Doctor Who*. When she had to 'cover up' by wearing a full-length period costume in 'The Talons of Weng-Chiang' (animal skins not being the fashion in late Victorian London), one (male) viewer wrote to the *Radio Times* to protest.[40] He need not have worried: the third episode saw Leela stripped to her (entirely decent) corsets and pursued through the sewer by a giant rat which entailed her getting wet and dirty.

'The Talons of Weng-Chiang' (#91) was the last serial supervised by Hinchcliffe before moving over to the police series *Target* (1977–1978) and the last directed by David Maloney before he became producer of *Blake's 7* (1978–1981). It is a pastiche of the world of the Victorian penny dreadful that demonstrates Holmes's imagination at its most fertile: fog, gas lamps, hansom cabs, secret societies, opium dens, a sinister Chinese magician and his murderous half-living puppet. On this occasion the *mise-en-scène* is used to assert a sense of period authenticity: the theatre interiors were shot at the Northampton Repertory Theatre and the costume designer was John Bloomfield, who had worked on the acclaimed drama serial *The Six Wives of Henry VIII* (1970). Holmes uses a range of historical and literary references that situate 'The Talons of Weng-Chiang' in a historically and culturally specific idiom. Arriving in late nineteenth-century London, the Doctor (wearing a deerstalker and cape in the manner of Sidney Paget's *Strand Magazine* illustrations of the Sherlock Holmes stories) and Leela investigate the disappearance of several young girls which they trace to Chinese magician Li H'sen Chang. The presence of oriental villains (the Tong of the Black Scorpion) brings to mind Sax Rohmer's *The Mystery of Dr Fu Manchu* (1913) and its sequels. Again the use of motifs from popular fiction also imports its cultural and ideological values, in this instance the spectre of the 'Yellow Peril' that threatens *fin-de-siècle* London. On this point there is no real defence against the charge that the serial reinforces racist stereotypes about 'Chinese ruffians' and 'opium-sodden scum' that have been present in the western cultural imagination since the nineteenth century. However, the major villain turns out to be not Li H'sen Chang but Magnus Greel, a time-travelling war criminal from the fifty-first century who survives by draining the 'life essence' of young women. It is here that the serial incorporates motifs from horror films such as *Murders in the Rue Morgue* (dir. Robert Florey, 1932) and *The Awful Dr Orloff* (dir. Jess Franco, 1962). The fifth-episode cliffhanger when Greel's mask is pulled away to reveal his hideously scarred face beneath is lifted directly from *The Mystery of the Wax Museum* (dir. Michael Curtiz, 1933).

With its sensationalist narrative and moments of visual excess, 'The Talons of Weng-Chiang' is a full-blown macabre melodrama in the best Grand Guignol tradition. It represents both a summation of and a conclusion to this period of *Doctor Who*. It is a period memorable for its extremes of emotion, characterisation and villainy, representing a Manichean universe of good and evil in which the Doctor's victories are achieved only after a prolonged and epic struggle against his supremely powerful foes. It features the most despicable and thoroughly evil examples of villainy in the series' history (Davros, Sutekh, Morbius, Greel), representing not the technological horror of the Daleks or Cybermen or the faceless alien menace of the Ice Warriors or Autons, but rather a form of individual psychological evil that expresses itself through insanity and megalomania. These villains are driven by irrational hatred: their aim is not to conquer but to destroy. They are the Hitlers, Stalins, Amins and Pol Pots of the *Doctor Who* universe. Given its content it is perhaps not surprising that this was also a time when *Doctor Who* attracted censure on account of its violence. It was this aspect of the series that would now come under close scrutiny.

5

High Camp

1977–1980

If you're supposed to be the superior race of the universe, why don't you try climbing after us?

The Doctor (Tom Baker) in 'Destiny of the Daleks'

'The violence and the pretty ladies – one was very conscious that the microscope was there, that the spotlight was on us.'[1] So remarked the new *Doctor Who* producer Graham Williams, replacing Philip Hinchcliffe in 1977. The popular historiography of *Doctor Who* has not been kind to Williams, often regarded as a weak producer whose inability to restrain the excesses of Tom Baker's performance allowed the series to drift further and further towards parody – a trend that was much to its detriment in the eyes of many aficionados. Thus *Doctor Who*'s period of High Gothic was followed by its period of High Camp. To lay the blame for the changes to the content and style of the series solely at Williams's door, however, is to ignore both the institutional and the cultural conditions that prevailed at the BBC in the late 1970s. Williams came to *Doctor Who* under strict instructions from his superiors to tone down the horror and violence that had characterised the previous three years of the series. The evidence of the BBC Written Archives, moreover, shows that Williams enjoyed much less of a free hand than had been extended to Hinchcliffe and that scrutiny of *Doctor Who* within the Drama Department was more intense than it had been at any time since the series began.

It is clear that the corporation had been rattled by the public criticism of *Doctor Who*. This was a time when the violent content of popular drama series was increasing, a trend that was most evident in the law-and-order police series such as ITV's *The Sweeney* (1975–1978) and American imports such as *Starsky and Hutch* (1975–1979). As a series that straddled the genres of family entertainment and drama, *Doctor Who* was always particularly vulnerable to the complaints of pressure groups like the NVALA in a way that late-evening post-watershed series such as *The Sweeney* were not. It was in response, largely, to the adverse publicity that had attended some of the Hinchcliffe-produced serials that *Doctor Who* now came under much closer scrutiny. Graeme McDonald, Williams's immediate superior as Head of Serials, exercised greater control over the scripts and was quick to jump on anything that might cause upset. After reading 'The Stones of Blood', for example, he told Williams: 'Please be careful how you handle the goat sacrifice … It could cause a lot of concern for children, adults *and* me.'[2] On another occasion he wrote: 'I liked "Nightmare of Eden". Please watch the drug culture bit though.'[3] It was McDonald, too, who imposed a doctrine of political correctness on the series. He took exception to phrases like 'female assistant' ('A sexist remark!') and 'junior female acolyte' ('A sexist remark again!') in the scripts of 'The Ribos Operation'.[4] It is evident that Williams enjoyed significantly less control over the content of his *Doctor Who* stories than Hinchcliffe had done.

If the aim was to reduce public criticism of *Doctor Who* for its horror, then this policy can be adjudged to have been largely successful. The popular historiography of *Doctor Who* maintains that the monsters of the late 1970s such as the Mandrels ('Nightmare of Eden') and the Kroll ('The Power of Kroll') were not as frightening as they used to be. This verdict is supported by Audience Research which found that 'some [children] were disappointed by the lack of monsters and "frightening bits"'.[5] Williams made the same point in reply to one correspondent: 'I am sorry to hear that your children found the monster in our recent programme more scary than usual – the vast majority of comments we have received is that the monsters have not been scary enough in recent episodes.'[6] The episode in question was 'The Creature from the Pit', in which the design of the creature itself had been somewhat unfortunate:

> 'The Monster' appeared in the studio resembling nothing so much as a giant green blancmange with a four foot phallus … The most easily available (and essential) function gave the impression of erection – both

common sense and what remains of our decorum dictated that the action
as planned should be abandoned and the view of the monster restricted to
three shots. We thus lost a vital dramatic point.[7]

What of the popularity of *Doctor Who* during the Williams era?
The average audience throughout Williams's three seasons was a very
healthy 9.4 million, which, to put it in context, was less than the three
Hinchcliffe-Holmes seasons but more than the Letts-Dicks-Pertwee era.
When the statistics are scrutinised more closely, however, they reveal
less consistency in viewing trends than at any time since the end of the
1960s. The fifteenth season in 1977–1978 averaged 8.9 million viewers
with a low of 6.7 million (for the first episode of 'Image of the Fendahl')
and a high of 11.4 million (for the second episode of 'The Invasion of
Time'). It was partly in response to the fluctuation during season fifteen
that Williams and script editor Anthony Read decided that the sixteenth
season in 1978–1979 should have a linking narrative in an attempt to
maintain viewers throughout. To this end they sent the Doctor and his
new companion on a quest to find six segments of something called the
Key to Time. Williams explained the intention thus:

> The Doctor will be seen to have six independent ventures, each linked by
> the common theme ... Those who wish to join him in episode one and follow
> him through to episode twenty-six will gain the momentum and bonus of
> following the story through. Those who choose to watch only one venture
> will enjoy it for its own sake – the scope in each venture is as wide and as
> free-ranging as ever – but should be encouraged as far as possible to see
> what happens next.[8]

The strategy was only partly successful: the season averaged 8.6 million
viewers but saw an even greater variation between individual episodes.
Thus, while the lowest audience for the entire season was 6.5 million for
the first episode of 'The Power of Kroll', the highest audience was 12.4
million for the very next episode of the same serial.

The seventeenth season in 1979–1980 is one of the most unusual
in the series' history, not least because its last serial, 'Shada', was never
completed due to a technicians' strike at the BBC. The first two serials
enjoyed significantly higher than usual audiences due to the fact that a
strike had taken the ITV network off the air between August and October

1979. It is fair to assume that the season opener, 'Destiny of the Daleks', which averaged 13.5 million over four episodes, would in any event have attracted a large audience, representing as it did the first new Dalek serial for over four years, though this was surpassed by the second serial, 'City of Death', which averaged 14.5 million over its four episodes. The 16.1 million viewers who tuned in for the last episode of 'City of Death' was the highest audience in the series' history. The season's average of 11.2 million was certainly inflated by the rather peculiar circumstances that affected the first two serials, especially when we consider that the lowest audience for the season was only six million for the first episode of 'The Horns of Nimon'.

While its overall level of popularity remained highly respectable, therefore, Williams-era *Doctor Who* enjoyed a less consistent presence in the audience ratings than previous regimes had achieved. To some extent this reflects the variable quality of scripts. The critic Richard Boston, for example, felt in autumn 1977 that 'this series is below standard. The pace is painfully slow, the characterisation is wooden, and the dialogue is made of baked beans.'[9] The fifteenth season of *Doctor Who* is in fact something of a hybrid that exhibits an uneasy tension between different styles: 'Horror of Fang Rock' and 'Image of the Fendahl' are throwbacks to the Hinchcliffe-Holmes style of Gothic melodrama – these were both commissioned while Holmes was still the series' script editor – whereas 'The Sun Makers' and 'Underworld' exemplify the trend towards satire and parody that would become increasingly dominant in the late 1970s. Williams experienced much difficulty in finding the right calibre of scripts during his three years in charge of *Doctor Who*. As he explained to McDonald in July 1979:

> We have discussed the problems of finding new writers for Doctor Who several times and the number of commissions we have made this year I believe demonstrates our willingness to go as far afield as possible in promoting new writers. Sadly, the number of rejections demonstrates the difficulty writers have in working within the unique brief. The scale of rewriting upon inexperienced Doctor Who writers' scripts has given me no ground to believe that the situation is improving.[10]

An unfortunate legacy of the Hinchcliffe-Holmes era was that *Doctor Who* had become over-dependent on a small pool of writers, including

Holmes himself, Terrance Dicks, Bob Baker, Dave Martin and newcomer Chris Boucher. Two Williams-produced serials ('The Invasion of Time' and 'City of Death') are credited to 'David Agnew', who was in fact Williams himself writing in association with the script editor of the time.

It is to Williams's credit that he attempted to encourage new writers, but several of those new writers, particularly Douglas Adams, were more inclined to comedy and parody. Williams seems to have endorsed this trend, but McDonald disliked it. He was particularly concerned that writers should not feed Tom Baker's increasingly wayward performance style. Of Adams' 'The Pirate Planet' he wrote: 'On the basis of the first two scripts this won't do … We're doing science fiction, remember, not comic cuts. The Captain with the parrot is a cod figure out of Treasure Island with jokey lines which will inevitably lead Tom to stop taking himself seriously again.'[11] David Fisher's 'The Creature from the Pit' met with an equally dismissive response from the Head of Serials: 'At first glance this serial hardly evidences the increased calibre of writing I expected this year. It's littered with schoolboy humour that will reduce Tom's authority and credibility hopelessly … If we allow Tom to get his hands on material like this surely it's an open invitation to him to become even more flippant and unmanageable.'[12]

The fact that McDonald was so apt to intervene in the production process does tend to reinforce the notion of Williams as a weak producer who was unable to impose his own style on the series. This, again, is somewhat unfair. Williams was as concerned as McDonald over Baker's tendency to improvise his lines and was critical of directors for allowing him to get away with it. In March 1978 he had 'to remind actors and Directors of the continual purpose of the script, and ensure that the contributions they offer are additional to the basic material and are not misguided substitutions or actual detractions from that purpose'.[13] Baker remarks in his autobiography that he and Williams did not get on:

> [There] was something about me that made Graham insecure. As time went by there was increasing tension between us and I'm sorry to say I was probably at fault. He was younger than I was and yet I thought of him as older. I grated on his nerves a bit and some of my notions just exhausted him … By the time he finished as producer things were very cool between us.[14]

Baker had now played the Doctor for longer than any previous actor and had become proprietorial about the part. There are moments in his later stories where his performance suggests that he was not merely playing an alien from another planet but appeared also to be living there.

There were other pressures on Williams, too, from outside the BBC. The late 1970s witnessed a science fiction boom in popular cinema sparked off by the extraordinary success of the space opera *Star Wars* (dir. George Lucas, 1977), the film which, more than any other, turned SF fantasy into a mainstream Hollywood movie genre. The record-breaking box-office success of *Star Wars* demonstrated a lucrative market for SF fantasy in film and television: it spawned a cycle of inferior imitations, including *The Black Hole* (dir. Gary Nelson, 1979), *Flash Gordon* (dir. Mike Hodges, 1980), *Battle Beyond the Stars* (dir. Jimmy T. Murakami, 1980) and the television series *Battlestar Galactica* (1978–1979) and *Buck Rogers in the 25th Century* (1979–1981), both produced by the enterprising Glen A. Larson. The post-*Star Wars* SF boom also precipitated the long-heralded revival of *Star Trek* in the form of *Star Trek – The Motion Picture* (dir. Robert Wise, 1979). It was in the wake of *Star Wars* that *Doctor Who* made its first significant incursion onto US television when 98 of Tom Baker's episodes (his first four seasons) were bought for syndication through the Public Broadcasting Service. *Doctor Who* was shown in America, albeit only on local stations and at different times, before *Battlestar Galactica* was aired on the ABC network in the autumn of 1978.[15]

The *Star Wars* factor inevitably impacted upon *Doctor Who*. Williams recognised that *Doctor Who* would never be able to match the glossy production values of *Star Wars* or even *Battlestar Galactica*, though the impressive model landscapes and space ships in both 'The Invisible Enemy' and 'City of Death' demonstrate that the BBC was able to produce special effects that were comparable in quality if not executed on the same scale. Williams asserted that the recourse to more character-driven scripts was a strategy of product differentiation: 'If we didn't go for the hardware, we had to go for something. And we went for character.'[16] The production discourse of *Doctor Who* stressed its 'quirky' characteristics and as there was no one more quirky than the Doctor himself this entailed allowing Baker scope to accentuate the eccentricity and individuality of the Time Lord. At the same time, however, the influence of *Star Wars* pervaded *Doctor Who*. It is a matter of faith amongst *Doctor Who* fans that the Doctor's robotic dog, K9, was introduced into the series before *Star Wars* was released in Britain (late 1977) and was not, therefore, a response to that film's loveable bickering robots C3PO and R2D2. Baker disliked 'the insufferable K9'.[17] So, too, did the production team, who soon tired of K9 coming to the Doctor's rescue with the ray gun in its nose. One of the promotional points listed for 'The Stones of Blood', for example, was that 'K9 is to be seen on this occasion not to be able to solve every problem!'[18] Audience Research, however, found 'much enthusiasm on the part of many children for the bionic dog, K9, their response to his introduction being much warmer than that of the adults in general'.[19] It was K9's popularity with children that kept it in *Doctor Who* for over three years, though some writers chose to confine it to the TARDIS for the duration of the story. *Doctor Who* might be held responsible for the presence of the 'cute' robot companion that seemingly became de rigeur in late-1970s SF series such as *Battlestar Galactica* ('Muffit') and *Buck Rogers* ('Twiki').

It may have been the epic narrative scope of *Star Wars* that persuaded Williams that a season with a continuous narrative thread running throughout offered a way in which *Doctor Who* might compete with SF cinema. The sixteenth season exhibits a clear 'story arc': a theme that links each story and builds towards a climax. The device was to have the Doctor undertake a quest for the Key to Time – 'a perfect cube which maintains the equilibrium of time itself' that is divided into six segments and 'scattered throughout the cosmos'. The Key contains 'the elemental force of the universe' and the Doctor needs to find it 'before the universe is plunged into eternal chaos'. What this amounted to, in a sense, was a reworking of 'The Keys of Marinus' over an entire season. The rationale behind the season is explained in a production document which Williams originally drafted for his first season in charge:

> The universe, as we know it, is held in delicate balance by forces which we do not yet fully understand ... The balance must be kept by someone, or something, which enjoys a greater sense of responsibility, and a greater sense of objectivity. A sense of right against a sense of wrong. A force for right against a force for wrong. If a force for good were to govern the balance there would *be* no balance. Therefore the force of evil must have an equal control. Must responsibility and objectivity lie solely in the hands of the good influence? Of our recent history there is no account nor any

evidence that Hitler believed in his principles less sincerely than Churchill did in his.[20]

Williams posited, therefore, a Manichean view of the universe in which the forces of good and evil, light and darkness, order and chaos, are equally matched. He devised an authority even more powerful than the Time Lords known as the Guardians – one White, one Black – who maintain the equilibrium of time and space. The theme of a Manichean universe is a familiar motif of fantasy and SF, of course, also informing *Star Wars* in which the balance between good and evil is maintained by the mystical energy field known as the 'Force'.

The Key to Time season also introduced another new companion in the form of Time Lord Romanadvoratrelundar (Romana for short). In this season Romana represents another feminine archetype: the cool 'ice maiden' whose intelligence and aristocratic demeanour are contrasted with the Doctor's irrational and impulsive behaviour. In this sense the 'instinctive' companion Leela had been replaced by the 'intellectual' companion, though Romana, at least in her first incarnation, presented the same problems as Liz Shaw had in the 1970 season: she is a scientist whose intellect matches the Doctor's own (in fact she graduated from the Time Lord Academy with a better class of degree) and who therefore limits dramatic exposition (there is little need for the Doctor to explain the plot to her). As Romana, Mary Tamm acts mostly with her cheekbones and plays the character with an icy, haughty aloofness. When she left after one season, the production team's answer, bearing in mind that Romana was a Time Lord, was to have her regenerate, modelling her new appearance on Princess Astra, played in 'The Armageddon Factor' by Lalla Ward, who now became a series regular as Romana II. The second Romana is an altogether more successful companion, representing in many ways an ideal counterweight to Baker's Doctor: she shares his sense of the absurd and exhibits an amused, detached response to the bizarre predicaments in which she finds herself ('I'm a Time Lord and I'm not used to being assaulted by a collection of hairy, grubby little men'). With her slim, boyish figure and unconventionally pretty face, Ward plays Romana as a sort of pantomime 'Principal Boy', reflected in her fashion sense which favours frock coats and breeches – or Earthly variations such as a St Trinian's schoolgirl outfit ('City of Death') or an Edwardian boy's bathing costume ('The Leisure Hive')

– in contrast to the more traditionally feminine attire of Romana I. There is an easy rapport between Baker and Ward (they were, briefly, married) that recalls the John Steed-Emma Peel relationship of *The Avengers* in its knowing innuendo and light-hearted banter. As a style of performance Ward's Romana could not have fitted into a more serious period of *Doctor Who*, but her ability to convey the sense that she did not take events entirely seriously and recognised the absurdity of their adventures made her the ideal heroine for this particular point in the series' history.

The narrative strategy that defines Williams-era *Doctor Who*, in the way that allegory informs the Letts-Dicks era and pastiche characterises the Hinchcliffe-Holmes era, is parody. Parody is different from pastiche in the sense that parody is sending up the conventions of a genre in order to expose their absurdities whereas pastiche employs them straight in the spirit of the original. This, perhaps, best summarises the differences between Hinchcliffe-Holmes *Doctor Who* and Williams-era *Doctor Who*. Holmes's textual references to classic adventure fiction treats the original sources with respect – indeed in stories like 'Pyramids of Mars' and 'The Talons of Weng-Chiang' they are used to good dramatic effect – whereas in many of the Williams-produced stories similar points of reference are incorporated in order to make fun of them. Or, to put it another way, whereas Holmes's scripts 'quoted' from an eclectic range of literary and visual texts, Williams-era *Doctor Who* does not merely 'quote' but also winks at the audience as it does so. To this extent Williams-era *Doctor Who* falls approximately halfway between pastiche and full-blown *Carry On*-style genre spoof.

David Fisher's 'The Androids of Tara' (#101), from the Key to Time season, perhaps best exemplifies the trend of late-1970s *Doctor Who* towards a more explicit inter-textuality that consciously parallels situations and devices from its source texts. This is an undisguised parody of Anthony Hope's novel *The Prisoner of Zenda*: the TARDIS arrives on the planet of Tara where Romana I is mistaken for a royal princess and she and the Doctor are caught up in a conspiracy to usurp the throne by the treacherous nobleman Count Grendel of Gracht. It is replete with all the trappings of Ruritanian romance: castles, coronations, courtly intrigues, swashbuckling derring-do and a climactic sword-fight replete with banter between the Doctor and Count Grendel. There were some, including Graeme McDonald, who felt that the parody had got out of hand and suggested that the inter-textual references should be more carefully disguised. After reading the scripts he pronounced it 'a rollicking adventure', but added: 'The sources of "Prisoner of Zenda" and "Rupert of Hentzau" are so obvious, however, that I hope they will be blurred by the design style. Art deco rather than Ruritanian, for example.'[21] This, of course, would have entirely defeated the point of the parody. To his credit, Williams stood his ground and the 'look' of 'The Androids of Tara' conformed to the accepted visual conventions of the 'Ruritanian' style: colourful costumes, chocolate-box uniforms and lots of pomp and pageantry. In contrast to the Robert Holmes-scripted literary pastiches, however, 'The Androids of Tara' does not merely borrow narrative devices from its source texts but also comments on the fact that it is doing so. Thus, when the notion of using an android copy of Prince Reynart at the coronation to foil an assassination attempt is mooted, the Doctor's reply ('Well, it has been done before') acknowledges that the story is using a narrative device from elsewhere. Count Grendel's escape by diving from the battlements into the castle moat would come as no surprise to those viewers who knew the original.

The parodic strategy of Williams-era *Doctor Who* can be seen as an attempt to appeal to a more sophisticated (i.e. older) audience. Various stories depend, for their full effect, on the audience 'getting' the references. In the case of 'The Androids of Tara' the sources are visual as well as literary, but in other stories the parody is more narrative-based and might require a greater level of cultural competence to decode. To be fair, however, the sources are barely disguised. Greek mythology is the source of both Baker and Martin's 'Underworld' (#96) and Anthony Read's 'The Horns of Nimon' (#108), for example, though in neither case is a degree in classics necessary to spot the references. 'Underworld' is the more subtle of the two. Perhaps to disguise that it was a reworking of the story of Jason and the Golden Fleece, the promotional materials described it as 'the most futuristic adventure "Doctor Who" has ever presented'.[22] On 'the edge of the cosmos' the TARDIS materialises on a colony ship carrying the survivors of the Minyan (Minoan) civilisation on an intergalactic quest to find the missing spacecraft P7E (Persephone) which carries the 'race banks' of Minyos. The Minyans are led by Jackson (Jason) and other characters include Orfe (Orpheus), Idmon and Idas (both unadulterated names of Argonauts). The notion of divine intervention in human affairs is raised in so far as the Minyans regard the Time Lords as gods, while the Oracle on this occasion turns out to be 'just another machine with megalomania'. At the end of the story, and for the benefit of any viewers who have not already identified the source, the Doctor accidentally refers to Jackson as 'Jason' and tells Leela: 'Jason was another captain on a long quest … He was looking for the golden fleece. Perhaps these myths are not just old stories of the past, but prophesies of the future, maybe.' It is an intriguing notion that, however, is left undeveloped.

'The Horns of Nimon' is a barely less disguised reworking of the story of Theseus and the Minotaur: Seth (Theseus), the young prince of Athene (Athens), travels to the planet of Skonnos (Knossos) to slay the Nimon (Minotaur), a bull-like creature which lives in a labyrinth and demands a tribute from Seth's people. 'The Horns of Nimon' is performed as a comedy and there is a strong pantomime element to the way in which the actors hide from the monster whilst remaining in clear view. Romana II's role as 'Principal Boy' is most evident here: on this occasion she has more of the conventional heroic action than the Doctor.

Holmes's 'The Sun Makers' (#95) is more a satire than a parody, recalling 'Carnival of Monsters' in exposing the bureaucratic excesses of officialdom, in this instance the Inland Revenue. The mid 1970s saw an increasing level of taxation, the Budgets of 1974 and 1975 imposing big rises in income tax and VAT (Value Added Tax), in response to price inflation. The Doctor and Leela arrive on Pluto, controlled by a corporation that imposes such a heavy tax burden on its citizens that they are forced into virtual slavery. 'The Sun Makers' (the title refers to fusion satellites that provide artificial suns around the planet) is another dystopian SF parable in which an oppressive regime controls the masses, monitoring its citizens through surveillance cameras and pacifying them with gas. The Doctor finds a group of 'tax criminals' hiding beneath the city and incites them to rebel, parodying Marx by telling them they have nothing to lose but 'your claims'. The narrative of oppressed workers rising against their capitalist overlords – recalling Fritz Lang's *Metropolis* – is further evidence of the occasional radical edge to the politics of *Doctor Who*. That Holmes meant the story as a satire of corporate greed is evident:

> *The Doctor*: Don't you think commercial imperialism is as bad as military conquest?

The Collector: We have tried war, but the use of economic power is far
          more effective.

The motif of individuals being processed by an oppressive, bureaucratic
state ('Shan't keep you pending for long. His Excellency has invoiced
your execution') was a recurring feature of 1970s SF, informing the
dystopian futures of *THX 1138* (dir. George Lucas, 1970), *Sleeper* (dir.
Woody Allen, 1973) and *Logan's Run* (dir. Michael Anderson, 1976). It
demonstrates, once again, that *Doctor Who* kept abreast of developments
in the SF genre and that its format was flexible enough to incorporate a
range of different narrative templates and themes. This particular story
was well received by viewers, who 'warmly welcomed the more realistic,
less "fantastic" nature of the theme (widely interpreted as an expose
of "super monopoly capitalism"), felt the story was well developed,
intriguing and exciting, and liked the "more recognisable characters",
considering them a nice change from monsters'.[23]

It was during its seventeenth season in 1979–1980 that *Doctor Who*
underwent what might best be described as its parodic 'turn'. There is no
question that this was due mainly to the influence of that season's script
editor Douglas Adams. A Cambridge graduate who had written comedy
sketches for the Footlights revue, Adams had recently achieved cult
success with his radio serial *The Hitchhiker's Guide to the Galaxy* (1978),
a spoof of many familiar SF themes and tropes that established Adams
in the tradition of American SF-comedy writers such as Robert Sheckley
and Kurt Vonnegut. Although, due to the cancellation of 'Shada', Adams
has only one solo writing credit for *Doctor Who* ('The Pirate Planet'),
his influence can be detected throughout the seventeenth season, to
which he added a plethora of 'in-jokes' that would be detected only
by a small minority of viewers. For example, when, in 'Destiny of the
Daleks', a temporarily trapped and immobilised Doctor passes time by
reading Oolon Colluphid's *The Origins of the Universe*, this is a reference
to Adams' *Hitchhiker's Guide* in which Colluphid is author of a 'trilogy of
philosophical blockbusters' (*Where God Went Wrong, Some More of God's
Greatest Mistakes* and *Who Is This God Person Anyway?*). This is the sort
of inter-textual in-joke that most viewers would certainly have missed.[24]

Adams' work, including not only *The Hitchhiker's Guide* but also
his 'Dirk Gently' novels and the computer game *Starship Titanic*, is
characterised by a sense of the absurdity of SF tropes and conventions.

This also manifests itself in his period of *Doctor Who*. 'Destiny of the Daleks' (#104), for example, has been the object of criticism within the fan culture for making fun of the Daleks. The Doctor and Romana II have arrived on Skaro in the future, discovering that the Daleks have returned to their home planet and are excavating the old Kaled city to find their creator Davros (who, it transpires, has been kept alive for centuries by his secondary life-support system). The Daleks are locked in a strategic stalemate in a war against the Movellans, a race of handsome androids, and believe that Davros will be able to provide them with a tactical advantage to break the impasse. The Doctor escapes from one Dalek by climbing up a shaft and mocking his pursuer to follow. To this extent *Doctor Who* was acknowledging one of the long-standing jokes about itself. Later, the Doctor disables a Dalek simply by throwing his hat over its eye stalk. Terry Nation disliked these additions to the script, feeling that they reduced the menace and plausibility of the Daleks: in the event 'Destiny' would turn out to be Nation's last *Doctor Who* script.[25]

The best-regarded of the Williams-era stories within fan culture is 'City of Death' (#105), jointly written by Williams and Adams, though the recurrence of tropes between this and *The Hitchhiker's Guide* would suggest that Adams was chiefly responsible. The serial is probably best understood as a parody of the 'Threat and Disaster' school that has been such a frequent device of *Doctor Who*. It begins in pre-history as Scaroth, the last of the Jagaroth, attempts to leave Earth in his damaged spaceship and the consequent explosion splits him into a number of 'splinters' scattered throughout time. In contemporary Paris, the Doctor and Romana II discover that Count Scarlioni, one of Scaroth's 'splinters', is planning to steal the Mona Lisa from the Louvre so that he can sell copies to art collectors in order to raise funds for the time-travel experiments that he hopes will return him to pre-history and thus prevent his own destruction. Scarlioni has seven genuine Mona Lisa copies, all painted by Leonardo da Vinci and commissioned by Tancredi, another splinter of Scaroth. As in 'The Dæmons', it transpires that Scaroth has shaped the course of human history to advance scientific knowledge to a stage where it will be possible for the last splinter to travel back in time. All of mankind's greatest inventions – the wheel, the pyramids, the Industrial Revolution – have been engineered by Scaroth. The Doctor knows that he has to prevent Scaroth when he realises that it was the explosion of Scaroth's spaceship that actually started life on Earth. This rewriting of history is also a feature of *The Hitchhiker's Guide*, in which the Earth is a giant computer built by 'a race of hyper-intelligent pan-dimensional beings' to work out 'the Ultimate Question of Life, the Universe and Everything', but which is demolished to make way for a new hyperspace bypass before the experiment can be completed. 'City of Death' is a slightly less absurd variation on the idea than *The Hitchhiker's Guide*, but it shares much the same intent: Adams is sending up not only the conventions of the SF genre but also all the underlying assumptions of historical causality that inform SF narratives. There is a sense, too, in which these stories are profoundly subversive: they challenge conventional narratives of great human achievements in scientific and technological advancement in their suggestion that the human race is nothing more than the by-product of a historical accident.

This subversion of grand narratives is evident on other levels. A recurring feature of 'City of Death' is the question of authenticity (or rather inauthenticity) in the arts: the Doctor writes 'This is a fake' across the canvases of the Mona Lisa copies (leaving a note to 'Dear Leo' to paint over them) and is able to identify the 'first draft' of *Hamlet* because he wrote it (Shakespeare having 'sprained his wrist writing sonnets'). Adams has much fun exposing the pretensions of art critics, exemplified by the famous sequence in which two critics (played by former Footlights performers John Cleese and Eleanor Bron) come across the TARDIS in the Louvre and mistake it for an exhibit:

Cleese: For me the most curious thing about the piece is its wonderful a-functionalism.

Bron: Yes, I see what you mean. Divorced from its function and seen purely as a work of art, its structure of line and colour is obviously counterpointed by the redundant vestiges of its function.

Cleese: And since it has no call to be here the art lies in the fact that it is here.

To drive the joke home, moreover, Cleese's 'the fact that it is here' is followed immediately by the dematerialisation of the TARDIS. 'Exquisite!' sighs Bron.

This parody of the language of intellectual criticism is another characteristic Adams touch: in *The Hitchhiker's Guide*, for example, Arthur Dent and Ford Prefect have a cod-discussion of the use of metaphysical imagery and rhythmic devices in Vogon poetry (recognised as the third worst in the universe) that 'counterpoint the surrealism of the underlying metaphor'. It is the sort of language one associates with 'Pseud's Corner' in the satirical magazine *Private Eye*, suggesting that Adams (who read English literature as an undergraduate) was looking to the large audience for *Doctor Who* amongst university students.

That 'City of Death' was highly regarded within the *Doctor Who* production team is evident in its use of authentic Parisian locations (it was the series' first overseas 'shoot') and in the casting of 'name' actors Julian Glover as Scarlioni and Catherine Schell as his wife. Its unusually large audience may have been the consequence of peculiar circumstances, though it would also seem to suggest that Adams' style of undergraduate humour was somewhat less alienating to viewers than some *Doctor Who* aficionados would claim. The uncompleted 'Shada' (#109) was an attempt to repeat the style of 'City of Death', once again featuring extensive location filming in picturesque locations and a tongue-in-cheek script that parodies SF conventions. 'Shada' is set against the background of Adams' Alma Mater of Cambridge University and concerns the attempt of the criminal Skagra to discover the secret knowledge of the Time Lords. This is contained in a book, *The Worshipful and Ancient Law of Gallifrey*, brought to Earth by Professor Chronotis, a Time Lord now living as a doddery old university don at St Cedd's College. The script is replete with university in-jokes and features narratively bizarre sequences such as the Doctor riding a bicycle and being pursued through the streets of Cambridge by flying spheres. The production was abandoned when a BBC technicians' strike meant that studio space was unavailable to complete the recording, though some scenes from the completed location work were later used in the twentieth-anniversary special 'The Five Doctors'. Adams, renowned for recycling his own ideas, later used many of the concepts and even names of 'Shada' for his novel *Dirk Gently's Holistic Detective Agency* (1987).

Although Douglas Adams' involvement with *Doctor Who* was relatively short-lived – he was script editor for only one truncated season and thereafter made no further contribution to the series – he nevertheless had a significant influence on its style and tone. The parodic 'turn' of *Doctor Who*, however, for all that it is disliked with certain constituencies of the fan community, needs to be seen within the wider cultural and institutional contexts of the BBC. That *Doctor Who* was able to negotiate this changing context at the same time as responding to the challenge presented by the rise of SF cinema is, yet again, testimony to the flexibility of its format. That it was also able to do so while maintaining its overall level of popularity, even if its ratings were less consistent than they had been in the mid 1970s, suggests that the comedy inflection was in tune with the tastes of most viewers. It is significant in this regard that the series' return to a more serious content and approach at the beginning of the 1980s would coincide with a marked downturn in its popularity.

6

New Directions

1980–1984

That's the trouble with regeneration – you never quite know what you're
going to get.

The Doctor (Peter Davison)
in 'Castrovalva'

The eighteenth season of *Doctor Who* in 1980–1981 is widely regarded
as representing a turning point for the series. A new producer (John
Nathan-Turner), a new script editor (Christopher H. Bidmead), a
new arrangement of the theme music and a new 'look' for the series
in terms of its visual style heralded a bold new era for *Doctor Who* as
it entered its third decade. In the popular historiography of *Doctor
Who*, John Nathan-Turner is almost as controversial a figure as Graham
Williams: admired by many fans for moving the series in a more serious
direction following the camp excesses of the late 1970s, but criticised by
others for his obsession with series continuity and for his penchant for
casting 'guest stars' from light entertainment which detracted from the
dramatic credibility of the series. Although no one could have realised
it in 1980, Nathan-Turner would be the last 'house' producer of *Doctor
Who* and would preside over its last decade in regular production at
the BBC. The 1980s are usually seen as a period of decline for *Doctor
Who*, but, while the quantitative evidence indicates that its popularity
was indeed diminishing in comparison to the preceding decade, it was
under Nathan-Turner's stewardship that the series experienced its most
conceptually ambitious phase.[1]

Nathan-Turner, who had been production unit manager of *Doctor Who* for three years before taking over as producer from Graham Williams, was acquainted with the series and its history in a way that previous producers were not. Nathan-Turner wanted to differentiate his approach from his predecessor, feeling that what he termed 'the undergraduate humour' had become too dominant. It is evident that Nathan-Turner set out to assert his authority from the outset: 'I think each new producer imposes some sort of style on the programmes and I would just like the comedy to fall more into the background.'[2] In particular he sought to reign in the excesses of Tom Baker's performance and to rediscover some of the moral seriousness that had been a hallmark of *Doctor Who* during its formative years. K9 was written out (the robotic dog did, however, feature in a Christmas special entitled *K9 and Company* in 1981), the comedy was downplayed and the in-jokes characteristic of Douglas Adams were dropped. In their stead was a more fallible Doctor less inclined to produce his jelly babies or resort to juvenile quip and jest. Baker's performance in this season, his last, is his most subdued: in his last serial 'Logopolis', especially, he is sombre and introspective as the Doctor nears the end of his fourth incarnation. Also characteristic of this season, and of the Nathan-Turner regime in general, was a greater sense of respect for the series' internal history than had been evident during Williams's period. This was due in some measure to the input of Ian Levine, a prominent figure in the *Doctor Who* fan community who became an unofficial consultant to the series. The magazine *Doctor Who Monthly* noted 'the superb continuity linking the serials not only with each other but with other serials long past' which, it felt, 'contribute nicely to an essential unity in the series that has been all but ignored in recent years'.[3] At first the continuity references are quite subtle – costumes left over from previous adventures and companions, for example – though later they would assume greater narrative significance to the extent that *Doctor Who* came to rely upon a sophisticated knowledge of the series' own history amongst its viewers.[4]

Critics of Nathan-Turner aver that *Doctor Who* under his stewardship lacked the more distinctive identity of other production regimes characterised by a particular content, such as Innes Lloyd (monsters), Barry Letts (action adventure), Philip Hinchcliffe (Gothic horror) or Graham Williams (comedy). It is true, certainly, that no single type of story dominates during the Nathan-Turner period, which is characterised by a greater diversity of narrative templates than perhaps at any time since the earliest years of the series. The eighteenth season includes allegorical satire ('The Leisure Hive'), horror ('State of Decay'), surreal fantasy ('Warriors' Gate') and universal catastrophe ('Logopolis') narratives, while during the nineteenth season the traditional action adventure ('Earthshock') and the pure historical story ('Black Orchid') would both return to *Doctor Who*. This greater diversity in content coincided with the series' most ambitious period in terms of exploring 'hard' SF themes. In large measure this was due to the input of eighteenth-season script editor Christopher H. Bidmead, a former scientific journalist who sought 'to anchor the show in terms of real science'. Bidmead's 'bible' for new writers stressed his desire to relate plots and devices to accepted scientific theories:

> The adventures of a time-travelling renegade Time Lord are of course built on a premise of wildest fantasy. But without inhibiting creative ideas, we'd prefer writers to work within this concept in a way that acknowledges the appropriate disciplines. Charged Particle Physics (to pick a topic at random) is mapped territory accessible to many of our viewers (there are *Doctor Who* Appreciation Societies in universities all over the world); and writers who want to bring the topic into the story should at least glance at the relevant pages of the encyclopedia. History of course deserves similar treatment. Imaginative extrapolation of 'the facts' should be preferred to gobbledegook.[5]

The eighteenth season, which Bidmead oversaw, includes stories informed by the theoretical science of tachyonics ('The Leisure Hive'), the idea of charged vacuum environments ('Full Circle') and the notion of entropy popularised by 'new wave' SF writers ('Logopolis'). Within the space of one season, therefore, *Doctor Who* had radically altered direction from a parody of the SF genre to a serious exploration of hard SF themes. Never before had a new production regime asserted itself so immediately and decisively upon the nature of the series.

These changes in the content of *Doctor Who* were also reflected in a new visual style. Nathan-Turner felt that the series had started to look 'stale' and wanted to refresh it visually: this was evident on several levels. Visual effects designer Sid Sutton devised a new opening title sequence in which the Doctor's face emerges from a pattern of stars (replacing the 'time tunnel' motif that had been used since 1974); new visual effects technologies were employed including Quantel 5000 (a digital image manipulator) and Scene-Synch (composites of two moving images); and certain serials (notably 'The Leisure Hive' and 'Earthshock') displayed a more 'filmic' style using more camera set-ups to enhance the pace and tempo of narrative. Costume designer June Hudson redesigned Baker's costume, maintaining the trademark scarf and hat but in a more subdued plum-coloured variant that reflected his more sombre style of performance during his last season. The fact that the Doctor's costume was designed so that its parts were coordinated in colour and tone is emblematic of a coherence between content and design that hitherto had only occasionally been in evidence. Britton and Barker aver that 'Nathan-Turner brought a stylistic coherence to *Doctor Who* that had been missing almost since its first year'.[6] Influenced to an extent by films such as *Star Wars* and *Alien*, the 'look' of *Doctor Who* became richer in detail, especially the costumes and set dressings which gave the series a more expensive-looking veneer that disguised its economy-conscious production values. Nathan-Turner adopted the old Cecil B. De Mille maxim to 'put the money on the screen', allocating a greater proportion of the budget to design, costume and visual effects. Serials shot mostly or entirely outside the studio became less frequent and location shooting was reserved either for historical stories ('Black Orchid', 'The Visitation') or for overseas shoots (Amsterdam for 'Arc of Infinity', Lanzarote for 'Planet of Fire') where the novelty gave the production a more expensive look.

However, the much-vaunted new style of *Doctor Who* did not meet with widespread popular approval. Ratings for the eighteenth season averaged only 5.8 million per episode – a marked decline following the previous year's success – and the 3.7 million who watched the second part of 'Full Circle' was the smallest audience for any single episode of *Doctor Who* to date. The conventional explanation for the disappointing ratings of Nathan-Turner's first season of *Doctor Who* is that ITV had finally won back Saturday evenings with the imported American space opera *Buck Rogers in the 25th Century*, which achieved twice the audience of *Doctor Who* by dint of being shown across the entire network. A slight upward trend for the last three serials ('Warriors' Gate', 'The Keeper of Traken', 'Logopolis') is explained by the time of *Doctor Who* being brought forward from 6.15 pm to 5.10 pm so that it started before *Buck*

Rogers. The greater success of the rival series is difficult to understand given that *Buck Rogers* has hardly endured in the popular imagination (except for the memory of Erin Gray's tight-fitting jumpsuit) to anything like the extent of *Doctor Who*. It suggests that early evening audiences preferred the action-oriented hokum of the American series to the more conceptual SF of this season of *Doctor Who*.

The eighteenth season of *Doctor Who*, indeed, represents probably the fullest extent of its excursion into the realms of imaginative fiction. This season displays a self-consciously philosophical and lyrical approach that makes significant demands upon the intelligence and sophistication of its viewers. Nowhere is this better exemplified than in the much underrated 'Warriors' Gate' (#114), probably the most oblique and surreal of all *Doctor Who* adventures. Written by Steve Gallagher and directed by Paul Joyce, 'Warriors' Gate' is the conclusion to the 'E-Space trilogy' (also comprising 'Full Circle' and 'State of Decay'). The TARDIS arrives at the Zero Point that marks the gateway between exo-space and normal space. This is represented by a white void containing only a stone archway and a crashed spaceship. It turns out that the vessel is a slave ship and that its navigator, Biroc, is from a race of time-sensitive Tharils who are able to 'ride the time winds'. The design of 'Warriors' Gate' is nothing if not a conscious homage to French art cinema, particularly *Beauty and the Beast* (dir. Jean Cocteau, 1946) from which it borrows the lion-like Tharils, and *Last Year at Marienbad* (dir. Alain Resnais, 1961) as the Doctor follows Biroc around a maze of black-and-white hallways and formal gardens. The script is self-referential ('It does have a certain legendary quality') and highly elegiac: at the end of the story Romana decides to remain in E-Space to help the Tharils rebuild their civilisation.

This self-conscious 'artiness' had been signalled at the very beginning of the season: the first episode of 'The Leisure Hive' (#110) opens with a long (90 seconds), slow camera pan across a deserted and windswept Brighton beach in a manner reminiscent of avant-garde film-makers such as Alain Resnais or Peter Greenaway. Britton and Barker suggest that 'The Leisure Hive' is 'a commonplace screenplay ... rendered memorable and cogent almost entirely by design, which appeals to the imaginative and evocative powers of the spectator's mind more directly than the fairly sketchy and formulaic script'.[7] David Fisher's script is an examination of the political economy of the leisure industries. Argolis, devastated by nuclear war, rebuilt itself as a 'leisure planet' but is now facing bankruptcy as new competitors have lured away its customers. The Argolins are conducting time experiments in the hope that they will be able to offer physical rejuvenation and thus stave off bankruptcy. Their experiments use tachyonics (a tachyon is a particle that travels faster than the speed of light), but it turns out that Pangol, one of the Argolins, intends to use the Tachyon Recreation Generator to duplicate himself and lead Argolis into another war. A sub-plot concerns the Foamasi, a reptilian race who bankroll Argolis, equating private enterprise with organised crime in that a breakaway faction (known as the 'West Lodge') are pressuring the Argolins to sell the Leisure Hive. It is an imaginative if somewhat uneven script that attempts, perhaps, to combine too many ideas. What is most remarkable about 'The Leisure Hive', however, is its extraordinary visual elegance: glossy geometric sets and an abundance of yellow and gold combine to create a sumptuous texture that suggests social order and wealth.

That Bidmead himself attached greater significance to imaginative concepts than to plotting is evident in his scripts for 'Logopolis' (#116) and 'Castrovalva' (#117), which span the transition from Doctor No.4 to Doctor No.5. 'Logopolis' is a remarkably multi-layered, complex story that explores the mythos of *Doctor Who* itself and to this extent anticipates the direction the series would take as it moved into the 1980s. Intellectually 'Logopolis' belongs to the 'new wave' of British SF emerging in the late 1960s and associated with *New Worlds* magazine under the editorship of Michael Moorcock. This 'new wave' was characterised by experimental storytelling (some would say it was 'plotless') and a greater pessimism of tone: it was particularly obsessed with the notion of entropy (as enshrined in the Second Law of Thermodynamics) which posits that the structure of the universe is unravelling and decaying. In 'Logopolis', entropy is explained by the Doctor as 'the more you put things together, the more they fall apart' and it is held at bay by pure mathematics. The city of Logopolis is a giant living computer where the Logopolitans, a race of master mathematicians, work on their endless calculations, which hold the fabric of the universe together. 'If you destroy Logopolis you unravel the whole causal nexus,' the Monitor, Logopolis's chief mathematician, tells the Doctor. This is precisely what the Master – who, at the end of the previous story, 'The Keeper of Traken', has taken over the body of Councillor Tremas – intends to do. The Doctor therefore has to prevent 'a change of circumstances that fragment the law that holds the universe together'.

It would be fair to say that 'Logopolis' is stronger on mood and atmosphere than it is on plotting and exposition. The opening scene – a policeman using a telephone box and being dragged inside to his death – establishes a sense of menace that pervades the serial, violating the comfortable association of the TARDIS with safety and security. The Doctor, deciding at last to repair the chameleon circuit of his own TARDIS that should allow its exterior shape to blend in with its surroundings, materialises it around a real police box in order to be able to measure its dimensions accurately: he needs the measurements for the Logopolitans to repair the TARDIS using something called 'block transfer computation'. However, the Master has already materialised his own TARDIS around the same police box and has killed not only the policeman but also a passing motorist. The Doctor realises that he is involved in a sequence of events over which he has no control when he meets the mysterious 'Watcher', a shroud-like figure observing events who turns out to be a projection of the Doctor's future self ('Nothing like this has ever happened before'). Continuity with the series' past is maintained through references to the chameleon circuit being left in 'a totter's yard' (a junkyard in Totter's Lane is where the TARDIS is located in 'An Unearthly Child') and through the flashback sequence of old enemies and companions that precedes the Doctor's regeneration (quite literally as if his life were flashing before him before death). The prevailing mood is highly pessimistic: the Doctor realises that the end for this incarnation is approaching, and, while he succeeds in saving the universe from destruction, the suggestion that it will eventually be overwhelmed by entropy makes this only a pyrrhic victory. 'Logopolis' leaves too many plot loopholes ever to be entirely satisfying as a narrative, but as an attempt to explore imaginative SF concepts, as much as for its historic significance as Baker's swansong, it can rightly be regarded as one of the landmark *Doctor Who* adventures. *Time Out* recognised this at the time: '"Logopolis", with its excellent performances throughout, its mind-boggling concepts and its exemplary direction by Peter Grimwade shows just how good a Doctor Who story can be.'[8]

'Castrovalva' begins where 'Logopolis' ends with the newly regenerated Doctor, who is experiencing physical and mental trauma ('I can feel it isn't going to be as smooth as on other occasions'), being helped back into the TARDIS by his companions. They narrowly escape destruction when the Master sends the TARDIS on a pre-set course to 'Event One' – the hydrogen in-rush that created the universe – and then head for the peaceful Castrovalva, 'dwellings of simplicity' where the Doctor can recover from the effects of his regeneration. Bidmead's inspiration on this occasion was the work of the Dutch graphic artist M.C. Escher, whose work explored visual illusions arising from playing with perspectives. Prints such as *Ascending and Descending* and *The Waterfall* depict the ambiguity between two-dimensional space and three-dimensional images with their 'impossible' pictures of staircases that appear to lead to the same destination and water that appears to flow against gravity. Once in Castrovalva the Doctor finds that he cannot leave as all routes lead back to the town square. He realises that he is caught in a 'recursive reclusion' in which space is 'being folded in on itself'. Castrovalva itself is a 'spatial anomaly' that turns out to have been created by the Master (using the Logopolitans' method of block transfer computation) solely for the purpose of trapping the Doctor and imprisoning him for eternity. Janet Budden's set designs are modelled visually on Escher's prints (all columns, staircases and squares) and the Quantel imaging process is used to represent the recursion as parts of the town break away. 'Castrovalva' is an attempt to translate a visual idea into a narrative form that is both highly innovative and, again, assumes a level of intellectual sophistication on the part of the viewer.

There is another narrative purpose to 'Castrovalva', of course, which is to introduce audiences to Doctor No.5. As the new incumbent, Peter Davison faced probably a greater challenge than any of his predecessors bar Troughton. Tom Baker had bestrode the series for seven years and for some younger viewers would have been the only 'Doctor Who' they had ever known. The Doctor's difficult regeneration in 'Castrovalva' might be interpreted as a commentary on the difficulties of replacing him: Bidmead includes references to the new Doctor's insecurity as he introduces himself to his companions ('I'm the Doctor – or at least I will be if this regeneration works out') and sees his own reflection in a mirror ('Well, I suppose I'll get used to it in time'). In this sense 'Castrovalva' is assuring viewers that they, too, will get used to the new Doctor in time. The scene in which Davison unravels Baker's famous scarf as a sort of Ariadne's thread to find his way through the labyrinthine corridors of the TARDIS sees him, quite literally, shedding the trappings of his predecessor.

It has become part of *Doctor Who* folklore that Nathan-Turner had a photograph of Peter Davison at a charity cricket match on the wall of his office when he was casting the new Doctor. This may or may not be one of those prophetic-in-hindsight stories, though it is worth noting that Nathan-Turner had worked on the BBC's comedy drama series *All Creatures Great and Small* (1978–1980), based on James Herriot's novels, in which Davison played a young Yorkshire vet called Tristan Farnon. Certainly Davison met Nathan-Turner's list of requirements for the new Doctor: that he should be a younger man than his predecessor (Davison was 30 when he took the role), that he would appear more vulnerable as an antidote to Baker's overpowering presence, that he would exhibit a more old-fashioned sense of heroism and that he should have straight hair as opposed to Baker's mop of unruly curls.[9] To a greater extent than any of his predecessors, Davison's existing television image (as the callow, gauche Tristan Farnon) informed his characterisation of the Doctor. He suggested that 'my Dr Who will look a bit like Tristan in *All Creatures* – only brave'.[10] Nathan-Turner was aware that the blonde, boyish-looking Davison had a large female fan following and hoped this would attract viewers. One (female) critic described him as 'the youngest, dishiest and most dashing Dr Who', but added that he 'seemed lacking in either authority or panache'.[11] Some critics derided Davison as a 'wet vet'. His Doctor lacks the masculine authority of, say, Pertwee or Baker: he is less confident than his predecessors, more reliant on his companions and more aware of his own mistakes and insecurities. Yet in an odd sort of way he is also the most heroic Doctor of them all: he displays great physical courage in dangerous situations (to a greater extent than Baker who, in his later years especially, had let Leela or K9 take care of the action) but does so in a casual, understated way (thus differentiating him from Pertwee's flamboyant action man). Davison's later television roles as gentleman detectives in *Campion* and *The Last Detective* can be seen as an extension of his Doctor in this regard.

Davison also represents the most quintessentially English of all the Doctors. This is most evident in his costume, a stylised version of an Edwardian gentleman cricketer with the addition of a Panama hat. For once the Doctor's costume has a narrative function: in the two-part story 'Black Orchid' he is mistaken for a replacement for a country-house cricket match and wins the game with bat and ball. The visual coding of Davison's Doctor as a retro-styled English gentleman hero has the effect of locating this period of *Doctor Who* in the context of so-called 'heritage' film and television. The early 1980s was a high water mark for sumptuous costume serials – exemplified by Granada's *Brideshead Revisited* (1981) and *The Jewel in the Crown* (1984) – that exhibited a cultural fascination with the past. These were successful both critically and commercially, being sold abroad, including to the USA. The return of historical and period stories to *Doctor Who* during the early 1980s can be seen in relation to the vogue for costume dramas that packaged a certain romantic image of 'Englishness' as an exportable cultural commodity. Davison's first season, moreover, coincided with the success in America of the film *Chariots of Fire* (dir. Hugh Hudson, 1981) – the surprise success of the Academy Awards in March 1982 – and there is a certain sartorial link between Davison's elegantly retro-styled cricket attire and the baggy 1920s-style running shorts worn in the film by actors Ben Cross and Ian Charleson. The opening of 'Mawdryn Undead' refers visually to *Chariots of Fire* with a long shot of a group of schoolboy athletes in white running kit against a heritage backdrop of a historic public school. And 'Black Orchid' anticipates films like *Gosford Park* (dir. Robert Altman, 2001) in its 1920s setting and its use of the country house mystery format to explore the social mores and hypocrisies of the English aristocracy.

Continuity with the end of the Baker period was maintained through the Doctor's companions. Davison inherited no fewer than three companions – two women and a boy – which made for a somewhat crowded TARDIS. Eric Saward, who took over as script editor during the nineteenth season, complained that 'there were far too many and that some should go'.[12] It was the irritating 'boy genius' Adric (Matthew Waterhouse) who was written out – quite decisively, as it turned out, in the last episode of Saward's 'Earthshock' – leaving the comely Nyssa (Sarah Sutton) and the bossy Tegan (Janet Fielding) as principal companions. The character of Tegan, an Australian air hostess, represents a return to the original concept of the companion in *Doctor Who*: like Barbara she is a professional woman who clashes with the Doctor when he is unable to return her to her own time and place. Later companions included an other-worldly public schoolboy Turlough (Mark Strickson) and an American student Peri (Nicola Bryant) whose cleavage assumed an iconic status of its own for *Doctor Who*'s male viewers. The introduction of an American companion reflected the growing popularity of *Doctor*

Who in the United States: it was now syndicated throughout two-thirds of the country by PBS, the Doctor Who Fan Club of America attracted over 30,000 members and in November 1983 a twentieth-anniversary convention in Chicago was attended by some 12,000 fans. In making the companions once again young people rather than adults, as had been the case throughout the 1970s, *Doctor Who* was again returning to its roots. That said, however, it could be argued that early 1980s *Doctor Who* reverses gender stereotypes: Nyssa (capable, intelligent) and Tegan (assertive, independent) are usually more proactive and successful than Adric (nerdy, sulky) and Turlough (vain, neurotic). Indeed, both the male companions prove to be weaker than the women and are all-too easily controlled by malign influences: Adric comes under the spell of the Master ('Castrovalva') and Monarch ('Four to Doomsday'), while Turlough, initially, is an agent of the Black Guardian. The return of the Master (now played by Anthony Ainley) as a semi-regular recurring villain was another link with the series' past. In contrast to the urbane menace of Roger Delgado, however, Ainley's performance was that of a pantomime villain with a silky voice and sinister chuckle.

This continuity with *Doctor Who*'s past can be seen as a strategy to persuade viewers that it was still the same series it had always been. This was particularly significant in light of the BBC's decision to move the series from its traditional Saturday teatime slot to weekday evenings (Mondays and Tuesdays at around seven o'clock). It would also become bi-weekly: thus, while the nineteenth season ran for 26 episodes, these were now condensed into just 13 weeks. This decision, taken by BBC Director-General Alasdair Milne, was in response to the disappointing ratings of the previous season. It had not passed unnoticed that weekday repeats of old serials as part of 'The Five Faces of Doctor Who' on BBC2 in the autumn of 1981 drew larger audiences than some of the last Baker episodes (over 7 million for a repeat of 'Carnival of Monsters', for example). Milne's decision, however, provoked widespread public opposition, indicating the extent to which *Doctor Who* had come to be regarded as a venerable British cultural institution. *The Guardian* even published a leading article deploring this 'sacrilege', maintaining that *Doctor Who* was 'an essential part of a winter Saturday as coming in cold from heath, forest or football, warm crumpets (or pikelets, if preferred) before the fire, the signature tune of Sports Report, and that sense of liberation and escapist surrender which can only come when tomorrow is a day off too'. 'Saturday will be smitten by the destruction of an essential ingredient,' it declared, 'and *Doctor Who* will be destroyed by this violent wrenching from its natural context.'[13] The paper's point was that the traditional family audience was less likely to be watching on weekday evenings: and to this extent its prediction of the series' demise would eventually be justified.

This was not evident at the time, however, as ratings for the nineteenth season would seem to have suggested that the combination of a new lead and a new slot had succeeded in winning back *Doctor Who*'s audience. An average of 9.3 million per episode represented a significant improvement on the previous season, and, moreover, the audience throughout the 13 weeks remained more consistent than at any time since the mid 1970s. Yet this apparent success should be nuanced in so far as *Doctor Who* was still lagging behind the competition on ITV, where the soap opera *Crossroads* and the travel programme *Wish You Were Here?* routinely attracted around 14 million viewers. In 1983, *Doctor Who* switched to Tuesdays and Wednesdays but lost around two million viewers in the process. This season was truncated to 22 episodes when 'Resurrection of the Daleks' was postponed to the next season, although there was an additional one-off 90-minute 'special' to mark the series' twentieth anniversary later in the year. 'The Five Doctors', broadcast as part of BBC1's *Children in Need* evening on Friday 25 November 1983, attracted 7.7 million viewers. The 1984 season, mostly broadcast on Thursdays and Fridays, again averaged seven million. The core *Doctor Who* audience during the early 1980s, therefore, stabilised at around seven million, respectable enough for its new time slot, perhaps, but less than it achieved during the 1970s.

The content of the series during these years exemplifies a tension between the old and the new. Eric Saward, who took over the reigns of script editing from temporary stand-in Antony Root during the nineteenth season, inherited intellectually ambitious scripts that had been commissioned by Bidmead ('Four to Doomsday', 'Kinda') and mixed them with more traditional fare (such as his own 'The Visitation' and 'Earthshock'). Saward and Nathan-Turner both recognised the popularity of old adversaries with *Doctor Who*'s loyalist fans and during these years revived the Cybermen ('Earthshock'), Omega ('Arc of Infinity'), the Black Guardian ('Mawdryn Undead', 'Terminus', 'Enlightenment'), Silurians and Sea Devils ('Warriors of the Deep') and, inevitably, the Daleks ('Resurrection of the Daleks'), as well as bringing back the Master as a semi-regular villain ('Castrovalva', 'Time-Flight', 'The King's Demons', 'The Five Doctors', 'Planet of Fire'). The recycling of ideas that inevitably affects long-running drama series is evident in the resort to familiar plot devices: 'The Visitation' (aliens arriving in England in 1666 attempt to spread a virulent plague virus) bears affinities with Robert Holmes's 'The Time Warrior'; 'The Awakening' (an alien presence called the Malus buried in a village church) is essentially a reworking of 'The Dæmons'; and 'Warriors of the Deep' (underwater base under siege) revives a tired old formula that was done rather better in the monochrome, claustrophobic 1960s than the colourful, glossy, brightly lit 1980s.

There are other ways, too, in which early 1980s *Doctor Who* combined elements from other periods. The device of linking one serial into the next, used throughout the 1960s but largely abandoned during the 1970s, was restored, so that, for example, 'Time-Flight' begins immediately after 'Earthshock', and 'Frontios' ends on a cliffhanger that leads directly into 'Resurrection of the Daleks'. The TARDIS interior underwent one of its periodic refurbishments: a new control console designed for 'The Five Doctors' replaced the old levers and switches with computerised keyboards, reflecting the desire to upgrade the technological 'look' of *Doctor Who* in relation to SF cinema and television. This was most apparent in the new-look Cybermen (Mark V in the series' internal history) with their sleek, streamlined silver costumes. The redesign of the Cybermen was 'symptomatic of the way in which *Doctor Who* tried to accommodate itself to design imperatives from sci-fi films'.[14]

Yet while the content of the series maintained strong continuity links with its past, the majority of scripts commissioned by both Bidmead and Saward were from new writers. This, again, was part of Nathan-Turner's strategy to refresh the series: 'If you don't entertain new writers, you'd be stuck with the same people who wrote it in 1963. We are concentrating on new writers who come with fresh ideas and a fresh outlook towards the programme.'[15] The most prolific *Doctor Who* writers of the early 1980s were Terence Dudley, Johnny Byrne, Peter Grimwade and Saward himself – all of whom wrote their first scripts for Nathan-Turner – though it was old stalwarts Terrance Dicks and Robert Holmes who were brought back for, respectively, the twentieth-anniversary special 'The Five Doctors' and Davison's highly regarded final story, 'The Caves of Androzani'. Following 'Androzani' – a powerful drama in which the Doctor sacrifices his fifth life to save not the universe but his new companion Peri, who is dying from spectrox toxaemia – the television critic of *The Scotsman* was moved to comment that *Doctor Who* 'is now breaking new ground, the feelings in it are of a more adult character ... For the first time in the whole time I've watched it, it was possible actually to believe that the ageless traveller actually feels anything at all.'[16]

'Earthshock' (#122) proved that *Doctor Who* had retained the ability to surprise its long-term viewers. The 'shock' elements – the untrailed reappearance of the Cybermen at the end of the first episode and the unexpected death of Adric in the fourth – are undoubtedly the dramatic highlights of that season. 'Earthshock' begins with the Doctor and his companions investigating the sudden deaths of members of an archaeological expedition in the year 2526 and discovering a bomb planted to destroy an intergalactic conference convened to form an alliance against the Cybermen. After the Doctor succeeds in defusing it, the Cybermen turn to their contingency plan of crashing a hijacked space freighter into the conference. When the freighter is caught in a time warp, with Adric trapped on board, the Doctor realises this was the object whose collision with the Earth wiped out the dinosaurs some 65 million years ago. 'Earthshock' exemplifies all the characteristic production traits of the Nathan-Turner regime: a fast-paced narrative, glossy production design, a strong sense of continuity with the series' past (clips from previous Cyberman serials show their defeats at the hands of the Doctor) and the presence of a familiar figure from television light entertainment (Beryl Reid improbably cast as a tough space captain). The Doctor's confrontation with the Cyber Leader recalls their first appearance in 'The Tenth Planet':

> *Cyber Leader*: I see that Time Lords have emotional feelings ... Surely a great weakness in one so powerful?
>
> *The Doctor*: Emotions have their uses.
>
> *Cyber Leader*: They restrict and curtail the intellect and logic [of] the mind.

> *The Doctor*:   They also enhance life. When did you last have the pleasure
>   of smelling a flower, watching a sunset, eating a well-
>   prepared meal?
>
> *Cyber Leader*: These things are irrelevant.
>
> *The Doctor*:   For some people, small, beautiful things is what life is all
>   about.

'Earthshock' contains too many plot loopholes to be one of the great *Doctor Who* stories, but its chief success was that it restored the menace of the Cybermen – always a more plausible adversary than the Daleks – following their ineffectual presence in 1975's 'Revenge of the Cybermen'.[17]

The high body-count of 'Earthshock' (there are some 16 violent deaths over its four episodes) exemplifies another means through which early 1980s *Doctor Who* differentiated itself from the previous regime. Yet again the series attracted adverse criticism for its violent content, though on balance this period is probably no worse than others. The violence tends to be restricted to 'old monster' stories and it is always presented in such a way that it demonstrates a clear moral position. Thus the Doctor is horrified by the wholesale massacre that concludes 'Warriors of the Deep' ('There should have been another way') and it is the violence she witnesses in 'Resurrection of the Daleks' that prompts Tegan's departure ('A lot of good people have died today … It's stopped being fun, Doctor'). Nathan-Turner, for his part, cultivated a casually off-hand attitude to criticisms of the series, later remarking, albeit with tongue firmly in cheek: 'Quite often I would pray that Mrs Whitehouse had watched the programme and thought it was too violent, because it automatically put two million viewers on our audience figures.'[18] It is difficult to avoid the impression that the production team was deliberately courting controversy through using images that had caused censure in the past, such as the Doctor's apparent death by drowning ('Warriors of the Deep') and killer policemen ('Resurrection of the Daleks').

While violence is a dramatically necessary ingredient of action adventure narratives such as 'Earthshock', the diversity of story templates under the Nathan-Turner regime meant that no one type of story ever dominates. 'Kinda' (#119), for example, was conceived in very different terms. Christopher Bailey, an English lecturer and part-time television writer, avers 'that I tried to set myself to write it without people being killed all along the way. Very often this type of programme gets its tension over a pile of dead bodies.'[19] With its dialogue-heavy script, 'Kinda' is perhaps the closest that *Doctor Who* has ever come to the world of literary SF. In particular it has drawn comparison with American novelist Ursula Le Guinn: Tulloch and Alvarado, for example, identify no fewer than twelve narrative and thematic parallels between 'Kinda' and Le Guinn's *The Word For World Is Forest* (1972).[20] Le Guinn's novel, itself an allegory of the Vietnam War, concerns a military-scientific expedition to the planet of Paradise where it is revealed that the indigenous inhabitants, far from being the primitives that the expedition has assumed, are in fact a highly advanced culture living in perfect equilibrium with nature. In 'Kinda' this takes the form of an expedition that has arrived to assess the suitability of the planet Deva Loka for colonisation. Expedition leader Sanders (played by another 'name' actor in the person of Richard Todd) regards the Kinda people as 'just a bunch of savages' and scorns the attempts of his science officer Dr Todd to learn more about their culture. To this extent the serial can be read as a critique of colonialism: Sanders is represented as a form of colonial overlord both through his name (a reference to Edgar Wallace's *Sanders of the River*) and his colonial-style pith helmet.

On another level, however, 'Kinda' also works as a complex Christian-Buddhist fable that combines ideas and imagery from both religions. The Kinda's equilibrium with nature is threatened by the Mara, a creature that inhabits 'the dark places of the inside' and appears in corporeal form as a snake. The Mara possesses Tegan and then takes over the body of Aris, one of the Kinda tribe. It seems reasonable to assume that the Christian imagery would have been recognisable to many viewers (a garden paradise, an apple, a serpent) and that the more obvious Buddhist influences (the Wheel of Life) might also have been recognised by some. That Bailey, himself a practising Buddhist, intended that the story should be read in this way is also evident through his use of Buddhist terms (Dukkha, Anatta, Anicca, Karuna) for the names of the Kinda, though these are not all revealed until the end credits and would in all likelihood have passed unnoticed by many. The demand this places upon the knowledge and cultural competences of viewers is evident in the equivocal reaction to 'Kinda' within *Doctor Who* fandom at the time: the plot was generally regarded as being 'far too complex', though the serial itself 'was one of the most visually striking stories since the Hinchcliffe era'.[21]

Bidmead's 'Frontios' (#133) represents another attempt to further the conceptual and narrative horizons of *Doctor Who*. The story is set in the distant future – so distant that even the Time Lords have no knowledge of it – and concerns a frontier-style colony of human survivors under siege on an inhospitable planet following the death of the Earth. The futurist survival narrative has been a staple SF template since the 1950s – it could even be argued that it has a biblical antecedent in the Book of Genesis – though this was the first occasion on which *Doctor Who* wholeheartedly embraced the concept. Bidmead's script can be compared to the BBC's mid 1970s series *Survivors* (itself written largely by Terry Nation) in that it posits a distinctly uncomfortable vision of the future in which technological regression and an increasing sense of paranoia combine to threaten the existence of the last remnants of the human race. The colonists on Frontios have lost much of their technological know-how following the crash of their colony ship, while the bombardment of the planet by meteorites has created a siege mentality that allows a petty tyrant to rule through martial law. A number of colonists have disappeared – literally pulled under the ground – and the Doctor discovers that they have been taken by the Tractators, a subterranean species controlled by the Gravis, a creature that plans to build a gravity motor to guide the planet and plunder other worlds. Bidmead disliked 'the monster element … partly because they tend to look cheap, and mainly because they are so limited on dialogue', averring instead that he was attracted to the situation in which the colonists find themselves: 'I wrote it around the time of the Beirut crisis and I was influenced by that. Without imposing any political angle I always felt that *Doctor Who* could much better reflect the sort of things that were happening in the 1980s.'[22] 'Frontios' was generally well received within *Doctor Who* fandom: it was admired as both 'a straightforward tale of ordinary people in a struggle for survival' and as 'an original, quite inventive story with hints of the atmosphere and style of the "classic" *Doctor Who* of old'.[23]

In contrast, the twentieth-anniversary special 'The Five Doctors' (#130) is nothing if not a celebration of *Doctor Who*'s history. Nathan-Turner had wanted 'to do something really spectacular' for the anniversary from early in his tenure and argued, albeit unsuccessfully, for the series to be restored to autumn transmission in order to facilitate this.[24] In the event the BBC's annual *Children in Need* jamboree provided the occasion for the 90-minute special, though 'The Five Doctors' was broadcast two days earlier in the USA in order to go out on the actual anniversary date of 23 November. Nathan-Turner and Saward had originally approached Robert Holmes to write the special, turning to Terrance Dicks when Holmes was unable to turn his draft scenario into a viable script. Dicks's brief was to include all five incarnations of the Doctor along with selected monsters and companions. Patrick Troughton and Jon Pertwee reprised their roles, while Richard Hurndall provided an uncannily accurate impersonation of the late William Hartnell. The one absentee was Tom Baker, who declined to appear on the grounds that it was too soon since he had left. Doctor No.4 therefore made a cameo appearance via unused location footage from 'Shada', while Baker was represented at the official photo-call by a wax effigy borrowed from Madame Tussaud's. 'Nobody noticed any difference,' he said later. 'So much for my acting.'[25]

Although it is handicapped by the necessity of including all five incarnations of the Doctor alongside companions past and present (Susan, the Brigadier, Sarah Jane Smith, Tegan and Turlough) and old enemies (a Dalek, a Yeti, Cybermen and the Master), 'The Five Doctors' succeeds, for the most part, in combining them into a coherent narrative. Dicks seems to have drawn inspiration from J.R.R. Tolkien's epic fantasy adventure *The Lord of the Rings*: not only does 'The Five Doctors' utilise the device of several groups of characters on their different quests, it also borrows freely from the imagery of Tolkien's 'Middle Earth'. Four incarnations of the Doctor are taken out of their own time streams by a 'time scoop' and deposited in the Death Zone on Gallifrey (Doctor No.4 is trapped in the temporal vortex) where they must reach the Black Tower and discover the secret of Rassilon. The Death Zone (which the Master calls 'the black secret at the heart of your Time Lord paradise') is an area sealed by an impenetrable force field where, in less enlightened days, the early Time Lords would amuse themselves by watching specimens of other races fight to the death (shades of 'The War Games'). The Doctors have been brought here by an unknown enemy, who in the event turns out to be none other than Lord President Borusa, using them as pawns in his attempt to discover the secret of immortality believed to be hidden in the Black Tower by Rassilon. Borusa, in several different incarnations, had been an occasional minor character since 'The Deadly Assassin' and the revelation that he, too, has been corrupted by power links to that serial's representation of Gallifreyan society as rotten and decadent. For this reason, it is implied, the Doctor turns down the offer of the presidency (he had once, briefly, held the office before in 'The Invasion of Time') and instead chooses to go on the run from his own people ('After all, that's how it all started').

'The Five Doctors' is invested with a sense of the series' history: it opens with a sepia clip of Hartnell's monologue to the departing Susan at the end of 'The Dalek Invasion of Earth' ('One day I shall come back – yes, I shall come back. Until then, there must be no regrets, no tears, no anxieties. Just go forward in all your beliefs and prove to me that I am not mistaken in mine'). It is also preoccupied with the theme of memory: 'A man is the sum of his memories – a Time Lord even more so,' remarks Doctor No.5, while Doctor No.2 says that 'it's a matter of memory' when coming face to face with his former companions Jamie and Zoë (he realises they cannot be real, as the Time Lords erased their memories of the time they spent travelling with him). There is respect, too, for continuity: 'It's *you* you!,' exclaims Sarah upon meeting Doctor No.3, while he does not immediately recognise the reincarnation of the Master. Therefore 'The Five Doctors' assumes a certain level of knowledge about the series' past – a shared memory amongst its fans. This is perhaps only to be expected in the context of a twentieth-anniversary special whose *raison d'être* was to celebrate the series and its history. Any television programme that runs continuously for twenty years is entitled to a degree of self-indulgence in celebrating its own legacy. For *Doctor Who*, however, this was to become the norm in the years that followed. Perhaps the long-term significance of 'The Five Doctors' is that it anticipated, and perhaps even started, the increasing tendency towards self-referentiality that characterised the series in the later 1980s. Hitherto the 'unfolding text' of *Doctor Who* had drawn upon and occasionally revised its own mythos. Later in the decade, however, it came to depend upon its audience's knowledge of that mythos. This dependency was to contribute significantly to the series' decline and to its eventual cancellation.

7

Trials of a Time Lord

1985–1989

In all my travellings throughout the universe I have battled against evil, against power-mad conspirators. I should have stayed at home. The oldest civilisation – decadent, degenerate and rotten to the core ... Daleks, Sontarans, Cybermen! They're still in the nursery compared to us.

The Doctor (Colin Baker) in 'The Trial of a Time Lord'

There are worlds out there where the sky is burning, where the sea's asleep and the rivers dream, people made of smoke and cities made of song. Somewhere there's danger, somewhere there's injustice, and somewhere else the tea is getting cold. Come on Ace, we've got work to do.

The Doctor (Sylvester McCoy) in 'Survival'

Throughout the last five years that *Doctor Who* remained in regular production at the BBC it is hard to avoid the impression that the series was not only in decline but was perpetually on trial as far as the corporation was concerned. There were changes to its format (the twenty-second season in 1985 experimented with 45-minute episodes without making any significant difference to the audience figures) and it was shifted around the schedules, returning to its traditional Saturday evening slot for two years (1985 and 1986) before reverting to weekdays for its final three years. In the mid 1980s, moreover, *Doctor Who* discovered an implacable new enemy in the person of Michael

Grade, Controller of BBC1, who disliked the series to the extent that he took the unprecedented step of suspending it for eighteen months and then effectively sacked Doctor No.6, Colin Baker. Although the series would survive for a further three years – during which time, ironically, it experienced one of its most creative periods – there was always a sense in which *Doctor Who* was now living on borrowed time.

Andrew Pixley has demonstrated that the changes imposed on *Doctor Who* in the mid 1980s represented a process by which its increasingly outdated format was brought into line with the norms of television drama production that had emerged in the 1980s.[1] A 26-episode half-hour series of serials was an anachronistic anomaly at a time when most drama series were produced in batches of thirteen episodes and when only soap operas (such as Granada's venerable *Coronation Street* and the BBC's new challenger *EastEnders* which started in 1985) clung to the half-hour format. The 1985 season of *Doctor Who*, back in its Saturday evening slot, comprised thirteen 45-minute episodes (five two-part serials and one three-parter), but the average audience throughout the season of 7.2 million remained at much the same level it had done for the last three years. It was during the course of this season that the BBC caused uproar amongst the show's fans when it announced that the next season would be postponed until the autumn of 1986 – an unprecedented eighteen-month gap – which prompted a 'Save *Doctor Who*' campaign in the popular press.[2] *Doctor Who*'s reprieve was due, to some extent, to the fact that its putative Saturday evening replacement – an ambitious adaptation of John Christopher's trilogy *The Tripods* (1984–1985) – failed to attract a large enough popular following and ended up being axed after only two of the planned three seasons had been made.

Although the view persists within certain sections of the *Doctor Who* fan community that the antipathy of Michael Grade was the sole reason for its suspension in 1985, this is to ignore the wider institutional and political circumstances affecting the BBC at this time. In 1985 the Thatcher government had set up a committee under Professor Sir Alan Peacock – an advocate of the 'new economics' based on the demands of the market place – to investigate the funding of the BBC. Knowing that Peacock was no supporter of the licence fee, the BBC was under pressure to demonstrate that it could keep costs down. The official reason given for the suspension of *Doctor Who* was a shortage of studio space and production funds which meant pushing the twenty-third season into the next financial year. The reported cost of the 1985 season of *Doctor Who* was between £100,000 and £200,000 an episode, which the BBC claimed it could not afford if it was also to fulfil its remit to develop new drama. An official statement declared: 'The BBC is committed to make a lot of new drama this year and we cannot afford to do that and *Dr Who*. The BBC is committed to the future of *Dr Who* and there is no question of the series being axed.'[3] When the Peacock Committee reported in 1986, however, its recommendations included several that would affect the future of *Doctor Who*. The freezing of the licence fee for two years meant that in real terms budgets would be reduced as they could not keep pace with inflation. And the decision that fewer programmes should be made in-house and more commissioned from outside producers (on the model of Channel 4) had consequences for 'house' producers like Nathan-Turner who wanted to move on to other projects. It has even been suggested that the reprieve for *Doctor Who* was due to Jonathan Powell, Head of Drama, having to find employment for his existing staff producers for cost-saving purposes and not having another series lined up for Nathan-Turner.[4]

As this period of instability for *Doctor Who* coincided with the all-too brief tenure of the Sixth Doctor, Colin Baker, it has sometimes been alleged that the suspension of the series was due to his unpopular characterisation of the role. This charge is entirely unfair. While the initial reaction to the Sixth Doctor – who made his debut in 'The Twin Dilemma', the last story of the 1984 season – was equivocal, this was no different from the response either to his immediate predecessor Peter Davison or to Tom Baker. 'The Twin Dilemma', arguably, focused too much attention on the Doctor's instability following his regeneration: he is nasty, unpredictable and violent, threatening to throttle his lissom companion Peri (a scene that is not entirely at odds with the Doctor's character, remembering his apparent intent to kill the caveman in 'The Forest of Fear') before he regains his self-control. It was this incident (one moment in the first episode) that coloured some critics' responses to the Sixth Doctor. Judith Simons of the *Daily Express* declared that 'I don't like the new Dr Who. Not yet, anyway'.[5] Other critics, however, liked this bad-tempered Doctor, such as Hilary Doling in the *Sunday Express*: 'I was worried that he was getting too good-tempered. But Colin Baker, our new Doctor, seems set to play him with all the crabbiness of the original.'[6]

The nastiness that some critics identified in Colin Baker's portrayal of the Doctor was to some extent a legacy of his previous television roles, including Paul Merroney in *The Brothers* (a forerunner of J.R. Ewing as 'the man viewers love to hate') and several parts as 'heavy' villains in *Blake's 7* (Bayban the Berserker in 'City at the Edge of the World') and, ironically, *Doctor Who* (Commander Maxil in 'Arc of Infinity').[7] ('In one episode I actually shot Peter Davison, but this was in no way an attempt on my part to get his job,' Baker would remark in interviews.) If Davison had been the 'Vulnerable Doctor', then Baker, C., was the 'Dangerous Doctor': the new incumbent was once again characterised in complete contrast to his immediate predecessor. Baker's highly physical bull-in-a-china-shop style of performance is eminently suited to a Doctor who is arrogant, conceited, insensitive and quick-tempered, though the nasty edge was toned down after 'The Twin Dilemma' as his regeneration settles down. Yet these characteristics have tended to obscure the fact that the Sixth Doctor is also erudite, witty, whimsical and humorous. There is a sense in which Baker's performance combines elements of his predecessors: the irascibility of Hartnell, the humour of Troughton, the flamboyance of Pertwee and the sheer zaniness of Baker, T. It is much to the detriment of *Doctor Who* that he was not given the opportunity to develop his portrayal over a longer period. Where he was let down, however, was in the variable quality of the scripts written for him and in his Harlequin-styled costume that was so gaudy it tended to obscure other, more subtle touches such as the Doctor's white cat lapel badge.

As his companion, Baker inherited Peri (short for Perpugilliam Brown), a spunky and pretty botany student who had joined him to get away from her boorish stepfather. A theme of their earlier adventures is Peri having to come to terms with the Doctor's regeneration when, it is hinted, she was quite attracted to the previous incarnation ('I really liked you – you were sweet!'). The casting of Nicola Bryant as the Doctor's first American companion was probably made with one eye on potential US sales and the other on the traditional physical attributes of the *Who* girl. Not since the heyday of Leela had male tabloid journalists devoted so many entirely gratuitous column inches (and photographs) to the subject of the Doctor's assistant, though in the changing cultural climate of the 1980s there were complaints from some female viewers that Peri's low-cut tops and shorts were 'tasteless and annoying'.[8] Bryant, like so many of her predecessors, found that her physical appearance overshadowed her performance, though a feature of the stories in which she appeared is that her beauty became a theme of the series. Peri is the first of the Doctor's companions to find herself the object of (usually unwanted) attentions from the villains – ever the fate of SF heroines since Flash Gordon's girlfriend Dale Arden was desired by the lecherous Ming the Merciless. Thus Sharaz Jek ('The Caves of Androzani') eulogises her beauty, the Borad ('Timelash') wants to make her his consort and the gourmet cannibal Shockeye ('The Two Doctors') covets her for lunch ('What a fine, fleshy beast. Just in your prime – and ripe for the knife!').

The six serials of the 1985 season represent the main body of Baker's *Doctor Who* adventures. It is a season of mixed quality, including two old monster stories ('Attack of the Cybermen' and 'Revelation of the Daleks'), the introduction of a sexy new female villain ('The Mark of the Rani'), a disappointing reunion for Patrick Troughton and Frazer Hines ('The Two Doctors'), one imaginative satire ('Vengeance on Varos') and one outright failure ('Timelash'). Simon Hoggart suggested that *Doctor Who* suffered from 'its sense of studio claustrophobia', but felt, nevertheless, that it possessed 'a certain charm' and that 'it is quite a frightening programme' for children.[9] The most frequently commented-upon feature of this season (other than Miss Bryant's cleavage) was, once again, the level of violence. 'Attack of the Cybermen' and 'Revelation of the Daleks', in particular, are both heavy on the killings, while 'Vengeance on Varos' (#139) features bodies being deposited in an acid bath and, notoriously, the Doctor's sub-James Bond quip ('Forgive me if I don't join you') as a guard meets a grisly end. While scenes such as this are no more realistic than the comic-book violence of the Bond films, such as the heavy electrocuted in the bath in *Goldfinger* (dir. Guy Hamilton, 1964) or the henchman speared by a harpoon in *Thunderball* (dir. Terence Young, 1965), they did stretch the limits of what was acceptable for early evening family viewing.

This is not to say that the violence of *Doctor Who* was entirely gratuitous. It is clear that the production team was alert to debates over the representation of screen violence, and, moreover, responded to those debates in the series itself. Philip Martin's 'Vengeance on Varos', for example, is a commentary on television's sensationalising of violence and the desensitising effect this has on viewers. Varos is a society of sadists, in which the elected governor remains in authority only as long as he is able to deliver the sort of violent entertainment that the people want. Thus the inhabitants are treated to live pictures of a rebel leader being tortured and of the Doctor being pursued through the Punishment Dome where a deadly trap awaits him. Martin includes an abundance of satirical comments on the public's appetite for sensationalism and on the responsibility of the television and video industries for providing it ('I'm sure the video of his execution will sell. You said we must export or die!'). 'Vengeance on Varos' came shortly after the moral panic of the early 1980s around so-called 'video nasties' (uncertified horror films that exploited a loophole in that video cassettes were not, as yet, subject to the process of classification and censorship applied to films) and to this extent belongs squarely to the long-established tradition of using *Doctor Who* as a vehicle for social satire. It is ironic, however, that a story about the media's fascination with violence as a form of public spectacle should itself be criticised for its violent scenes, including, in addition to the notorious acid bath, a sequence where Peri is nearly transformed into a bird by a molecular transformation device operated by the odious slug-like villain Sil which, Hoggart predicted, would 'cause plenty of youthful nightmares'.

Another trend that emerged during the 1985 season was towards an increasing sense of self-referentiality. Continuity references were an established hallmark of Nathan-Turner's regime, of course, but they began to assume greater narrative significance from 'Attack of the Cybermen' (#138). This serial, credited to one Paula Moore, is an unnecessarily convoluted story about the Cybermen's attempt to prevent the destruction of their home planet Mondas (in 1986) by time travelling (to 1985) and causing Halley's Comet to crash into the Earth. It refers to the events of both 'The Tenth Planet' and 'The Tomb of the Cybermen' – unfairly so as, at the time, the latter was a 'lost' story – and contrives to confuse any new viewers with its garbled account of the history of the Cybermen's presence on Telos. To some extent this can be seen as a strategy to shore up the popularity of *Doctor Who* with its core audience, but at the same time it ran the risk of alienating new or casual viewers who would probably feel alienated by references to the series' past that were essential for understanding the plot. This sense of alienation would seem to be borne out by the audience ratings: the 8.9 million who watched the first episode dropped to 7.2 million for the second. 'Paula Moore' was in fact a pseudonym covering the input of several writers, including Eric Saward,

Paula Woolsey and Ian Levine. The involvement of unofficial 'consult-ant' Levine in the script-writing process reinforced the notion that *Doctor Who* was now being made more for its most dedicated aficionados than for the general audience that it needed to attract.

There was a sense during the eighteen-month hiatus in 1984–1985, therefore, that *Doctor Who* was under the microscope to a greater degree than it ever had been before. Grade made public his opinion that it had become 'too tired and too violent'.[10] Although the production team had been working on scripts for the next season (including a sequel to 'The Celestial Toymaker', entitled 'The Nightmare Fair', by former producer Graham Williams), their plans had to be scrapped when the BBC decreed that the twenty-third season would revert to the traditional 25-minute format and that it would comprise only 14 episodes. The best that Nathan-Turner and Saward could devise was a series of linked stories under the umbrella title of 'The Trial of a Time Lord' (#144). The irony was not lost on the series' fans. Nathan-Turner attempted to appease Grade by declaring that 'we toned down the action and substituted the violence with humorous intercourse between the actors'.[11] 'The Trial of a Time Lord' had a troubled production history. It was written by committee (Robert Holmes, Philip Martin and husband-and-wife team Pip and Jane Baker were responsible for individual segments), with Saward in overall editorial control. The production ran into trouble when Holmes, who had been commissioned to write the concluding episode that wrapped up the loose ends (of which there were many), died before it could be finished. Saward completed it, but clashed with Nathan-Turner, who felt that his proposed ending was both too downbeat and too open-ended. Saward thereupon resigned as script editor and refused permission to use any of his script. Another conclusion therefore had to be devised by the Bakers, who had to write it to fit locations that had already been selected. 'The Trial of a Time Lord' was broadcast in the autumn of 1986 but was a major ratings disappointment, averaging only 4.8 million viewers. The production team's argument that the low ratings were down to the series being screened opposite the popular American action series *The A-Team* on the ITV network did not disguise the fact that this was consistently the poorest performance in the series' history. The jury was still out as far as the future of *Doctor Who* was concerned.

The narrative of 'The Trial of a Time Lord' displays its troubled production history. It is inconsistent, at times incoherent, and poorly structured. The linking narrative is that the Time Lords are conducting an inquiry into the Doctor's actions and behaviour, particularly his habit of interfering in the affairs of other civilisations which is expressly against the laws of Gallifrey. The inquiry is presided over by the Inquisitor (Lynda Bellingham) and the case against the Doctor is presented by the Valeyard (Michael Jayston). The 'evidence' consists of three separate adventures that are shown to the court, via the Matrix (the repository of all knowledge), two of which are presented by the Valeyard as evidence of the Doctor's reckless and dangerous conduct, and another which the Doctor presents in his own defence. The main problem with 'The Trial of a Time Lord' is that none of the individual segments are engaging enough in their own right to be regarded as anything more than mediocre *Doctor Who* adventures and that, in each case, any tension is dissipated by frequent cutaways to the court for the Doctor to contest the evidence (it soon becomes apparent that someone has tampered with the Matrix) and to engage in sarcastic repartee with the Valeyard. Nor do the somewhat repetitive courtroom scenes succeed in providing a dramatically coherent framing device as there are too many *longeurs* and *non sequiturs* over the fourteen episodes. While audiences picked up slightly at the very end (the highest audience was 5.6 million for the last episode), they were confronted with a convoluted and generally unsatisfying resolution. It transpires that the evidence against the Doctor has been adulterated and that the culprit is the Valeyard. The Master appears, from inside the Matrix, to reveal to the Doctor that the Valeyard is 'an amalgamation of the darker side of your nature, somewhere between your twelfth and final incarnation'. The Doctor then has to enter the Matrix to fight the Valeyard.

The unevenness of 'The Trial of a Time Lord' also extends to its production design. It begins and ends with a visual tour de force. The first episode opens with the most ambitious effects sequence in the series' history at that point, as the TARDIS is caught in a tractor beam and drawn inside a massive space station (rather like *2001: A Space Odyssey* executed on a BBC Visual Effects budget) and the scenes inside the Matrix towards the end involve a surreal Dickensian 'Fun Factory' that is a triumph of nightmarish imagination. The courtroom where so much of the exposition takes place, however, is flat and uninspiring (one critic wrote that it 'looks like a heavenly hairdressing salon, with ludicrous helmets on every head'),[12] and the prevalence of the usual economy-conscious sets for the individual segments would seem to suggest that much of the budget was indeed spent on the opening and concluding sequences.

Saward had intended that the climax of 'The Trial of a Time Lord' should feature the Doctor and the Valeyard locked in combat inside the Matrix. This would have been an 'open' and suitably ambiguous ending not unlike the resolution of 'The War Games', which was similarly written when the future of the series was uncertain. Perhaps Nathan-Turner felt this would have been tempting fate: what chance the renewal of the series if its protagonist had apparently been killed off? In the ending as broadcast the Doctor escapes and the charges against him are dropped; but a final twist reveals that the Valeyard has also survived. Grade, for his part, reserved judgement. Shortly before the series was broadcast he had declared: 'It seems to have improved but I want to see future episodes before I make a final decision.'[13] In the event it was decided that the series would continue for the time being, but that it was again time for a change of star. Baker refused the offer of one more serial at the start of the next season to facilitate the transition and his regrettably brief tenure came to an end amidst some acrimony and recrimination.[14]

While *Doctor Who* would continue for another three years – albeit again in seasons of only 14 episodes – it was evident to all concerned that the future of the series was perpetually under threat. The lukewarm reception of 'The Trial of a Time Lord' had convinced the BBC that *Doctor Who* was no longer the popular family show it had once been and that the nature of its audience had changed since its 1970s heyday. Audience Research reported that reaction to 'The Trial of a Time Lord' had been mixed, but revealed, significantly, that *Doctor Who* was now failing to connect with the important teenage (10–15) and young adult (16–24) age groups. It was now seen as 'a cult show with a small but vocal following which lacked the potential to reclaim the affection of the mainstream audience'.[15]

So what had happened to the *Doctor Who* audience? Although any explanation needs, of necessity, to be somewhat speculative, it should probably be seen in relation to changing demographics and cultural tastes. The enduring success of *Doctor Who* over two decades was due in large measure to its ability to appeal across age groups (from young children to adults) and to the fact that several successive generations had, as it were, 'grown up' with the series. This was no longer the case by the mid 1980s, however, for a variety of reasons. Perhaps the foremost amongst these was that the original concept of the 'loyalty' programme was itself no longer a widely recognised aspect of television culture. The trend in the 1980s, marked by the launch of Channel 4 in 1982 and later in the decade by the arrival of satellite and cable television, was towards an increasingly segmented and compartmentalised view of audiences: more programming was directed towards particular age, gender and ethnic groups, while less was being made for the traditional family audience. Furthermore, the increasing popularity of the home video cassette recorder – by the mid 1980s, half of British homes owned a VCR – meant that the notion of families sitting down to watch television at particular times was no longer an accurate reflection of viewing habits. While the family audience was dissipating, moreover, *Doctor Who* was no longer appealing to its core audience of teenagers and young adults, many of whom now preferred the 'adult' themes of the new generation of soap operas such as *Brookside* and *EastEnders*. It is significant in this context that Phil Redmond, the creator of *Brookside*, previously produced the children's school drama series *Grange Hill* for the BBC: his mixture of melodrama and controversy seemed more in tune with the interests of teenagers than the staid heroics and morality plays of *Doctor Who*.[16]

Thus it was that in its final years *Doctor Who* became a marginal series made for a 'cult' rather than a mainstream audience. The response of *Who* fans to the series' suspension in 1985 had served to create the impression that there was a large and dedicated fan base for the series. As ratings demonstrated in the late 1980s, however, the fan base, while dedicated, was not especially large. Audiences remained disappointingly low, averaging 4.9 million in 1987, 5.3 million in 1988 (the twenty-fifth anniversary season) and 4.2 million in 1989. That *Doctor Who* was now broadcast at 7.35 pm on Mondays (season 24) or Wednesdays (seasons 25 and 26) against the popular soap opera *Coronation Street* on ITV – an even more venerable and long-running television institution than *Doctor Who* – did nothing to help its ratings.[17] Indeed, it is difficult to avoid the impression that the BBC, having lost interest in *Doctor Who*, had deliberately scheduled it in a slot where it was almost bound to fail to attract a significant audience, with a view to cancelling it at the first opportunity. In this context, the fact that the series survived as long as it did represents quite a considerable achievement in its own right.

Yet at a time when its quantitative popularity was diminishing, *Doctor Who* itself was experiencing a revival in quality and innovation. The television critic of the *Daily Telegraph*, for example, remarked at the start of the twenty-fourth season in September 1987: 'The new script is self-consciously whimsical, almost self-parodying: perhaps this odd little genre, like all art forms, is pushing in its late maturity against its own boundaries.' At the end of the next season, *The Scotsman* felt that '*Who* has gone imaginative and very stylish and there is a lot of galactic go in the old police box yet.'[18] The arrival of a new script editor, Andrew Cartmel, who presided over the last three years of *Doctor Who*, was instrumental in opening up the series to new writers and new ideas.

The appointment of Cartmel, an untried writer who worked for a computer company, might be taken as another indication that the BBC no longer had any real interest in *Doctor Who*. Yet it soon became clear that Cartmel had definite ideas about the content and direction of the series and was keen to promote like-minded writers such as Ben Aaronovitch, Ian Briggs, Marc Platt and Stephen Wyatt. Cartmel would later claim (not without reason) that 'before I joined the show, *Doctor Who* had been entering a bit of a slump … and the stories showed a certain lack of inspired commitment'. In particular Cartmel, the first *Who* script editor to be a seasoned reader of SF literature, sought to introduce more SF content in place of the action-adventure narratives favoured by his predecessor Eric Saward: 'Crucially, there was no feeling for science fiction or fantasy in the show at the point where I took over. Basically the scripts were failed thrillers full of confusing incident and boring characters with science fiction *detail* arbitrarily heaped on, but nothing genuinely science fictional about them.'[19] If Cartmel's dismissive attitude towards the previous regime is somewhat unfair, there is no question that the nature of the series did change, and arguably for the better, during his tenure. That said, however, there still remained an abundance of confusing incident.

Three particular developments characterise the Cartmel 'era' of *Doctor Who* and are unique to this period of the series: the suggestion of a darker side of the Doctor's character, an increased stylisation, and a greater emphasis placed on the role of the companion. These elements are present, in different degrees, throughout the last three seasons of *Doctor Who*. These years are uneven – the twenty-fifth anniversary season with its commemorative Dalek and Cyberman serials is probably the best in overall quality – due in large measure to the annual uncertainty hanging over the renewal of the series. Yet, taken overall, during these three years the series enjoyed a sustained level of narrative sophistication, thematic depth and visual invention marred only by an incessant use of synthesised incidental 'muzak'. It is ironic that the series was taken off the air just as this new approach was beginning to gel into a coherent and consistent style. This came too late, however, for *Doctor Who* to be saved following the severe drop in its ratings in 1989.

Perhaps Cartmel's most significant contribution to *Doctor Who* was to restore some of the mystery surrounding the Doctor himself. He explains:

> The trajectory of his mysterious character had been one of steady decline. First, we had no idea of who or what he was. Then we learned he was a Time Lord. Then we learned he was a Time Lord among other Time Lords. And, the next thing you know, he was the kind of chump who could be put on trial by the other Time Lords, and generally be pushed around with impunity.
>
> So I set about restoring the awe, mystery and strength to the character. With the help of Marc Platt and Ben Aaronovitch, the two writers I was working with who were interested in the *Doctor Who* mythos and had a knowledge of it, I set about making the Doctor once again more than a mere chump of a Time Lord.[20]

Cartmel was aided in this task not only by writers with a knowledge of the *Who* mythos, but also by the casting of Sylvester McCoy as Doctor No.7. McCoy, a Scottish actor in his mid 40s, was best known for his roles in children's television which prompted speculation that he would play a 'comedy' Doctor in the manner of Patrick Troughton. In his first story, 'Time and the Rani', indeed, McCoy's Doctor seems very much a 'chump', unsure who he is and given to uttering malapropisms ('Absence makes the nose grow longer', 'He who dares spins', 'Time and tide melt the snowman'), though this is explained by his having been given an amnesia-inducing drug by the Rani who intends to use his scientific knowledge to create a Time Manipulator and thus bring order to the universe ('Creation is chaotic. I shall introduce order. Where evolution has taken the wrong route, I shall redirect it.'). Later adventures – and in this context it should be noted that Nathan-Turner had commissioned

'Time and the Rani' before Cartmel's appointment – would reveal a more mysterious, calculating character who often seems to have foreknowledge of the events in which he is a participant.

If Baker had been the 'Dangerous Doctor', McCoy would take this even further as the 'Dark Doctor'. The motif that recurs most frequently during these years is that of a cosmic chess-player (literally so in 'Silver Nemesis' and 'The Curse of Fenric'), manipulating events and people to his own ends. His apparent forgetfulness (a Hartnell characteristic) conceals a deep intelligence and an analytical, calculating mind. It is hinted that what we know about the Doctor is incorrect, that he has a dark and secret past and that he was a contemporary of the legendary Time Lords Rassilon and Omega. McCoy characterises the Seventh Doctor as a conjuror and a magician – in 'Battlefield' it is even suggested that he once assumed the identity of Merlin and sided with King Arthur against Morgaine – who has a penchant for jazz and speaks with a slight Scottish burr. His costume is a pot-pourri that combines elements of his predecessors – checked trousers (Troughton) and Panama hat (Davison) – with a '?' motif incorporated into his sweater and into the elaborately curved handle of his ubiquitous umbrella.

The idea of the Doctor as a master strategist and a manipulator of events is explored in both Ben Aaronovitch's 'Remembrance of the Daleks' (#149) and Kevin Clarke's 'Silver Nemesis' (#151). Both serials have much the same plot: an old enemy arrives on the Earth in pursuit of a 'MacGuffin' only to find that they have played into the hands of the Doctor who has anticipated their arrival and set a trap.[21] In 'Remembrance of the Daleks', two rival Dalek factions – Imperial Daleks and Renegade Daleks – are seeking something called the Hand of Omega, a remote stellar manipulator that the First Doctor removed from Gallifrey and hid in London in 1963. The narrative takes place in and around some of the same locations as 'An Unearthly Child' (the junkyard at 76 Totter's Lane and Coal Hill School) and at one point a television announcer can be heard introducing the first episode of a new television series called '*Doctor* …' This self-referentiality displays Aaronovitch's knowledge of the series' past, though 'Remembrance' is neither a celebration of the *Doctor Who* legacy (such as 'The Five Doctors') nor an exercise in fan-obsessive continuity (like 'Attack of the Cybermen'). In fact, the discontinuities between 'Remembrance' and previous Dalek serials suggest that it is offering a revisionist exploration of the *Doctor Who* mythos that is deliberately questioning the series' received internal history. It turns out that the Emperor Dalek (previously seen in 'The Evil of the Daleks') is none other than Davros himself. The Doctor allows Davros to acquire the Hand of Omega and goads him into using it: Davros cannot control its power, with the result that Skaro's sun becomes a supernova and renders the Dalek home planet a 'burnt cinder'. It is implied that the Doctor has planned this all along in order to destroy the Daleks once and for all, but, as it involves a plot revelation that pre-dates the Doctor's first encounter with the Daleks, it opens up, retrospectively, the possibility that the First Doctor's presence on Earth may have been part of some grand design.

'Silver Nemesis' – the silver anniversary serial – is a less effective version of the same plot. This time it is the Cybermen who come to Earth in search of the MacGuffin, here the Nemesis comet, actually composed of a 'living metal', validium, a substance created by Omega and Rassilon for 'the ultimate defence of Gallifrey', but for some (unexplained) reason removed and launched into space by the Doctor. The comet is in a decaying orbit and will return to Earth on 23 November 1988 (thus coinciding with the twenty-fifth anniversary of the series) and the Doctor has set a trap for the Cybermen, whose attempt to use Nemesis brings about the destruction of the Cyber fleet. 'Silver Nemesis' is a confused and incoherent narrative that contrives also to include a band of neo-Nazis dedicated to setting up the Fourth Reich and a seventeenth-century sorceress who travels forward in time by alchemy (defying one of the 'rules' of a series that hitherto had not allowed 'magical' apparatus) in order to get her own hands on Nemesis. It turns out that Lady Peinforte has met the Doctor before and knows about his past ('I shall tell them of Gallifrey. Tell them of the old time – the time of chaos'), though how she knows this is not explained. The Cybermen, however, prove to be disappointingly uninquisitive ('The secrets of the Time Lords mean nothing to us').

The revisionist narratives of 'Remembrance of the Daleks' and 'Silver Nemesis' have been compared to the trend in the 1980s to revisit and reinterpret the origin myths of comic-book characters. This was a time of increasingly adult-oriented comic books, most famously Frank Miller's revisionist reinterpretation of the Batman myth in *The Dark Night Returns* and *Batman: Year One*, notable for introducing a greater sense of psychological realism into the motivation of the tortured protagonist and for their representation of an urban world of chaos and disorder. British comic writers such as Grant Morrison and Alan Moore, who cut their teeth on the comic paper *2000AD*, were acclaimed for their 'adult' comics characterised by a dystopian and morally ambiguous view of past and future fantasy worlds. Moore's work in particular, such as *V for Vendetta*, *Swamp Thing* and *Watchmen*, is notable for its satirical and self-referential style, later finding its fullest expression in his 'graphic novel' *The League of Extraordinary Gentlemen*. Cartmel even approached Moore, who earlier in his career had contributed to *Doctor Who Magazine*, to write for the series.[22]

The trend in 1980s comic books towards more complicated and morally ambiguous stories, punctuated by striking and often horrific visuals, is exemplified by late 1980s *Doctor Who* stories like 'The Curse of Fenric' (#155) and 'The Greatest Show in the Galaxy' (#152). 'The Curse of Fenric', by Ian Briggs, may have been inspired by Moore's *Swamp Thing* story 'Still Waters' (underwater vampires terrorise a flooded town in America's Midwest) and also bears strong visual and narrative similarities to *The Fog* (dir. John Carpenter, 1979). Another sign of the increasing cultural confidence of *Doctor Who* during this period is that it attempts to combine motifs from different genres, the wartime spy thriller and vampire/zombie horror, and, while it suffers from a confusing narrative it is memorable for its striking visuals such as the vampiric Haemovores rising from the sea (a recurring *Who* image, also employed to good effect in both 'The Sea Devils' and 'Full Circle'). The action is set around a naval base on the North Yorkshire coast in 1943, but 'The Curse of Fenric' is very far from the standard base-under-siege story characteristic of 1960s *Doctor Who*. It is revisionist in that it questions the received popular narrative of the Second World War: there are references to the controversial bombing of German cities and to the onset of the Cold War. A group of Russian commandos attempt to steal the 'Ultima' decoding machine from their erstwhile allies, little realising that Commander A.H. Millington (note the initials) is expecting them and has booby-trapped it with a deadly chemical agent. Millington's apparent fetish for chemical warfare ('Just think what a bomb full could do to a city like Dresden or Moscow') might be interpreted as a reference to the destructive power of the atomic bomb. It is neither the Russians nor the Germans who are the real enemy, however, but rather Fenric, a distilled force of pure evil that has existed from the dawn of time but has to assume corporeal form in order to do harm. Once again the Doctor has to confront an old foe ('We play the contest again – Time Lord!') and has foreknowledge of the events that he does not impart to his companion ('You know what's going on, don't you? You always know and you never tell anyone! It's like some kind of game and only you know the rules!').

Similar characteristics of an oblique narrative and striking visuals are also evident in 'The Greatest Show in the Galaxy'. Stephen Wyatt's script can be located squarely within the sinister fairground tradition of Charles G. Finney's *The Circus of Dr Lao* and Ray Bradbury's *Something Wicked This Way Comes*, as well as harking back to the nightmarish fantasies of 'The Celestial Toymaker' and 'The Mind Robber'. The Doctor and his companion arrive on the planet Segonax and visit the sinister Psychic Circus where unfortunate visitors are forced to entertain the Family who watch every performance – or die. It turns out that the Family are in fact the Gods of Ragnarok, powerful creatures from another dimension who exist on the misery of others, and who, once again, the Doctor has met before ('I have fought the Gods of Ragnarok all through time'). It is tempting to interpret the Doctor's performance before them as a commentary on *Doctor Who*'s struggle to appeal to the family audience that it had once enjoyed: in their humanoid form they appear as a nuclear family of mother, father and child. Wyatt's script is populated with grotesque eccentrics in true comic-book tradition, including 'eminent intergalactic explorer' Captain Cook (a Blimpish ex-military type) and the sinister Chief Clown (whose make-up resembles that of Batman's arch-enemy the Joker). Most memorable about 'The Greatest Show in the Galaxy', however, is its remarkable imagery: pink skies, an ominous black hearse (also a motif of the 1967 *Avengers* episode 'Epic') and the psychedelic colours and costumes of the circus itself. Director Alan Wareing even succeeds, for once, in investing a quarry with a sense of atmosphere that suggests an alien landscape. It would be fair to say that 'The Greatest Show in the Galaxy', like 'The Curse of Fenric', demonstrates the increasing prominence of visual stylisation over narrative coherence that was a feature of late 1980s *Doctor Who*. It is a further indication of the cultural confidence of the production team in experimenting with the *Doctor Who* format during its mature period.

This is not to say, however, that late 1980s *Doctor Who* simply privileged style over substance. The political satire of Wyatt's 'Paradise

Towers' (#146) and Graeme Curry's 'The Happiness Patrol' (#150), for example, is explicit enough to suggest that the production team were deliberately using the series to put forward a message. To this extent the late 1980s can be linked back to the allegorical period of the early 1970s. 'Paradise Towers', set in a run-down tower block populated by rival gangs and policed by the sinister black-uniformed caretakers, is an allegory of urban decay and social alienation in 1980s Britain. The early 1980s, especially, had witnessed violent race riots in deprived urban areas such as Brixton in London, Toxteth in Liverpool and Moss Side in Manchester. Is it entirely too fanciful to see the rival 'kangs' – Red Kangs and Blue Kangs – as representing the Labour and Conservative parties, and the inflexible Chief Caretaker (who wears a 'Hitler' moustache) as a comment on the failure of the government to respond to social dislocation? That a political meaning was overlaid onto 'The Happiness Patrol' is confirmed by Cartmel, who avers that it 'was intended, on some level, to be a satire of Thatcher's Britain'.[23] Helen A (the surname initial indicates an individual's place in the social hierarchy) is the tyrannical ruler of Terra Alpha where sadness is illegal and malcontents are ruthlessly hunted down by the gun-toting happiness patrol. Sheila Hancock's vocal impersonation of Margaret Thatcher leaves no doubt exactly whom Helen A is modelled on. The style of 'The Happiness Patrol' again eschews naturalistic presentation in favour of extreme stylisation, exemplified by the appearance of the robotic executioner known as the Kandyman whose similarity to the figure of 'Bertie Bassett' – used in commercials for the confectionery manufacturer Bassett's – was a brilliantly subversive touch that provoked a complaint from the company's chairman.[24]

If these stories recall the 'message' narratives of the 1970s presided over by Barry Letts and Terrance Dicks, other Cartmel-commissioned *Doctor Who* stories hark back to the parodic style of Douglas Adams. 'Delta and the Bannermen' (#147), for example, is posited on an idea that could almost have come straight from *The Hitchhiker's Guide to the Galaxy*: a company called Nostalgia Tours provides holidays for time-travelling tourists, and when their spaceship 'bus' is attacked and knocked off course it ends up not in Disneyland, but in the Shangri-La Holiday Camp in Wales *c*. 1959 ('Are you telling me that you are not the Happy Hearts Holiday Club from Bolton, but instead are spacemen in fear of an attack from some other spacemen?'). And 'Dragonfire' (#148) includes a scene where the Doctor engages in a mock philosophical discussion with a guard who turns out to be a repressed intellectual ('What do you think of the assertion that the semiotic thickness of a performed text varies according to the redundancy of auxiliary performance codes?'). Cartmel averred that 'I lifted [the] passage about semiotics from a very pretentious text book about *Doctor Who* I happened to have on my shelves'.[25] Thus the series was poking fun not only at SF conventions (guards are rarely versed in cultural studies) but also at the conventions of intellectual criticism.

The greater maturity and sophistication of late 1980s *Doctor Who* was also reflected in the more adult characterisation of the Doctor's companion. McCoy's first companion had been a 'screamer' with the unfortunate name of Mel Bush (played by a controversially cast Bonnie Langford), but a change of direction was indicated with her replacement at the end of 'Dragonfire' by the character of Ace (Sophie Aldred). Not only did Ace represent an entirely different archetype from all previous *Who* companions – a streetwise teenager with a troubled past and something of an attitude problem – but she was also written with a greater sensitivity and subtlety than had usually been afforded to the role of the companion. Ace's real name is Dorothy (she dislikes her parents for having given her such a 'naff' name): like her namesake in *The Wizard of Oz* she has been dislocated from her home (Perivale rather than Kansas), though unlike Frank L. Baum's heroine she has no desire to return there as 'nothing ever happens'. Ace is no sex symbol in the mould of Leela or Peri, but a tomboy who wears Doc Martens and a bomber jacket emblazoned with badges – thus reflecting contemporary 'street' fashion – and is not afraid to set about bashing a Dalek with a super-charged baseball bat. She is also a dab hand at concocting something called 'Nitro-9' (a highly explosive derivative of nitroglycerine which caused her to be expelled from school when she blew up the chemistry lab). The character 'stood for the disaffected and disenfranchised portion of British society that the series had generally overlooked'.[26]

As the character became more established, and Aldred's performance more assured, the writers allowed Ace something that had been denied most previous companions: space to grow and mature as a character. It is instructive here to compare her to the first companion, Susan, another contemporary teenager who was never really allowed to grow up. *Doctor*

Who was now, belatedly, making amends for its limited representation of female companions. A theme of the last season, especially, is her growing awareness of her own sexuality, which she uses, for example, to distract a guard in 'The Curse of Fenric' ('Professor, I'm not a little girl') and which causes her to try on 'girl clothes' in 'Ghost Light'. A moment in 'The Curse of Fenric' anticipates the 2005 *Doctor Who* episode 'Father's Day', when Ace saves the life of a baby who turns out to be her own mother – a revelation that causes her to rethink her own future ('I used to think I'll never get married, but now I'm not so sure'). In 'Ghost Light' (#154) the Doctor takes Ace back to a 'haunted house' in nineteenth-century Perivale (a house, it transpires, that she burned down in 1983) in order to make her face her own fears and phobias. In this regard *Doctor Who* was following an entirely new tack: the reform of a juvenile delinquent in which the Doctor plays the role of mentor and guardian.

The final serial broadcast as part of the regular *Doctor Who* series, 'Survival' (#156), is a fitting summation to this period even if it was not intended to be the 'last' *Doctor Who*. It is stronger on imagery than plot; it employs motifs from a range of different sources; and it focuses attention more than ever before on the character of Ace. The Doctor takes her back to Perivale, where she finds that her old friends have disappeared and that young children are being drilled in self-defence and survival techniques by the self-styled 'Sergeant' Patterson. The children of Perivale have been carried away by the Cheetah People, inhabitants of an unnamed planet who are able to transport themselves through time and space in order to hunt their prey. Once on this planet, humans succumb to its influence and become Cheetah People themselves. It is a characteristically complex narrative that combines diverse elements from *The Lord of the Flies*, the psychological horror film *Cat People* (dir. Jacques Tourneur, 1942) and, more prosaically, *Tarzan and the Leopard Woman* (dir. Kurt Neumann, 1946). The image of Ace being chased through a children's playground by a giant cheetah on horseback is as frightening an image as the series has ever produced (all the more so due to its everyday location), while the sequence in which she starts to turn into a cheetah herself might be interpreted as a covert metaphor for her character's sexual awakening. The association of female sexuality with feline imagery extends as far back as the representation of the Egyptian goddess Isis as a cat and has persisted in popular culture, exemplified in different forms by Batman's adversary, by the cat-suited Emma Peel of *The Avengers* and by Nastassja Kinski in the sexually explicit remake of *Cat People* (dir. Paul Schrader, 1982).

'Survival' turned out to be the last new televised *Doctor Who* adventure for more than six years. The series could no longer sustain the low ratings: the twenty-sixth season had started poorly with a mere 3.1 million for the first episode of 'Battlefield' and, while audiences improved over later stories, the decision had already been made not to commission another season. The last episode of 'Survival' includes a tacked-on voiceover at the end which serves as a eulogy for the series as well as an endorsement of the Doctor's favourite hot beverage. Officially the series was being 'rested' and the BBC maintained that it would come back, though without ever setting a specific time frame for its return. In late 1989 it was announced that if or when *Doctor Who* did return it would no longer be an in-house production but commissioned from an outside producer. There was persistent speculation during the early 1990s about the future of the series and a vocal campaign amongst aficionados for the BBC to restore it to the schedules.[27] A celebratory documentary to mark the thirtieth anniversary in November 1993, *Doctor Who: 30 Years in the TARDIS*, concluded with a cryptic remark by BBC1 Controller Alan Yentob in response to a rumour that Hollywood film-maker Steven Spielberg was involved in negotiations about a new *Doctor Who* ('You may have heard that, but I couldn't possibly comment'). In late 1995, it was announced that a co-production deal had been agreed between the BBC and Universal Television and that a television movie of *Doctor Who* would be forthcoming in 1996 as the possible pilot for a new series. It would seem that there was life in the 950-year old Time Lord yet.

8

Millennial Anxieties

1996

> It was on the planet Skaro that my old enemy the Master was finally put on trial. They say he listened calmly as his list of evil crimes was read, and sentence passed. Then he made his last, and I thought somewhat curious, request. He demanded that I, the Doctor, a rival Time Lord, should take his remains back to our home planet, Gallifrey. It was a request they should never have granted.
>
> The Doctor (Paul McGann)

'He's back … And it's about time.' The return of *Doctor Who*, after a hiatus of over six years, in the form of a £3 million co-production between BBC Worldwide and Universal Television was welcomed by aficionados but overall met with the sort of response from television critics that is perhaps best described as 'mixed'. *Doctor Who* had been to all intents and purposes 'dead' throughout the early 1990s, though the corpse had refused stubbornly to be buried and there were persistent rumours of its revival. The 1996 'Doctor Who' – strictly speaking the only individual *Doctor Who* story with the same title as the series itself[1] – was the outcome of the shifting political economy of the BBC as it responded to both institutional and cultural change within the wider television industry. As the putative pilot episode for a series that was not commissioned, the *Doctor Who* 'movie' tends to be seen as a failure. This, however, is to ignore both its many points of special interest and its unique place in the series' history.

The 'new' *Doctor Who* needs to be understood in the context of changing broadcasting ecologies in the 1990s. These changes were heralded by the advent of satellite television in the form of the Rupert Murdoch-owned Sky, which began broadcasting via the Astra satellite in 1989, and by the Broadcasting Act of 1990 which extended the deregulatory policies of the Conservative government to television and radio and thus paved the way for a proliferation of new channels over the following years. The BBC, under pressure during the 1990s from governments hostile to its privileged status and struggling to protect the principle of the licence fee on which it relied for its funding, became increasingly market-oriented (a process dubbed 'dumbing down' by its critics) at the expense of its traditional public-service remit. The popular and critical acclaim lavished upon its 1995 adaptation of Jane Austen's *Pride and Prejudice* and on the drama series *Our Friends in the North* (1996) perversely indicates how rare such 'quality' drama had become in the midst of a seemingly ubiquitous diet of game shows, quiz shows, chat shows and 'makeover' shows.[2]

The fate of *Doctor Who* exemplifies three processes occurring in parallel inside the BBC during the 1990s. The first was the introduction, under Director-General John Birt, of a new mechanism for securing funding which meant that individual programmes, rather than being part of an allocated budget, now had to bid against each other. This was dressed up in terms of 'producer choice' but what it effectively amounted to was the introduction of an internal market into the BBC of a sort that had already crippled the National Health Service. (Birt was caricatured in *Private Eye* as a bureaucratic Dalek, indicating that the cultural legacy of *Doctor Who* persisted even while the series was in hiatus.) The second development was the requirement that a quarter of its entire programme output should be commissioned from independent producers, which effectively brought the corporation into line with the ITV franchise holders and Channel 4. The third development was an increasing trend towards co-productions with international partners in recognition of the fact that television had become a global rather than a purely national enterprise.

Co-productions were advantageous in two ways: they allowed the corporation to share the costs of production at the same time as providing access to an international audience. In 1995, BBC Enterprises, a commercial arm originally set up in the 1960s to sell programmes to overseas broadcasters, became BBC Worldwide with an expanded remit to invest in co-productions with overseas partners. It did not go unnoticed that one of BBC Enterprises' major revenue sources since the late 1980s had been from the sale of *Doctor Who* videos for the home retail market. A plan to mark the thirtieth anniversary in 1993 with a feature-length special, 'The Dark Dimension', produced solely for video, had to be aborted.[3] (In the event the anniversary was marked by a woeful pantomime piece for *Children in Need*, entitled 'Dimensions in Time', featuring all the surviving Doctors – Pertwee, Davison, McCoy and the two Bakers – and assorted villains and companions caught in a time loop on the set of the soap opera *EastEnders*.)

Evidence that there remained a strong fan base for *Doctor Who* can be found in the success of the *New Adventures* novels published under licence by Virgin Books, charting the further adventures of the Seventh Doctor and Ace, which began in 1991. Another line of *Missing Adventures* featuring previous Doctors and companions was added in 1994. Barry Letts wrote two *Doctor Who* radio serials featuring Jon Pertwee and Elisabeth Sladen, 'The Paradise of Death' (1993) and 'The Ghosts of N-Space' (1996), though neither excited much interest. In the meantime rumours persisted about a 'new' *Doctor Who* on television or film, most of them wildly inaccurate, some containing a morsel of truth. One of the most persistent stories was that a *Doctor Who* feature film would be produced by a consortium backed by pop singers Bryan Ferry and John Illsley, with Alan Rickman as the Doctor and to be directed by Leonard Nimoy, 'Mr Spock' of *Star Trek* who had successfully directed two *Star Trek* continuation films. A court case was threatened when the consortium sued the BBC for reneging on the film deal.[4] In late 1993 a story was leaked that Steven Spielberg's Amblin Entertainment was in negotiations to buy the rights to the series. According to which report one prefers, the candidates to play the Doctor included Eric Idle, Dudley Moore, David Hasselhoff and Tom Cruise.[5] Yet again, the initiative did not progress, perhaps because Amblin was committed to producing another SF adventure series, *Seaquest DSV* (1993–1996), for Universal Television.

However, it was largely through the agency of former Amblin executive Philip Segal that *Doctor Who* was commissioned in late 1995. Fans' concerns that the BBC had 'sold out' to an American network were partly redressed by the fact that Segal, writer Matthew Jacobs and director Geoffrey Sax were all British and that a British actor, Paul McGann, was to play the Doctor. The television film was shot in Canada early in 1996, with Vancouver standing in for San Francisco where the story was located.[6] It was broadcast by the Fox network in the USA and by the BBC in Britain in May 1996.

Segal later averred that the production of *Doctor Who* was compromised by having to meet the demands of four constituencies: Fox, Universal, BBC1 and BBC Worldwide. The US network Fox 'insisted on it being an Americanised version' and on the casting of 'special guest star' Eric Roberts as the Master. At the same time, however, Segal 'had to make sure that I kept my promise to Alan [Yentob, Controller of BBC1] in terms of the integrity of the show and its Britishness'. BBC Worldwide just wanted something 'terribly commercial'.[7] Given the circumstances of its production, therefore, it is hardly surprising that *Doctor Who* betrays the competing cultural and ideological demands of the various interested parties. It represents an uneasy compromise between British cultural capital and American commercial enterprise, between the different cultural competences of British and American audiences, and between the liberal ethos of the 'old' BBC series and the innate conservatism of the US networks. In attempting to be all things at once – both a revival of an old series and the start of a new one – it failed to satisfy any of the constituencies for whom it was intended.

The response of British critics, predictably perhaps, was that *Doctor Who* had lost its distinctive British identity. It was described, variously, as 'a classic mid-Atlantic fudge', 'a vulgar American reincarnation', 'awfully, awfully American' and as 'stranded somewhere in mid-Atlantic and about as interesting as Rockall'. One critic thought that the producers 'seem to have missed the joke. There is no point to the Doctor if he's just another vaguely eccentric Englishman culture-clashing [*sic*] in America.' Even those commentators who were more favourably disposed towards it, such as the SF critic and author Kim Newman, felt that 'this regeneration hasn't taken yet. There's still extraneous American DNA floating around the matrix.' These responses demonstrate that *Doctor Who* had now become a site of cultural contestation for British critics keen to protect its 'Britishness' against the encroaching effects of Americanisation. The terms of this opposition are familiar: 'British' equals small, quaint, eccentric and individual, whereas 'American' equals big, brash, conformist and corporate. Thus critics disliked the intrusion of those 'Hollywood' ingredients deemed necessary for American audiences. Newman, for example, felt that '*Doctor Who* is really hurt by the need for car chases, a cocky ethnic sidekick, [and] a second-rate straight-to-video villain'. Others waxed nostalgic for the Heath Robinson production values of the original ('special effects consisting of loo rolls, washing-up bottles and sticky-backed plastic'), claiming that 'there was something very British about the refusal to espouse anything flashy.' This was a view shared within the fan community. The spokesman of the 'Dalek Appreciation Society' wrote: 'Once again the Americans have used their Midas touch on an original, inventive British masterpiece and created an over-the-top, Batmanesque nightmare.'[8]

There were some dissenting voices, however, whose response was not coloured by the parochial 'Little Britain' discourse of most critics. 'Does everything that claims "Britishness" have to be quaint, quirky and amateur?' asked one correspondent, who thought it 'a very worthy successor' to the original series and remarked that 'it was a pleasure to see it given the production values and funding that it has always deserved'. Newman, whose review is amongst the most balanced and considered, felt that the production had been much enhanced by spending more money: 'The revelation of seeing a shot-on-film "Who" that is well-lit and atmospheric – something the show hasn't been since its very earliest studio monochrome days – is so strong that, in his first-reel cameo, even Sylvester McCoy comes across well, suggesting the melancholy of an outcast from his own planet who can never fit in on Earth.'[9]

The presence of McCoy – referred to in the publicity as 'The Old Doctor' – is the most direct testament of this *Doctor Who*'s continuity with the original series. It is evidence that the producers were keen to keep faith with the fans and to respect the legacy of *Doctor Who*. The transition from McCoy to McGann is much better handled than the transition from Baker to McCoy had been, with McCoy allowed his valedictory performance as the Doctor. The film begins with the Doctor transporting the remains of the Master back to Gallifrey when the TARDIS is forced to make an emergency landing in San Francisco. (Here there are some glaring *non sequiturs* with the series' internal history: had not Skaro been destroyed at the end of 'Remembrance of the Daleks', and since when did the Daleks, whose voices can be heard in the background, go in for legal process and judicial execution?) Stepping out of the TARDIS the Doctor is shot by gun-toting members of a street gang. Taken to hospital, his unusual physiology ('Two hearts! That can't be right') confuses the surgeon operating on him and he dies following a cardiac seizure. The body of the unknown 'John Doe' is sent to the morgue, where it regenerates. Also consistent with the series' past is that the regeneration leaves the Doctor shaken and disoriented. He has temporarily lost his memory, until a chance encounter with the surgeon who operated on him (but of course does not recognise him now) starts to bring it back. Some of the dialogue can be read as a commentary on the nature of this new *Doctor Who*: McGann's anguished 'Who am I?' reflects its schizophrenic identity (is it British, American or a mixture of both?) and his subsequent realisation of what has happened ('I was dead too long this time. The anaesthetic almost destroyed the regenerative process') is an ironic comment on the 'death' of *Doctor Who* which had been absent from television screens for so long that some had begun to doubt whether it would ever be revived.

What, then, of the new 'Doctor Who'? McGann was described both as 'the best actor ever cast as Doctor Who' and as 'the sexiest Time Lord in light years'.[10] McGann had first come to notice in the BBC's Great War drama *The Monocled Mutineer* (1986) and possessed the necessary acting credentials to make his interpretation of the Doctor acceptable to fans, whilst his appearances in Hollywood films (*Alien³*, *The Three Musketeers*) lent him a certain 'star' cachet for the US market. A chisel-jawed and handsome-faced actor, McGann plays the Doctor as a Romantic hero: passionate, energetic, extravagant, sensual, idealistic, quixotic. He imbues the Doctor with a youthful vigour that recalls Davison, while at the same time possessing the flamboyance and élan of Pertwee. His outfit, a 'Wild Bill Hickock' fancy-dress costume that he appropriates following his regeneration (neck-tie, waistcoat, frock coat), is strikingly similar to Hartnell's. There is a sense, therefore, in which Doctor No.8 is a composite of his predecessors, an idea further alluded to by the reintroduction of props such as his jelly babies and sonic screwdriver. The suggestion of a romantic attraction between the Doctor and cardiologist Dr Grace Holloway (Daphne Ashbrook) was anathema to some fans, but it is entirely consistent with the McGann characterisation of the Doctor as a heroic, handsome and youthful figure. Perhaps this is also why the Doctor is revealed here to be half human. In any event, the romance is understated (it amounts to two rather chaste kisses) and the film ends with Grace deciding not to go off with the Doctor in the TARDIS. It would probably be fair to say that McGann's Doctor represents an American idea of the modern British gentleman: courteous, mild-mannered and slightly foppish. This was the archetype personified by

Hugh Grant in the hugely successful romantic comedy *Four Weddings And A Funeral* (dir. Mike Newell, 1994), and to an extent the 1996 *Doctor Who* belongs in the same tradition. Indeed, the Doctor is here explicitly coded as British through his encounter with a traffic policeman. The Doctor, challenged by the policeman, puts his hand into his pocket, apparently searching for some form of identification. The traffic cop interprets this as a hostile move and reaches for his gun. Grace intervenes:

Grace: Wait! Stop! He's... er... he's British.

The Doctor: Yes, I suppose I am. Jelly baby, officer?

It is an incident that irresistibly brings to mind Hugh Grant's much-publicised encounter with the Los Angeles Police Department in 1995, though, unlike the Doctor, Grant did not offer the excuse that he was looking for some jelly babies at the time of his arrest.

If McGann's Doctor is, in a sense, a pastiche of all his predecessors, the *Doctor Who* film is itself a pastiche that references various film and television sources. Rather than being a deliberately postmodernist production strategy, as with cult series such as *Moonlighting* (1985–1989) or *Twin Peaks* (1990–1991), the various generic and cultural references would seem to indicate the production's acute anxiety about who its audience actually was. The notion of pairing an other-worldly hero with a career-minded heroine suggests that Fox saw it as their answer to ABC's *Lois & Clark: The New Adventures of Superman* (1993–1996), whilst making the heroine a surgeon also tapped the audience of the medical drama *ER* (1994–). Almost all reviews drew comparisons with *Terminator 2: Judgment Day* (dir. James Cameron, 1991) on the grounds of the special effects that turned the Master into a pool of liquid slime and the chase sequence which saw the Doctor and Grace on a motorcycle pursued by an ambulance. The opening title sequence, with its voiceover narration, planetary fly-past and 'wormhole' effect, refers explicitly to *Star Trek: The Next Generation* (1987–1994). As one critic remarked: 'Add a dash of *Indiana Jones*, a hint of *ER*, a smidge of *Candyman*, a pinch of *Point Break* and verbal inflections from *Bill and Ted* and you've got an idea.'[11]

This is not to say, however, that the television movie is entirely unoriginal. In some instances the imagery it draws upon is employed for symbolic effect rather than as mere pastiche. The best example is the regeneration sequence, in which the Doctor's physical metamorphosis is intercut with the mortuary attendant watching a television screening of the classic horror film *Frankenstein* (dir. James Whale, 1931). The 'birth' of the Monster in an electrical storm is paralleled with the 'rebirth' of the Doctor in a special-effects sequence replete with crackling energy and flashes of lightning. Throughout the film there are references to the Frankenstein story: Grace, like Frankenstein, became a doctor because she wanted to be able 'to hold back death', while the Doctor, like Frankenstein's Monster, is initially regarded as a lunatic. The most explicit manifestation of the promethean theme that pervades the film is the resolution in which the Doctor is able to circumvent the deaths of Grace and Chang Lee (Yee Jee Tso) by returning them to a point in time before they died – a direct violation of the Laws of Time, though this transgression passes without comment.

Another form of symbolism that pervades the film is its use of Christian imagery. The Doctor is (quite literally) resurrected: he emerges from the mortuary wearing only a white shroud in what seems a conscious reference to the Gospel of St Mark where Christ's disciples discover in the holy sepulchre 'a young man … clothed in a long white garment' (Mark 16.5). If this might seem a fanciful interpretation, the imagery is even more explicit at the climax of the film where the Doctor, as one critic put it, 'is manacled to a crucifix and garlanded with a crown of nails'.[12] In invoking both Frankenstein and Christ, the film is attempting to reconcile the contradictory discourses of scientific rationality and religious faith. In this context the Doctor himself becomes a more complex figure than in the BBC series: both a Prometheus defying the forces of creation and 'a gentlemanly Jesus come to save the world as it prepares to party on December 31, 1999'.[13]

The scientific and religious themes of this *Doctor Who* are also apparent in its take on the familiar 'Threat and Disaster' narrative. The Master plans to open the Eye of Harmony in the Doctor's TARDIS, which will cause the destruction of the Earth by altering its molecular structure and turning it inside out. Quite how or why he should want to do this is never fully explained. Critics were divided about this device: one felt that 'the worst sci-fi cliché is the countdown to eternal oblivion', but *Time Out* observed that it reflected the contemporary concerns of 'global destruction and millennial malaise'.[14] *Doctor Who* can be located within a social and intellectual *zeitgeist* of the mid and late 1990s that found expression in the term 'millennial anxieties'. This *zeitgeist* was both similar to and different from the *fin-de-siècle* uncertainty that had marked the end of the nineteenth century. Of course the doom-merchants have always declared that 'the end of the world is nigh' and the prophesies of Nostradamus continue to be the subject of much speculation and debate. Events such as the siege at Waco, Texas, in 1993, in which 77 members of the Branch Davidian sect died, fuelled the fantasies of those millennialist groups, particularly in the USA, who believed that an apocalyptic confrontation between the forces of Good and Evil was imminent. In the 1990s, furthermore, the doom-merchants found a new cause in the 'millennium bug' that would, or so it was feared, cause all the world's computer systems to crash on 1 January 2000 and thus precipitate a catastrophic global meltdown. There were hysterical predictions of aeroplanes falling from the skies and hospital life-support machines failing. Millennial anxieties found expression in the vogue for 'end-of-the-world' narratives in popular cinema, ranging from disaster movies such as *Deep Impact* (dir. Mimi Leder, 1998) and *Armageddon* (dir. Michael Bay, 1998) in which comets collide with the Earth, to action films such as *End of Days* (dir. Peter Hyams, 1999) in which Arnold Schwarzenegger is all that stands between mankind and biblical apocalypse. The *Doctor Who* movie is an early manifestation of the 'end-of-the-world' narrative in the 1990s that taps into millennial anxieties by positing that the world will end at midnight on 31 December 1999/1 January 2000. It is an epic confrontation between the forces of Good (the Doctor) and Evil (the Master) that is replete with allusions to Armageddon and the Day of Judgement. Never before had *Doctor Who* drawn so explicitly on biblical allusion.

Geoff King has argued that the millennial disaster narrative is a means of displacing real social and political issues onto 'a "higher" realm of biblical inevitability'.[15] This process of displacement is evident in *Doctor Who*, which on this occasion dresses up its apocalyptic scenario as a biblical struggle rather than responding to the sort of topical issues, such as the misuse of technology, pollution and eco-catastrophe, that it had addressed in the past and that remained relevant in the 1990s. This demonstrates an ideological conservatism on the part of the 1996 film that can probably be explained by its American semi-parentage. It is difficult to imagine the heavily industrialised nation that five years later refused to sign the Kyoto Treaty on greenhouse gas emissions accepting a *Doctor Who* story as radical as 'The Green Death'. In this regard it is difficult to escape the conclusion that one of the great strengths of *Doctor Who*, its willingness to address social and political concerns, was lost in this version.

Another criticism of the millennial catastrophe narrative is that it lacks the charm of the 'old' *Doctor Who*. Some critics bemoaned the absence of familiar ingredients. Tom Cussock in the *Sunday Telegraph*, for instance, professed his disappointment that there were 'no interesting beasties or gadgets, no guards with strange salutes, no nerve-centre of power, no underground rebels'.[16] The visual style of the film, *pace* Newman, is indistinguishable from any other US television film. The sole exception is the design of the TARDIS interior: a spacious, cavernous, temple-like space that now includes a library and stone staircase. One critic described it aptly as 'a mad-scientist mixture of Jules Verne's *Nautilus* and the British Library reading room'.[17] Its 'retro' appearance of mechanical levers, switches, dials and overhanging wires recalls both the secondary control room featured in the 1976–1977 season and the two Peter Cushing films. The TARDIS design marks *Doctor Who* as different from the smooth, touch-sensitive surfaces of the *Star Trek* continuation series. But Grace's reaction on entering the TARDIS ('This looks pretty low-tech') might be seen as a comment on the American opinion of *Doctor Who*.

The television movie was successful enough in Britain (it attracted nine million viewers on a Bank Holiday Monday) to suggest that there might yet be a popular audience for the show, but its reception in the all-important American market was lukewarm at best and there was insufficient interest from the networks to commission the proposed series. Its main problem, in terms of attracting a new audience to *Doctor Who*, is that it is too respectful of the series' past. There are too many continuity references and too much prior knowledge of the series is assumed. As the series had never been shown on network television in the USA, American viewers could be forgiven for asking what had happened to the first six Doctors. Even in Britain there was a feeling that *Doctor Who* had had its day. Sean Day-Lewis felt that the Doctor 'deserved to be left to rest in peace' and regretted that he had been 'summoned from beyond the grave and asked to achieve the impossible … to be accessible to a mass American audience, previously unaware of his existence, while not offending the sensibilities of British fans ready to spot any detail out of place'.[18] In comparison to the high-tech American space operas of the 1990s (*Babylon 5*, *Space: Above and Beyond*, *Earth: Final Conflict*, *StarGate SG-1*, *Farscape*, *Andromeda* and the various different incarnations of *Star Trek*), *Doctor Who* looked rather quaint and old-fashioned, despite its much-vaunted special effects makeover. The future for the ailing time traveller remained highly uncertain.

9

Second Coming

2005

I'm a Time Lord. I'm the last of the Time Lords. They're all gone. I'm the only survivor. I'm left travelling on my own 'cos there's no one else.

The Doctor (Christopher Eccleston) in 'The End of the World'

The second return of *Doctor Who* in 2005 represented more than just the successful revival of an old television series. The success of the new series confounded those commentators who had argued, following the 1996 television film, that *Doctor Who* had passed its sell-by date. Nicholas Cull, for example, had remarked in 2001 that '*Doctor Who* seemed like a cultural dead end', while Mark Campbell asserted even less equivocally that '*Doctor Who* is dead and buried'.[1] That *Doctor Who* was able to reinvent itself so successfully for the vastly different cultural conditions of the early twenty-first century was due in large measure to the fact that it was produced, and promoted, as a brand new series in its own right rather than as a direct continuation of the series that had run between 1963 and 1989. A new 'Doctor Who' (Christopher Eccleston) would be introduced without any reference to previous incarnations, and while it would soon become clear that the Doctor had a past, the new series would not be weighed down with the sort of continuity references that could be understood only by fully paid-up members of the *Doctor Who* Appreciation Society. The fact that the revived *Doctor Who* has attracted new audiences while maintaining faith with fans of what is now known as 'classic' *Who* (most of them at least) suggests that, unlike the 1996 film, it has successfully negotiated the terrain between 'mainstream' and 'cult' television.

The resurrection of *Doctor Who* again needs to be understood in relation to changing cultural and institutional contexts. From the late 1990s there is evidence of different attitudes towards *Doctor Who* within the BBC itself. On the one hand, in the eyes of programme- and policy-makers, *Doctor Who* seems to have been regarded as something of a joke – a subject suitable only for mockery. This, at least, is the impression given by the 1999 *Comic Relief* spoof 'The Curse of Fatal Death' (written by professed *Who* fan Steven Moffat) and the skits included in BBC2's themed '*Doctor Who* Night' the same year.[2] However, when the 'real' *Doctor Who* was resurrected, in the form of repeats of the first two Jon Pertwee serials on BBC2 ('Spearhead from Space' and 'Doctor Who and the Silurians'), poor ratings meant that a proposed run of all the colour episodes was aborted. (The failure to attract new audiences is curious, given that repeats of Gerry Anderson's 'Supermarionation' series *Thunderbirds* and *Captain Scarlet and the Mysterons* in the same weekday 6 pm slot had created a whole new generation of fans.) On the other hand, however, for the corporation's commercial arm, BBC Worldwide, *Doctor Who* remained a profitable 'franchise' that generated a steady income through sales of licensed merchandising, including books, videos and DVDs. Undeterred by the relative failure of the 1996 *Doctor Who* television film, BBC Worldwide pushed ahead with an expanding range of *Doctor Who* spin-offs, including original novels, computer games and audio dramas. It is instructive here to make a comparison with both the *Star Wars* and *Star Trek* franchises, which similarly branched out into other media during the 1990s.

The world of *Doctor Who* fandom has been much exercised by the vexed question of whether non-televised *Who* is or is not part of the 'canon' – the officially mandated version of the *Doctor Who* fictional universe and continuity.[3] From 1999, for example, the production company, Big Finish, was licensed to produce original *Doctor Who* audio dramas on CD: these included new adventures for Doctors Davison, Baker, C., McCoy and McGann – and recently also for Baker, T. – but also various 'alternative' Doctors including Geoffrey Bayldon, David Warner and Arabella Weir. The Big Finish audios were produced by 'professional fans' who had grown up with the classic series, such as Gary Russell and Julian Richards. The audio format meant that these stories were able to be as epic and ambitious as they liked: they exhibit what Matt Hills has called 'televisuality without television'.[4] And, from 1997, BBC Books published new ranges of 'Eighth Doctor Adventures' and 'Past Doctor Adventures' which took over from Virgin's 'New Adventures' and 'Missing Adventures'. The real significance of these continuation books and audios is not the issue of their 'canonicity' but rather that they kept the *Doctor Who* 'brand' alive in the imagination of its fans while allowing the BBC to gauge the response of the public towards the prospect of a new television series.

It was almost certainly the success of these *Doctor Who* spin-offs that prompted the BBC to test the water regarding the possibility of reviving the series in the early 2000s. It did this through an unusual channel. Since the mid 1990s the World Wide Web had developed from its original form as an information network to become, in effect, the fifth mass medium following press, cinema, radio and television. The availability of increasingly powerful home computers and the growing number of Internet service providers made domestic and leisure use of the Web widely available by the turn of the millennium. While predictions that the Internet would spell the end of film and television proved to be very wide of the mark, it is nevertheless an indication of a changing media culture that, for example, the trailers for much-anticipated films like the *Star Wars* prequel trilogy were first released via the Internet. It is in this context that the four *Doctor Who* 'webcasts' broadcast on BBCi between 2001 and 2003 can be seen. The webcasts progressed technologically from what were essentially audio recordings with cartoon images to a fully fledged animated adventure, 'Scream of the Shalka', visualised by the animation specialist Cosgrove Hall (responsible for *Danger Mouse* and *The Wind in the Willows*) and broadcast in the autumn of 2003. The Doctor of 'Scream of the Shalka' was based on the actor Richard E. Grant, who had also appeared in 'The Curse of Fatal Death' and who was, briefly, officially recognised as the Ninth Doctor.[5]

The BBC's decision to 'have another crack at the series', as BBC1 Controller Lorraine Heggessey put it, has been explained by the fact that the generation of BBC senior executives in the early 2000s included a number of dedicated fans who had grown up with *Doctor Who*. It was the then-editor of *Doctor Who Magazine* (*DWM*), Clayton Hickman, who coined the term '*Doctor Who* Mafia' in reference to the senior echelons of the BBC: 'That's why the show's coming back. If it wasn't for all the fans in high places, it would have just faded away.'[6] The 'Doctor Who Mafia' included Heggesey herself, Mal Young, Controller of BBC Continuing Drama Series, and series producer Phil Collinson. Young, in particular, had been quietly agitating to revive Doctor Who for years: he would be co-executive producer of the new series alongside writer-in-chief Russell T. Davies (also a Who fan of long standing) and Julie Gardner, the newly-appointed Head of Drama at BBC Wales. In fact Heggessey had 'revealed plans to revive the world's longest-running sci-fi series' in the autumn of 2002, although the process of clearing rights – BBC Worldwide still harboured unrealised ambitions to make a Doctor Who film – meant that it would be another full year before a new series of thirteen 45-minute episodes was commissioned in September 2003.[7]

Yet the revival of Doctor Who cannot be explained solely through the influence of the 'Doctor Who Mafia'. It was also an outcome of the institutional contexts of the corporation at the time. The decision that production of Doctor Who would be based in Cardiff rather than London, for example, needs to be understood as part of the BBC's 'nations and regions' strategy to diversify its programme-making activities. BBC Wales had hitherto produced mostly Welsh language content and, unlike other regional production centres – such as Bristol (Casualty), Belfast (Ballykissangel) and Glasgow (Monarch of the Glen) – had not produced any major network dramas. The BBC's Annual Report for 2005–2006 explicitly linked Doctor Who to its strategy of regional diversification: 'The BBC is committed to increasing programme production outside the M25 . . . BBC Cymru Wales has been notably successful in supplying the network with memorable programming across a range of genres. Drama has been particularly strong and includes some of the high points of BBC One, such as Doctor Who and Life on Mars.'[8] However, there were some local concerns that Doctor Who was not sufficiently 'Welsh' in content. 'On a personal note,' confided Russell T. Davies, 'I still find plenty of moaners complaining that the much longed-for BBC Wales Drama Department isn't what they wanted, simply because it's making huge primetime dramas with worldwide sales, instead of small, intense shows called I Was Born In Wales And I'm Cross.'[9]

In another sense, the revival of Doctor Who provided a direct echo of the origin of the series in 1963: the contest for Saturday evening ratings. It is clear that right from the outset Heggesey intended 'to reinstate it in its teatime slot on Saturdays – a time that has recently consistently underplayed in the ratings'.[10] In 2003 it was reported that Saturday evening – once the highlight of the weekly television schedules – had become the least watched day of the week.[11] This was widely blamed on the prevalence of celebrity-led 'reality TV' shows and tired light entertainment formats that no longer appealed to the traditional cross-generational family audience. Consequently Saturday evening television had become 'a ratings disaster and a cultural wasteland'.[12] Heggesey wanted an early evening drama with broad-based popular appeal – and Doctor Who fitted the bill. As she later told DWM: 'We wanted to bring some drama to early Saturday evenings, and I think, if Doctor Who hadn't come back, we'd have had to reinvent it as something else. Given that it did exist, it seemed better to bring it back for today's generation, rather than start something else from scratch.'[13]

However, the new Doctor Who was to be more than just a television series. Its revival can also be seen as part of an ambitious and wide-ranging strategy to launch a multi-media franchise along the lines of Star Trek or Star Wars. Frank Collins avers that 'the BBC saw Doctor Who as the perfect vehicle to offer multiple points of entry into a franchise, to develop new modes of engagement, and increase fan involvement'.[14] This is evident on several levels. The new series would be supported by a 'making of' programme, Doctor Who Confidential, broadcast after each episode on BBC3. There was particularly innovative use of online and interactive media, including episode commentaries in the form of downloadable podcasts and additional content for digital viewers 'via the red button'. Several fake websites were created specifically for the 2005 series in order that eagle-eyed viewers could actually find information about organisations such as UNIT (which features in the episodes 'Aliens of London' and 'World War Three') or Henry Van Statten's Geocomtext Corporation ('Dalek'). The first episode features an Internet conspiracy theorist who runs a website entitled 'Who Is Doctor Who?': the URL would lead fans to the BBC's official Doctor Who website.[15] Nor were traditional print media forgotten: BBC Books launched a new series of Ninth Doctor novels whose content was approved by the Doctor Who production team. While the classic series had spawned a wide range of spin-off merchandising, especially in the mid 1960s, the new series demonstrated an entirely new approach. In this sense the television series itself would be the engine that drove and sustained an even bigger cross-media franchise.

To this extent, the decision to 'have another crack' at *Doctor Who* was much more than that comment implied. The new series was evidently intended both to appeal to a wide audience and to attract new viewers to the BBC. Much was riding on its success. Here there is a major difference from the origin of the classic series. In 1963, *Doctor Who* had been conceived to fill a gap in the schedules: it had not been foreseen that it would prove to be such a long-running or successful series. In contrast, the 2005 version of *Doctor Who* was intended from the outset as flagship primetime entertainment. This much is evident from the level of resources afforded to it. The reported cost of the 2005 series was £900,000 an episode, placing it firmly in the upper cost bracket of BBC drama production. At last *Doctor Who* was to be made with something approaching the level of production values that had become the norm for blockbuster American SF series such as the new *Battlestar Galactica* (2005–2009). This would not be the *Doctor Who* of popular memory with its wobbly sets and papier-mache models. In particular, *Doctor Who* would make extensive use of CGI (Computer-Generated Imaging) in order to realise its aliens and spacecraft. BBC1's launch trailers for the new series emphasised visual spectacle, the most oft-repeated shots being a spaceship crashing into Big Ben and flying past Tower Bridge.

The production discourses of new *Doctor Who* positioned it as 'quality' drama rather than a science fiction series. This was most evident in the recruitment of Russell T. Davies as writer-in-chief and co-executive producer of the new series. Davies is one of a select number of British television writers – others include Dennis Potter, Tony Garnett, Alan Bleasdale and Stephen Poliakoff – who can be regarded as genuine auteurs both on account of the recurring themes of their work and the extent to which having their name attached to a project carries a degree of cultural weight.[16] Davies's oeuvre combines the issues-led social realist import of Garnett or Bleasdale with the formal innovation of Potter or Poliakoff. Davies had cut his teeth in children's drama, writing the fantasy serials *Century Falls* (1991) and *Dark Season* (1993) for the BBC and producing *Children's Ward* for Granada in the early 1990s. He graduated to adult drama, via a stint as story editor of the long-running soap opera *Coronation Street*, with the period hotel drama *The Grand* (1997–1998). Davies's breakthrough came with his drama of gay life in Manchester for Channel 4, *Queer as Folk* (1999–2000), one of the boldest (and consequently one of the most controversial) original television dramas of the

1990s. He followed with *Bob & Rose* (2001), *The Second Coming* (2003) and – immediately prior to *Doctor Who* – *Casanova* (2005). There were some, such as the *Sun*'s television critic Gary Bushell (a long-standing critic of *Doctor Who*), who complained about what they perceived as Davies's 'gay agenda'.[17] But most fans were reassured by the fact that Davies was, first and foremost, a *Doctor Who* fan. He had written one of the Virgin 'New Adventures' novels (*Damaged Goods*, 1996) and famously referenced *Doctor Who* in an episode of *Queer as Folk* in which the character Stuart dumps his boyfriend because he is unable to name all the actors who have played the Doctor. Davies was astute enough to recognise the importance of keeping faith with fandom: to this end he wrote an occasional 'Production Notes' column for *DWM* in which he revealed gossipy tidbits about the new series.

It has been argued that the idea of 'authored' television drama is incompatible with the essentially genre-based format of a series like *Doctor Who*. Matt Hills characterises these arguments as '"cult TV" versus "television-as-culture" discourses'.[18] Yet there is no reason why television drama cannot be both 'authored' and 'cult'. For one thing, the fan discourses of classic *Who* have always privileged certain writers, such as Robert Holmes, whose scripts reveal a distinctive tone and style.[19] For another, Davies's role as *Doctor Who*'s principal 'showrunner' – a term imported from American television where it refers to writer-producers who exercise a tight degree of control over the entire creative process – also collapses the distinction between authored and genre-based drama. Davies's role is comparable with US showrunners such as Chris Carter (*The X Files*), Joss Whedon (*Buffy the Vampire Slayer*) and J.J. Abrams (*Alias, Lost*). Indeed, Davies is on record to the effect that he took *Buffy the Vampire Slayer* as a point of reference for new *Doctor Who*.[20] Furthermore, the other writers recruited by Davies for the new series were all drawn from the world of *Doctor Who* fandom. Mark Gatiss ('The Unquiet Dead') and Steven Moffat ('The Empty Child' and 'The Doctor Dances') had written television skits of *Doctor Who*, while Robert Shearman ('Dalek') and Paul Cornell ('Father's Day') had each written both novels and audio dramas.[21] Shearman's episode, 'Dalek', was commissioned on the basis of his Big Finish audio, 'Jubilee', which had focused on the relationship between the Doctor's companion and a lone Dalek.

Another indication of the 'quality' status of the new *Doctor Who* was the casting of Christopher Eccleston in the title role.[22] As a television actor, the 40-year-old Eccleston was best known for 'serious' dramas such as Peter Flannery's *Our Friends in the North* (1996), Jimmy Mc-Govern's *Hillsborough* (1996) and Davies's own *The Second Coming* in which he played the Son of God reincarnated in Manchester. Eccleston was a surprise choice – Bill Nighy, Alan Davies and *Buffy the Vampire Slayer*'s Anthony Head had been the bookies' favourites – but he was a perfect fit for what Davies wanted to do with the character. Davies averred that he wanted to get away from 'the nonsense that started taking over the series, the poshness, the frilly language and frilly shirts . . . I started stripping that away when I was writing the first episodes, before Christopher Eccleston was cast, but when you cut out the nonsense, you end up with something very like Chris.'[23] Accordingly, Eccleston's Doctor eschews the Edwardiana and eccentricity of his predecessors in favour of a minimalist, contemporary look consisting of leather jacket with plain sweater and trousers. Tall, gaunt and crop-haired, Eccleston is a highly physical actor whose body movements are studied and precise. He was also the first 'Doctor Who' to suggest a regional, working-class identity, playing the part in his own distinctive northern accent (Eccleston was born in Salford) rather than standard received pronunciation. The first episode even acknowledges as much:

Rose: If you are an alien, how comes you sound like you come from the north?

The Doctor: Lots of planets have a north.

Eccleston's authentic northernness identifies his Doctor as a spiritual successor to characters such as Albert Finney's Arthur Seaton and Richard Harris's Frank Machin.

Another facet of Eccleston's persona that feeds into his portrayal of the Doctor stems from his film roles as a 'damaged Everyman', such as Derek Bentley in *Let Him Have It* (dir. Peter Medak, 1991) and as the tormented protagonist of *Jude* (dir. Michael Winterbottom, 1996).[24] Eccleston's characterisation of the Doctor fits this portrayal of damaged masculinity in that it becomes apparent over the course of the series that he has a traumatic back story. There are fleeting references throughout the series to the apocalyptic events of the Time War, which it transpires was 'the war between the Daleks and the Time Lords, with the whole of creation at stake' ('The Parting of the Ways'). The Doctor is revealed to be the last survivor of the Time Lords and is plagued by guilt over what happened to his people. Eccleston's performance imbues the Doctor with a brooding, dangerous quality. For the first time we see a Doctor who seems genuinely afraid (when he has to face an enemy he thought had been destroyed in 'Dalek') and who expresses real anger and rage. He is unpredictable, irrational and impulsive. These character traits are nowhere better seen than at the end of 'Bad Wolf', where the Daleks have captured his companion Rose Tyler but, rather than accede to their demands, the Doctor vows to 'wipe every last stinking Dalek out of the sky'.

If Eccleston was an unusual choice for the Doctor, controversy also attended the casting of the new *Who* companion, with former teenage pop songstress and pin-up, Billie Piper, in the part of Rose. Piper had revealed her acting credentials in the BBC's modernised rendering of *The Canterbury Tales* (2003). A.A. Gill, for one, felt that Piper 'was well cast as a modern, chavishly smart sidekick who runs well'.[25] While, on one level, Piper's casting was consistent with *Doctor Who*'s usual strategy of providing 'something for the dads', her engaging and sympathetic performance ensured that she also became a point of identification for female viewers. To an extent the character of Rose, who lives with her mother on a South London council estate, represents continuity with the final years of classic *Who*: like Ace she is sassy, streetwise and fashion-conscious. Rose represents the 'Girl Power' generation of young British women: determined, outspoken, opinionated and independent. Her association with modernity is indicated, for example, in 'The Empty Child', where she finds herself in wartime London conspicuously 'wearing a Union Jack across my chest': the Union Jack T-shirt, first popularised in the 1960s, had become voguish again in the 1990s as part of the sixties cultural revival that came to be branded as 'Cool Britannia'. The inclusion of Rose's mother, Jackie Tyler (Camille Coduri), and on-off boyfriend, Mickey Smith (Noel Clarke), as semi-regular characters was indicative of Davies's desire to provide a social context for the companion in the form of a family and a normal life. The introduction of this 'soap opera' element would be one of the defining characteristics of Davies's reinvention of *Who*.

The challenge facing the producers of new *Doctor Who* was how to revive the series for those viewers who remembered the original, while also introducing it to a new generation of children who had no memory of classic *Who*. The problem of how to deal with the *Doctor Who* 'legacy' was identified by the BBC's own market research:

> Its legacy could be a help and a hindrance. On the whole, dads thought that the new show would be for their children (since the dads had watched it when they were young), but the children thought that the new show would be for their dads (since their dads already knew who Doctor Who was and they didn't).[26]

In this regard there were lessons to be learned from the television film, where promotional materials had focused on the return of the Doctor ('He's back . . . And it's about time'). In the event the trailers for the 2005 series avoided references to the series' past and instead emphasised its fantasy-adventure elements as Eccleston asked viewers 'Do you wanna come with me?' and promised them 'the trip of a lifetime' against a montage of some of the more spectacular moments.

The decision not to over-emphasise the *Doctor Who* legacy was also part of the narrative strategy of the new series. There are no references to any of the Doctor's previous incarnations – though Davies confirmed in *DWM* that Eccleston was officially the Ninth Doctor – and no re-generation sequence to explain the change from McGann to Eccleston. The opening episode, 'Rose', introduces a character calling himself 'The Doctor' who appears out of the blue to save shopgirl Rose Tyler from a group of Autons – referred to as such in the end credits though not in the episode itself – but there is no reference to the previous Auton invasions of Earth. That the Doctor has a past and an association with the Earth is established through the character of Clive (Mark Benton), an Internet nerd who has been tracking his appearances – including at the eruption of Krakatoa, the embarcation of the *Titanic* and the assassination of Kennedy ('The Doctor is a legend, woven throughout history. When disaster comes, he's there . . . And he has one constant companion – Death!'). Davies includes hints of a larger fictional universe, with references to the Time War and the Shadow Proclamation without (at this stage) explaining what they are. As he told *DWM*: 'Now, if you're new to the series, or just dipping in, it doesn't matter if you're following these hints or not . . . But if you want to follow the links, then maybe the stories get a bit more interconnected.'[27]

The new *Doctor Who* was an immediate popular and critical success. The 'overnight' audience for 'Rose' was 9.9 million (later adjusted to 10.8 million to include the Sunday repeat on BBC3 and those who recorded it to watch later) and the average audience for the series as a whole was 8.2 million. This represented a major success in the Saturday 7 pm slot, where *Doctor Who* was aired against ITV-1's popular light entertainment programme *Ant and Dec's Saturday Night Takeaway*. The independent network later replied with repeats of blockbuster movies such as *The Phantom Menace* and *X-Men* without making any dent in the ratings for *Doctor Who*. The BBC's Audience Research found that the core audience for the new series comprised children under 15 and adults in the 35–44 age bracket (the age of those who would have remembered *Doctor Who* from their own childhoods during the 1960s and 1970s) and that over 90 per cent of those questioned regarded it as 'good family viewing'.[28]

The success of *Doctor Who* was no accident: on the contrary it showed every sign of a carefully planned and executed strategy to ensure that it made an immediate impact and that it maintained the loyalty of viewers. The 2005 series was launched with a blitz of publicity – including several *Doctor Who*-themed specials in the week leading up to the series' première – and was structured in such a way as to ensure that audiences stayed with it. As Davies explained: 'We built in "sweeps" episodes – event episodes and two-part stories placed strategically throughout the run, designed to boost ratings. The last in the series quickly became the "season finalé".'[29] (The notion of 'sweeps' episodes is an American term referring to the four weeks in the year when the Nielsen Ratings are used to set advertising rates for the next quarter: accordingly the networks plan their flagship dramas with 'event' episodes for these weeks.) *Doctor Who* was launched on the Easter Bank Holiday weekend (26 March) and ran for thirteen consecutive weeks: three two-part stories were strategically placed during the run, while the reintroduction of an iconic monster ('Dalek') mid-way through was an 'event' episode coinciding with the early May Bank Holiday weekend (30 April). The success of this strategy can be measured by the fact that, even with fluctuations for individual episodes – 'The Doctor Dances' had the lowest overnight audience at 6.9 million – *Doctor Who* maintained an average audience share of around 40 per cent throughout.[30]

The critical response to the new series was overwhelmingly positive. *Doctor Who* was credited with 'resurrecting family TV viewing virtually single-handedly'.[31] Most reviewers felt that the formula had been successfully reinvented and would appeal to a broad audience. Henry Venning in *The Stage*, for example, thought it 'a fabulous, imaginative, funny and sometimes frightening reinvention of the esteemed, if somewhat time ravaged, Time Lord'.[32] Ceri Thomas in the *Daily Mail* found it 'more emotional and infinitely more satisfying' than before.[33] *The Times* simply declared that 'this new *Doctor Who* is an unqualified triumph'.[34] For the first time in its history, *Doctor Who* was recognised by the World Science Fiction Society: 'The Empty Child'/'The Doctor Dances' won a Hugo Award for Best Dramatic Presentation (Short Form), with 'Dalek' and 'Father's Day' also among the runners-up. These were also among the favourite episodes of *DWM* readers, along with the concluding story 'Bad Wolf'/'The Parting of the Ways'.[35] The new series even won over one of *Doctor Who*'s oldest foes. Michael Grade, now Chairman of the BBC Governors, congratulated all those involved with the series for what he called '[a] classy, popular triumph for people of all ages and all backgrounds – [and] real value for money for our licence fee payers'.[36]

This is not to say, however, that *Doctor Who* was uncontroversial. In one respect the reception echoed responses to the classic series: the charge that *Doctor Who* was too horrific and too violent for younger children. In particular the reanimated corpses of 'The Unquiet Dead' ('The stiffs are getting lively again!') and the monstrous child of 'The Empty Child' ('Are you my mummy?') were accused of giving some children nightmares. The BBC had to put out a statement that '*Doctor Who* has never been intended for the youngest of children . . . We would suggest it would be a programme which eight-year-olds and above would enjoy watching with their parents.'[37] It was decided to cut a sound effect of a cracking skull from 'The Empty Child' prior to transmission as it was deemed 'a bit too horrible'.[38] The British Board of Film Classification (BBFC) endorsed the view that some episodes were unsuitable for younger children when it awarded a '12' certificate to the DVD releases of 'The Unquiet Dead' and 'Dalek'. The BBFC objected to 'Dalek' on the absurd grounds of cruelty towards science fiction's foremost genocidal killing machines: 'We were concerned at the use of violence to resolve problems. The Doctor is a role model for young children but he takes out his cruelty on the Dalek. A good role model should not use torture to satisfy his desire for revenge.'[39]

This prompted a leader in *The Times* condemning the BBFC's decision as 'the interfering arm of the nanny state, intent on exterminating all free thought'.[40] However, these controversies can also be seen, if somewhat perversely, as an indication that *Doctor Who* was in good health: in the past the loudest complaints against the series had usually coincided with its periods of greatest popularity.

The 2005 series of *Doctor Who* demonstrates that it is indeed possible for a television series to be both 'authored' and 'cult'. Davies, who wrote eight of the thirteen episodes, was clearly the guiding creative influence on the content and tone of the series. While there is a range of SF templates – including invasion/infiltration ('Rose', 'Aliens of London', 'Boom Town'), futuristic histories ('The End of the World', 'The Long Game'), action-adventure ('Dalek'), period horror ('The Unquiet Dead', 'The Empty Child'), intimate drama ('Father's Day'), satire ('Bad Wolf') and all-out epic space opera ('The Parting of the Ways') – episodes are linked by a structured 'story arc' in the manner of American series such as *Babylon 5* and *Buffy the Vampire Slayer*. A story arc is an underlying narrative that maintains a degree of seriality between otherwise discrete stand-alone episodes. This is apparent in several ways in Series One of *Doctor Who*. Thus the dislocation caused by the Time War – a war visible only to the 'higher life forms' – provides a background for the attempted invasions of the Earth by the Nestene Consciousness ('Rose') and the Gelth ('The Unquiet Dead') whose home planets have been destroyed. The discovery of a rift in time and space in nineteenth-century Cardiff ('The Unquiet Dead') in turn provides a reason for the Doctor to return to the city in the present ('Boom Town'), to draw energy from the rift in order to replenish the power supply of the TARDIS. There are also references throughout the series to the phrase 'Bad Wolf', whose meaning is explained only at the climax of the final episode.[41]

Other signs of Davies's authorship can be found in the tone of the scripts. Davies's so-called 'gay agenda' is in fact little in evidence: the secondary character of 'omnisexual' Captain Jack Harkness (John Barrowman) – a Time Agent from the fifty-first century – is the series' most overt engagement with the cultural politics of male sexuality, but his behaviour amounts to little more than mild flirtation (with men, women, humans and aliens alike). The question of the Doctor's own sexuality is hinted at through veiled references in 'The Doctor Dances', but this seems to have passed unnoticed by most viewers. It would be more accurate to suggest that Davies pursues a progressive agenda – an agenda that is entirely consistent with the ethos of *Doctor Who* itself. The Doctor stands, as ever, for the disadvantaged and the oppressed, and maintains a genuine belief in the human race's potential for good. Davies includes his own equivalent of Tom Baker's famous 'homo sapiens' speech (from 'The Ark in Space') in the first episode: 'This planet is just starting! These stupid little people have only just learned to walk but they're capable of so much more!' ('Rose'). Davies's influence can also be detected in the popular culture references – 'The End of the World', for example, includes the music of Soft Cell and Britney Spears – and in a particular style of undergraduate humour reminiscent of Douglas Adams: an alien species known as Adherents of the Repeated Meme reminds us that Davies read English Literature at Oxford University.

The style and 'look' of new *Doctor Who* marked a significant change from the classic series, reflecting technological and stylistic changes in the television industry since the 1980s. In particular, new *Who* can be placed within the discourse of 'televisuality' that the US critic John Thornton Caldwell argues has transformed the visual style of high-end television drama. Caldwell shows how the adoption of new technologies from the mid to late 1980s, especially improvements to camera lenses and high-definition video recording, transformed the 'murky' style of much television drama by enhancing image resolution. One consequence of this was the way in which series such as *Miami Vice* (1984–1989), *Moonlighting* (1985–1989), *Beauty and the Beast* (1987–1990) and *Twin Peaks* (1990–1991) privileged visual style and *mise-en-scène* over narrative and characterisation. Caldwell labels this 'televisuality' and suggests that it is particularly appropriate for fantasy genres where it 'developed a system/genre of alternative worlds that tolerated and expected both visual flourishes – special effects, graphics, acute cinematography and editing – and narrative embellishments – time travel, diegetic masquerades, and out of body experiences.'[42] Jan Johnson-Smith has demonstrated, furthermore, how the discourse of televisuality may be applied to American SF series, such as *Star Trek: The Next Generation* (1987–1994), *Babylon 5* (1994–1998), *Space: Above and Beyond* (1995–1996) and *StarGate SG-1* (1998–2007), where advances in special effects technology made possible 'the creation of a sustainable and plausible future history'.[43]

British television may have been slower to adopt the new (and expensive) production technologies, but the revival of telefantasy from the 1990s – exemplified by special effects-heavy Saturday evening shows such as *Bugs* (1995–1998), *Crime Traveller* (1997) and *Randall & Hopkirk (Deceased)* (2000–2001) – paved the way for the more ambitious project of *Doctor Who*. The two major technological differences from classic *Who* were digital shooting (new *Who* is shot using the DigiBeta format) and Computer-Generated Imaging (CGI). The special effects for the new series were provided by a company called The Mill, which had been responsible for the Academy Award-winning visual effects for Roman epic *Gladiator* (dir. Ridley Scott, 2000). The extensive use of CGI technology made possible both a 'sustainable and plausible future history' – demonstrated in the futuristic settings of 'The End of the World', 'The Long Game', 'Bad Wolf' and 'The Parting of the Ways' – and also a spectacular recreation of the London Blitz in 'The Empty Child', with its panoramic shots of the night sky criss-crossed with barrage balloons, searchlights and a fleet of bombers. The new series' visualisation of the future seems to have been influenced by *Blade Runner* (dir. Ridley Scott, 1982) – a clear point of reference for Satellite Five in 'The Long Game', with its crowds and fast-food stalls – and by the space station settings of *Babylon 5* and *Star Trek: Deep Space Nine* (1994–1999).

Perhaps the two most striking differences between new and classic *Who* are the faster pace and greater narrative scope of the new series. The narrative pace of television drama has quickened significantly since the 1980s: hence new *Who* compresses complete stories into 45 minutes that in the classic series would have been told over four 25-minute episodes. (The experience of watching classic *Who* has changed as a consequence: even serials by acclaimed directors like Douglas Camfield and David Maloney now seem to have some padding and *longueurs*.) The narration of new *Who* is nothing if not slick: a mobile camera, elliptical editing and film-style montage all create a sense of pace and movement. The opening scenes of 'Rose' are a case in point: a montage of short scenes lasting in total one minute of screen time (Rose getting up, having breakfast, greeting her mother, travelling to work, establishing her job at a department store, meeting her boyfriend for a picnic lunch in Trafalgar Square) shows with brilliant economy everything we need to know about her life and daily routine. In particular, new *Who* largely eschews the long, static dialogue scenes in the TARDIS that were a prominent feature of the old series. Unlike, say, costume drama, where individual shots may be lovingly composed for their aesthetic and pictorial effect, new *Who* uses a mobile camera to move the action forward. A good example, again, is a scene in 'Rose' where a long tracking shot picks up the Doctor and Rose leaving her tower block and follows them around the estate as he strides purposefully ahead and she follows demanding an explanation. The shot duration is 88 seconds (an eternity in modern television drama where 'MTV'-style editing is the norm) and is reminiscent of the famous long tracking shots that open *Touch of Evil* (dir. Orson Welles, 1958) and *The Player* (dir. Robert Altman, 1992). It is a means of maintaining visual fluidity in exposition scenes without needing to resort to a conventional two-character shot/reverse shot dialogue sequence.

The higher production values of new *Doctor Who* in relation to the classic series also invest it with a much greater narrative scope: put simply, the stories are told on a bigger scale. This is evident, again, from the very beginning. 'Rose' replays several scenes from 'Spearhead from Space', including the opening zoom-in to the Earth and the famous sequence of shop-window dummies coming to life and shooting passers-by: on each occasion the effect is to assert that new *Who* has been conceived on an altogether grander scale than the old series. Whereas in 'Spearhead from Space', for example, the Autons' killing spree takes place on a conspicuously empty high street (due to the fact that it was filmed early one Sunday morning), in 'Rose' they wreak havoc in a busy shopping centre. Similarly, the first two-part story of new *Who*, 'Aliens of London'/'World War Three', is an invasion narrative involving UNIT and an attempted alien take-over of the British government. Whereas in a UNIT story from the 1970s the spaceship would have landed in a quarry outside London, here it collides with Big Ben and flies under Tower Bridge before crashing into the River Thames. The destruction of Big Ben is an image borrowed from Hollywood SF films such as *Independence Day* (dir. Roland Emmerich, 1996): here it amounts to nothing less than a declaration of intent that new *Who* is aspiring to the epic scale of SF cinema.

It will be apparent, therefore, that new *Doctor Who* offers a much more spectacular viewing experience than the classic series. This is evident, too, in the frequent shots of iconic London landmarks – the London Eye, Tower Bridge, the Houses of Parliament – that feature prominently in the contemporary episodes (despite most of the series being shot in Cardiff) and function as signifiers of its Britishness. However, for all the expensive production values and special effects, there is much more to new *Who* than spectacle. Russell T. Davies has consistently iterated that his focus is on human drama rather than SF apparatus. In an interview with *DWM* after the 2005 series, for example, he explained his outlook thus:

> [T]here's so much potential in science fiction, but you read the listings magazines and under *Star Trek: Enterprise* it'll say, "The Crystals of Poffnar have been hidden in a cave, and so-and-so argues with the Federation that they have to be retrieved." What is there to watch in that!? But one of *Buffy*'s billings might be, "Buffy falls in love, and discovers he's a monster." Brilliant! It speaks to your heart. That's a great model to follow.[44]

To this end, the character focus of Series One of *Doctor Who* is not so much on the Doctor but on Rose: she is introduced to the audience before the Doctor makes his first appearance and events are seen from her perspective rather than the Doctor's. The early episodes, especially, focus on Rose's responses to visiting the future ('The End of the World') and the past ('The Unquiet Dead'). Not since the very first companions, Ian Chesterton and Barbara Wright, has *Doctor Who* associated itself so closely with the point of view of the companion.

A consequence of the human-drama element of new *Who* is the much greater degree of emotionality invested in the series. Some critics have derided the 'soap opera' element of Davies-era *Who*: characters such as Rose's mother Jackie, a working-class single mother, and Rose's boyfriend, Mickey, would not have seemed out of place in *EastEnders*. Yet this 'soap' element is integral to the strategy of new *Who*, which, for all its SF elements, seeks to locate itself within a discourse of psychological realism. One of the themes of new *Who* is the idea that the companion might have a life independent of the Doctor and to examine the impact of her travelling with the Doctor on her family and friends. A theme of Series One, for example, is the gradual estrangement between Rose and Mickey. And the opening of 'Aliens of London' examines how the companion's prolonged absences affect their loved ones. Rose returns home after two adventures with the Doctor only to discover that a year has passed (on this occasion the TARDIS remains as unreliable as ever) and that she has been reported missing. (This develops an idea from 'Survival', where it is reported that Ace's mother has also listed her as a missing person.) Jackie's relief at seeing her daughter again is tempered by her suspicion that the Doctor has ulterior motives ('Did you find her on the Internet? Did you go online and pretend you're a doctor?'). This positions Jackie's response to her daughter's absence within a plausible psychological framework. At the same time, Rose's experiences have given her a new perspective on life that her family can never understand: 'The Doctor's shown me a better way of living your life ... that you don't give up, you don't just let things happen, you make a stand, you say no, you have the guts to do what's right when every one else runs away' ('The Parting of the Ways').

The best example of the human-drama element of new *Doctor Who* is Paul Cornell's 'Father's Day' (1.8). This is essentially a character-driven emotional drama that just happens to be a science fiction story. It is a time-travel narrative that easily stands comparison with Harlan Ellison's acclaimed *Star Trek* episode 'The City on the Edge of Forever'.[45] Rose asks the Doctor to take her back to 7 November 1987 – the day her father died in a hit-and-run car accident – so that she can be 'there for him' rather than letting him die alone. When the time comes, however, Rose impulsively pushes her father away from the oncoming car and in so doing saves his life. The Doctor is angry with her for changing the past – especially as her action causes a rift in time that summons terrifying flying Reapers 'to sterilise the wound'. But on this occasion the special effects are secondary to the emotional drama that unfolds as Rose meets the father she has never known. Having grown up with an idealised image of her father, she has to come to terms with the fact that he is 'a born failure' (in his words) and 'a sort of Del Boy' (her words) rather than the successful businessman she had been brought up to believe. In one of the most affecting scenes, after Pete has discovered she is his daughter, Rose constructs an idealised childhood for herself:

Pete: Am I a good dad?

Rose: You told me a bed-time story every night when I was small. You were always there – you never missed one. And, erm, you took us on picnics in the country every Saturday. You never let us down. You were there for us all the time. Someone I really could rely on.

Pete: That's not me.

At this point Pete does not know that he is supposed to be dead: when he realises what has happened he throws himself in front of the car (caught in a time loop) and heals the temporal disturbance. Rose comforts him as he dies: and her mother later tells the infant Rose how an unknown girl sat with her father as he died. Rose's loss also strengthens her relationship with the Doctor: when the Doctor touches her face at the end of the episode, repeating a gesture made by Pete earlier, he is in effect assuming the role of surrogate father. The visual style of 'Father's Day' – filmed around a grim estate with dilapidated buildings and under grey skies – locates it within the 'kitchen sink' tradition of British social realism.

'Father's Day' is an atypical episode that demonstrates how far the production team of new *Doctor Who* was prepared to push the boundaries of the genre. Elsewhere the series is squarely within what two BBC staff writers in 1963 had labelled the 'Threat and Disaster' school of SF. The presence of monsters is a *sine qua non* of new *Doctor Who* – the Reapers, for example, were added after the first draft of 'Father's Day' when it was felt monsters were needed – though there are some imaginative variations on the familiar invasion tropes. Steven Moffat's acclaimed two-parter 'The Empty Child' (1.9) and 'The Doctor Dances' (1.10) is an interesting story for several reasons – not least of which is its association between childhood and the monstrous. In wartime London a mysterious and sinister small boy in a gas mask is seeking his 'mummy': he is one of numerous people with identical injuries. The Doctor has arrived on the trail of an alien vessel that has crashed there. It turns out that the boy had died in an air raid and his body was 'repaired' by nanogenes from the alien vessel. However, the nanogenes are unfamiliar with human physiology, and have mistakenly fused the child's gas mask to his face. On this occasion, therefore, the alien presence turns out to be benign.

'The Empty Child'/'The Doctor Dances' – which topped *DWM*'s readers' poll of Series One – is also notable for its revisionist interpretation of an aspect of the British historical experience. It is only the second *Doctor Who* television story (following 'The Curse of Fenric' in 1989) set during the Second World War. Moffat uses the story as an opportunity to examine both the myth and the reality of 'the people's war'. The familiar view of heroic British resistance to Nazi tyranny is expressed in an admiring soliloquy by the Doctor:

The Doctor: Amazing! 1941. Right now, not very far from here, the German
                war machine is rolling up the map of Europe. Country after
                country falling like dominoes, nothing can stop it – nothing.
                Until one tiny, damp little island says 'No!' No, not here. A
                mouse in front of a lion. You're amazing, the lot of you. Don't
                know what you do to Hitler, but you frighten the hell out of
                me!

However, this is contrasted with another side of the wartime experience
that has been written out of many historical accounts of 'their finest
hour'. A young woman called Nancy (clearly intended as an allusion to
Oliver Twist) acts as a surrogate mother to a group of orphans and street
urchins who sneak into houses during air raids while the occupants are in
shelters in order to scavenge food ('It's *brilliant!* Not sure if it's Marxism
in action or a West End musical'). The story's focus on the traumatising
effects of war (one boy hints at being abused when he was evacuated)
is far removed from the rosy nostalgia of the idyllic *Goodnight Mr Tom*
or John Boorman's autobiographical film *Hope and Glory* (1987). Like
'Father's Day', 'The Empty Child' and 'The Doctor Dances' sit outside
the story arc – though Moffat's story is the vehicle for the introduction
of John Barrowman's Captain Jack Harkness.

Early indications of a grand narrative design emerge in the two-part
story 'Aliens of London' (1.4) and 'World War Three' (1.5). An alien
spaceship crash landing in London reveals publicly the existence of alien
life. The unfolding saga is reported by television news bulletins – a
device that Davies would use frequently throughout his tenure as writer-
in-chief. In fact the crash turns out to be an elaborate hoax intended to
bring together all the world's leading experts on extra-terrestrials to a
conference at Downing Street in order to assassinate them and so clear the
way for the takeover of the government by the Slitheen. The Slitheen are
not a species but a criminal family, who disguise themselves as human by
inhabiting the skins of their victims. Their plan is to infiltrate the British
government and trigger a nuclear war in order 'to reduce the Earth to
molten slag and then sell it'. At the end of 'World War Three' a cover-up
by the media – the first instance in the series of a recurring theme of
the role of the mass media as an agency of social and political control –
writes the incident out of history. And with all the senior members of
the government killed by the Slitheen, Harriet Jones (Penelope Wilton),

the fussy MP for Flydale North, leads the task of reconstruction. Davies uses this to create an alternate political history of contemporary Britain that will inform later episodes of *Doctor Who*: 'I thought I knew the name! Harriet Jones. Future prime minister. Elected for three successive terms, the architect of Britain's golden age.' 'Boom Town' (1.11) is a direct sequel in which the Doctor, Rose and Captain Jack track down the surviving Slitheen to Cardiff, where she has assumed the guise of mayor Margaret Blaine and plans to build a nuclear reactor in the city centre, knowing that the release of energy from the rift will cause a catastrophic meltdown.

Robert Shearman's 'Dalek' (1.6) is the pivotal episode of Series One. Responding to an alien distress signal, the TARDIS materialises in an underground bunker in Utah, in 2012, where billionaire Henry Van Statten has built a private museum of extra-terrestrial artefacts. These include the arm of a Slitheen and the head of a Cyberman ('The stuff of nightmares reduced to an exhibit,' the Doctor muses). Shearman's script posits a secret history where all the major technological developments of the recent past have been based on technology cannibalised from crashed alien ships: broadband Internet, for example, is derived from the Roswell flying saucer. However, Van Statten has one living specimen, a damaged and largely immobilised Dalek that has fallen through time and space and was discovered in the South Pacific. 'Dalek' interprets the antagonism between the Doctor and his oldest enemy as a psychological drama of war guilt and racial hatred. The Doctor, overcoming his initial fear, reveals a pathological hatred of the Daleks (Eccleston literally spits out the word 'Dalek!'), delights in taunting the impotent creature ('Look at you – the great space dustbin! If you can't kill, then what are you good for – Dalek?') and boasts that he helped to bring about the destruction of the Daleks during the Time War ('I watched it happen! I made it happen!'). The Dalek, for its part, realises that it and the Doctor are both the last of their kind ('I am alone in the universe. So are you. We are the same') and accuses the Doctor of cowardice because he survived when the rest of the Time Lords were destroyed. The Doctor's bitter and deep-rooted hatred of the Dalek is contrasted with Rose, who, having never encountered a Dalek before, feels sympathy for it when it is being tortured by Van Statten's engineers who try to penetrate its casing with drills. Rose touches the Dalek's casing, whereupon it absorbs her DNA to initiate cellular reconstruction. Consequently the Dalek breaks free, restores its power, and proceeds to follow its natural instinct to exterminate everyone in sight.

The principal achievement of 'Dalek' is that it successfully restores the classic *Who* monster as a formidable, thoroughly nasty and genuinely menacing antagonist. The Dalek design is essentially the same as in the classic series, but now it looks like an armoured fighting machine rather than a flimsy fibreglass shell: the image of this lone Dalek undamaged by the combined firepower of an entire SWAT team illustrates perfectly the apparent impregnability of the Doctor's deadliest foe. It is also able to levitate: thus rendering stairs rather less useful as an escape route.[46] The Doctor calls it 'the ultimate in racial cleansing' – a familiar idea explained for a new generation of viewers – and for a while the creature seems unstoppable as it embarks upon a ruthless killing spree. However, the Dalek has been 'contaminated' by its contact with human DNA, which causes it to start to feel compassion – an emotion it is unable to understand. There are parallels here with a *Star Trek: The Next Generation* episode 'I, Borg' in which a captured Borg drone is imbued with a sense of individuality, though 'Dalek' does not in the end offer the possibility of humanising the creature. Instead the Dalek starts to hate itself for having become, in its eyes, racially impure: its self-loathing finally causes it to destroy itself ('This is not life. This is sickness. I shall not be like you').

The narrative of alien intervention in human affairs is developed in Davies's linked stories 'The Long Game' (1.7) and 'Bad Wolf' (1.12). In 'The Long Game' the TARDIS materialises on an orbiting space station in the year 200,000 at what should be the zenith of 'the Fourth Great and Bountiful Human Empire – planet Earth at its height'. Satellite Five is a television satellite broadcasting 600 news channels throughout the empire – but the news is controlled by the mysterious Editor whose aim is 'to prevent mankind from ever developing'. To this end 'The Long Game' rehearses debates over the control of the media and the abuse of corporate power. The Editor himself turns out to be the servant of a creature known as the Mighty Jagrafess of the Holy Hadrojassic Maxarodenfoe, which has taken over Satellite Five and has used its control of the media to retard mankind's social and political development. The topicality of this story is readily apparent at a time when there were 1,500 satellite, digital and cable television channels in Western Europe and when ownership of the broadcast media was increasingly vested in a handful of transnational media conglomerates, such as Time Warner, Viacom and

News International. The Communications Act of 2003, moreover, was seen by some media analysts as paving the way for the possible future sale of the ITV network to one of those conglomerates. 'The Long Game', therefore, is a commentary on the institutional and cultural contexts of the television industry that produced *Doctor Who*.

'Bad Wolf' is yet more explicit in its satirical critique of the culture of broadcasting. The Doctor and his companions return to Satellite Five a century later and find that events have again taken a disturbing turn. Bereft of news programmes following the destruction of the Jagrafess (for which the Doctor was responsible), the satellite, now known as the Game Station, is broadcasting nothing but grotesque parodies of light entertainment programmes where contestants who fail are (apparently) disintegrated. Thus the Doctor finds himself a guest in the *Big Brother* house, Rose faces the prospect of disintegration as the weakest link and Captain Jack is about to be dismembered by two fashion-guru robots. The episode is a satire of the entertainment shows *Big Brother* ('reality TV'), *The Weakest Link* (a popular quiz show) and *What Not To Wear* (one of the then voguish 'makeover shows'). It is perhaps an indication of the prestige attached to *Doctor Who* that the producers and presenters of all these shows were complicit in the process: *Big Brother* presenter Davina McCall, *Weakest Link* host Anne Robinson and fashion 'experts' Trinny Woodall and Susannah Constantine all voiced their android equivalents. It was the proliferation of programmes such as these that brought accusations of the 'dumbing down' of television – though of course this was nothing new as much the same criticism had been made ever since the launch of ITV in 1955.

'The Parting of the Ways' (1.13) completes the story arc, providing a resounding action climax as well as tying together the various narrative threads. The Daleks – revealed at the end of 'Bad Wolf' as the malign influence secretly manipulating human history – prepare to launch a full-scale invasion of the Earth. It is revealed that the Daleks survived the Time War through the agency of the Emperor Dalek who escaped the Doctor's 'inferno' and has been cultivating a new race of Daleks bred from 'the waste of humanity'. The Emperor's description of the 'harvest' is consciously redolent of industrial mass slaughter: 'The bodies were filleted, pulped, sifted. The seed of the human race was perverted – only one cell in a billion was fit to be nurtured.' Davies creates a new mythology for *Doctor Who* in suggesting that the Emperor Dalek thinks he has become a deity ('I am the God of all Daleks!') and that the others worship him to such a degree that they will not tolerate blasphemy ('Since when did the Daleks have a concept of blasphemy?' asks an incredulous Doctor). In this context the desperate battle between the human defenders of Satellite Five and the invading Dalek army becomes an epic confrontation between the forces of Good and Evil characterised by their entirely different belief and value systems. The Daleks no longer function just as a historical allegory of Nazism: their racial hatred of everything else and their genocidal urges clearly have contemporary resonances in the wake of 'ethnic cleansing' in Rwanda and Kosovo, while their ideological commitment to an apocalyptic war against humanity (for which read liberal democracy) might be equated with terrorist extremism.

The resolution of 'The Parting of the Ways' provoked controversy in some quarters of *Doctor Who* fandom for its resort to a *deus ex machina* (literally 'God in the machine') plot device. The Doctor, surrounded by Daleks and facing certain death, is rescued by the sudden reappearance of Rose, whom he had sent back to her own time on a pre-arranged programme in the TARDIS. Rose, determined to save the Doctor, has accidentally looked into something called the Time Vortex in the heart of the TARDIS. This has imbued her with what amounts to divine power, including the power over life and death. It turns out that Rose herself is the 'Bad Wolf' and has scattered the words (Bad Wolf Corporation is the name of the company that runs Satellite Five) throughout time and space in order to bring herself to this moment. Her power is such that she simply wishes the Daleks out of existence ('I can see the whole of time and space, every single atom of your existence, and I divide them') and even resurrects the slain Jack Harkness. It is a moment of high drama – enhanced by the epic orchestral music of Murray Gold – but it was regarded by many fans as a cheat because such *deus ex machina* moments are supposedly outside the scriptwriting practices of *Doctor Who*. It has been argued that the device – which Davies would employ again in later series – 'suggests a tongue-in-cheek awareness by Davies of the storytelling *faux pas* he was committing and that the use of the device was a conscious decision rather than an oversight'.[47]

The immediate popular success of *Doctor Who* was such that the commissioning of a second series and a Christmas special was announced only days after the broadcast of the first episode.[48] That the next series would be without Christopher Eccleston had already become public knowledge, so the 'surprise' regeneration scene at the end of 'The Parting of the Ways' was in fact widely expected. The news of Eccleston's departure had provoked something of a backlash – the popular online forum *Outpost Gallifrey* was even suspended for a while until the storm of protest as fans vented their anger subsided – and the BBC attempted to repair the damage by insisting that it had always been planned that the actor would make only the one series of *Doctor Who*.[49] Davies was upset with the way in which the news was leaked and blamed the policy of 'openness' at the BBC for revealing the 'spoiler': 'That's why the leak about Christopher Eccleston leaving could not be plugged. Once asked by *The Mirror*, Jane Tranter [Controller of Drama Commissioning] could not deny it. Even though it ruined the surprise cliffhanger to Series One . . . It's all still the consequences of the Hutton Inquiry.'[50] (The Hutton Inquiry had investigated the BBC following a controversial report by Radio 4's *Today* programme that the government of Tony Blair had 'sexed up' its dossier on Saddam Hussein's 'weapons of mass destruction' in order to justify British participation in the US-led invasion of Iraq in 2003: the inquiry was highly critical of the BBC but later events have proved the original report was substantially correct.) David Tennant was quickly confirmed as the new 'Doctor Who' before bookmaker William Hill had even been able to lay odds on possible successors. Nevertheless, Eccleston has one of the series' best exit lines, which might also stand as a verdict on the 2005 series as a whole: 'Rose, before I go, I just want to tell you – you were fantastic! Absolutely fantastic! And you know what? So was I.'

10

Love and Monsters

2006–2009

I'm the Doctor – and I've just snogged Madame de Pompadour!

The Doctor (David Tennant) in 'The Girl in the Fireplace'

The immediate success of new *Doctor Who* – two further series were confirmed before the first had finished, and a spin-off entitled *Torch-wood* was in development by the year's end – was nothing if not an unalloyed triumph for the BBC Wales production team. Matt Hills contends that 'the "Russell T. Davies era" must surely be counted, by fans, critics and scholar-fans alike, as a golden age for the series'.[1] The 'golden age' label places this 'era' of *Doctor Who* on a par with the Letts–Dicks and Hinchcliffe–Holmes periods: not since the 1970s had *Doctor Who* enjoyed a period of such sustained popularity and cultural visibility. It received critical acclaim with an award from BAFTA (the British Academy of Film and Television Arts) for Best Drama Series of 2005 and won the accolade of Most Popular Drama Series at the National Television Awards – voted for by the general public – for five consecutive years from 2005 to 2009. Viewing figures remained consistent, with consolidated averages of 7.9 million for Series Two (2006), 7.6 million for Series Three (2007) and 8 million for Series Four (2008), while some individual episodes, including the fourth-series finale 'Journey's End' and several of the Christmas specials, drew audiences over 10 million.[2] *Doctor Who* was not only back on television: it was back to stay.

It can legitimately be argued that, even more than the 'Dalekmania' of the mid 1960s, the 'Whomania' of the 2000s marked the zenith of

Doctor Who's success both as a television series and as a 'brand'. As Davies told *DWM* in 2006: 'In a business sense – and we don't often get a chance to talk about it as a business – it's achieved the most important thing for its longevity: it's re-established itself as a brand, just as everything tilts towards a new media world.'[3] The ambition to relaunch *Doctor Who* as the engine for a multi-media franchise saw fruition with innovations such as new online adventures and 'Tardisodes' (short fictions that could be downloaded onto mobile phones) to supplement the television episodes. From 2005 ('The Christmas Invasion' introducing David Tennant as the Tenth Doctor) the *Doctor Who* seasonal special became an integral part of BBC1's Christmas Day schedule. The best indication of the success of the franchise was the launch of two fully-fledged spin-off series, *Torchwood* and *The Sarah Jane Adventures*, which each built upon the popularity of *Doctor Who* while at the same time establishing their own fan bases. For a while British television seemed saturated by *Doctor Who*: the height was reached during the Christmas and New Year period in 2006–2007 which in the space of one week saw the second *Doctor Who* Christmas special ('The Runaway Bride'), the final two episodes of the first series of *Torchwood* and the premiere episode of *The Sarah Jane Adventures* ('Invasion of the Bane'). And it was not only in Britain that *Doctor Who* was so visible. The new series was sold to over 50 countries – including Australia, Canada, India, Hong Kong, Japan, Brazil, Chile, Colombia, the United Arab Emirates and much of Europe – and established itself as one of BBC Worldwide's three 'global brands' alongside *Top Gear* and *Planet Earth*.[4]

The consistent popularity of *Doctor Who* throughout this period was a reflection of a production team confident about its formula and in tune with the tastes of its audiences. An indication of the BBC's confidence in its 'new' hit series was that a purpose-built new drama studio was opened at Upper Boat, Pontypridd, specifically for *Doctor Who*.[5] This facility would also serve as the production base for both *Torchwood* and *The Sarah Jane Adventures*. Davies remained the major creative influence as *Doctor Who*'s 'showrunner'. The extent of his involvement is seen in the fact that he wrote 31 of the 60 episodes between 'Rose' (1.1) and 'The End of Time Part 2' (4.18), whereas the next most prolific contributor during this period, Steven Moffat, wrote six.[6] While Moffat was the heir apparent as showrunner, this period was very much Davies's 'era' of *Doctor Who* and he implanted his imprimatur on it at every level, from scripts and casting to publicity and press releases.

It is evident that, following the success of the 2005 series, Davies was laying down a long-term strategy for *Doctor Who* to ensure its future. He was concerned that the series did not become stale but remained fresh in the eyes of audiences. And it is clear that he also gave thought to what might be termed succession planning. His published correspondence with journalist Ben Cook throughout the pre-production and shooting of Series Four demonstrates the extent of this forward planning. In an email of 31 May 2007, for example, Davies wrote:

> The plan for 2009 and beyond? Well . . . we'll transmit Series Four next year, then a 2008 Christmas Special, and then two hour-long Specials in 2009, most likely Easter and Christmas Day. Then a third Special in 2010 should segue into a brand new Series Five, with a new production team. We've planned this for ages . . . The show, by 2009, will simply need a rest. We need to starve people a bit. We're producing 14 movie-sized episodes a year, which are then repeated ad infinitum, and ratings are bound to decline, even just a little. *Doctor Who* is a phenomenon right now, but nothing stays a phenomenon. Not without careful management. People need to be begging for new *Doctor Who*, instead of just expecting it.[7]

This was indeed what happened: after four series between 2005 and 2008 *Doctor Who* took a partial hiatus during 2009 (in the event there would be four specials between Easter 2009 and New Year's Day 2010) before returning with a full new series in 2010.

An important factor in ensuring the long-term success of *Doctor Who* was stability at the level of production. The same core production team – series producer Phil Collinson and executive producers Davies and Julie Gardner – remained at the helm until the end of Series Four, when Collinson left to take over *Coronation Street.* Another reason for the stability of *Doctor Who* was that the pool of writers during this period was relatively small. Davies, rather like Graham Williams in the late 1970s, found it difficult to find writers who understood the unique nature of *Doctor Who.* There were new commissions for Steven Moffat, Mark Gatiss and Paul Cornell. Otherwise Davies either followed the tried and tested strategy of recruiting writers from the world of *Doctor Who* fandom – including Gareth Roberts ('The Shakespeare Code', 'The Unicorn and the Wasp' and co-author of 'Planet of the Dead') and Matt Jones ('The Impossible Planet'/'The Satan Pit') – or promoting writers who, while not necessarily 'Whovians' themselves, had worked on

Doctor Who in some capacity, such as script editor Helen Raynor, who wrote the two-part Dalek story for Series Three and the equivalent Sontaran story for Series Four, and Chris Chibnall ('42'), co-producer of its spin-off *Torchwood*.[8] The new writers brought in from outside *Doctor Who* tended to have experience of creating their own programmes: Toby Whithouse ('School Reunion') with *No Angels* and *Being Human*, Matthew Graham ('Fear Her') with *The Last Train* and *Life on Mars*, and Stephen Greenhorn ('The Lazarus Experiment', 'The Doctor's Daughter') with *River Cut* (a regional soap opera for BBC Scotland). James Moran ('The Fires of Pompeii') had written the British horror film *Severance*, while Keith Temple ('Planet of the Ood') was an experienced television hand with many episodes of *Emmerdale* and *Casualty* under his belt.

This is not to say that scripting *Doctor Who* was a straightforward process. Davies admitted to frequently extensive rewriting of others' scripts, telling *DWM*: 'People with huge drama reputations such as Steven Moffat and Matthew Graham, you wouldn't dream of rewriting, and they would come on board with that proviso. The other writers have significantly less experience of writing drama than me, and I am a full showrunner in the true American sense of rewriting the scripts – sometimes to a lesser extent, sometimes to a huge extent, whatever I think is necessary to get the programme up to scratch.'[9] There is evidence that, behind the scenes, Davies was frustrated by the limitations of some writers. On one occasion he told Cook: 'I just got an email from A. N. Other Writer. Having trouble with the "basic linear causality" of an episode. *Basic linear causality?* Do you see the crap that writers talk?'[10] And following the broadcast of 'Human Nature', he confided: 'I had a whole Sunday of people saying "That was brilliant", and specifically "What a brilliant script. Paul Cornell is a genius." Which he is. But I'm thinking, if only you knew how much of that I wrote!'[11] For Series Four Davies had to write an additional script when one did not work out:

> I admitted to Julie today that Tom MacRae's Episode 8 simply isn't right. Tom's script is good, and we could make it great, but I don't think it can ever be great enough. This is entirely my fault: I don't like the concepts I gave him . . . I'm left with the prospect of having to write a replacement script myself. But I've no time. I'd have about three days![12]

In the event Davies did produce the extra script, 'Midnight', in the process altering the order of broadcast for Series Four. 'Midnight' was what is known as a 'bottle episode': one written with an eye to economical production with a small cast and few special effects.

The expense of *Doctor Who* became a matter of some speculation. It was reported in the press that the series was under pressure to reduce costs – the BBC licence fee was under intense scrutiny during these years – and it was even suggested that the reason for Christopher Eccleston leaving the series was that his salary demands had been too expensive to sustain.[13] These stories were ill-informed. It is correct, certainly, that the *Doctor Who* production team was concerned to economise where it could without compromising the quality of the series. Accordingly each series was planned with one or two lower-cost episodes such as 'Love & Monsters' (2.10), 'Fear Her' (2.11), 'Blink' (3.10), 'Midnight' (4.10) and 'Turn Left' (4.11). And a recurring theme of the email correspondence between Davies and Cook is the need to reduce the number of 'SFX days' per episode.[14] Oddly enough, the pressures on the budget were not always down to expensive special effects. Davies explained how such a mundane matter as the logistics of location shooting affected the scripting of 'Partners in Crime' (4.1): 'We can afford the stunt, the Adipose, the End of the Sodding World, but not that confrontation scene. (The reasons are too dull to go into. It involves the number of nights – just one, apparently – for which we can afford a crane and an actual cradle, as opposed to the cradle that we'll build in the studio for the stunt sequence against the green screen.)'[15] But the BBC was keen to support what had become one of its flagship programmes, and, while there was never a blank cheque as such, *Doctor Who* was evidently afforded a considerable degree of latitude. When Davies struggled to compress the script of 'Journey's End' (4.13) into 45 minutes, for example, a solution was quickly forthcoming: 'Julie read it, loved it, phoned Jane [Tranter] and got instant authorisation for a 60-minute Special! It's not that simple, of course – Julie now needs to find funding and contract Graeme [Harper] and all departments and the actors for another week . . . What support, though. Amazing.'[16]

A crucial factor in the success of *Doctor Who* during this period was the casting of David Tennant as Doctor No. 10. The adverse reaction in some quarters of *Doctor Who* fandom to Eccleston's departure after just the one series made it all the more desirable that his successor should stay the course. The 34-year-old Tennant proved a popular choice, not least because he was a self-confessed *Doctor Who* addict, impressing fans from the outset with his genuine enthusiasm for the role and his knowledge of the series' history. Tennant would play the Doctor in 47 episodes of *Doctor Who* – and in addition two *Children in Need* shorts, two episodes of *The Sarah Jane Adventures* and voiced the animated adventures 'The Infinite Quest' and 'Dreamland' – and in the process established himself so definitively in the role that he even surpassed Tom Baker as the favourite Doctor of *DWM*'s readers.[17] Unlike Eccleston, whose reputation was built on his work in film and television, Tennant was more associated with the stage, having performed at the Royal Shakespeare Company where he had played Romeo, Lysander (*A Midsummer Night's Dream*) and Edgar/Poor Tom (*King Lear*). His much-publicised (and critically acclaimed) starring role in the RSC production of *Hamlet*, at Stratford-upon-Avon in 2008, was one of the most successful in the company's history.[18] At the time of his casting in *Doctor Who*, Tennant was on the cusp of stardom following the police drama *Blackpool* (2004) and Davies's *Casanova* (2005), as well as playing the role of Barty Crouch in *Harry Potter and the Goblet of Fire* (dir. Mike Newell, 2005).

Tennant's Tenth Doctor represents yet another variation on the Britishness of *Doctor Who*. In contrast to Eccleston's austere look, Tennant's pinstripe suit and trainers embody a hybrid smart/shabby look in line with the voguish fashion styles known as 'business casual' or 'dress-down Friday', while in contrast to Eccleston's pronounced northernness his broadly 'estuary' accent is less class-specific. (Tennant had originally wanted to play the Doctor with his natural soft Scottish accent, but this was reportedly vetoed by Davies on the grounds that he did not want the Doctor to be seen as 'touring the regions'.)[19] Tennant is a Doctor for the X-Box and iPod generation: he lacks the patrician authority of previous incumbents (it is impossible to imagine William Hartnell or Jon Pertwee shouting 'perfectomundo!') but he is thoroughly versed in popular culture (he refers to *The Lion King*, *Scooby Doo*, *Ghostbusters*, *Harry Potter* and *Monty Python's Big Red Book* among many others). One of the reasons for Tennant's popularity, especially with younger viewers, is that his Doctor employs the same terms of reference as they do: 'How to explain the mechanics of the infinite temporal flux? I know – it's like *Back to the Future*!' ('The Shakespeare Code'). And he is also a much more touchy-feely Doctor than previous incumbents: except for the cast's photo-calls there had never been this much hugging in classic *Doctor Who*.

Tennant was the first star of *Doctor Who* whose sex appeal was integral to the series. Although Tennant described himself as a 'skinny, gawky freak boy' – a quotation that found its way into the series where companion Donna Noble calls him 'skinny boy' – this was not reflected in the response of female journalists such as Caitlin Moran of *The Times*, whose review of his debut in 'The Christmas Invasion' was entitled simply 'Timephwoard'.[20] Tennant's sexiness is not the beefcake masculinity of Hollywood action stars, but rather a sort of 'geek chic' that combines intelligence and boyish charm. Another female critic described Tennant's Doctor as 'an entirely new kind of sex symbol, redefining sexy for the noughties, for a more technologically savvy, liberal, free thinking generation . . . like Professor Brian Cox, but with better hair and a sexier voice'.[21] Whereas, in the past, it was the female companion who had provided the sex appeal, now it is the Doctor himself who is objectified. Thus Lady Cassandra finds him 'slim and just a little bit foxy' ('New Earth'), the Wire thinks 'this one is tasty – I'll have lashings of him!' ('The Idiot's Lantern'), and the returning Captain Jack Harkness remarks 'this new regeneration [is] kinda cheeky' ('Utopia').

Tennant's romantic image – no doubt boosted by playing the Great Lover himself in *Casanova* – suited Davies's intention of writing more emotionality into *Doctor Who*. Thus, for the first time we see the Doctor falling in love: with Madame de Pompadour in eighteenth-century France ('The Girl in the Fireplace') and with Edwardian school nurse Joan Redfern ('Human Nature'/'The Family of Blood'). The Doctor, in turn, is the object of Martha Jones's unrequited love in Series Three – another instance of the 'soap opera' sensibility that Davies had brought to *Doctor Who*. The romantic element is most fully explored in the development of the relationship between the Doctor and Rose. It is tempting to draw a parallel with Davies's previous *Bob & Rose* (the female protagonist's name may or may not be coincidental) which examines the love affair between a gay man and his female best friend: the relationship between the Doctor and Rose similarly grows from close friendship to romantic attraction. Agonisingly the Doctor loses Rose twice: first at the end of Series Two – when she is trapped in a parallel universe after declaring her love for him ('Doomsday'); and again at the end of Series Four ('Journey's End') when – Rose having travelled across universes to be reunited with him – the Doctor leaves her with a human doppelgänger of himself.

These years saw the development of a new mythology for the Doctor that was ideally suited to Tennant's performance. The Doctor is elevated to mythical status as a defender and champion of the Earth. In Tennant's introductory episode 'The Christmas Invasion' (2.X), for example, he sees off the Sycorax – assuming the uncharacteristic role of action hero in the process – with the warning: 'And when you go back to the stars and tell others of this planet, when you tell them of its riches, its people, its potential, when you talk of the Earth, then make sure that you tell them this: It is defended.' And in 'Last of the Time Lords' (3.13), when the human race has been subjugated by the regenerated Master whose Toclafane allies have decimated the world's population, and the Doctor himself has been incapacitated, his companion Martha Jones travels the world as a resistance fighter spreading the legend of the Doctor: 'There's someone else. The man who sent me out there. The man who told me to walk the Earth. His name is the Doctor. He's saved your lives so many times and you never even knew he was there. He never stops, he never stays, he never asks to be thanked. But I've seen him. I know him. I love him. And I know what he can do.'

One commentator noted a 'worrying trend' in the tendency of *Doctor Who* 'to cast the tenth Doctor . . . as a messianic hero'.[22] In some stories he is characterised in terms that invoke – both visually and narratively – the story of Christ. The regeneration sequence at the end of 'The Parting of the Ways' and the partial regeneration of 'Journey's End' (wherein the Doctor uses the regeneration energy to heal himself following a Dalek blast) seem to mimic the Crucifiction as the Doctor stands with his arms spread in a cruciform pose. In 'Voyage the Damned' (4.X) he is carried aloft by angelic-visaged robots known as 'heavenly hosts'. 'Gridlock' (3.3) explicitly presents the Doctor as a messiah figure whose coming has been 'waited for . . . these many years'. He heals the sick ('New Earth'), shares bread with the poor ('Daleks in Manhattan') and even has his own cult of devoted followers who regard him with awe and seek to spread his message ('Love & Monsters'). The presence of the Devil is invoked in 'The Impossible Planet' and 'The Satan Pit' (2.8–2.9) in which it is prophesied that 'the beast and his armies shall rise from the pit to make war against God'. And in 'Last of the Time Lords' the Doctor is quite literally resurrected through the power of prayer. He has been reduced to a Golem-like creature by the Master's genetic manipulation device and imprisoned in a cage. But – thanks to Martha travelling the world spreading word of the Doctor like a latter-day St Paul, and another one of Davies's *deus ex machina* plot devices – he is restored to his normal state when all the people of the world chant his name in unison. The Doctor's resurrection is accompanied by that most Christian of values: forgiveness. He holds the Master in his arms and whispers: 'I forgive you.' Davies, an atheist, nevertheless acknowledged: 'The series lends itself to religious iconography because the Doctor is a proper saviour. He saves the world through the power of his mind and his passion.'[23]

This is not to suggest, however, that *Doctor Who* was consciously being used for the promotion of a Christian world view. The prominence of Christian imagery and symbolism is as much a reflection of the extent to which they are embedded in Western culture as evidence of an authorial agenda. (This is also the case with *Torchwood*, which features an abudance of Christian motifs but which espouses a much more pessimistic world view than *Doctor Who*.) Moreover, the messianic Doctor is just one motif of the Tenth Doctor stories and far from the only one. Another tendency – and probably the dominant trend overall – is to cast the Doctor in the role of a tragic hero. He remains a lonely, isolated figure – 'the last of the Time Lords' – despite the presence of companions. Madame de Pompadour sees into his mind and calls him 'my lonely Doctor . . . Doctor Who?' ('The Girl in the Fireplace'). The story arc of Series Three is partly based around a cryptic message to the Doctor from the Face of Boe – the oldest creature in the universe – telling him that 'You are not alone' ('Gridlock'). The theme of loss pervades the Tenth Doctor stories. Encountering the Daleks in 1930s New York, for instance, he is dismayed to find that his oldest enemies have once again escaped destruction: 'They survived! They always survive, while I lose everything!' ('Daleks in Manhattan'). It takes Davros (of all people!) to bring home to the Doctor 'how many have died in your name' with a montage of all the characters who have lost their lives while helping him ('Journey's End'). One critic has suggested that this period of *Doctor Who* is characterised by 'the immediacy of the emotional and the classically tragic grief and isolation of the epic'.[24]

It almost became a cliché of Davies-scripted *Doctor Who* that each series would end with an emotional 'goodbye' sequence between the Doctor and his companion. There had been instances of this in classic *Who* – the departure of Jo Grant at the end of 'The Green Death' is perhaps the best example – but Davies would return to it time and again.

These character-based scenes serve as a dramatic counterweight to the spectacular action climaxes of the series finales in which the fate of the Earth or even the universe as a whole is at stake. The first (and best) of these moments is the ending of 'Doomsday' where the Doctor projects a holographic image of himself into the parallel universe where Rose is trapped, in order to say goodbye properly: she tells him 'I love you' but the projection is cut off before he can reply. Davies explained the impact of the scene thus: 'When the Doctor and Rose were separated into parallel universes at the end of "Doomsday", that felt like every love you've ever lost – even if it's only the ones that you've lost in your head, like teenage virgins pining over love songs in their bedroom.'[25]

For Davies, the investing of emotionality into *Doctor Who* was essential to its success as drama. It would be fair to say that the real dramatic focus of Davies's *Doctor Who* was not so much the return of old monsters and villains – these included the Cybermen (Series Two), the Master (Series Three) and the Sontarans and Davros (Series Four) – but rather the relationship between the Doctor and his companions. This is at the heart of some of the best episodes. Toby Whithouse's 'School Reunion' (2.3), for example, is an exploration of the nature of love and friendship that suggests that the Doctor consciously distances himself from having any emotional involvement with his companions. 'School Reunion' is a vehicle for the return of Sarah Jane Smith (again played by Elisabeth Sladen) and is the first new episode to refer explicitly to the memory of classic *Doctor Who*. Sarah Jane's initial joy at meeting the Doctor again 30 years after their parting ('You've regenerated!') is followed by resentment at what she regards as his dumping of her ('I thought you'd died! I waited for you. You didn't come back, and I thought you must have died!').[26] It is implied that Sarah Jane was in love with the Doctor and that he left her behind because of this. It is a bittersweet episode in that Sarah Jane accepts she is now too old to be a romantic partner for the younger Doctor ('You know you're getting older – your assistants are getting younger,' she remarks upon meeting Rose) but clearly still yearns for her old life of adventure. Rose, for her part, is worried that one day the Doctor will abandon her too as he did Sarah Jane. The Doctor tries to explain to Rose why he cannot form lasting relationships: 'I don't age. I regenerate. But humans decay. You wither and you die . . . You can spend the rest of your life with me, but I can't spend the rest of my life with you.'

The emphasis on emotionality accounts for the introduction of terms like 'character arc' and 'emotional journey' into the production discourse of *Doctor Who*. In scripting the Doctor's new companions Davies continued his 'soap' strategy of creating a life for them beyond the TARDIS that they will return to at the end of their time spent travelling with the Doctor. Both Martha Jones (Freema Agyeman) in Series Three and Donna Noble (Catherine Tate) in Series Four have families who feature prominently as a means of grounding their adventures in some sort of social reality. Martha is a medical student who meets the Doctor when the hospital where she works is transported to the Moon in 'Smith and Jones' (3.1). Martha is attracted to the Doctor but he does not notice: for much of the time he is still grieving over the loss of Rose. As Martha does not become a romantic interest for the Doctor, her role is closer to the companions of classic *Doctor Who*: she is granted little narrative agency in her own right until her world-saving role in 'Last of the Time Lords'. At the end of the series Martha decides to resume her studies rather than continue travelling with the Doctor: she explains this by talking about her friend, Vicky, who was in love with her housemate and 'wasted years pining after him . . . because while he was around she never looked at anyone else. And I told her, time and time again, I told her: "Get out." So this is me – getting out.'

The most developed companion 'character arc' is perhaps that of Donna Noble in Series Four. Donna – introduced in the 2006 Christmas special 'The Runaway Bride' and now returning as a fully-fledged companion – is older than both Rose and Martha and much less in awe of the Doctor. Their relationship is friendly rather than romantic: a recurring joke of Series Four is that they constantly have to explain they are not a married couple. Tate was best known as a comedy performer, and her scenes with Tennant recall the bantering nature of the Tom Baker–Lalla Ward partnership in classic *Who*. She is characterised in terms that constantly emphasise her ordinariness ('I'm just a temp from Chiswick') and who believes that 'I'm no one special'. Yet Donna is not only allowed space to develop as a character – her initially shrill, abrasive, insecure personality gives way to a more mature, compassionate and confident Donna – she is also afforded much greater narrative agency than either Martha or even Rose (at least until Rose's return as a Dalek-blasting action heroine with a Very Big Gun in 'The Stolen Earth'). The notion that various time lines converge around Donna is demonstrated when her encounter with a 'time beetle' in 'Turn Left' creates an entire parallel universe around her. And in 'Journey's End' Donna becomes 'the most important woman in the whole wide universe' when she acquires all the Doctor's knowledge and skills due to a 'human–Time Lord biological meta-crisis' – yet another one of Davies's *deus ex machina* plot devices – though she is denied a happy ending when the Doctor is obliged to wipe her memory to prevent a mental breakdown. It is an ending characterised both by its sadness (on an emotional level) and its conservatism (at the level of gender politics): even twenty-first century *Doctor Who* does not have space for female intelligence equal to the Doctor.

Paul Cornell's much-admired 'Human Nature' and 'The Family of Blood' (3.8–3.9) – which he adapted from his Seventh Doctor novel *Human Nature* for the 'New Adventures' – marks the fullest extent of the introduction of emotionality into *Doctor Who*. Like the same writer's 'Father's Day', it is really a character-driven emotional drama that just happens to be an SF story. The Doctor is being hunted by an alien family who need to consume the bodies of others to survive and who believe they will live forever if they can take the body of a Time Lord. In order to hide – knowing that the Family of Blood have a limited life span and will simply die if they cannot get to him – the Doctor uses a device known as a chameleon arc to rewrite his own biology and turn himself into a human. In so doing he erases his memory and knowledge of his real identity: he leaves Martha with instructions on how to restore him to his real self once the danger has passed. Arriving in England, in 1913, the Doctor assumes the identity of schoolmaster John Smith and falls in love with widowed nurse Joan Redfern. This is the cause of much distress to Martha, posing as a maid ('He had to go and fall in love with a human – and it wasn't me!'). The arrival of the Family of Blood obliges Martha to tell an unbelieving John Smith who he really is. Smith is shocked that the Doctor's contingency plans did not envisage that he might form any sort of romantic attachment during his human existence ('Falling in love, that didn't occur to him? What sort of man is that?'). In the event, of course, John Smith does change back into the Doctor, though not before he has a dream in which he marries Joan and they raise a family together. This brief sequence develops an idea from the Tenth Doctor's (first) goodbye to Rose in 'Doomsday', when he refers to 'living your life, day after the day, the kind of life I can never have'.

Davies defended the introduction of 'adult' emotional drama into *Doctor Who* on the grounds that good drama would work for viewers of all ages:

> There's this great misconception that the Slitheen are for kids and episodes like 'Human Nature' and 'The Family of Blood' are for adults. In fact, adults can enjoy daft green monsters, and kids can appreciate emotional, grown-up drama. Pixar understands that perfectly. J. K. Rowling does. If kids are upset, then they're feeling something, and kids feel things vividly. The death of a goldfish is like the end of the world. It's keen, real and powerful for them. But that doesn't make it something to be avoided. If they can reach that state through fiction, well, they're actually experiencing something wonderful.[27]

The response of viewers to 'Human Nature' and 'The Family of Blood' – judged by the sample of letters published in *DWM* – confirmed Davies's assessment of its emotional impact. The story was appreciated by long-term *Doctor Who* fans ('without doubt the finest story ever put on screen in *Doctor Who* history!') and by younger viewers ('The episode "Human Nature" was amazing, it was really original, very different, a clever piece of writing').[28] Cornell's story came second in *DWM*'s Series Three poll, with one respondent calling it 'quality drama of the highest order', and another (male) viewer writing: 'I've never cried during an episode of *Doctor Who* before, but this was exceptionally moving.'[29]

This is not to say that *Doctor Who* had become a sort of science fiction equivalent of *Brief Encounter*. The Davies-supervised series of *Doctor Who* can be understood in terms of a contrast between the intimate and the epic, the personal and the public. It continued to offer all the action and spectacle that had characterised the series since its 2005 relaunch. Davies expanded the narrative scope of new *Doctor Who* with the first off-world adventures ('New Earth', 'The Impossible Planet'/'The Satan Pit') and the first locations outside Britain. 'Fires of Pompeii' (4.2) is notable for a particularly epic feel: it was shot partly at the Cinecittà Studios in Rome using sets left over from the HBO/BBC co-production *Rome* (2005–2007). And the landscapes for 'Planet of the Dead' (4.15) were shot in the desert outside Dubai rather than at Camber Sands. For the first time in its history, *Doctor Who* was able to suggest that alien invasions of the Earth were on a planetary scale and not confined solely to London and the Home Counties. 'Army of Ghosts' (2.12), for instance, has Cybermen stomping around in front of national landmarks including the Eiffel Tower and the Taj Mahal. This can again be seen as a statement of intent that *Doctor Who* was seeking to emulate end-of-the-world films such as *Independence Day* (dir. Roland Emmerich, 1996) and *Armageddon* (dir. Michael Bay, 1998) – albeit that the effects in *Doctor Who* are achieved on a smaller scale. However, Davies drew the line at destroying New York in 'The Stolen Earth' (4.12) on the grounds that 'it leaves heavy repercussions for the rest of *Doctor Who* history, because there's no reset button . . . Series Five is bound to have episodes set on modern-day Earth – and that might be hard to establish, because it'd be a very wounded world.'[30] It might also have been thought tasteless to have Daleks laying waste to the city so soon after the events of 9/11.

Davies continued the strategy of structuring each series of *Doctor Who* around a story arc, wherein narrative hooks are laid down throughout the series that build to a climax in the series' finale. These became more ambitious as the series progressed, including cross-overs with both *Torchwood* and *The Sarah Jane Adventures*. Consider, for example, Series Three of *Doctor Who*, which SF critic Graham Sleight describes as 'the most intricately constructed' of the Davies period.[31] The Series Three story arc weaves together several apparently unrelated incidents, including the Face of Boe's prophetic message 'You are not alone' ('Gridlock') and several references to a vaguely sinister politician called Harold Saxon – a name that also links to the 'Vote Saxon' posters that appear in later episodes of the first series of *Torchwood*. The return of Captain Jack Harkness also carries over from *Torchwood*. It is in 'Utopia' (3.11) that the seemingly disparate plot strands start to come together. At 'the end of the universe' the kindly Professor Yana – engaged in a project to try to save the last surviving humans by sending them to a mythical utopia – has a fob watch identical to the one that held the Doctor's chameleon arc in 'Human Nature'/'The Family of Blood'. Yana (whose surname of course is an acronym of 'You are not alone') is a Time Lord – and not any Time Lord, but none other than the Master himself ('The Professor was an invention – so perfect a disguise that I forgot who I am!'). His memory restored, Yana (Derek Jacobi) is transformed from benevolent philanthropist to malevolent psychopath. A regenerated Master (John Simm) travels back in time to contemporary Britain, where he assumes the identity of Harold Saxon, and – by planting subliminal messages in a mobile phone network – is elected Prime Minister. It is now revealed that the Master was behind a genetic research experiment earlier in the series ('The Lazarus Experiment') which has provided him with the technology to subject the Doctor to premature ageing ('The Sound of Drums'/'Last of the Time Lords'). The whole series is structured around a temporal paradox – for the Doctor and Martha the events of 'The Lazarus Experiment' happen before they meet Professor Yana and he turns into the Master – which Davies conveniently sidesteps by inventing a device known as a Paradox Machine. A final twist is the revelation that the Face of Boe – the oldest creature in the universe – is none other than 'immortal' Captain Jack towards the end of his life.[32]

A feature of each new series of *Doctor Who* became the reintroduction of an old monster. This can be seen as a strategy for building in 'event' episodes: the 'old monster' stories were usually placed in the first half of the series and were heavily publicised. Series Two, for example, saw the return of the Cybermen in Tom MacRae's 'Rise of the Cybermen' and 'The Age of Steel' (2.5–2.6). MacRae provides an entirely new origin story for the series' second-favourite monsters, set in a parallel universe where the Cybermen are the creation of crippled business tycoon John Lumic, whose agents are rounding up homeless people from the streets and implanting their brains into robotic suits. There are echoes of the *Terminator* films in the name of Lumic's Cybus Industries and of the *Avengers* episode 'The Cybernauts', which similarly featured a wheelchair-bound automation expert who seeks to conquer the world in the name of efficiency. The new series' Cybermen are equated with computer technology: Lumic calls them 'the ultimate upgrade' and the Cybermen themselves parody the language of Information Technology ('You are not compatible – you will be deleted'). The return of another old monster in 'The Sontaran Stratagem' and 'The Poison Sky' (4.4–4.5) was rather less successful. The Sontarans themselves no longer seem so frightening (a UNIT soldier contemptuously calls one of them 'Humpty Dumpty') and their performance of a Maori-style haka ('Sontar-ha! Sontar-ha!') before going into battle is an embarrassment. It is perhaps no surprise that they would soon cross-over into *The Sarah Jane Adventures*, where their childish resentment at being excluded from the Time War ('The finest war in history and we weren't allowed to be part of it!') seems more fitting.

The reintroduction of old monsters can also be seen as part of a strategy to keep faith with the world of *Doctor Who* fandom. Davies clearly enjoyed fuelling speculation about the series. On one occasion, for example, he advised *DWM* to avoid 'spoilers' – fandom's term for advance knowledge of plot details that might spoil the viewing experience – in television listings magazines: 'I guarantee, you'll wake up on a Saturday morning, feeling that essential *Doctor Who* Saturdayness, only to discover a little box next to the TV listings saying "The Doctor and Rose visit New Earth and discover the evil plans of the Macra".'[33] (This was actually a disguised spoiler: in Series Three the Doctor and Martha would visit New Earth and encounter the Macra in 'Gridlock'.) The trailers for Series Two included what seems to have been a deliberate piece of misdirection: a brief shot of guest star Anthony Head next to an office door that apparently says 'Master' prompted feverish speculation in online forums. In fact Head obscures part of the sign, which actually says 'Headmaster' ('School Reunion'). But this misdirection may have helped to disguise the major surprise of Series Two: the unannounced return of the Daleks at the end of 'Army of Ghosts'. This sets up a battle between Daleks and Cybermen in 'Doomsday', an example of what has come to be known as 'fanwank' – something included specifically to appeal to the world of fandom. For some of the more emotionally repressed fans, the outcome of the Daleks vs. Cybermen battle was more significant an event than Rose's departure in the same episode.[34]

The 'old monsters' stories nevertheless represent only a small number of *Doctor Who* episodes in the twenty-first century. Most of the new monsters differ from the classic series in that their ambitions are rarely territorial conquest alone (hence there has been – to date – no return for fan favourites such as the Ice Warriors or the Zygons), but rather the need for their species to survive. The Carrionites ('The Shakespeare Code') and the Pyrovars ('The Fires of Pompeii'), for example, have lost their home worlds and are seeking to establish themselves elsewhere. Other alien species, such as the Assoloth ('Fear Her') and the Adipose ('Partners in Crime'), do not have hostile intent but are trapped on the Earth and unaware that they are causing harm. The idea of creatures feeding off waste and pollution, such as the Nestene Consciousness (Series One's 'Rose') and the Macra ('Gridlock'), rehearses a theme that featured in several 1970s *Doctor Who* stories and had become topical again given the debate around climate change in the early twenty-first century. A recurring trope of new *Doctor Who* is parasitic species, such as the Weeping Angels ('Blink') and the Vashta Narada ('Silence in the Library'/'Forest of the Dead') who feed off the energy of others. The Weeping Angels are 'the only psychopaths in the universe to kill you nicely ... They just zap you into the past and let you live to death', while the Vashta Narada are 'the piranhas of the air – the shadows that melt the flesh'. These two monsters were both created by Steven Moffat, whose scripts have provided *Doctor Who* with some of its most frightening stories. Other episodes borrow from SF and horror cinema: the werewolf of 'Tooth and Claw' is a close relation of *An American Werewolf in London* (dir. John Landis, 1981), while *The Fly* (dir. David Cronenberg, 1986) is clearly the inspiration for the human mutation in 'The Lazarus Experiment'.

The politics of *Doctor Who* continue to reflect the liberal-progressive ethos that characterised the classic series. 'Planet of the Ood' (4.3), for example, makes an association between slavery and corporate capitalism. The Ood are a slave species (first introduced in 'The Impossible Planet'/'The Satan Pit' in Series Two) who seem content with their subservient status. In 'Planet of the Ood' the Doctor and Donna discover that the Ood are bred on farms and then lobotomised by the Ood Corporation which sells them as slaves ('Buy one new   now only 50 credits'). When several Ood exhibit symptoms of 'red eye', a condition that causes them to become violent, the corporation's solution is simply to slaughter them ('Kill the livestock – the classic Foot and Mouth solution from the olden days'). Where 'Planet of the Ood' differs from classic *Doctor Who* stories on similar lines, is that it is not the Doctor's intervention alone that frees the enslaved species but also the efforts of an undercover group, known as 'Friends of the Ood', who have spent years infiltrating the corporation to effect their freedom. For Una McCormick this is 'a rare acknowledgement in *Doctor Who* that substantive political change results more from years of dedicated work under duress than from the passing kindliness of strangers, toppling empires in a single night'.[35]

'The Doctor's Daughter' (4.6) is a variation on the conflict-resolution narrative. On the planet Messaline, a colony of humans have been fighting a generations-old war against a race of fish people called the Hath. The war has been raging 'longer than anyone can remember' and the human beings are using a technology of genetic replication to breed new soldiers who emerge as fully-developed adults. A tissue sample from the Doctor is fed into the progenation machine and creates a young adult female whom Donna christens 'Jenny' (from 'generated anomaly'). The Doctor is shocked that his 'daughter' exhibits a militaristic attitude, though under his influence she mellows. The warmonger Colonel Cobb imprisons the Doctor ('Don't think you can infect us with your pacifism!') but he is rescued by Jenny. In the meantime, Donna has worked out that the supposedly age-old war is in fact only seven days old: the combatants think it is longer because each new generation of genetically-bred soldiers has created its own history. The Doctor succeeds in bringing about a ceasefire: Jenny takes a bullet intended for him and apparently dies – though a coda reveals that she has been reborn and has taken off in a spaceship for adventures of her own. 'The Doctor's Daughter' is chiefly notable for the fact that Jenny is quite literally the Doctor's daughter: she is played by Peter Davison's daughter (and future wife of David Tennant) Georgia Moffet.

Another narrative template that features prominently in this period of *Doctor Who* – and one that was very much an invention of the new series – is what has come to be known as the 'celebrity historical'. The model for this was provided by the appearance of Charles Dickens (played by Dickens enthusiast and scholar Simon Callow) in 'The Unquiet Dead' in Series One. Each series would feature a similar story: the Doctor and Rose meet Queen Victoria ('Tooth and Claw'), the Doctor and Martha meet William Shakespeare ('The Shakespeare Code'), the Doctor and Donna meet Agatha Christie ('The Unicorn and the Wasp'). There are two points to make about these episodes. One is that Davies himself seems to have been less interested in the historical stories than in contemporary and futuristic stories: during his tenure as writer-in-chief, the only period episode he scripted was 'Tooth and Claw' (2.2). The other point is that the new series' representation of the past is very far removed from the seriousness and psychological realism of the early historical stories in classic *Doctor Who*. Instead, the model would seem to have been the film *Shakespeare in Love* (dir. John Madden, 1998), which treats the past with a postmodern playfulness. This is also the strategy adopted in the 'celebrity historicals', which are replete with anachronisms and non-sequiturs. Thus the past is interpreted through the lens of contemporary celebrity culture: Dickens ('You're not a *fan* are you?') and Shakespeare ('No autographs!') have grown tired of the cult of celebrity that surrounds them. In 'The Shakespeare Code' (3.2) and 'The Unicorn and the Wasp' (4.7) there is less interest in representing historical periods authentically than there is in working in references to Shakespeare's plays or Christie's books: in the former the Doctor quotes from *Hamlet* and *Macbeth* (thus implanting the poetry in Shakespeare's imagination), while in the latter the Doctor and Donna even keep a tally of how many Christie titles are name-checked. And in 'Tooth and Claw' Rose spends most of the episode trying to prompt Queen Victoria into saying 'We are not amused!' In these episodes, journeys into the past are represented rather like visits to a theme park: even the spectacular CGI landscape of Elizabethan London in 'The Shakespeare Code' seems artificial in contrast to the scenes shot on location in the Globe Theatre – itself a recreation of the original rather than an authentic location.[36]

An exception to this largely inauthentic and parodic view of the past is Paul Cornell's aforementioned 'Human Nature' and 'The Family of Blood', which is notable for its attempt to provide a critical examination of the past rather than treating it anachronistically. We have already seen how this story is essentially an existential exploration of what it is to be human: but Cornell also uses the setting – a minor English public school in 1913 – to examine the social values of the time. It is significant, for example, that this is the only occasion in Series Three when Martha's ethnicity is an issue: as a black woman she is treated as second class by the supercilious public schoolboys, and even a sympathetic character like Joan Redfern expresses the views of the time ('Women *might* train to be doctors, but hardly a scivvy and hardly one of your colour'). In particular, Cornell focuses on the role of the public schools in promoting patriotism and imperialism to the boys of England. Interestingly, it is more sympathetic to the public school system and its values than might be expected in a series characterised for the most part by its liberalism and progressive social politics. In fact, the story rehearses both sides of the debate. Thus the headmaster's assertion of the value of the school cadet system in instructing the boys in military values ('I hope, Latimer, that one day you may have a just and proper war in which to prove yourself') is contrasted with the foreknowledge of the horrors of the Great War by the time-travelling Family of Blood ('War is coming, in foreign fields, war of the whole wide world, with all your boys falling down in the mud. Do you think they will thank the man who taught them it was glorious?'). The ethos of the public schools, so often derided today, is seen as a force for good ('This school teaches us to stand to-gether!'), and the boys' cadet training proves useful when they are called upon to defend the school against an army of living scarecrows. A slow-motion sequence of the scarecrows being mown down by machine-gun and rifle fire is clearly meant to represent the slaughter of the Western Front. The conclusion is beautifully judged. A sensitive boy called Tim Latimer, who has befriended the Doctor and whose 'low-level tele-pathic field' has allowed him some insight into the future, arrives to say goodbye:

> *Tim*:   I've seen the future and I now know what must be done. It's
>   coming, isn't it? The biggest war ever.
>
> *Martha*: You don't have to fight.
>
> *Tim*:   I think we do.

This insistence on understanding the past on its own terms rather than imposing upon it the different values of the present – Tim rejects Martha's twenty-first century outlook and instead reasserts the public school ethos of duty and patriotism – links this story back to early *Doctor Who* historicals. A coda shows that Tim survives the Western Front – his life saved by the Doctor's fob watch at a crucial moment. In a poignant final scene, Tim as an old man attends a Remembrance Day service and glimpses the Doctor and Martha in the distance.

As well as the specific story arcs built into each series, several under-lying themes run throughout this period of *Doctor Who*. Davies seems to have been particularly interested in the question of moral legitimacy: by what right does the Doctor act as he does? This had often been a theme of the classic series, most famously in the Fourth Doctor's 'Do I have that right?' dilemma in 'Genesis in the Daleks'. In the new series, this issue tends to be addressed on a personal rather an abstract philosoph-ical level. 'The Fires of Pompeii' (4.2) is a good example. This episode again rehearses the debate over the rights and wrongs of intervention in history – an issue over which *Doctor Who* has been very flexible over the years depending on the preferences of the production regime and the needs of the plot. As Davies put it:

> If the Doctor goes to Pompeii and he knows what's going to happen, why doesn't he help? He saves the world, so why not this one? What makes history established? Lord knows, there's never been a good answer to this in the history of the programme, but we could think of some fascinating dialogue – and it's a great attitude for Donna, marks her out as a new companion. None of the others have asked this essential stuff.[37]

The answer offered in 'The Fires of Pompeii' is the idea of fixed points in time. The Doctor tells Donna that they cannot warn people to evacuate the city because 'Pompeii is a fixed point in history – what happens, happens. There is no stopping it.' Quite why this is the case is not fully explained. In the event, the Doctor is rather let off the hook when it comes to the moral question: it transpires that a race of alien 'Fire Creatures', called Pyrovars, are living inside Mount Vesuvius and the Doctor is forced to engineer the volcano's explosion in order to prevent them from turning the entire human race to stone ('It's Pompeii – or the world . . . It's me – I make it happen!'). As a concession to Donna, however, he uses the TARDIS to save Caecilius and his family from the inferno.

Davies also affords greater attention to exploring the consequences of the Doctor's actions than before. The fullest exploration of this theme is in 'The Waters of Mars' (4.16), one of the longer specials produced towards the end of the Tenth Doctor's reign. Here the question posed is not about changing the past but changing the future. The Doctor arrives at Bowie Base One, the first human settlement on Mars, on 21 November 2059. He knows this is the day the base is destroyed in a massive explosion and tries to leave. He tells Captain Adelaide Brooke that 'certain moments in time are fixed – tiny, precious moments – everything else is in flux . . . but these certain moments, they have to stand . . . What happens here must always happen.' The fixed point here is Adelaide's death: the Doctor knows it will inspire her granddaughter to become a scientist-astronaut who thirty years in the future will pilot the Earth's first light-speed ship to Proxima Centuri ('Your death creates the future!'). There are parallels here with *Star Trek: First Contact* (dir. Jonathan Frakes, 1996), in which the first human light-speed flight is also seen as a pivotal moment in the history of the human race. Meanwhile, the base is under siege from a water-borne viral life form that is deadly to humans. Adelaide prepares to evacuate the base, but then, realising that the virus will spread to Earth if they return, instead initiates Action Protocol Five which will blow it up. At this point, the Doctor has a change of heart: he rescues Adelaide and the two other surviving crew members and returns them to Earth in the TARDIS. His action sparks a heated exchange:

> *Adelaide*:   You should have left us there.
>
> *The Doctor*:   Adelaide, I've done this sort of thing before, in small ways, saved some little people. But never anyone as important as you. Oh, I'm good!
>
> *Adelaide*:   Little people!? What, like Mia and Yuri? Who decides they're so unimportant – you?
>
> *The Doctor*:   For a long time now, I thought I was just a suvivor, but I'm not. I'm the winner, that's who I am. The Time Lord Victorious.
>
> *Adelaide*:   And there's no one to stop you. This is wrong, Doctor! The Time Lord Victorious is wrong!
>
> *The Doctor*:   That's for me to decide.

The Doctor's 'Time Lord Victorious' speech was controversial within fandom as it suggests he has assumed some divine right to decide who lives and who dies. In the event, however, Adelaide takes matters into her own hands: she commits suicide by shooting herself, and the future unfolds as it should. Her action makes the Doctor realise that on this occasion he has transgressed ('I've gone too far!') and hastens the end of his tenth incarnation.

As well as questions of moral legitimacy, *Doctor Who* also raises the issue of political legitimacy. Series Two, especially, problematises the relationship between the Doctor and state authority: this is the theme of the 'Torchwood' story arc. The Torchwood Institute is founded by

Queen Victoria in 1879 following her encounter with the Doctor and an (alien) werewolf: 'I saw last night that Great Britain has enemies beyond imagination and we must defend our borders on all sides. I propose an institute to investigate the strange happenings and to fight them' ('Tooth and Claw'). Later in the series, Torchwood's modern-day director, Yvonne Hartman, tells the Doctor: 'You're actually named in the Torchwood foundation charter of 1879 as an enemy of the Crown' ('Army of Ghosts'). The idea of Doctor as 'an enemy of the Crown' is lent credence by his actions at the end of 'The Christmas Invasion', when he reacts angrily to Harriet Jones ordering Torchwood to destroy the departing Sycorax spaceship ('That was murder!') and in response starts a rumour about her health ('Don't you think she looks tired?') that undermines her authority and leads to her downfall as Prime Minister. It is an uncharacteristically machiavellian act for the Tenth Doctor: he is responsible for deposing a democratically elected politician and 'architect of Britain's golden age'. It will also turn out to be an act with unforeseen consequences: Harriet Jones's downfall creates a political space that will be filled by Harold Saxon. The idea of the Doctor 'lording it over us and assuming alien authority over the rights of man' (as Hartman puts it) extends into later episodes. Even when he is working alongside UNIT to combat the Sontaran invasion, the Doctor has to be remined that 'You're not authorised to speak on behalf of the Earth' ('The Poison Sky').

The Torchwood story arc is linked to a narrative of British power that is much more overt than in previous eras of *Doctor Who*. Harriet Jones defends the destruction of the Sycorax in terms that echo the arguments in favour of a nuclear deterrent: 'You said yourself, Doctor, they'd go back to the stars and tell others about the Earth . . . In which case we have to defend ourselves' (The Christmas Invasion'). The incident has also been understood as a reference to Margaret Thatcher's controversial order to sink the Argentinian cruiser *General Belgrano* during the Falklands War of 1982.[38] Yvonne Hartman is a super-patriot who asserts the right to utilise alien technology 'for the good of the British Empire . . . We must defend our border against the alien' ('Army of Ghosts'). While Hartman's rhetoric of British imperialism may seem somewhat anachronistic in the early twenty-first century ('There isn't a British Empire!' 'Not yet!'), the reference to border security would be topical in light of the polit-ical debates around immigration current at the time: not for the first time in *Doctor Who*, the alien threat is equated with foreigners. The Torchwood narrative, furthermore, is consistent with a theme of contemporary British SF, especially in graphic novels such as Ian Edginton's *Scarlet Traces* (a sequel to *The War of the Worlds* where Britain uses technology cannibalised from the Martian war machines to support imperial expansion) and Warren Ellis's *Ministry of Space* (wherein it is the British who grab the German rocket scientists at the end of the Second World War and develop a space programme). These graphic novels ultimately expose the hubris of Britain's imperialistic ambitions – a theme also apparent in *Doctor Who* in that it is Torchwood itself that inadvertently opens a bridge between parallel worlds that enables the invasion of the Cybermen. Yet imperial values are not presented as entirely bad: Yvonne is ultimately redeemed by the strength of her patriotism ('I did my duty for Queen and Country!'), which proves resistant to Cyber conditioning.

Another theme that may to some extent have been influenced by comics – including Bryan Talbot's *The Adventures of Luther Arkwright* and Alan Moore's *The League of Extraordinary Gentlemen* – is the projection of an alternate history of Britain. This is an idea that classic *Doctor Who* had explored only once in 'Inferno'. Davies had originally planned this for Series Two, where 'there was a great, complicated version of "Tooth and Claw" in my mind, where, at the end of the episode, Queen Victoria is killed, and that creates the parallel universe, which becomes the world of "Rise of the Cybermen" and "The Age of Steel" . . . It's a brilliant moment, but its legacy is too complicated, and too dark.'[39] Having decided that the death of Queen Victoria should remain a fixed point in history, Davies instead wrote an alternate history of the future. 'Turn Left' (4.11) is based on the premise that a seemingly inconsequential decision can change the course of history – an idea that Davies based on the film *Sliding Doors* (dir. Peter Hewitt, 1998).[40] Donna Noble's encounter with a 'time beetle' on the planet Shan Shen creates an alternate universe in which she never meets the Doctor – and therefore is not present to save his life in his confrontation with the Empress of Racnos in 'The Runaway Bride'. As in *It's A Wonderful Life* (dir. Frank Capra, 1946), the Doctor's death changes the course of events already seen in episodes such as 'Smith and Jones' (Martha Jones and Sarah Jane Smith are both among the dead when the Royal Hope Hospital is transported to the Moon) and 'Voyage of the Damned' (the *Starship Titanic* crashes into Buckingham Palace and the royal family are all killed).

With London destroyed in a nuclear explosion, millions are displaced and there is massive unemployment. The withdrawal of US economic aid leads to the collapse of social order, an emergency government and the rise of extreme nationalism ('England for the English') that sees immigrants sent to labour camps. Davies here draws an explicit parallel with events in Germany in the 1930s ('Labour camps – that's what they called them last time!'). It is perhaps the most dystopian episode *Doctor Who* has ever done, because its alternate history is all too plausible: the success of the British National Party in some local elections and the rise of organisations like the English Defence League were fuelled by hysteria around immigration. Fortunately, Rose Tyler and UNIT are on hand to send Donna back in time so that history can revert to its proper course.

The inclusion of an episode like 'Turn Left' indicated that *Doctor Who* was willing to stretch the boundaries of its genre. In its quiet way it typified the Russell T. Davies era of *Doctor Who* as eloquently as the epic space opera of episodes such as 'The Stolen Earth' and 'Journey's End' or the two-part special 'The End of Time' (4.17–4.18) that brought the Tenth Doctor's reign to a suitably apocalyptic conclusion. 'The End of Time' features not only the return of the Master, but also the resurrection of the Time Lords themselves who – having seen a prophesy of their destruction in the Time War – retrospectively implant a signal in the Master's brain (the noise that torments him 'The Sound of Drums' and 'Last of the Time Lords') that will cause him to break the time lock that prevents the outcome of the Time War from being rewritten. The episode provides a resolution of sorts to the back story of the Time War in its revelation that the Doctor destroyed the Time Lords because the war had made them even more ruthless and genocidal than the Daleks. This time it is Rassilon (Timothy Dalton) who seeks to bring about nothing less than 'the end of time itself' ('You see now, that's what they were planning in the final days of the war – I had to stop them!'). There are suggestions of horrors beyond imagination as the Doctor refers to 'the Skaro Degradations, the Horde of Travesties, the Nightmare Child, the Could Have Been King with his army of Meanwhiles and Neverweres' that will engulf the Earth if the time lock is broken. For Davies, however, the real dramatic point of 'The End of Time' is in the final act, when the Doctor – knowing that his body is dying from radiation poisoning – spends his last moments travelling the universe to revisit his companions one last time. This was Davies's way of providing dramatic closure for the main companions (and in the process addressing Sarah Jane's charge in 'School Reunion' that the Doctor just abandons them) and clearing the slate for the next production regime.

For all that the Tenth Doctor's protracted final act ('I don't want to go!') and his 'farewell tour' of his companions prompted mirth and even derision within some sections of fandom, 'The End of Time' was nevertheless a fitting conclusion to the Davies era of *Doctor Who*. Its audience of 12.2 million was by some distance the biggest for the final adventure of any incumbent, and David Tennant had the satisfaction of leaving the series at the height of its popularity. Furthermore, its balance between the epic and the intimate was the hallmark of Davies-era *Doctor Who*. It was a highly successful formula that had not only re-established *Doctor Who* as one of the jewels in the BBC's crown, but had also transformed a 'creaky old science fiction show' into 'must-see' television for the twenty-first century.

11

Aliens of Cardiff

2006–2011

We don't just catch aliens. We scavenge the stuff they leave behind, find ways of using it, arming the human race for the future. The twenty-first century is where it all changes and you've gotta be ready . . . We're separate from the government, outside the police, beyond the United Nations.

Captain Jack Harkness (John Barrowman) in 'Everything Changes'

Although *Torchwood* is invariably referred to as a spin-off of *Doctor Who*, its origin predated the 2005 resurrection of its parent series. Russell T. Davies has said that he had the idea for a hybrid science fiction/crime drama before his appointment as showrunner of *Doctor Who*: it was originally to have been called *Excalibur* and was conceived in the style of *Buffy the Vampire Slayer* and its spin-off *Angel*.[1] The idea was revived following the success of Series One of *Doctor Who* when it became a vehicle for John Barrowman, whose character of Captain Jack Harkness had been introduced in *Doctor Who* and who Davies felt 'had so much more to offer'.[2] *Torchwood* was commissioned by Stuart Murphy, then Controller of BBC3, a new digital channel launched in 2003 whose target audience was the 16–34-year-old age group and whose remit was 'to bring younger audiences to high quality public service broadcasting through a mixed-genre schedule of innovative UK content featuring new UK talent'.[3] Hitherto BBC3's most successful programmes had been comedies such as *Little Britain* and *Two Pints of Lager and a Packet of Crisps*. The premiere 'double bill' of *Torchwood* on 22 October 2006 set a viewing record for the channel (2.4 million) that to date has been surpassed only by its live coverage of the London Olympic Games of 2012.[4] So successful was *Torchwood* that its second series in 2008 was broadcast on BBC2 (episodes of the first series had been repeated on BBC2 a week after their premiere on BBC3), while its third (a five-part serial entitled *Torchwood: Children of Earth*) and fourth series (a ten-part serial known as *Torchwood: Miracle Day*) were shown in a primetime evening slot on BBC1. The scheduling history of *Torchwood* can therefore be seen in terms of its move from the margins (a niche digital channel) to the mainstream of British television culture.[5]

The production of *Torchwood* demonstrated continuity with the production of *Doctor Who*. It had the same executive producers (Russell T. Davies and Julie Gardner) and drew upon several of the same writers (including Chris Chibnall, Matt Jones, James Moran, Helen Raynor and Toby Whithouse) and directors (Euros Lyn, James Strong, Colin Teague, Alice Troughton) as its parent series. Other writers who contributed to *Torchwood* included Noel Clarke, who played Mickey Smith in *Doctor Who*, and Peter J. Hammond, creator of the cult British telefantasy series *Sapphire & Steel* (1979–1982) to which *Torchwood* owed more than a small debt in its basic premise. Like *Doctor Who*, the production was based in Cardiff, though unlike *Doctor Who* there was a conscious effort to showcase the city and its environs. As Davies put it: 'It's got everything a city should have – and Cardiff Bay . . . I wanted it to look like a city does in an American show. They aren't ashamed about putting what they've got on the screen.'[6] This might be seen as a response to those who had complained that *Doctor Who* was not sufficiently 'Welsh' in content and that BBC Wales should focus instead on drama as a vehicle for exploring Welsh culture and identity. However, the projection of Wales in *Torchwood* would focus very much on the modern and the contemporary: there would be no space for male voice choirs or the Blaenau Ffestiniog Miniature Railway. *Torchwood* would owe more to the urban-realist Wales of films such as *Twin Town* (dir. Kevin Allen, 1997) than to the rural-mythic Wales of *How Green Was My Valley* (dir. John Ford, 1941).

The premise of *Torchwood* – a group of alien hunters based in Cardiff who investigate crimes involving extra-terrestrials and supernatural phenomena – was hardly original in itself. *Torchwood* can be positioned in relation to two lineages within popular television. One is the tradition of telefantasy dealing with alien incursions and/or the supernatural that extends back to the *Quatermass* serials of the 1950s and includes American series such as *Kolchack: The Night Stalker* (1974) and *The X Files* (1993–2002). *Kolchack*, about a newspaper reporter who investigates supernatural crimes involving zombies, vampires, werewolves, demons and even Jack the Ripper, bears a number of similarities to *Torchwood*. And *Torchwood* itself acknowledges the influence of *The X Files* when a minor character (PC Andy) refers to Jack and Gwen Cooper (Eve Miles) as 'Mulder and Scully'. The BBC's *Doomwatch* (1970–1972), about a special unit investigating abuses of science and technology, is a more distant relation. The other major influence on *Torchwood* came from modern American crime dramas with an emphasis on forensic investigation such as *NCIS* (2003–) and the successful *CSI* franchise: *CSI: Crime Scene Investigation* (2000–), *CSI: Miami* (2002–2012) and *CSI: New York* (2004–). The visual style of these series, with their glossy cinematography and realistic forensic detail, would influence the 'look' of *Torchwood*. That *Torchwood* was identifying itself with this genre – but at the same time also distancing itself to a degree from its American cousins – is established in the first episode when PC Andy (again) remarks: 'It's like that *CSI* bollocks. *CSI: Cardiff* – I'd like to see that! They'll be measuring the velocity of a kebab.'

The relationship between *Torchwood* and *Doctor Who* may be understood in terms of theoretical concepts such as 'hyperdiegesis' and 'palimpsest'. A hyperdiegesis is the idea of a shared fictional universe. *Torchwood* clearly inhabits the same fictional universe as *Doctor Who*. There are references to events in *Doctor Who* (notably the destruction of 'Torchwood One' during the Battle of Canary Wharf in the *Doctor Who* episode 'Doomsday') and several characters cross-over from the parent series. These include, in addition to Jack Harkness, scientist Toshiko Sato (Naoko Mori), who had appeared working for UNIT in the *Doctor Who* episode 'Aliens of London', and the Doctor's former companion Martha Jones (Freema Agyeman), now attached to UNIT, who guest stars in three episodes of the second series of *Torchwood*. The fact that Cardiff is built on an invisible rift in space and time, established in *Doctor Who*, is the plot device that explains why so many aliens turn up there. There are also points of intersection between the narratives of *Torchwood* and *Doctor Who* as each fills gaps in the diegesis of the other. The presence of politician Harold Saxon (who is part of the story arc of Series Three of *Doctor Who*) is indicated towards the end of the first series of *Torchwood*, for example, while Jack's absence from Cardiff between 'End of Days' (1.13) and 'Kiss Kiss, Bang Bang' (2.1) is explained by the fact that he was travelling with the Doctor in the *Doctor Who* episodes 'Utopia', 'The Sound of Drums' and 'Last of the Time Lords'.

Torchwood may also be seen as a palimpsest of *Doctor Who*. This is a term imported from classical studies referring to a text that is written over, but where traces of the original may still remain. A good example of this idea is the *Torchwood* episode 'Cyberwoman' (1.4). In this episode, Torchwood member Ianto Jones (Gareth David-Lloyd) has secretly preserved the body of his girlfriend Lisa, partially converted into a Cyberman, in the basement of the Torchwood 'Hub' (the name for their base hidden underneath Cardiff's Millennium Centre). Lisa's conversion into a Cyberman was aborted when the power to the conversion units failed during the Battle of Canary Wharf. However, the appearance of the Lisa/Cyberwoman, which includes her own flesh and face, is markedly different from the Cybus Industries Cybermen of the new *Doctor Who*. These are not augmented human bodies, as per the Mondasian and Telosian Cybermen of classic *Doctor Who*, but rather entirely robotic bodies into which a human brain is implanted. In other words, the new series' Cybermen should not have any recognisable human body parts at all. This is explained away in the *Torchwood* episode, however, in a casual reference explaining that the Cyberwoman's half-human/half-cyborg appearance was due to the Cybermen adopting a new conversion process when they required urgent reinforcements during their battle with the Daleks: 'They started upgrading whole bodies instead of transplanting human brains, using Earth technology.' This is a palimpsest in the sense that *Torchwood* rewrites what was known about the Cybermen in *Doctor Who*. If nothing else, it is a useful theoretical concept for resolving continuity problems.

All that said, however, there were very significant differences between *Torchwood* and *Doctor Who*. *Torchwood* was conceived from the outset as a more 'adult' drama than *Doctor Who*. It would be shown after the 9 pm watershed and would include more violent content and sexual references than its parent series. Davies told *SFX* magazine: 'We can be a bit more visceral, more violent, and more sexual, if we want to ... It's the essential difference between BBC One at 7 pm and BBC Three at 9 pm. That says it all – instinctively, every viewer can see the huge difference there.'[7] And Stuart Murphy emphasised the darker tone of the new series: '*Torchwood* is sinister and psychological – Russell was really keen to play with your head – as well as being very British and modern and real. But at the centre of the drama are warm, human relationships and the overcoming of adversity.'[8] The more 'adult' content of *Torchwood* was signalled in the first episode, which includes its first swear word after just two minutes ('There's no procedure any more – it's a fucking disgrace') and a gruesome death inside the first quarter-hour. In particular, *Torchwood* includes more direct sexual references, including several same-sex kissing scenes and brief moments of male (though not female) nudity.[9] *Torchwood* would provide further fuel for those who accused Davies of pursuing a 'gay agenda', though in fact the regular series includes only one fully-fledged male homosexual/bisexual relationship, which all things considered hardly seems excessive.

It would be fair to say that critics were initially unsure how to respond to *Torchwood*. For those who (however wrongly) regarded *Doctor Who* as a children's show, the idea of an 'adult' spin-off was evidently problematic. James Walton, the television critic of the *Daily Telegraph*, complained that 'this isn't really *Doctor Who* for adults, as promised. Instead it's *Doctor Who* with added sex and swearing – which isn't the same thing at all.'[10] His colleague Christopher Howse added: 'If it weren't for things like the sex in the lavatory, I'd say this was merely enjoyable tosh . . . Countless little children will stay up to watch, but I don't think I'll bother again.'[11] Thomas Sutcliffe of *The Independent* was equally dismissive: 'It was fun, if you like this sort of thing, but then I can't work out why you would if you are more than 16 years old. Surely now Russell T. Davies can write something for the grown-ups again.'[12] The gist of comments such as these is that the 'adult' intentions of *Torchwood* were misconceived and compromised as, even in a 9 pm slot, it would surely attract some of the younger fans of *Doctor Who*. (The BBC recognised this fact and for the second series aired a 'child-friendly' edit on Sundays at 7 pm followed by an 'adult' version later in the week at 9 pm.) A more sympathetic assessment of the series came from Pete Clark in the *Evening Standard*, who called *Torchwood* an 'impressively multi-layered, visually dazzling world of weird wonders' and who appreciated it on the grounds 'that drama is endlessly refreshed by what might loosely be termed science fiction because the impossible is allowed to happen'.[13]

Academic critics have also been divided on the merits of *Torchwood*. Sue Short, for example, complains that its main characters (excepting Ianto) are 'consumed by narcissism or neurosis . . . and the premise proves equally disappointing', and is dismissive of its leading man: 'Seemingly cast to appeal to straight women and gay men, John Barrowman's good looks fail to conceal the fact that he is out of his depth in the acting stakes.'[14] (Barrowman was best known as a song-and-dance man from stage musicals prior to his casting as Captain Jack Harkness. Moreover, the version of Captain Jack who appears in *Torchwood* is notably darker and psychologically more complex than the time-travelling con man introduced in the first series of *Doctor Who*.) For Andrew Ireland, however, *Torchwood* is 'a unique television drama series . . . that is forever challenging the accepted norms of the genre', while Captain Jack is 'arguably one of the most fleshed-out, unique and multi-dimensional [characters] in recent television history'.[15] How can we account for these very different assessments?

It would probably be fair to say that the quality of *Torchwood* – in terms of scripting, characterisation and performance – is inconsistent. One fan writer pinpointed this problem at an early stage: 'My main complaint about the first season of *Torchwood* is that, in spite of it having the illusion of continuity, none of the writers appears to be actually working on the same show.'[16] The series lacks the presence of a full showrunner in the style of *Doctor Who*: Russell T. Davies devised the basic situation and characters but wrote just the first episode ('Everything Changes') after which he received no further writing credits until *Torchwood: Children of Earth* in 2009. The most prolific writer, with 8 of the 26 episodes from Series One and Two, was co-producer Chris Chibnall. Even so there are basic inconsistencies, including in the relationships between the characters and the nature of the organisation they work for: Torchwood is supposed to be a top-secret organisation but the team drive noisily around Cardiff in an SUV emblazoned with the name 'Torchwood' and even have pizzas delivered to their headquarters under that name! Captain Jack's costume, consisting of a heavy Second World War-era RAF greatcoat and service revolver, is hardly inconspicuous. Barrowman, for his part, is required to play both the extrovert action hero (in which role he excels) and a lonely, brooding tragic hero struggling to come to terms with a fundamentally life-changing experience (Jack is immortal, having been resurrected by Rose/Bad Wolf in the *Doctor Who* episode 'The Parting of the Ways'). Furthermore, the formula of *Torchwood* proved unstable, changing mid-way through the series from an investigative/procedural genre framework to something akin to an SF version of *The Fugitive* with the team operating outside the law.

The first two series of *Torchwood* comprise what can best be described as 'monster of the week' stories. Among the various extra-terrestrial threats encountered by the Torchwood team are a gaseous cloud creature that emits powerful sex pheromones ('Day One'), demonic fairies ('Small Worlds'), an emotionally conflicted cyborg ('Cyberwoman'), a carnivore who feeds on human hearts ('Greeks Bearing Gifts'), an advance guard of aliens who have taken human form as the prelude to a full-scale invasion ('Sleeper') and a shape-shifting creature whose progeny has been implanted in a human surrogate mother ('Something Borrowed'). One does not need to look far to identify some familiar genre motifs. *Torchwood* draws upon the imagery and iconography of SF cinema, including *Metropolis* (the shapely female cyborg of 'Cyberwoman'), *Quatermass 2* (the gas exploding from a meteorite in 'Day One'), *Alien* (the larvae bursting out of a victim's stomach in 'Reset'), and the *Terminator* and *Predator* films (the aliens of 'Sleeper' whose arms turn into stabbing weapons). There are also points of reference from outside science fiction. 'Countrycide', for example, is nothing if not an homage to *Straw Dogs* (dir. Sam Peckinpah, 1970) in its representation of a rural backwater as a site of horror, and its murderous 'yokels' who turn violently upon the urban outsiders who trespass into their isolated community, while 'Combat' reworks the basic premise of *Fight Club* (dir. David Fincher, 1999) as Owen Harper (Burn Gurman) goes undercover to investigate an underground fight-ring involving captured aliens.

The alien threat in *Torchwood* is usually presented as both malignant and intrusive. A frequent motif is the alien that either takes on the form of human beings ('Day One', 'Greeks Bearing Gifts', 'Sleeper') or seeds itself inside a human host ('Reset', 'Something Borrowed', and the backstory of Owen's fiancée in 'Fragments'). In this sense, *Torchwood* can be placed in the sub-genre of 'body horror' that characterises the work of film directors such as Ridley Scott (*Alien*, *Prometheus*) and David Cronenberg (*Shivers, Rabid, The Fly*). It also rehearses the horror motif that, following Barbara Creed, has been termed the 'monstrous-feminine'.[17] It is instructive to note how often in *Torchwood* the alien assumes female form. In 'Day One' (1.2) a gaseous life form that feeds on sexual energy takes over the body of a woman, who works as a receptionist in a sperm bank, and turns her into a sex-crazed fiend whose lovers are vapourised at the moment of climax. In 'Greeks Bearing Gifts' (1.7) Toshiko is seduced by another highly sexualised woman who turns out to be an alien political prisoner who has escaped her own world and is able to assume human form. And in 'Something Borrowed' (2.9) Gwen Cooper is impregnated by the bite of a Nostrovite ('a shape-shifting carnivore with a taste for human flesh') and finds herself carrying an unnatural offspring on the eve of her wedding to her long-suffering fiancé Rhys (Kai Owen). The episode explicitly addresses the motif of the monstrous-feminine both in its dialogue ('An alien egg in your belly and its mother come to rip you open', Owen rather unhelpfully remarks) and in the figure of the female Nostrovite that, as a shape-shifter, assumes various guises including an attractive female wedding guest and Rhys's own mother. The moment when a heavily pregnant Gwen shoots her mother-in-law-to-be is no doubt ripe for all sorts of Freudian interpretations.

'Cyberwoman' (1.4) is a key episode in this respect as it represents the female body as both monstrous and erotic. In the basement of the Torchwood headquarters, Ianto has secretly kept the half-cyborg body of his girlfriend Lisa on a life-support machine. Ianto hires an expert in cybernetics to try to reverse the Cyber conversion, but Lisa/Cyberwoman rejects any attempt to remove her robotic implants, escapes and embarks upon a destructive rampage around the Hub. The cyborg regards itself as monstrous, reacting in horror to its appearance in a mirror ('The upgrade is incomplete – I am disgusting') and seeking the technology to complete its conversion. Yet, at the same time, the cyborg is presented in a highly fetishistic manner: patches of Lisa's bare skin are contrasted with the grotesque 'handlebar' head gear, while her conical bra and silver metallic briefs recall the outrageous stage costumes of pop stars such as Madonna and Lady GaGa. A further dimension is overlaid onto the episode's cultural politics by Lisa's ethnicity: the fact that she is black represents the monstrous not just as feminised but also as racialised.[18] 'Cyberwoman' borrows from a range of SF and horror films – including *Metropolis* and *Frankenstein Created Woman* (dir. Terence Fisher, 1967) – and is further evidence of the extent to which *Torchwood* draws upon other genre texts.

This is not to say that *Torchwood* is wholly preoccupied with alien-taking-over-the-world stories. Some episodes reverse the binary by casting aliens as the victims and human beings as the oppressors.

'Combat' (1.11) is one such example: the humans running the alien fight club are more monstrous than the Weevils they exploit, as they have chosen to take part in the violent spectacle whereas savagery is in the nature of the Weevils. On this occasion, Jack is cast as protector of the alien life form: 'These creatures are to be left alone – go back to your lives!' In the similarly-themed 'Reset' (2.6) Torchwood discover that a bio-tech company is incubating alien larvae in human beings in an attempt to find a cure for diseases such as HIV and cancer. The head of the bio-tech company has entirely lost his moral compass ('We're on the edge of the greatest discovery in history – that's got to be worth a few sacrifices'), whereas Jack is horrified ('This place is a torture chamber! You abused the Mayflies . . . This is slavery – exploitation – a war crime') And 'Meat' (2.4) concerns a criminal gang who have captured a blubberous alien creature that regenerates itself when they cut away its flesh. They are using it to sell cheap meat, oblivious to the pain the creature is suffering. Jack is disgusted at the treatment of the alien ('Imprisoned, chained and drugged – welcome to planet Earth!') and even the usually cynical Owen is saddened at having to kill the creature to put it out of its misery. The theme of human beings as monstrous had been raised in *Doctor Who* – when the Sycorax spaceship is destroyed at the end of 'The Christmas Invasion' the Doctor remarks that 'the monsters are coming – the human race!' – but the darker-themed *Torchwood* is able to take the idea further than its parent series ever could.

There are several recurring narrative templates in *Torchwood*. Peter J. Hammond's episodes, for example, revolve around the themes of dream and memory. In 'Small Worlds' (1.5) Jack is haunted by nightmares of an incident in Lahore, in 1909, when a platoon of soldiers he was commanding all suddenly died while vomiting red petals. A number of similar deaths in the present indicates the presence of a 'malignant race' known as the Mara ('that's where the word nightmare comes from') who appear as fairies and who prey upon lonely children. The episode refers to the infamous hoax of the Cottingley fairies: Gwen identifies a child taken by the Mara as one of the 'fairies' in the photographs by Elsie Wright and Frances Griffiths in 1917. The monsters in 'From Out of the Rain' (2.10) are the Night Travellers, fairground performers from the nineteenth century who 'left a trail of damage and sorrow wherever they performed' but who now exist only as subliminal images in old films. The Night Travellers are nitrate-based creatures who have been trapped on celluloid: when old films are projected at a cinema museum they take on corporeal form. The episode shares with 'Small World' the theme of memory (Ianto recognises Jack in old films of the travelling circus) and the motif of creatures trapped in photographic records of the past. Ianto refers to travelling fairs as 'part of history trapped in film form': this is also what the Night Travellers have become. The episode belongs to the tradition of horrific fairgrounds also exemplified by *The Circus of Dr Lao* and classic *Doctor Who*'s 'The Greatest Show in the Galaxy'.

Another template – and one that demonstrates the generic hybridity of *Torchwood* – is the police procedural. This being *Torchwood* there are no 'straight' detective stories, but in some episodes the SF apparatus is downplayed to the extent that the tone is more *CSI* than *The X Files*. 'Everything Changes' (1.1) opens in the style of a procedural narrative, as police arrive at a crime scene only to be elbowed out by the arrival of the Torchwood team. In this episode, the SF device is an alien glove that is able to bring the dead back to life for a brief moment: Torchwood are using the 'resurrection gauntlet' to investigate a series of grisly murders by a serial killer at work in Cardiff. The killer turns out to be Torchwood's own Suzie Costello, who has been carrying out the murders in order to better her experience of using the alien technology: 'I needed the bodies . . . It was the only way. The more I use the glove, the more I control it. If I get enough practice, then think what the glove could do!' In 'They Keep Killing Suzie' (1.8) Torchwood use the glove to resurrect Suzie – shot dead at the end of 'Everything Changes' with her body kept in cryogenic suspension – believing that she holds the answer to another spate of murders that seem to implicate Torchwood itself. This time it turns to be a ploy by Suzie from beyond the grave to cause Torchwood to resurrect her in order that she can kill her own father. In these episodes the SF content is secondary, and the genre conventions are essentially those of the investigative/procedural thriller.

The narrative of temporal displacement is another recurring template. Several stories revolve around characters who are out of their own time. In 'Captain Jack Harkness' (1.12) Jack and Toshiko find themselves in 1941 where they meet the 'real' Captain Jack Harkness, an American volunteer serving in the Royal Air Force whose identity Jack assumed after the real Harkness's death. The dramatic focus of the episode is not so much on the efforts of the Torchwood team to restore the temporal anomaly, but rather on the character of the real Jack who it turns out is a repressed homosexual trapped in an unwanted heterosexual relationship with a Welsh girlfriend: his meeting with (and attraction to) Torchwood's Jack is presented as a liberating experience. In 'To the Last Man' (2.3) Toshiko is caught in a time loop with a soldier from the First World War who has to be sent back to 1918 in order to repair a rift in time. This time matters are complicated because Toshiko has fallen in love with the soldier and knows that he is being sent back to face certain death: he is suffering from shellshock and will be executed for cowardice. Tommy is understandably riled at being used as a pawn in the effort to restore time to its proper course: 'You're no better than the generals, sitting safely behind the lines, sending the men over the top.' Perhaps the best of these temporal displacement stories – in the sense that the emphasis is on character and the fate of the world is not at stake for once – is 'Out of Time' (1.10). A small passenger aeroplane from 1953 passes through a 'transcendental portal' and arrives in the present. Here the real drama arises from the passengers' adjustment to their new environment. As Jack puts it: 'There's no puzzle to solve, no enemy to fight, just three lost people who've suddenly become our responsibility.' The episode draws the expected humour from their reactions to present-day prices and social mores, but also includes highly poignant moments, such as the middle-aged John Ellis's discovery that his wife has died and that his (now elderly) son is suffering from Alzheimer's Disease. John decides there is nothing left for him and Jack helps him commit suicide ('Let me go with some dignity – don't condemn me to live').

It will be evident from these examples that *Torchwood* is more rooted in a discourse of psychological realism than *Doctor Who* (even Davies's *Doctor Who* with its investment in characterisation and emotionality). At times, indeed, *Torchwood* verges on existential drama: an interlude where one or more of the main characters discuss the Meaning of Life is never too far away. Hence Gwen can remark that 'there's Torchwood, then there's real life' ('Out of Time') and even a heinous villain can try to rationalise his actions as 'ordinary blokes just trying to find meaning in a world that doesn't have any' ('Combat'). A recurring theme of the series is the question of whether there is an afterlife. This is addressed principally through the character of Jack Harkness, whose immortality has invested him with a particularly unique outlook towards life and death. Jack regards his immortality as a curse – echoes here of the classic *Doctor Who* story 'The Five Doctors', in which Rassilon came to the same conclusion – and throughout the series feels a sense of empathy with those who want to die. Hence his actions in helping John Ellis commit suicide by carbon monoxide poisoning ('Out of Time') and in the mercy killing of the alien creature suffering in agonising pain ('Meat'). *Torchwood* is sceptical in the extreme about an afterlife. When a murder victim is briefly resurrected at the start of the first episode, his reaction to Jack's question 'What did you see?' is 'Nothing . . . Oh my God, there's nothing!' ('Everything Changes'). Other characters brought back from the dead all testify to a similar experience. For Suzie Costello there is 'nothing, just nothing' ('They Keep Killing Suzie'), while following Owen's death and resurrection in Series Two, he says that he saw 'nothing . . . just darkness' ('Dead Man Walking').

The pessimistic tone of *Torchwood* is in stark contrast to the philosophical and moral optimism of its parent series. At the same time, however, *Torchwood* is, somewhat paradoxically, also invested with a strong undercurrent of Christian symbolism. Examples of this include the Torchwood team taking a form of communion reminiscent of the Last Supper – albeit that Jack is passing around amnesia pills to counteract the effects of an alien able to alter people's minds ('Adam') – and the image of Owen proving to a suicidal woman that he is dead by allowing her to touch the gunshot wound in his chest in a manner recalling Doubting Thomas ('A Day in the Death'). The most overtly Christian metaphor in the series is Jack offering himself as a sacrifice to the reawakened satanic monster, Abaddon, and his subsequent resurrection ('End of Days'). This motif is taken even further in 'Day Two' of *Torchwood: Children of Earth* in which Jack's dismembered body is sealed away in a vault only to re-emerge fully restored two days later. This is not to suggest that *Torchwood* is consciously promoting a Christian worldview – especially given that any such message is consistently undercut by the series' extreme scepticism about an afterlife – but rather, as with *Doctor Who*, simply indicates how deeply the symbols of Christianity are rooted in society.[19]

By far the most contentious aspect of *Torchwood* is its representation of sexuality. This positioned many critics' responses to the series and has set the framework for much of the academic discussion of *Torchwood*. At one extreme there has been hostility towards the series' inclusion of 'gay sex scenes'. In 2011, for example, *Pink News* reported that the BBC 'has received hundreds of complaints over gay sex scenes' in *Torchwood:*

Miracle Day.[20] It is instructive to note that this hostility was directed particularly at male same-sex scenes and not female same-sex scenes: scenes of Gwen and Toshiko experiencing same-sex encounters (in 'Day One' and 'Greeks Bearing Gifts') were seemingly deemed less offensive than those featuring Jack and other men. At another extreme, *Torchwood* has been criticised, in effect, for not being gay enough. Critics have pointed out that none of the series' main characters are strictly homosexual: Jack is bisexual (Toshiko remarks that 'he'll shag anybody if they're gorgeous enough'), Ianto asserts that he is attracted specifically to Jack but not to other men, and Gwen and Toshiko's same-sex encounters are induced under alien influence and are not consistent with their otherwise normative heterosexuality (Gwen is in a long-term relationship with Rhys, whom she marries in Series Two, while Toshiko is – albeit inexplicably – attracted to Owen).

For Davies the aim of making the main character bisexual was to challenge normative views of sexuality as being either/or. In an interview for *Gay Times* he said: 'Without making it political or dull, this is going to be a very bisexual programme. I want to knock down the barriers so we can't define which of the characters is gay. We need to start mixing things up, rather than thinking, "This is a gay character and he'll only ever go off with men."'[21] The idea that sexuality is defined simply as either straight or gay is challenged in a scene in 'Day One' where Gwen passionately kisses another woman ('Okay, first contact with an alien not quite what I expected') and is witnessed on CCTV by a surprised Owen:

Owen: She said she had a boyfriend!

Jack: You people and your quaint little categories.

The idea that heterosexuality and homosexuality are merely categories that do not explain the complexities of human sexuality is a recurring theme throughout *Torchwood*. This explains why Jack can have relationships both with women (in 'Small Worlds' it is revealed that he was in love with Estelle, now an elderly woman, during the Second World War) and with men (such as the roguish Captain John Hart, another Time Agent from the fifty-first century, played by James Marsters – Spike in *Buffy the Vampire Slayer* – in 'Kiss Kiss, Bang Bang' and 'Exit Wounds'). It is also implied that Jack has romantic and sexual feelings for Gwen even while he is carrying on an affair with Ianto during the second series: he (semi-jokingly) invites her to join them for a threesome when she walks in on them engaged in a sexual act ('Adrift').

While, on the face of it, *Torchwood* may be thought progressive in its representation of sexual identities as fluid and its refusal to pigeonhole characters as either gay or straight, it has been argued, counter to this view, that the sexual politics of *Torchwood* are in fact quite conservative. Christopher Pullen, for example, sees 'the representation of bisexuality within *Torchwood* as both pleasurable and problematic. It is pleasurable as it vividly represents male to male intimacy and same sex desire; it is problematic as it does this by employing a preferred bisexual representation as a substitute for homosexual identity.'[22] In this reading, *Torchwood* suppresses homosexual desire by suggesting that male same-sex relationships are really an expression of bisexuality rather than homosexuality: in other words men can have sexual relationships with other men if they also have relationships with women. And Sherry Ginn argues 'that much of the overt sexual overtones of the series play into the usual stereotypes about gender and sexuality'.[23] Hence Jack is characterised in a very conventionally heroic mould and Gwen is characterised as a career woman trying to reconcile her job with her domestic life – both very familiar constructions of gender – while Jack's promiscuity simply reinforces stereotypes about gay male behaviour. And the representation of women in the series – with the partial exception of the aviatrix Diane Holmes in 'Out of Time' – can hardly be described as progressive: if they are not being taken over by monsters they are being laid either by Owen or by Jack. However, the social politics of *Torchwood* are probably as much a reflection of the conventions of genre as an expression of authorial agency.

Torchwood: Children of Earth, a five-part serial broadcast in 2009, marked a change of direction for the series. It moved to BBC1 and was planned as a piece of 'event' television screened across five consecutive evenings (6–10 July 2009). Davies averred that it was 'the most ambitious serial we've ever made'.[24] It was written by Davies, James Moran and John Fay, and directed by Euros Lyn, an experienced *Doctor Who* director making his *Torchwood* debut. *Torchwood: Children of Earth* features three of the regular Torchwood team – Jack, Gwen and Ianto – with Toshiko and Owen having been killed at the end of the second series. Davies had also envisioned roles for Martha Jones and Mickey Smith from

Doctor Who, though this did not transpire as actors Freema Agyeman and Noel Clarke were unavailable.[25] *Torchwood: Children of Earth* has a more epic, even cinematic, feel than previous episodes. It was a popular success, averaging 5.8 million viewers in what was supposedly a summertime 'graveyard slot' for drama. To some extent, its success can be attributed to the absence of *Doctor Who* for much of 2009: this was the year of the Tenth Doctor 'Specials'. It also succeeded in its aim of producing 'event' television. Daniel Martin, who followed fan forums in a daily blog for the *Guardian*, observed that 'something remarkable happened this week. These forums have been rife with reports of people who never even watched nu-Who turning out, and the casual fans there became die hards... From its hideous Sex Alien vs Cyberwoman beginnings, *Torchwood* has become a true treasure.'[26]

Torchwood: Children of Earth institutes a significant narrative and ideological shift from the first two series. It posits an overt, rather than covert, alien attack on the Earth, with a species known only as the '456' materialising in London and demanding that each nation on Earth offers up one in ten of their children: 'We want a gift... We will take your children... We want ten per cent of the children of this world.' It turns out that the 456 have visited once before, to Britain in 1965, when the government allowed them to take twelve children from an orphanage in return for an anti-virus to prevent a pandemic of deadly Indonesian flu. This time the 456 threaten to release a virus that will kill the entire population of the Earth unless they are given the children. The chief negotiator for the British government, a senior civil servant called John Frobisher (Peter Capaldi), has meanwhile issued an order for the assassination of Jack and his colleagues because Jack has knowledge of what happened in 1965. The Hub is blown up and the Torchwood team go on the run pursued by sinister black-clad special police. This represents an ideological realignment for the series as the team are no longer quasi-official alien-fighters but fugitives operating outside any official framework.

On one level, *Torchwood: Children of Earth* can be seen as a pastiche of various SF and other sources. The 456 communicate through the collective hypnosis of children: scenes of groups of children eerily chanting 'We are coming' reference John Wyndham's novel *The Midwich Cuckoos* – filmed as *Village of the Damned* (dir. Wolf Rilla, 1960) – and recall the *Doctor Who* episode 'The Empty Child'. There are elements of paranoid conspiracy thriller in the style of *Edge of Darkness* (1985) and *State of Play* (2003) as the government attempts to hide its complicity and orders the assassination of Jack and his team. The main influence, however, is to be found in the *Quatermass* serials, and particularly in the little-regarded final serial of 1979, known in Britain simply as *Quatermass* and released in cinemas overseas as *The Quatermass Conclusion*. The premise of *Quatermass* is that an unseen race of aliens are 'harvesting' the young people of Earth (for what reason is never explained) and its resolution is nihilistic in the extreme: with no other solution possible the elderly professor (John Mills) destroys the aliens (and himself) with an atomic bomb. In *Torchwood: Children of Earth* the aliens also remain largely unseen and are carrying out a sort of harvest in that they feed off chemicals in pre-pubescent children's bodies that make them 'feel good' ('You're shooting up on children?' as Colonel Odeya of UNIT puts it). And, like *Quatermass*, the conclusion is extremely unsettling. Jack, finally in a position to try to broker a solution, fails in his attempt to frighten the aliens off – inadvertently causing the death of Ianto in the process – and while he finally succeeds in defeating them, the price is the death of his own grandson. (Specifically he employs the aliens' own communication technology against them and uses all the children of the Earth to transmit a 'counter wave': but he knows that the child at the epicentre of the wave will die – and the only child available is his 10-year-old grandson.)

On another level *Torchwood: Children of Earth* introduces a political subtext that had been absent from previous *Torchwood* stories. It is not just that the government attempts to murder Jack and his colleagues in order to prevent its guilty secret from the past being made public – such duplicity is to be expected in the world of the paranoid conspiracy thriller – but rather that politicians are shown colluding with the aliens and lying to their own public. It is impossible to see certain aspects of *Torchwood: Children of Earth* as anything other than a commentary on the political culture of contemporary Britain. The Cabinet's initial response to the situation is to attempt to negotiate with the aliens by offering them a few thousand children – nominating the offspring of failed asylum seekers as the sacrificial lambs – but when this is rejected they have to find a way of explaining the loss of 325,000 children to the public. At the height of the crisis a government media advisor is more concerned with how to 'spin' the story to the electorate than with the fate of the children themselves:

> *Prime Minister*:   What are you suggesting – a cull of ten per cent will do
>   us good?
>
> *Rich*:   I'm just saying that if we need to spin this to the public –
>   and God knows at the moment spin is all we can do – then
>   in an age when we're terrified by the planet's dwindling
>   resources, a reduction in the population could possibly,
>   just possibly, if presented in the right way, be presented
>   as good.

This extreme cynicism about the culture of 'spin' – the dark art that had reached its nadir on 11 September 2001 when a government advisor infamously suggested that saturation news coverage of the terrorist attacks on the United States made it 'a good day to bury bad news' – is one indication of a political subtext in *Children of Earth*. Another is the discussion that follows around the Cabinet table regarding the selection process. The suggestion of a blind ballot is quickly dismissed: this might see their own children among the victims. Instead it is agreed that the decision should be made on the basis of saving children from 'good schools . . . the workforce of the future' and sacrificing those from 'failing schools . . . full of the less able, the less socially useful, those destined to spend their life on benefits'. The scene plays like a grotesque parody of debates current at the time over the existence of an underclass and the quality of education. As one Cabinet member asks: 'If we can't identify the lowest achieving ten per cent of the country's children, then what are the school league tables for?'

The grimly nihilistic final episode of *Torchwood: Children of Earth* can also be seen as a means of separating the spin-off decisively from its parent series. It posits the breakdown of social order as the army is mobilised to transport children to their collection points. The government puts out a cover story that they are being sent for inoculation against the alien virus. Frobisher, who has acted as middle-man in the negotiations between the government and the aliens, is told that his own children will be sacrificed: 'You will be seen to offer your children for inoculation . . . This action will help the public, show them there is no cause for alarm.' (Is it entirely too fanciful to suggest that a parallel is being drawn here with the infamous occasion in the early 1990s when a certain Minister for Agriculture responded to a scare over so-called 'mad cow disease' by parading his own children eating beefburgers?) Frobisher, now thoroughly disillusioned with the political masters he has served, shoots his two daughters, his wife and himself. In the meantime, Gwen is recording a video diary that documents the panic as parents try to prevent their children from being rounded up by troops: 'There's one thing I always wanted to ask Jack . . . I wanted to know about that Doctor of his. The man who appears out of nowhere and saves the world, except sometimes he doesn't . . . Sometimes the Doctor must look at this planet and turn away in shame.'

Torchwood: Children of Earth seems to have been set up as a possible conclusion to the series. The revelation that Gwen is pregnant suggests that motherhood and domesticity beckon, while Jack, who has seen the deaths of both his lover Ianto and his own grandson, decides to leave the Earth behind: 'I began to like it – and look what I became. I've lived so many lives – it's time to find another one.' However, its popular success meant that another series was commissioned. *Torchwood: Miracle Day*, a ten-part serial broadcast in 2011, was a co-production between BBC Wales, BBC Worldwide and Starz, an American subscription channel that broadcasts mostly first-run films but also includes some original premium drama. Davies explained the US co-production arrangement in terms of expanding the scope of the series and reaching new audiences:

> For the show to hit America, I think it's a new start without being a reboot . . . We have different producing partners, and it has added a new influx of imagination, and frankly, a bigger budget as well . . . And it's a new audience. We're very, very proud of the *Torchwood* fan base, but I never believe these programmes should be cult or small. I think everyone in the world should be watching them.[27]

Davies recruited writers experienced in American telefantasy, including Jane Espenson (*Buffy the Vampire Slayer*), Doris Egan (*Smallville*) and John Shiban (*The X Files*, *Smallville*). The locations for the series included Wales, Colorado and California. *Torchwood: Miracle Day*, rather like the 1996 *Doctor Who* telefilm, achieved reasonable ratings in Britain (where its average audience was 5.2 million) but did less well in America (where its average of around one million was 'slightly below expecations' for the Starz channel).[28]

Like most co-productions, *Torchwood: Miracle Day* is something of a polyglot that reveals traces of its production context in its content. The necessity of casting American actors in key roles – Mekhi Phifer as disavowed CIA agent Rex Matheson and Alexa Havins as computer analyst Esther Drummond – means that the new Torchwood is reconfigured as an Anglo-American team. To this extent *Miracle Day* has some echoes of the 'transatlantic' ITC telefantasy series of the 1960s such as *The Champions* (1967) and *Department S* (1969). The early episodes, especially, rehearse some of the familiar political and cultural tensions between Britain and America. Thus Jack and Gwen are extradited to the United States by the CIA (an instance of the so-called 'extraordinary rendition' that had become an issue over the extradition of terrorist suspects), while the Americans are ignorant of Celtic sensibilities ('If you're the best that England's got to offer, then God help us,' quips one CIA agent, to which Gwen retorts 'I'm Welsh!' before punching her in the face). The parallel narratives in Wales (focusing on Gwen's family) and America ultimately become quite cumbersome and create a number of implausible situations: Gwen is supposedly a fugitive on both sides of the Atlantic, yet is able to fly freely back and forth apparently under her own name.

Torchwood: Miracle Day follows the pattern of *Torchwood: Children of Earth* in that it features a major global crisis and again sees the Torchwood team operating outside the law as they are hunted by the intelligence services as well as by the villains. This time, the crisis is occasioned by a virus that prevents anyone from dying either from disease, age, accident or suicide. This apparent 'miracle' has far-reaching social consequences, as health care systems are unable to cope with an ever-increasing population of the sick and elderly, religion starts to lose its meaning as no one can die, and crime soars as people can (literally) get away with murder. As in *Children of Earth*, the official response to the crisis exposes the worst in human behaviour: governments across the world create 'overflow camps' where the 'category one' patients (those suffering from chronic illnesses) are sent to be incinerated. The parallels with the Holocaust are made explicit when Gwen – whose father has been shipped to one such camp in South Wales following a heart attack – declares: 'This isn't a hospital – this is a concentration camp! We let our governments build concentration camps – they built ovens for people in our names!' As in *Children of Earth*, the Torchwood team are cast in the role of defenders of individual rights against the excesses of bureaucratic control.

Like its predecessor, *Torchwood: Miracle Day* can be seen in part as a commentary on aspects of contemporary society. The target this time was America. America's obsession with televangelists is satirised in the character of Oswald Danes (Bill Pullman), a convicted child-murderer who escapes his death sentence and emerges as an evangelical spokesman for the 'dead' – the outcasts and unwanted who have been abandoned by society. The right-wing Tea Party is represented by a caricature female politician who argues that the 'dead' should be treated as illegal immigrants with no civil or legal rights. The main target is the health care system – a topical subject given the fierce debate raging in America around 'Obamacare' at the time. Thus a progressive doctor recognises that the crisis necessitates a radical rethink of health care priorities ('We have to rebuild the entire system of health care in our country, right now') and there are several references to the treatment of those without medical insurance. It is established early in the serial that a giant pharmaceutical corporation (known as Phicorp) is benefiting from the crisis: it has been stockpiling drugs and now backs a US Senator who introduces legislation to make all drugs available to the public without prescription – thereby increasing demand tenfold – while also having lucrative contracts to build and run the overflow camps. The close association between the pharmaceutical industry and Capitol Hill suggests, quite irresistibly, that the alliance of big business and politics is an obstacle to health care reform. The politics of *Miracle Day* are firmly to the left of the American political spectrum: this might be one reason for its less than entirely enthusiastic reception in the United States.

Otherwise, *Torchwood: Miracle Day* serves to detach the narrative of *Torchwood* even further from its parent series. For the first time there are no diegetic links with *Doctor Who*: this is *Torchwood* symbolically severing its ties with its original source and striding out on its own. This was partly a consequence of Davies handing over the reins of *Doctor Who* to a new showrunner in 2009, and partly a consequence of the new production context – as Starz did not show *Doctor Who* and so had no interest in the wider franchise of which *Torchwood* was a part. This distance from *Doctor Who* means that the content of *Torchwood: Miracle*

Day is able to be more extreme in its representations of sex and violence. The 'gay sex scenes' that some viewers took exception to are more explicit than in previous *Torchwood* episodes and the violence is more visceral. Episode 7 ('Immortal Sins'), for example, features a sequence wherein Jack is strung up in an abattoir and repeatedly stabbed to death that seems to have been inspired by so-called 'torture porn' films, such as the *Saw* series. Another sign of *Miracle Day*'s distance from *Doctor Who* – indeed its distance from all previous *Torchwood* – is that there is very little in the way of SF content. Even the explanation for the 'miracle' itself – caused when Mafia families fed some of Jack's immortal blood to 'The Blessing', an unusual (and unexplained) living rock formation beneath the Earth – is left obscure. The absence of aliens disappointed some fans who felt that *Torchwood* had ceased to be science fiction.

There are various reasons why *Torchwood: Miracle Day* was less well received than its predecessor. The polyglot nature of the production was undoubtedly a factor: it lacks the distinctively British flavour of previous episodes of *Torchwood* but at the same time seems to have been too 'unAmerican' for US audiences. Another reason was pinpointed by Dan Martin in his blog for *The Guardian*: 'The wisdom established on our episode blogs, over and over and over again, is that while *Miracle Day* might have worked as a five-parter in the style of the lauded third series *Children of Earth*, there simply hasn't been anywhere near enough story to go round.'[29] The decline in viewing figures over the course of the series, especially during the middle episodes, suggests that audiences lost interest. It is structurally flawed: the most shocking moment (the unexpected death of Dr Vera Huarez at the end of Episode 5) comes half way through, and the second half of the story contains too many episodes that feel like padding (including the back story of Jack and Angelo Colasanto, which turns out to have no connection to the 'miracle'). The addition of the new characters is only partly successful. And unlike *Children of Earth*, which for all its pessimistic ending nevertheless had a sense of narrative closure, the end of *Miracle Day*, while more optimistic, leaves so many plot strands unresolved, even after ten episodes, that it remains a much less satisfying experience.

At the time of writing, the future of *Torchwood* is uncertain: there are no confirmed plans for any further episodes and Davies has said that the series is in 'indefinite hiatus'.[30] Its legacy is mixed. On the one hand *Torchwood* exemplifies both the possibilities and the limitations of the spin-off series. It struggled initially to establish sufficient distance from its parent series: it came into its own with *Children of Earth* but by the time of *Miracle Day* had severed its links with *Doctor Who* to such an extent that it no longer seemed part of the same fictional universe. If there is a future for *Torchwood* it is most likely to be as something entirely independent of *Doctor Who*. On the other hand, when compared to other SF series that failed to make the grade – including Joss Whedon's *Firefly* (2002), which was cancelled after only fourteen episodes, the remake of *The Bionic Woman* (2007), which ran for only eight, or the BBC's own *Bonekickers* (2008), which totalled just six – the 41 episodes of *Torchwood*, not to mention the spin-off novels and radio plays, represent a significant achievement in their own right. In the last analysis, *Torchwood* was to *Doctor Who* what *Angel* was to *Buffy the Vampire Slayer*: the darker and more adult-themed relation that owed its existence to the parent series but which at its best became a television event in its own right.

12

Sarah Jane and Company

2007–2011

I saw amazing things out there in space, but there's strangeness to be found wherever you turn. Life on Earth can be an adventure too – you just need to know where to look.

Sarah Jane Smith (Elisabeth Sladen) in 'Invasion of the Bane'

The Sarah Jane Adventures was the second attempt at creating a *Doctor Who* spin-off built around its most popular companion. The first, *K9 and Company*, got only as far as a pilot episode in 1981.[1] *K9 and Company* had been the outcome of two processes. The first was an idea by the incoming *Doctor Who* producer, John Nathan-Turner, to reintroduce the character of Sarah Jane Smith to the series in order to smooth the transition from Tom Baker to Peter Davison – an idea that went nowhere when actress Elisabeth Sladen declined on the grounds that the series had moved on since she left in 1976 and that 'I'd just be an anchor from the past'.[2] The second was the problem of K9, the robot dog introduced to *Doctor Who* in 'The Invisible Enemy' in 1977, which had featured intermittently in the series for several years. For writers and actors K9 soon became an albatross, because the remote-controlled prop was both unreliable and dramatically limiting. As Tom Baker recalled: 'Every time the shot was the same because the dog was on the floor. Two shots had to be realized by me kneeling down. If there happened to be a matchstick on the ground K9 stopped abruptly.'[3] Nathan-Turner had decided that K9 should be written out of *Doctor Who*; but at the same time he was aware that the robot dog was popular with children. This time Elisabeth Sladen agreed to reprise Sarah Jane in a show that was originally to have been called *Sarah and K9*. She later wrote:

> I had to agree that it sounded a fabulous idea: Sarah Jane striding out into the world on her own, pursuing her journalistic instincts to solve crimes – with her trusty robot dog at her side. Even when they changed the title to *Girl's Best Friend* I was still on board. The plan was to shoot a pilot then hopefully be picked up for a full series the following year . . . I didn't have a clue what K-9 was – I'd never seen him. But, I figured, if Tom Baker had worked with him then it must be all right. Of course, that was before I heard the stories of Tom booting the thing across the studio in frustration every time it ruined a scene.[4]

Sladen would also be frustrated by the technical shortcomings of K9 ('"I'm going to save the universe but first I want to stop and open a door for a dog?" I asked') and felt that the script of the pilot episode 'was terrible'. Nevertheless 'A Girl's Best Friend' attracted an audience of 8.4 million when it was broadcast during the Christmas holiday period in 1981 – more than recent episodes of *Doctor Who* – and it came as something of a surprise that a full series was not commissioned. This was due to 'a change of faces at the top of the Beeb – the new suits wanted to distance themselves from *Who*'.[5] *K9 and Company* had been approved by the outgoing Controller of BBC1, Bill Cotton, but his successor, Alan Hart, was less keen.

The context for the commissioning of *The Sarah Jane Adventures* would be entirely different. The popularity of *Doctor Who* with children prompted CBBC (Children's BBC) to ask Russell T. Davies and the BBC Wales production team to develop a juvenile version of the series. Audience Research indicated that one-fifth of the audience for *Doctor Who* were under sixteen, while the CBBC magazine programme *Totally Doctor Who* could boast a peak of 1.5 million viewers. According to the authorised history of *Doctor Who*, Davies vetoed the suggestion of 'Young *Doctor Who*' in preference for *The Sarah Jane Adventures*: 'Somehow the idea of a fourteen-year-old Doctor, on Gallifrey inventing sonic screwdrivers, takes away from the mystery and intrigue of who he is and where he came from. So instead I suggested doing a series with Sarah Jane Smith, because she'd been so popular in "School Reunion".'[6] According to Elisabeth Sladen's autobiography, however, she was asked

by Davies and Julie Gardner 'shortly after New Year's Day, 2006', which
would have been some months before the broadcast of 'School Reunion'
(29 April 2006).[7] In any event, the momentum behind it was so strong
that *The Sarah Jane Adventures* was commissioned without a pilot. A
one-hour introductory episode ('Invasion of the Bane') would be broadcast on New Year's Day 2007 followed by a full series of ten half-hour
episodes in the autumn of 2007. The regular series would eventually run
for 52 half-hour episodes between 2007 and 2011.

The Sarah Jane Adventures needs to be understood in the context of
developments in children's drama programming in the early twenty-
first century. The progressive deregulation of broadcasting meant that
the ITV network had all but abandoned late-afternoon children's programming in favour of quiz shows and repeats of detective series such
as *Inspector Morse* and *Midsomer Murders* before the early-evening national news. CBBC had been launched as a dedicated digital channel
for children in 2002, providing programmes for 6–12 year-olds, shar-
ing content with BBC1 in the late afternoon between approximately
4–5.30 pm. This was a time when audiences – and consequently budgets – for children's television were declining. *The Sarah Jane Adventures*
can be seen in part as an attempt to shore up declining audiences in the
traditional late-afternoon children's drama slot.[8] That it was successful
in this regard is evident from the fact that the average audience of 1.25
million for the first series in 2007 (representing an 11 per cent audience
share) was 'significantly higher' than most children's programmes in the
same time slot.[9] Abi Grant, reviewing Series One for the *Daily Telegraph*,
also attested to its success in this regard: 'With all the debate about the
future of children's TV still rumbling, this is what the BBC does best,
and despite lacking the production values of *Doctor Who*, it's still top
tea-time programming. More please.'[10]

There is a sense in which *The Sarah Jane Adventures* represents something of a throwback to the 'golden age' of children's television drama
in the 1970s and 1980s. It can be seen as a modern heir to the lineage of
juvenile telefantasy exemplified by the likes of *Timeslip*, *The Tomorrow
People*, *Ace of Wands*, *Catweazle*, *Children of the Stones* and *The Box of
Delights*. Davies's own 1991 SF serial, *Dark Season*, was itself a late addition to this lineage, providing a link between the likes of *The Tomorrow
People* (which had been a childhood favourite of his) and *The Sarah Jane
Adventures*. Since the 1980s, however, there had been a gradual transition

from adventure serials and plays (such as ITV's *Shadows* and *Drama-rama*) to longer-running soap opera-style dramas such as *Grange Hill*, *Byker Grove* and *Children's Ward* (for which Davies had served as script editor in the early 1990s). Davies himself saw *The Sarah Jane Adventures* as harking back to the tradition of juvenile telefantasy. In a BBC press release announcing *The Sarah Jane Adventures* he declared: 'Children's TV has a fine history of fantasy thrillers – I loved them as a kid, and they were the very first things I ever wrote. So it's brilliant to return to such a vivid and imaginative area of television.'[11]

At the same time, of course, *The Sarah Jane Adventures* was also very much part of the *Doctor Who* franchise that was built around its parent series following its return in 2005. Indeed, there is good reason to believe that *The Sarah Jane Adventures* was regarded as an integral part of that franchise. Evidence that it was more than a mere spin-off is that it had the same core production team as *Doctor Who* (including executive producers Russell T. Davies, Julie Gardner and Phil Collinson) and shared production facilities with its parent series at Upper Boat. Davies himself co-wrote the introductory episode and would remain on board as an executive producer even after relinquishing his role as showrunner of *Doctor Who*. In so far as younger children who might start with *The Sarah Jane Adventures* would then graduate to watching *Doctor Who*, there is even a sense in which the junior series was a more important part of the franchise than *Torchwood* – especially once *Torchwood* began to distance itself from *Doctor Who*. The target audience for *The Sarah Jane Adventures* was also more likely to offer a market for licensed merchandise, such as toys and action figures. There was even a body of opinion that maintained that the quality of *The Sarah Jane Adventures* as drama was superior to *Torchwood*.[12] It certainly demonstrates a greater consistency of tone and style than its adult relation. This was due in large measure to the bulk of scripting duties being shared by two writers (Gareth Roberts and Phil Ford) and perhaps also to some extent to the need to conform to the generic conventions of children's drama.[13] If *The Sarah Jane Adventures* did not have the licence to be as edgy as *Torchwood* in content, the much stricter institutional guidelines regarding content for children's drama meant that it was always likely to adhere to a more consistent formula and genre conventions.

Like *Torchwood*, *The Sarah Jane Adventures* shares the same hyperdiegesis (fictional universe) as *Doctor Who*. Indeed the relationship between

The Sarah Jane Adventures and its parent series is more complex and multi-layered than it might seem to a casual viewer.[14] The protagonist of Sarah Jane Smith provides a diegetic link to both classic *Doctor Who* and new *Who*, while Elisabeth Sladen is the only actor to have played the same character in both the classic and the new series. Sarah Jane's special status as a 'favourite' companion meant that *The Sarah Jane Adventures* would have some nostalgic appeal for grown-up fans of the classic series as well as those new to the *Doctor Who* mythos.[15] There are other points of intersection with classic and new *Doctor Who*. *The Sarah Jane Adventures* includes guest appearances by classic series companions Brigadier Lethbridge-Stewart (Nicholas Courtney) in 'Enemy of the Bane' and Jo Grant (Katy Manning) in 'Death of the Doctor', while Sarah Jane herself and her adopted son Luke (Tommy Knight) appear in new *Doctor Who* episodes 'The Stolen Earth' and 'Journey's End' and have a cameo appearance in David Tennant's farewell story 'The End of Time'. The most significant diegetic cross-overs, however, are the appearances in *The Sarah Jane Adventures* of both David Tennant's Tenth Doctor ('The Wedding of Sarah Jane Smith') and Matt Smith's Eleventh Doctor ('Death of the Doctor'). The inclusion of the 'star' character from the parent series can be understood both as a means of providing 'event' episodes for *The Sarah Jane Adventures* (ratings for those episodes were significantly higher than usual) and as a narrative strategy designed to anchor *The Sarah Jane Adventures* securely within the fictional world of *Doctor Who*. In this sense there is a closer intertextual relationship between *The Sarah Jane Adventures* and *Doctor Who* than between *Torchwood* and *Doctor Who*: the Doctor himself has never appeared in *Torchwood*.

The production discourse of *The Sarah Jane Adventures* was keen to assert that while this was children's drama it was not to be seen as a childish drama. According to script editor Gareth Roberts: 'We're all determined that this will be a big, full-blooded drama; that nobody should ever think of it as "just" a children's programme.'[16] The narrative strategy of the series also reflects this. *The Sarah Jane Adventures* is more sophisticated than a lot of juvenile drama in that it offers two points of viewer identification. On the one hand there is Sarah Jane herself, the titular 'star' of the series who functions as an aspirational role model for younger viewers and as a point of identification for any parents who might be watching. It is unusual for the central protagonist of a children's drama series to be a middle-aged woman (Elisabeth Sladen was 60 at the time of the first series), but *The Sarah Jane Adventures* casts its star as part action heroine and part surrogate mother to her 'Scooby Gang' of teenage sidekicks. As Daniel Martin remarked in his blog for the *Guardian*: 'Sarah was always more hockey mistress than sex kitten, and this time she's a bizarre hybrid of Mary Poppins and Tank Girl, defending the earth with a (yes) Sonic Lipstick and a gang of children.'[17] On the other hand, Sarah Jane's juvenile associates represent the point of view of younger audiences. The surrogate 'family' that congregates around Sarah Jane includes her adopted son Luke, a 14-year-old born as the result of an alien genetic experiment ('Invasion of the Bane') whose intelligence marks him out as a somewhat 'unearthly' teenager, rather like Susan Foreman in early *Doctor Who*, and his schoolfriends, streetwise Clyde Langer (Daniel Anthony), sensible Maria Jackson (Yasmin Paige) and, replacing Maria in the second series, aspiring reporter Rani Chandra (Anjli Mohindra). In a sense *The Sarah Jane Adventures* follows the formula of early *Doctor Who* in providing 'loyalty' characters designed to appeal to boys and girls up to the early teens: the major difference here is that the supporting cast is ethnically diverse in a way that classic *Doctor Who* had not been. Martin noted the 'completely BBC patchwork family' but added that 'after one adventure it's already more convincing than *Torchwood*'.

The main challenge for a series like *The Sarah Jane Adventures* was to provide a full share of exciting adventure while not being too frightening or horrific for younger viewers. Davies explained his approach thus:

> The one thing I demanded is that the threat would always be real rather than comic, though we make it a lot lighter and with a lot less fear. On *Doctor Who* we consider the eight-year-olds or the 10-year-olds, but with this you seriously have to think of six-year-olds. It doesn't sound like there is much difference between 6 and 8, but they are actually a vastly different creature. Part of you also has to remember that the six-year-olds watching the series last year are seven-year-olds now, and they are into it, they get the mythology and want to see things dealt with in detail.[18]

The Sarah Jane Adventures would provide a home for some of the more child-friendly monsters from its parent series, such as the Slitheen, Sontarans and Judoon. On the Slitheen, for example, Martin felt that 'they were beyond annoying in the first series of *Doctor Who*, but in a *children's* children's programme they are actually pretty funny'.[19] It might be argued that *The Sarah Jane Adventures* can be situated in the tradition of juvenile adventure serials extending back to the likes of *Flash Gordon* and *The Perils of Nyoka*, in that characters will be placed in jeopardy but will invariably escape unharmed: this becomes such a convention that viewers instinctively know their heroes will escape whatever dire peril they may face. Indeed, the two-part stories of *The Sarah Jane Adventures* saw the restoration of the episode cliffhangers that had been a convention of classic *Doctor Who*. As James Walton noted in his review of 'Revenge of the Slitheen' for the *Daily Telegraph*: 'Traditional *Who* fans will also have appreciated the cliffhanger ending with our heroes apparently facing imminent death. On a less traditional note, the trailer for the next episode showed them all still alive.'[20]

The Sarah Jane Adventures can be understood as part fantasy and part realist drama. To this extent it differs from *Doctor Who*, which is essentially a fantasy adventure, albeit one that under Davies had acquired some 'soap opera' elements. In *The Sarah Jane Adventures* the extraordinary – aliens, robot dogs, a super-computer in the attic – is rooted in the ordinary. The Earthbound nature of *The Sarah Jane Adventures* recalls *Doctor Who* of the early 1970s. While Sarah Jane and her friends do not come across the proverbial Yeti 'sitting on your loo in Tooting Bec', they encounter all manner of aliens in and around the West London suburb of Ealing, and most of their adventures take place in everyday locations such as schools, shops, high streets, tower blocks and housing estates. Sarah Jane is the most mobile character – her profession as a journalist licences her to move across different social and work contexts – whereas her young companions constantly find themselves contrasting their extraordinary adventures with the mundane realities of school and family life. This juxtaposition between the ordinary and the extraordinary locates *The Sarah Jane Adventures* in the same context as contemporary juvenile fiction such as the Harry Potter and Alex Ryder novels, or – albeit for a slightly older audience – *Buffy the Vampire Slayer*.

Like all the best juvenile drama, *The Sarah Jane Adventures* succeeds largely because it does not patronise its viewers. There are episodes addressing issues that in all likelihood some of its viewers would have been exposed to, including Alzheimer's Disease ('Eye of the Gorgon') and broken families ('The Mark of the Beserker'). There is a reference to one boy's father having been killed in Iraq ('Warriors of Kudlak'). One episode ('The Lost Boy') even touches upon the theme of child abduction when Luke's (apparent) 'real' parents accuse Sarah Jane of kidnapping him – though it turns out they are Slitheen in disguise. A recurring theme of the series is the problematic nature of dysfunctional family relationships. Maria's parents have recently separated, while Clyde's father abandoned his mother when Clyde was small. The moral lessons are subtle and never too intrusive, such as when Sarah Jane explains the 'rules' to the newcomer: 'We look out for each other, we respect all life whatever planet it's from, and we tell no-one!' (The insistence on keeping secrets – essential for a team of alien-fighters – is seen as problematic by some commentators on juvenile fiction, who relate it to the manipulative strategies of child abusers who use emotional blackmail to compel their victims to secrecy. The imperative of secrecy in *The Sarah Jane Adventures* is better understood as akin to the secret identities of *Zorro* or *Batman*, neither of whom, as far as I am aware, have been exposed as paedophiles.) Occasionally *The Sarah Jane Adventures* rehearses the sort of moral dilemmas that have also featured in *Doctor Who*. Sarah Jane's regret over the death of an alien child in 'Revenge of the Slitheen' ('He was a child – twelve years old'), for example, is a counter of sorts to the scene in 'Genesis of the Daleks' when the Doctor compared destroying the Daleks at birth to the killing of a child.

The theme of parenthood pervades *The Sarah Jane Adventures*. In the introductory episode, 'Invasion of the Bane', Sarah Jane is introduced as a somewhat aloof character who has become resigned to a life of spinsterhood. This is rudely brought home by the villainess Mrs Wormwood: 'I take it, Miss Smith, that you're single? . . . No children? . . . Such a wasted life!' Sarah Jane's adoption, at the end of the episode, of Luke – a genetic experiment who has been brought into existence without biological parents – is seen as providing her with the emotional fulfillment that her life has lacked. The idea that an adult's life remains unfulfilled without children is repeated on numerous occasions throughout the series: hence Sarah Jane remarks over and again that Luke has made her life 'complete' ('Revenge of the Slitheen') or 'gave me my life back' ('The Nightmare Man'). While Sarah Jane occasionally doubts her competence, exemplified by her comment that 'I'm not cut out for being a parent – children have no place in my life' ('The Lost Boy'), she is nevertheless presented as a better parent than either Maria's mother (self-absorbed) or Clyde's father (untrustworthy). Sarah Jane is cast in the role of the 'good adult' who acts *in loco parentis* to her teenaged charges – even for Rani, the only one of the juvenile sidekicks from a conventional nuclear family.

The Sarah Jane Adventures also exemplifies the delightfully subversive theme within children's fiction that adult authority is not to be trusted. In the first episode of the series proper ('Revenge of the Slitheen') it turns out that the local comprehensive school has been taken over by aliens and that the teachers are Slitheen (a motif borrowed from the *Doctor Who* episode 'School Reunion' where the school had been taken over by the Krillitanes). The series is replete with 'bad' adults, such as the fake army officers in 'Enemy of the Bane' and 'Death of the Doctor' (UNIT seems to have become particularly susceptible to infiltration), while even the 'good' adults, such as Rani's parents, are usually ineffectual in a crisis. Indeed one of the pleasures of *The Sarah Jane Adventures* is that it is invariably the children who prove more resourceful and courageous than the adults who exercise authority over them. This is taken to its fullest extent in 'The Empty Planet', when adult authority is entirely absent: Rani and Clyde wake up to find that everyone else on Earth has apparently vanished and have to work out for themselves how to save the day. And 'Lost in Time' finds Sarah Jane and the children separated in different time periods as they search for segments of something called the Chronosteen (rather like the Key to Time): Rani finds herself a lady-in-waiting to Lady Jane Grey, while Clyde has to foil a Nazi invasion plot in 1941. These later episodes ('The Empty Planet' and 'Lost in Time' were both in Series Four) acknowledge that the child protagonists are themselves growing up. The maturing of the juvenile protagonists – also seen when Luke leaves for university in Series Four – is another feature that *The Sarah Jane Adventures* may have consciously borrowed from J.K. Rowling's Harry Potter novels.

Some of the best episodes of *The Sarah Jane Adventures* are those which use fantasy frameworks for creating situations of emotional drama. This, of course, is a strategy that we have also seen in new *Doctor Who*. 'The Temptation of Sarah Jane Smith' (2.5), for instance, can be seen as a *Sarah Jane* equivalent of the new *Who* episode 'Father's Day'. Sarah Jane travels through a time portal to the village of Foxgrove in 1951 where she meets her parents and sees herself as a baby. Sarah Jane knows that her parents died in a car accident and wants to know why they left her behind on the fateful day: she has grown up thinking that she was forgotten or abandoned. It turns out that she has stepped into a trap set by a creature known as the Trickster – a recurring antagonist whose entire purpose is to create chaos and confusion – who knows that she will intervene to prevent her parents' death. As in 'Father's Day' the proper timeline is restored when Sarah Jane's parents realise for themselves who she is and what needs to happen: they drive off to what they know will be their deaths, while the adult Sarah Jane realises it was her intervention that caused her parents to leave the infant Sarah Jane behind. The Trickster appears again in 'The Wedding of Sarah Jane Smith' (3.3), where Sarah Jane has fallen in love with the dashing Peter Dalton only to discover at the altar that Peter should in fact be dead, and is alive only due to a Faustian pact with the Trickster. (This is something the Trickster has done before: in 'Whatever Happened to Sarah Jane?' he trapped Sarah Jane in limbo by making a pact with her childhood friend Andrea, who had died in an accident, to swap places with Sarah Jane.) It is a trap by the Trickster to cause Sarah Jane to relinquish her old life of saving the world and so allow chaos to reign. On this occasion, Sarah Jane faces a choice between her own personal happiness and the safety of the world ('I love you – but I can't love you'): naturally she chooses the latter.

These wholly Sarah Jane-focused stories are exceptions rather than the norm: there is usually one story of this type per series. Otherwise *The Sarah Jane Adventures* adheres more or less to the 'Threat and Disaster' narrative – albeit with some differences from its parent series. It would be fair to say that the plotting of *The Sarah Jane Adventures* is less complex than *Doctor Who* – understandably so given its target audience – though this is not to suggest that the stories are in any way anodyne. On the contrary *The Sarah Jane Adventures* reveals a degree of narrative imagination that surpasses many supposedly more adult dramas. Among the weird and wonderful delights are ghostly nuns in a rest home for the elderly ('Eye of the Gorgon'), an astrologer possessed by aliens ('Secrets of the Stars') and paintings that come to life ('Mona Lisa's Revenge'). A favourite motif is that old Earth myths and legends may have some basis in fact, such as the Pied Piper of Hamleyn ('The Day of the Clown') and a Native American curse ('The Curse of Clyde Langer'). Other stories include the obligatory haunted house ('The Eternity Trap') and sinister fun fair ('The Mad Woman in the Attic'). These episodes are all best described as fantasy rather than science fiction: on the whole *The Sarah Jane Adventures* is more willing to embrace magical or supernatural motifs than its parent series. Other stories are more straightforward SF alien invasion narratives, such as 'Invasion of the Bane', 'Revenge of the Slitheen', 'The Last Sontaran' and 'Enemy of the Bane'. 'Invasion of the Bane' is slightly unusual for *The Sarah Jane Adventures* in that it includes an element of social satire that otherwise is mostly absent from the series. Alien invaders attempt to subdue the Earth's population with an addictive substance in a soft drink called Bubble Shock. That this is intended as a comment on modern dietary habits and the obesity epidemic is evident from Mrs Wormwood's somewhat over-the-top speechifying: 'The people are hungry, Miss Smith, for new food, new drinks, new tastes. All the Western world does is eat, all day, every day, eating, they gorge and feast and chew and bite, everything sweet and hot and cold and sticky, just food and drink, that's the human race!' Otherwise *The Sarah Jane Adventures* largely avoids the sort of satire that occasionally characterises *Doctor Who.*

While the absence of satire is, again, an indication of the nature of the target audience for *The Sarah Jane Adventures*, this is not to say that the series makes no demands on the cultural competences of young viewers. There are numerous popular culture references: 'Revenge of the Slitheen', to take just one example, includes references to *Jamie's School Dinners* and *High School Musical*. And particular episodes would seem to have been inspired by other SF and horror sources. 'Warriors of Kudlak' – in which a laser-tag arcade game turns out to be a means of testing the fighting prowess of British children prior to conscripting them into an alien war – is clearly based on the film *The Last Starfighter* (dir. Nick Castle, 1984). 'The Nightmare Man' – in which a ghostly manifestation (somewhat resembling The Joker in *Batman*) 'feeds on every nightmare that every man, woman and child has ever had' – is essentially a watered down version of the *Nightmare on Elm Street* films. Evidence that the writers assumed some adults might be watching can be found in 'The Eternity Trap', where Sarah Jane explains a haunted house as 'a stone-tape manifestation' – which for anyone who remembered would be understood as a reference to Nigel Kneale's television play *The Stone Tape* (1972). To this extent *The Sarah Jane Adventures* varies and extends the range of narrative templates employed in its parent series. This lends credence to Ross P. Garner's assertion that *The Sarah Jane Adventures* 'is born out of a context governed by commercial imperatives, and capitalises upon the success of a previous text, but nevertheless offers its audience different pleasures in terms of character and narrative by making subtle alterations to the generic structure implemented for *Doctor Who*'.[21]

The Sarah Jane Adventures maintained its popularity and its narrative imagination to the end. The Royal Television Society awarded it the accolade of Best Children's Drama in 2010, and it was consistently among the best-performing programmes in its time slot. There is every reason to believe that the series would have continued for many years had it not been for the untimely death of its star. Elisabeth Sladen was diagnosed with cancer early in 2011 and died on 19 April. The BBC announced shortly afterwards that the series would not continue without Sladen: while the Doctor could regenerate, it is impossible to conceive of anyone else playing Sarah Jane.[22] The completed episodes of what became a truncated fifth series of *The Sarah Jane Adventures* – which had introduced a new young companion in the character of alien child called Sky (Sinead Michael) – were broadcast posthumously. Davies would devise another juvenile telefantasy series in its place, *Wizards vs Aliens*, which began on CBBC in 2012. However, this has no diegetic link with *Doctor Who*. And in December 2012 the BBC announced that thereafter there would be no more children's programming on BBC1: all children's content would now be shown exclusively on the digital channel CBBC.[23] While there was a minor backlash against this decision in some sections of the media, with some commentators claiming that it effectively ghettoised children's television, the decision merely reflected the fact that audiences for children's programmes on BBC1 had dwindled to minuscule levels and that most viewers were already watching the same content on CBBC. In this regard, *The Sarah Jane Adventures* marked the end of an era in more ways than one.

13

Golden Jubilee

2010–2013

We're all stories in the end. Just make it a good one . . . A daft old man who stole a magic box and ran away . . . Oh, that box, Amy, you'll dream about that box. It'll never leave you. Big and little at the same time. Brand new and ancient. And the bluest blue ever. The Doctor and Amy Pond.

The Doctor (Matt Smith) in 'The Big Bang'

Just as, in the history of classic *Doctor Who*, a new production regime had generally heralded a change in the style and content of the series, so it would prove for new *Doctor Who*. The simultaneous arrival of a new 'showrunner' (Steven Moffat) and a new Doctor (Matt Smith) for the fifth series in 2010 would mark a turning point for *Doctor Who* that in its way was as decisive as any in the series' history. This was evident both in the new 'look' of *Doctor Who*, with its redesigned TARDIS, fresh title sequence and yet another rearrangement of the theme music, and in its content. The Moffat 'era' would see a shift away from the emotional drama and epic space opera of Davies's *Doctor Who* and the transition to a more fantasy-based style rooted in fairy tale and fable. It would also see a reassertion of the essential Britishness of *Doctor Who* and the re-emergence of the eccentricity of the Doctor himself. This occurred against the background of an increasing visibility for *Doctor Who* in the United States, as the world's longest-running science fiction series approached its fiftieth anniversary.[1]

As ever, the continuing evolution of *Doctor Who* must be understood in relation to its institutional contexts. This was, somewhat paradoxically, a period of both expansion and retrenchment for *Doctor Who*. The *Doctor Who* franchise was now firmly established as the BBC's most successful 'global brand' and the series itself was BBC Worldwide's biggest-selling television show. In 2011 it was reported that revenue from the *Doctor Who* franchise (including spin-off merchandise as well as television sales) had increased by 49 per cent over the previous year 'thanks to significant growth in the US'.[2] America – the one market that had hitherto proved resistant – was eyed as the big prize. *Doctor Who* was now a co-production between BBC Wales and BBC America, which provided additional funding to support some Stateside location shooting. The significance attached to breaking the US market can be seen in the increasing prominence of American-themed stories and locations – including the sixth-series opener 'The Impossible Astronaut'/'Day of the Moon' and the seventh-series episodes 'A Town Called Mercy' and 'The Angels Take Manhattan' – as well as in the return of Alex Kingston, familiar to US audiences as Dr Beth Corday in the long-running medical soap *E.R.*, in a semi-regular guest starring role as the mysterious River Song. 'The US shoot is great for the ambition of our show,' Steven Moffat told the media at the launch of Series Six. 'We made significant inroads last year, but I would hope that we can make it much bigger this time around.'[3] This strategy can perhaps most fairly be assessed as a qualified success: 'The Impossible Astronaut' scored BBC America's highest audience to date (1.3 million) but of course this was only a fraction of the audiences for the major networks.[4]

Yet the continuing growth of the *Doctor Who* franchise took place in a context of some uncertainty about the future of the series itself. There was much speculation about its cost, especially at a time when the BBC was undergoing a period of retrenchment following the freezing of the licence fee by the Conservative-led coalition government elected in 2010. Moffat's response was pragmatic: 'There will never be enough money to make *Doctor Who*. We could spend *Avatar*'s budget and still ask for more . . . Budget cuts are tough. I don't like them, but they force you to be more creative.'[5] There is certainly no evidence of lessening production values: indeed the visual style of *Doctor Who* looks more sumptuous than ever following its switch to High Definition. Nevertheless, it was suggested in some sections of the media that the popularity of *Doctor Who* was declining during these years. In particular, the impression given by the British tabloid press was that the series was haemorrhaging viewers at an alarming rate.[6] This was blamed variously on the increasingly convoluted story arcs and on the new star, who some fans regarded as too young for the role.[7] However, such reports were misleading as they failed to take account of changes in audience viewing habits. The declining viewing figures reported in the *Daily Mail* and elsewhere were the 'overnight' figures that did not include those who recorded the programme to watch at a later date. There had been a significant increase in 'time-shift' viewing between the series' return in 2005 (when the consolidated viewing figures for *Doctor Who* taking into account repeats and those who recorded to watch later usually added about half a million to the overnight figures) and 2011 (when consolidated figures typically accounted for a further 2–2.5 million viewers).[8] The reasons for this change in viewing behaviour include the earlier transmission times for some of the more recent episodes and the launch in 2008 of the BBC's iPlayer service that allowed people to watch online up to a week after the broadcast. In fact, the consolidated average audiences for Series Five (7.8 million) and Series Six (7.5 million) were consistent with each series of *Doctor Who* since its relaunch in 2005.

Where fans did have some cause for concern, however, was the apparent reduction in the number of new episodes of *Doctor Who*. Series Five in 2010 followed the pattern established since 2005, with a full series of thirteen episodes starting on the Easter weekend, but Series Six in 2011, while still comprising thirteen episodes, was split between two runs of seven in the spring and six in the early autumn. This was billed somewhat disingenuously as 'two new series' when in reality it was one series split in two. Moffat told *DWM* that this was his idea and was intended to address the decline in ratings usually experienced during the warmer summer months: the split series meant 'twice as many event episodes as we had before'.[9] However, the launch of Series Seven was put back to the end of the following summer, and was split between six episodes in 2012 and a further eight in 2013. This meant that what should have been the 2012 series was actually split over two years. This time Moffat was rather vague about whose decision it had been. He told the website *DigitalSpy*: 'I don't know, on this occasion, that the thinking particularly came from me, actually . . . I think that decision actually came from the BBC.'[10]

The strategy of splitting series into shorter chunks prompted much speculation within *Doctor Who* fandom. Some thought it was simply a cost-cutting exercise, others suggested it was to facilitate Moffat working on the successful new detective series *Sherlock* at the same time as *Doctor Who*. The official explanation put forward was that rationing new episodes enhanced the audience's appetite for *Doctor Who*. Moffat rationalised it thus:

> I've been well up for anything that we can do to shake up the trans-mission pattern, the way we deliver it to the audience and how long we make the audience wait, simply because that makes *Doctor Who* an event piece . . . The more *Doctor Who* becomes a perennial, the faster it starts to die. You've got to shake it up, you've got to keep people on edge and wondering when it will come back . . . So keeping *Doctor Who* as an event, and never making people feel 'Oh, it's lovely, reliable old *Doctor Who* – it'll be back about this time, at that time of year.' Once you start to do that, just slowly, it becomes like any much-loved ornament in your house – ultimately invisible.[11]

Another possible explanation, especially for splitting the 2012 series over two years, is that this would allow the costs to be spread over two budgeting periods rather than one. However, the rationing of new *Doctor Who* episodes as the series approached its fiftieth anniversary in 2013 seemed to some fans more than a little perverse.

Steven Moffat's appointment to replace Russell T. Davies as executive producer and writer-in-chief of *Doctor Who* had been widely welcomed within fandom. Towards the end of Davies's period in charge there had been some sections of the fan community who had tired of what they regarded as the formulaic nature of the series. In particular criticism was directed against the perceived over-reliance on old monsters (the Daleks had featured in each one of Davies's four full series of *Doctor Who*) and the introduction of 'soap opera' elements in the characterisations of the Doctor's companions. In contrast, Moffat was seen by many fans as a more 'authentic' *Doctor Who* writer. He had not only provided some of the favourite stories of the Davies era, winning three successive Hugo Awards (for 'The Empty Child'/'The Doctor Dances', 'The Girl in the Fireplace' and 'Blink'), but had also devised some of the most frightening new monsters in the Weeping Angels and the Vashta Narada. Following his appointment as the series' new showrunner, Moffat suggested that he wanted to move *Doctor Who* away from its reliance on old monsters: 'We're not in the business of being nostalgic, we're making nostalgia for the future... *Doctor Who* is at its best when it's brand new and you've always got to remember that there's a new bunch of eight-year-olds watching every year – it has to belong to them.'[12]

Like Davies before him, Moffat was a lifelong *Doctor Who* fan. He joked that his whole career had been 'a secret plan to get this job... I applied before but I got knocked back 'cos the BBC wanted someone else. And I was seven.'[13] He had written a *Doctor Who* short story ('Continuity Errors') for Virgin's *Decalog 3* anthology and the 1999 *Comic Relief* spoof 'Doctor Who and the Curse of Fatal Death'. In television, Moffat was best known as a sitcom writer (*Joking Apart, Chalk, Coupling*) though his oeuvre also includes modernised versions of classic Victorian popular literature in *Jekyll* (2007) and *Sherlock* (2010–). He also worked on the early script development of Steven Spielberg's *The Adventures of Tintin: The Secret of the Unicorn* (2012) before he withdrew from the project in order to take on *Doctor Who*, declaring that it was 'the proper duty of every British subject to come to the aid of the Tardis'.[14] Moffat had a distinct view about the style and nature of *Doctor Who*:

> For me, *Doctor Who* literally is a fairytale. It's not really science fiction. It's not out in space, it's set under your bed... Although it is watched by far more adults than children, there's something fundamental in its DNA that makes it a children's programme and it makes children of everyone who watches it. If you're still a grown up by the end of that opening music, you're not paying attention![15]

It is tempting to see Moffat-era *Doctor Who* as a reflection of his own childhood memories of watching the series. Hence the Doctor is often seen through the eyes of children, notably in episodes such as 'The Eleventh Hour' and 'The Doctor, the Widow and the Wardrobe'. The Doctor even remarks that 'the scariest place in the universe [is] a child's bedroom' ('Night Terrors'). His new companion, Amy Pond, remarks that the Doctor 'never interferes – unless there's children crying' ('The Beast Below'). A recurring theme of this period is the Doctor coming to the rescue of children who say they are afraid of monsters. A scene in 'The Hungry Earth', for example, where the Doctor reassures a frightened young boy ('Have you met monsters before? Are you scared of them?' 'No – they're scared of me!') recalls a similar moment in Moffat's

'The Girl in the Fireplace' ('What do monsters have nightmares about?' 'Me!') where the monster had been (literally) hiding under young Reinette's bed.

Moffat's view of *Doctor Who* as a fairytale is evident from the very beginning in 'The Eleventh Hour' (5.1), arguably the best introductory episode for any Doctor since William Hartnell. 'The Eleventh Hour' opens with an 8-year-old girl alone in a house thanking Santa for her Christmas presents but also asking him to send someone to fix the mysterious crack in her bedroom wall: as if on cue the newly-regenerated Doctor's TARDIS crash lands in her garden. The Doctor himself likens it all to a fairytale ('Amelia Pond – like a name in a fairytale') and this idea is reinforced through the idea of 'the Raggedy Doctor' who becomes Amelia's 'imaginary friend'. Moffat employs a device he had previously used in 'The Girl in the Fireplace' in that the Doctor has to leave Amelia briefly, promising he will be back in five minutes: it turns out that for her it is a full twelve years before he returns and meets her again as a young adult. The grown-up Amelia has clung to her belief that the Doctor was real ('Twelve years – and four psychiatrists . . . I kept biting them . . . They said you weren't real'), though she prefers to be known as Amy (Amelia is 'too fairytale') and works as a kissogram (when the Doctor meets her again she is dressed as a policewoman with an improbably short skirt). If, as has often been suggested, the role of the companion in *Doctor Who* is to act as a surrogate for the viewer, then Moffat seeks to position the viewer as an eternal child:

> *Amy*:   You told me you had a time machine!
>
> *The Doctor*: And you believed me.
>
> *Amy*:   Then I grew up.
>
> *The Doctor*: Aw, you never want to do that.

The fairytale motif recurs throughout the rest of the series. In later episodes the Doctor will dismiss the story of something called the Pandorica as 'a fairytale, a legend, it can't be real' ('The Pandorica Opens'), while the mysterious River Song suggests that she and the Doctor are themselves fairytales ('Flesh and Stone'). The resolution of Series Five, indeed, will depend upon Amy still believing in 'the Raggedy Man' following a 'total event collapse' that causes him to be taken out of existence when the entire universe is 'rebooted' ('The Big Bang').

With David Tennant having handed in his TARDIS key following 'The End of Time', it fell to Moffat to introduce Doctor No. 11. Moffat has suggested that initially he was thinking of an older Doctor, so the choice of Matt Smith, at 27 the youngest actor to take on the mantle of the ageless Time Lord, came as something of a surprise.[16] Smith was a relative unknown (prompting the inevitable 'Matt Who?' headlines) and it has been suggested that this fact, and his youth, were deliberate tactics to ensure that the new star would stay with the series at least until its golden anniversary in 2013.[17] There were concerns within fandom that Smith was too young to suggest the necessary gravitas for the Doctor and some comments to the effect that he would turn out to be 'another Peter Davison'. (This is curious in itself as Davison is now highly regarded by many fans of the classic series who believe that his subtle performance has not been given the credit it truly deserves.) However, these concerns were soon allayed as Smith proved to be a charismatic and energetic Eleventh Doctor. He plays the Doctor as a character older than his years who alternates between youthful zeal and world-weary introspection. There are echoes of Patrick Troughton in the way that he acts as a sort of mentor to his companions: indeed Smith has said that he was particularly fascinated by the Second Doctor episodes he watched while preparing for the role.[18] He also restores some of the eccentricity that had been stripped away in the Eccleston and Tennant incarnations. This is most evident in his choice of costume: his tweed jacket, braces and bow tie suggest the persona of a dotty academic. Smith's floppy-haired 'geek chic' endeared him to female fans and made bow ties an essential fashion accessory for 8-year-old boys across Britain.

Moffat's *Doctor Who* would refigure the relationship between the Doctor and the role of the companion. Davies's *Doctor Who* had opened the possibility of the female companion as a romantic interest for the Doctor. This is rejected as a possibility in Moffat's *Doctor Who* when a clearly embarrassed Doctor first fails to understand and then spurns the overtly sexual advances of his companion Amy Pond (Karen Gillan) at the end of 'Flesh and Stone'. This scene provoked a great deal of controversy within fandom. One *DWM* reader complained: 'I have suffered in silence over the Doctor's unnecessary canoodlings with a variety of fellow travellers during the last five years, but the sight of Amy Pond fawning over our Time Lord with all the panache of a tuppenny tart is just too much.'[19] Some male viewers were equally nonplussed as to how anyone could reject the overtures of the smouldering Karen Gillan who, with her flowing flaxen hair and penchant for the shortest of mini-skirts, was certainly cast in the 'sex bomb' mould of previous companions such as Jo and Peri. Yet the point of the scene is that, in the Doctor's eyes, Amy is still a child: he met her when she was 8 years old and still thinks of her as 'a little Scottish girl in an English village'. In the event, Amy would have to make do with her somewhat hapless fiancé Rory (Arthur Darvill) whom she marries at the end of Series Five and who becomes a regular companion in his own right. Rory functions mainly as comic relief through his bemused reaction to the unusual situations in which he finds himself ('I'm trapped inside a giant robot replica of my wife – I'm really trying not to see this as a metaphor'), though it is testament to Darvill's performance that his transformation into action hero in 'A Good Man Goes to War' is convincing.

The Doctor's rejection of Amy's advances is not to say, however, that this is a sexless Doctor. Far from it in fact: there are references to the Doctor marrying Marilyn Monroe ('A Christmas Carol') and he is even caught *in flagrante* hiding under the skirt of a royal ward ('The Impossible Astronaut'). More significantly Moffat develops the character of Dr (later – or previously – Professor) River Song, who had first appeared in the David Tennant story 'Silence in the Library'/'Forest of the Dead' where it was hinted that she was the Doctor's wife from his future. Moffat seems to have been inspired by Audrey Niffenegger's novel *The Time Traveller's Wife* in which two lovers experience their relationship in a different sequence from each other: River knows the Doctor's future (which is her past), while the Doctor does not know how their relationship begins but knows how it ends. The relationship between the Doctor and River serves several purposes in *Doctor Who*. On one level it can be seen as a means of shoring up the interest of adult viewers given Moffat's suggestion that *Doctor Who* was essentially 'a children's programme'. The scenes between Matt Smith and Alex Kingston are written and played rather like a bickering married couple from a sitcom – reminiscent as much of *I Love Lucy* as Moffat's own *Coupling* – while the age difference between them is emphasised through references to *The Graduate* (dir. Mike Nichols, 1967) with Smith as the shy young man ('Hello, Benjamin') and Kingston as the sexy older woman ('Mrs Robinson'). On another level it is a means of interacting with fandom: the warnings about revealing the future ('Spoilers!') serving as a plea not to spoil others' enjoyment by revealing plot twists. The revelation of River's true identity – at the end of 'A Good Man Goes to War' – was one of the series' best-kept secrets and was filmed under conditions of high security.[20]

The unfolding narrative of the Doctor–River Song relationship was one of the means through which Moffat implanted his signature on *Doctor Who*. The problematic nature of romantic relationships is a recurring theme of his work, seen in *Joking Apart* and *Coupling*. (It should be pointed out here that Moffat himself has denied consciously exploring themes: 'They happen accidentally. You repeat yourself once too often and it becomes a theme. We tell stories – that's what people talk about, not themes.'[21] In which case it would perhaps be more appropriate to say that the problematic nature of romantic relationships is a recurring story pattern in his work.) There are other ways, too, in which Moffat has sought to distance his *Doctor Who* from the previous regime. For example, Davies had located his Earthbound *Doctor Who* stories in an urban realist setting, with recognisable London locations prominent throughout his tenure. In contrast, Moffat's *Doctor Who* is set mostly outside the metropolis, with the Doctor finding alien threats in a quaint and sleepy English village ('The Eleventh Hour', 'Amy's Choice') and a remote Welsh valley ('The Hungry Earth'/'Cold Blood'). To put it another way: if the Britain of Davies's *Doctor Who* had been the realist-contemporary Britain of *EastEnders* or *Coronation Street*, then the Britain of Moffat's *Doctor Who* is the essentially imaginary and fantasy Britain of *The Avengers* or *The League of Gentlemen*. And while Davies had demystified the character of the Doctor during the David Tennant stories, for instance by normalising his relationships with his various surrogate families (the Tylers, the Joneses, the Nobles), Moffat has sought to restore the mystery and enigma of the Doctor. Indeed, as the series approached its anniversary, Moffat returned to the question raised in the very first episode of *Doctor Who* – albeit in a rather more elaborate way: 'On the Fields of Trenzalore, at the Fall of the Eleventh, where no living creature can speak falsely or fail to answer, a question will be asked . . . The oldest question in the universe, the question that hides in plain sight. Doctor – Who?' ('The Wedding of River Song'). 'Doctor – *Who*?' became a recurring question in Series Seven in 2012–2013, which featured more verbal references to the classic series, as *Doctor Who* prepared to celebrate its golden anniversary.

Moffat's imprimatur as *Doctor Who*'s showrunner is most evident in his fondness for intricately plotted story arcs. These can be seen as a strategy for maintaining audience loyalty (though they also risk alienating casual viewers) and for appealing to the US market where this has been a common feature of high-end drama series. They also negated the need for the sort of *deus ex machina* resolutions that had characterised the Davies era. For many fans, Davies's series finales had depended too often upon previously unsignalled plot twists, such as the revelation that Rose is the 'Bad Wolf' ('The Parting of the Ways') or the creation of an alternate half-human Doctor whose knowledge conveniently saves the day ('Journey's End'). Moffat's series-finale cliffhangers, in contrast, are resolved through carefully laid plotting. Thus the Doctor is able to escape from the Pandorica ('The Big Bang') and avert his own death at a fixed point in time ('The Wedding of River Song') because he has already planned his way out. Moffat would include both visual and narrative clues throughout each series that lay the groundwork for a climactic denouement. In Series Five, for example, there is an apparent continuity error in 'Flesh and Stone' (5.5) where the Doctor leaves Amy alone in the forest only to reappear to offer her reassurance: eagle-eyed viewers will spot that his costume is different in this scene. In the series finale 'The Big Bang' (5.13), however, it is revealed that this is the Doctor from the future crossing his own timeline to impart an essential piece of plot information. Series Six is by far the most intricately plotted. The Doctor's apparent death at the beginning of 'The Impossible Astronaut' (6.1) sets in train a sequence of events that will have far-reaching consequences for his companions. However, the answer to how the Doctor escapes his death has already been offered in Amy's response ('He can't be dead . . . maybe he's a clone or a duplicate or something') as at the end of the series it is revealed that the Doctor has substituted a robot double of himself. A further irony is that the Amy who says 'maybe he's a clone or a duplicate or something' will turn out to be a duplicate herself. For some critics, however, this trend became just as annoying as Davies's 'cheat' endings. As Gavin Fuller observed in his review of 'Day of the Moon', for example: '"Day of the Moon" is clearly aimed as an installment in an over-arching storyline, but it seems this is a storyline that will require the audience's concentration over many weeks; any casual viewer turning in this week, and I suspect not a few fans, will have been left baffled by the goings-on.'[22]

Moffat is particularly fond of a plot device known as the temporal or causal loop. This is different from the temporal paradox of a classic *Doctor Who* story such as 'Day of the Daleks', where resistance fighters from the future travel back in time to prevent an event (the outbreak of World War Three) only to discover that they actually caused it in the first place: they are unable to change the course of events and become trapped in a paradox. In contrast the temporal loop is based on the idea of two events at different points in time that exist in a cause-and-effect loop: one cannot have happened without the other having already happened and vice versa. This is consistent with one of the philosophical theories of time travel, known as the Novikov Self-Consistency Principle, which maintains that while events that cancel each other out (a paradox) could not happen, events that are consistent with each other could. The Doctor explains this in rather different terms by suggesting that time is not linear but should be understood as 'a big ball of wibbly-wobbly timey-wimey stuff' ('Blink'). Moffat's Hugo Award-winning episode 'Blink' (3.10) is posited on the notion that the Tenth Doctor and Martha – stranded in 1969 without the TARDIS, having been thrown back in time by the Weeping Angels, creatures who feed off time energy – are able to communicate with a young woman called Sally Sparrow in the present by leaving messages in the 'easter eggs' of DVDs. They have a conversation across time in which the Doctor is able to answer Sally's questions because in the DVD he is reading a transcript of their conversation taken by Sally's friend and then passed on to the Doctor when Sally meets him in the present. Another example is the 2007 *Children in Need* special 'Time-Crash', which Moffat wrote as a two-hander for David Tennant and Peter Davison. A temporal anomaly caused when the TARDIS crashes into itself is resolved when the Doctor recalls watching himself from his other self's point of view. Or as Davison puts it: 'You remembered being me watching you doing that!'[23]

The temporal loop motif fitted Moffat's predilection towards non-linear narrative and elliptical storytelling. One of its consequences in *Doctor Who* is to refashion the nature of the cliffhanger. Consider, for example, the climax of Series Five. At the end of 'The Pandorica Opens' (5.12) the Doctor is trapped inside the ultimate prison beneath Stone-henge in AD102. The Pandorica is a trap constructed by an alliance of all his enemies to contain 'the most feared thing in all the universe' and it has been established that it is impossible to open from the inside. The following episode 'The Big Bang' opens '1,894 years later' and shows young Amelia Pond being taken to see the Pandorica, now a museum exhibit, whereupon it opens to reveal that it contains the adult Amy Pond ('Okay, kid, this is where it gets complicated!'). It is then explained that the Doctor was released from the Pandorica by Rory (or, rather, by an Auton replica of Rory reincarnated as a Roman centurion) and replaced with Amy (who has been shot by Auton–Rory but whom the Doctor believes will survive inside the Pandorica). Rory knows how to do this because he has been told by the Doctor, travelling back in time after being released from the Pandorica. The causal loop is that the knowledge to release the Doctor from the Pandorica is provided to Rory by the Doctor after Rory has released him. Even the Doctor is confused ('Time travel – you can't keep it straight in your head') and no doubt he was also speaking for many viewers on this occasion.

It will be clear that Moffat's *Doctor Who* employs an extremely intricate and highly complex style of storytelling. Moffat rewrites the known history of the *Doctor Who* universe through a multitude of alternate time lines and parallel realities. This may be understood as a response to those fans who obsess over internal consistency. Moffat told the San Diego Comics Convention that 'a television series which embraces both the ideas of parallel universes and the concept of changing time can't have any continuity errors – it can't.'[24] Moffat's 'Whoniverse' is one in which the entire universe is 'rebooted' ('The Big Bang') and where the rewriting of a fixed point in time creates a world where 'all of history is happening at once' ('The Wedding of River Song'). Amy Pond experiences at least four alternate time lines, while Rory is, variously, alive, dead, never existed in the first place, an Auton replica of himself, alive again, then briefly a military commando, before finally dying twice on the same day in order to create a paradox that rids the world of the Weeping Angels. Further narrative complications occur in 'A Good Man Goes to War', wherein it is revealed that River Song is actually Amy and Rory's daughter, and in 'Let's Kill Hitler!' where Amy's childhood friend Melody turns out to be a younger version of River. Indeed the story arc of Series Six became so convoluted that there was a conscious decision in Series Seven to shift back to stand-alone stories.[25] It is difficult to avoid the conclusion that Moffat's 'wibbly wobbly timey-wimey' narratives are intended as a parody of SF conventions à la Douglas Adams. To the extent that it foregrounds the mechanics of storytelling over substance and content – and even draws attention to its own narrative complexity ('You named your daughter after – your *daughter*?') – Moffat's *Doctor Who* is genuinely postmodern.

Beyond the highly complex story arcs, Moffat would orient *Doctor Who* further towards fantasy and away from its reliance on old monsters. The Daleks have appeared less frequently since 2010, and the only classic series monsters resurrected during the first three Moffat series were the Silurians ('The Hungry Earth'/'Cold Blood') and the Ice Warriors ('Cold War'). The return of the Great Intelligence in the 2012 Christmas special 'The Snowmen', now taking corporeal form in the person of Dr Simeon (Richard E. Grant), fuelled speculation that the Yeti would be the next classic series monsters to put in an appearance, though in the event its foot soldiers turned out to be a new creature known as Whispermen ('The Name of the Doctor'). The introduction of recurring characters such as 'good Sontaran' Strax and Madame Vastra (a Silurian detective in Victorian London) is another indication that Moffat sought to refresh the formula by imbuing old villains with a sense of their own individuality. At the same time, Moffat has been careful to use his best monsters, the Weeping Angels, sparingly. Moffat's monsters play upon elemental childhood fears: the Weeping Angels are unable to move as long as you can see them, while the Silence are forgotten the moment you turn your back. In this sense they represent a form of psychological horror that is much more frightening and nightmare-inducing than the antics of ranting Daleks, stomping Cybermen or haka-chanting Sontarans.

Moffat-era *Doctor Who* is characterised by a wider range of narrative templates than the preceding Davies period. Davies had varied the 'Threat and Disaster' formula of *Doctor Who* in some more quirky and experimental episodes such as 'Love & Monsters' and 'Turn Left', though these had always been bound by the extent of their difference to remain one-off examples. The tradition of more experimental episodes continued into the Moffat period with the likes of 'The Lodger' (5.11), which adopts the genre of a flat-share sitcom as the Doctor – temporarily marooned without the TARDIS – finds himself lodging with his new best friend Craig (played by comedy actor James Corden) while investigating the invisible spaceship parked on the roof. ('The Lodger' was another example of a story recycled from other *Doctor Who* media: Gareth

Roberts based it on a comic strip he had written for *DWM* featuring the Tenth Doctor lodging with Mickey.) A significant trend that emerged during this period was the recycling of plots and motifs from Hollywood films. While pastiche or parody had never been far beneath the surface of *Doctor Who*, it became more explicit than ever during this period. Thus 'The Time of Angels' and 'Flesh and Stone' (5.5–5.6) – in which a detachment of space marine/clerics led by a female specialist (River Song) have to fight off a ruthless foe (Weeping Angels) in the wreck of a space liner – owes more than a little to the basic scenario of *Aliens* (dir. James Cameron, 1986). 'The Curse of the Black Spot' (6.3) – where the Doctor and his friends find themselves on a pirate ship menaced by 'a stroppy homicidal mermaid' – is a fantasy swashbuckler in the mould of the *Pirates of the Caribbean* films. 'Let's Kill Hitler!' (6.8) – an adventure romp set in Berlin in 1938 – is a sanitised version of *Inglourious Basterds* (dir. Quentin Tarantino, 2009). 'Asylum of the Daleks' (7.1) – in which the Doctor is sent (by the Daleks) to infiltrate a high-security prison – is somewhat reminiscent of *Escape from New York* (dir. John Carpenter, 1981). 'A Town Called Mercy' (7.3) – where a cyborg gunslinger menaces the American West – borrows from *The Terminator* (dir. James Cameron, 1984) and *Westworld* (dir. Michael Crichton, 1973). 'Cold War' (7.8) – an Ice Warrior on the loose in a Soviet-era submarine – is *Aliens* (dir. Ridley Scott, 1979) meets *The Hunt for Red October* (dir. John McTiernan, 1990). And the title of 'Dinosaurs on a Spaceship' (7.2) is nothing if not an homage to the infamous *Snakes on a Plane* (dir. David R. Ellis, 2006).[26]

The increasing diversification of narrative templates and conceptual frameworks in this period of *Doctor Who* can be attributed in some measure to the wider pool of writers that Moffat brought to the series. On the one hand there were more commissions for established new series writers, such as Mark Gatiss, Toby Whithouse, Gareth Roberts and Chris Chibnall. On the other hand, Moffat also brought in new writers from outside *Doctor Who* fandom, including two best known for comedy in Simon Nye (*Frank Stubbs Promotes, Men Behaving Badly*) and Richard Curtis (*The Vicar of Dibley, Four Weddings And A Funeral, Notting Hill*). However, the biggest 'name' recruited to *Doctor Who* at this time was the acclaimed comic-strip and fantasy fiction author Neil Gaiman. Gaiman, best known for the *Sandman* comics of the 1980s, was the first major fantasy author to contribute to *Doctor Who*: his recruitment is indicative of Moffat's strategy to steer the series further towards fantasy. Gaiman's episode 'The Doctor's Wife' (6.4) – originally planned for Series Five but held over to Series Six due to its effects-heavy budget – is one of the most conceptually imaginative and visually stunning *Doctor Who* stories ever made. (The title is a longstanding in-joke of *Doctor Who*: it had been a phoney title used in the production office in the 1980s to misdirect fans.) Here the Doctor's 'wife' is the living embodiment of the TARDIS incarnated as an ethereal woman. The Doctor, receiving what he believes is a signal from other Time Lords, traces its source to a place 'outside the universe' only to discover that it is a trap devised by a disembodied entity known as House which seeks to take over the TARDIS and feed off its energy. As House is unable to destroy the TARDIS matrix directly, he contrives to transfer it to the body of a woman, Idris, where it will die. The episode develops an idea introduced into *Doctor Who* in the early 1970s that the TARDIS is as much 'a living consciousness' as a machine: and its appearance as a woman ('Did you wish *really hard*?' Amy asks the Doctor) is consistent with Jon Pertwee's frequent references to the TARDIS as a 'she'. The episode represents the relationship between the Doctor and the TARDIS as a sort of love affair ('You were the most beautiful thing I'd ever known' says the Doctor) and it is suggested that it was the TARDIS as much as the Doctor who experienced a form of wanderlust on Gallifrey all those years ago ('I wanted to see the universe so I stole a Time Lord and ran away'). There is also an explanation of why the TARDIS has proved so unreliable over the years:

The Doctor: You didn't always take me where I wanted to go.

Idris: No, but I always took you where you *needed* to go.

Gaiman is evidently steeped in *Doctor Who* lore: he includes oblique references to the classic series, including the junkyard setting ('An Unearthly Child') and the Time Lord Emergency Messaging System ('The War Games'), while the TARDIS console that the Doctor and Idris build from left-over parts recalls the Third Doctor's attempts to repair it in 'Inferno'. It is the closest example to date in new *Doctor Who* of the more conceptual type of storytelling that occasionally featured in classic series stories such as 'Logopolis' and 'Castrovalva'.

'The Doctor's Wife' exemplifies a trend in Moffat-era *Doctor Who* towards what one former script editor (Terrance Dicks) had described as 'stories set in dreamland, fairyland, limbo or any other metaphysical setting'. This type of story had remained largely absent from the series since 'The Mind Robber' in 1968 but it returned to prominence under Moffat. The original planning documents for *Doctor Who* had envisaged what were termed 'sideways' adventures as well as those set in the past and future: to this extent it could be argued that the re-emergence of 'sideways' stories represented Moffat consciously returning *Doctor Who* to something closer to its origins. The difference now was that rather than using outright fantasy to examine characters' responses to spatial and/or temporal displacement (as in 'Planet of the Giants', for example) it now became a vehicle for exploring existential questions of choice. This is explicit in the title of 'Amy's Choice' (5.7), where the Doctor, Amy and Rory find themselves simultaneously experiencing two crisis situations: in one the TARDIS has lost power and is drifting into a cold star, while in another they are battling an army of zombies in Amy's home village of Ledworth. Simon Nye's script is based on the premise that 'you can't spot a dream while you're having it'. It turns out that these scenarios have been conjured up by the mysterious and sinister Dream Lord who tells them: 'If you die in the dream, you wake up in reality . . . Ask me what happens if you die in reality . . . You die, stupid, that's why it's called reality!' The episode recalls the classic *Doctor Who* stories 'The Celestial Toymaker' and 'The Mind Robber', while the character of the Dream Lord seems to have been inspired by 'Q' in *Star Trek: The Next Generation.* (There is also an echo of the Valeyard in 'Trial of a Time Lord' in the revelation that the Dream Lord is a dark version of the Doctor himself, conjured into existence when a few grains of 'psychic pollen' fell into the TARDIS's time rotor.) In Tom MacRae's similar-themed 'The Girl Who Waited' (6.10) Amy is accidentally caught in a faster time stream in which she ages 36 years. This happens in a 'kindness facility', where victims of a plague that proves fatal within one day are sent to an alternate reality where their last day is spread over decades so that they can experience a longer life. MacRae uses the premise to consider how people's decisions may affect their future. Rory has to choose between two versions of his wife: 'The future won't have happened . . . She's not real . . . There can only be one Amy in the TARDIS. Which do you want?'

Moffat's conception of *Doctor Who* as a fairytale is most apparent in his treatment of the Christmas specials, which have tended to feature the Doctor without his regular travelling companions. Davies's Christmas specials had all been 'Threat and Disaster' narratives on a grand scale as the Doctor defeats invasions by Sycorax ('The Christmas Invasion'), Racnoss ('The Runaway Bride') and Cybermen ('The Next Doctor') or averts catastrophe onboard the *Starship Titanic* ('Voyage the Damned'). In contrast, Moffat's Christmas specials have tended to be fables that draw upon literary fantasy. The inspiration for 'A Christmas Carol' (5.X) is clear enough: the Doctor reforms a Scrooge-like moneylender (who takes family members as collateral on loans and places them in cryogenic suspension) by reintroducing him to the girl he had loved as a young man. 'The Doctor, the Widow and the Wardrobe' (6.X) similarly reworks its source material in a *Doctor Who* style: two children evacuated with their mother to the country during the Second World War are displaced into a forest of living trees. (As an aside, it might be remembered that in 1963 the BBC felt that the SF stories of C. S. Lewis were 'clumsy and old-fashioned': his fantasy novels evidently were a different matter.) 'The Snowmen' (7.X) is a pastiche of Victoriana rather than being based on a particular source, but is replete with suitably Dickensian imagery and moments of pure fantasy, such as an invisible staircase that ascends to the TARDIS hidden in the clouds above London. The style of these episodes is more whimsical than most: their settings and costumes seem deliberately unreal. Hence 'The Snowmen' makes no attempt at a realistic depiction of Victorian London but visualises it in the style of Christmas cards. The pastiche of well-known literary sources with added horror (especially in 'The Snowmen') is reminiscent of Robert Holmes.

The Britishness of *Doctor Who* is reasserted in the Moffat era. Of course it has been a recurring theme of the series that it acts as a commentary on aspects of the British historical experience. This takes a particularly distinctive turn under Moffat. 'Victory of the Daleks' (5.3) by Mark Gatiss, for example, although one of the least-favourite episodes of this period, is nevertheless ideologically fascinating in its subversion of one of the dominant motifs of the series. The Doctor is summoned to wartime London by Winston Churchill – who turns out to be an old friend of the Doctor with a direct line to the TARDIS – to witness Britain's 'secret weapon' in the war against the Nazis. Churchill's 'Ironsides' are in fact Daleks, apparently serving the British war effort as the inventions of Professor Bracewell. Given that the Daleks have so often been equated with Nazism, the motif of khaki-coloured Daleks decorated with Union Jacks ('I am your soldier . . . Would you care for some tea?') is in its way as subversive as it is ridiculous, while it is Churchill's rhetoric of 'total war' that is more reminiscent of the Daleks themselves. Of course it all turns out to be an elaborate ruse: Professor Bracewell is a robot created by the Daleks themselves in order to set a trap for the Doctor that in turn will bring about the creation of a New Dalek Paradigm. (The new series' Daleks are 'impure' on account of being cloned from human cells: they have found a source of 'pure' Dalek DNA but it will not recognise them as Daleks due to their impurity. Hence the Daleks have devised a scenario to trick the Doctor into declaring 'I am the Doctor – and you are the Daleks!'). It is an imaginative but not entirely satisfactory episode, rather undermined by the *Star Wars*-style special effects sequence in which a squadron of Spitfires surrounded by gravity bubbles attack the Dalek spaceship in orbit around the Earth.

Moffat's 'The Beast Below' (5.2) may be understood as a satire of British politics in the early twenty-first century: to this extent it recalls classic *Doctor Who* stories such as 'The Sun Makers' which have been understood (not least in this book) as commentaries on Britain in the 1970s. In 'The Beast Below' the Doctor and Amy land on the *Starship UK*, which is carrying the people of the United Kingdom to a new world after the Earth's surface has been ravaged by solar flares. The world of the starship is a pastiche of British society and culture – including red telephone boxes, London Underground signs, ice cream vans and bowler-hatted City gents – but it has been 'bent out of shape'. This Britain has become a police state where the monarch ('Liz Ten') is a mere figurehead and citizens are under constant observation as in *Nineteen Eighty-Four*. It is suggested that totalitarianism is 'the price that has been paid for the security of the British people'. The pretence of participatory democracy is maintained but is illusory: the citizenry are brain-washed by party political broadcasts into voting to preserve the status quo. It turns out that *Starship UK* is being powered by a giant Star Whale tethered to the underside of the ship – a motif that suggests the influence of the *Discworld* fantasy novels of Terry Pratchett – and every five years people are asked to vote either to 'protest' at its treatment or to 'forget' what they have been told about its exploitation. As the consequences of a protest vote would be to end the journey, the result of the referendum is always to choose to forget. The Doctor is cast in the role of revolutionary ('Hold on, we're bringing down the government!') whose intervention brings about the end of the totalitarian state. Much was made of the fact that 'The Beast Below' was aired in the run-up to a general election in Britain: the sinister puppet Smilers have been compared to former Prime Minister Tony Blair, who was often depicted by cartoonists with a Cheshire-cat grin.[27] It was certainly the most overt political satire in *Doctor Who* since 'The Happiness Patrol' in 1988.

If the series' commentary on Britishness was consistent with *Doctor Who*'s past, then a possible new direction is opened up by its embracing of America. Nicholas Cull observes that classic *Doctor Who* had always defined itself in opposition to American SF such as *Star Trek* and *Star Wars*: the low-budget British series could not match the production values of its expensive transatlantic cousins so instead opted for quirkiness and eccentricity in contrast to their space opera and military-themed SF. And American themes 'had never been lucky for *Doctor Who*': 'The Gunfighters' had the lowest appreciation index for any *Doctor Who* story, Terry Nation had tried and failed to market the Daleks in America in the 1960s, and the 1996 television film suggested that *Doctor Who* was simply not fitted to the American market.[28] The new series of *Doctor Who*, however, has made concessions to American tastes and sensibilities without compromising its essential Britishness. In particular the sixth-series opener 'The Impossible Astronaut' and 'Day of the Moon' (6.1–6.2) – the first two-part opening story since the relaunch of *Doctor Who* – seemed like a homage to classic Americana with its location shooting in Arizona and the Doctor even wearing a stetson. It is a typically complex Moffat story in which Amy, Rory and River Song witness the apparent death of the Doctor at Lake Silencio in the present – shot dead before he can regenerate by what appears to be an Apollo astronaut – and then travel to Washington DC in 1969 with a younger Doctor, from earlier in his own time stream, where they meet Richard Nixon in the Oval Office and uncover a plot by an alien order known as the Silence to change the course of history. Incredibly, this marked the first occasion on which *Doctor Who* had made any reference to the Apollo space programme: it turns out here that it has been engineered by the Silence who (like the Jagaroth in 'City of Death') have secretly been influencing the evolution of the human race over millennia. Nixon also becomes the first real head of state to appear in *Doctor Who*: his sympathetic characterisation might be seen as a way of making amends for the assassination of the (fictional) president in 'The Sound of Drums'.

The success of *Doctor Who* in America needs to be qualified of course: it has a large audience by the standards of BBC America, though remains very much a niche or cult series in relation to the big US network dramas. Nevertheless – and to paraphrase Neil Armstrong – one small step for a Time Lord may yet turn out to be a giant leap for British television. As it reaches its fiftieth anniversary *Doctor Who* is bigger and more popular than it has ever been. It has become the BBC's – indeed British television's – biggest global brand. This is no small achievement for a cultural product that remains quintessentially British in so many ways. The success of new *Doctor Who* has been so phenomenal, indeed, that there is little hint of hubris in Steven Moffat's statement that 'I truly believe it could be a show that outlives everybody . . . it could make money forever.'[29] While the history of the series reveals that institutional and cultural contexts rarely remain fixed for very long, and with the caveat as ever that popular culture is inherently unstable and subject to rapid transformation and flux, there is, nevertheless, good reason to believe that the immediate future of *Doctor Who* is assured. It seems highly likely that the adventures of the Last of the Time Lords will continue to excite, thrill and frighten audiences both young and old for many years to come.

Appendix I

Lost Episodes

Until 1958, when the introduction of magnetic videotape into the British television industry made it possible to record programmes in advance of transmission, the majority of television drama in Britain was performed and broadcast 'live' from the studio with occasional inserts shot on film to link scenes together. When *Doctor Who* began in 1963, video recording had become standard practice, though the cumbersome process of editing video meant that studio recording was still carried out as if it were live with only limited scope for retakes if actors fluffed their lines or monsters collided with the scenery (as clearly happens, for example, to one of the Zarbi in 'The Web Planet'). Following transmission the usual process was for the master tapes to be 'wiped' so that they could be re-used. Repeat transmissions were very rare: only eight episodes of *Doctor Who* (the first episode 'An Unearthly Child' and the seven-part 'The Evil of the Daleks') were repeated during the 1960s. Between the late 1960s and early 1970s the majority of *Doctor Who* master tapes were wiped. What survives of 1960s *Doctor Who*, therefore, are usually 16-millimetre film prints copied from the tapes for overseas sales. *Doctor Who* was sold around the world to countries as diverse as Australia, New Zealand, Hong Kong, Cyprus and Nigeria. Following transmission these prints would either be junked, forwarded to another broadcaster or returned to the BBC. In the 1970s BBC Enterprises junked many of the prints returned, partly for reasons of storage space and partly because it was assumed that following the introduction of colour there would be no interest in old monochrome prints.

prints would either be junked, forwarded to another broadcaster or returned to the BBC. In the 1970s BBC Enterprises junked many of the prints returned, partly for reasons of storage space and partly because it was assumed that following the introduction of colour there would be no interest in old monochrome prints.

It was not until the establishment of the BBC Film and Videotape Library in 1978 that the corporation began to give serious consideration to the notion of archiving. Its motive was commercial as well as historic: the introduction of domestic video recorders was starting to open up a new means of distribution for which archival materials would in time become a valuable source. By this time many episodes of 1960s *Doctor Who* had apparently been lost. More by chance than by design BBC Enterprises still held prints of most of the first two years of the series, though for the period between 1965 and 1968 the archive was scarce indeed. In addition some of the colour episodes existed only as black-and-white prints, or, in the case of the first episode of 'Invasion of the Dinosaurs', did not exist at all. This was the context in which the BBC began the ongoing process of searching out the missing episodes.

In 1983 there were a total 134 episodes of *Doctor Who* that were 'missing, believed lost'. Over the next 21 years, 26 of these episodes were retrieved. They came from various sources, such as the vaults of overseas broadcasters which had not destroyed or returned them and from private collectors who had purchased or otherwise acquired 16-millimetre prints. A black-and-white copy of the first episode of 'Invasion of the Dinosaurs', for example, was retrieved in 1983. Most of the retrieved material comprised single episodes, though in 1983 two episodes of 'The Daleks' Master Plan' turned up in the basement of the Church of Latter Day-Saints in Wandsworth. In 1985 six Hartnell episodes were tracked down in Nigeria by Ian Levine, and in 1988 four episodes of Troughton's 'The Ice Warriors' were discovered during demolition work at Ealing Studios. To date the only serial to have been retrieved in its entirety is 'The Tomb of the Cybermen', which turned up in good condition in Hong Kong in 1992 and was quickly released on home video. Some serials (such as 'The Time Meddler' and 'The War Machines') have been put back together with prints recovered from different sources. The holy grail of *Doctor Who* collectors is the last episode of 'The Tenth Planet'. The first three episodes exist, and so does a short extract of the sequence in which William Hartnell metamorphoses into Patrick Troughton, due to this having been shown on the children's magazine programme *Blue Peter*. While there have been numerous reports that the last episode of 'The Tenth Planet' has been found, however, these have all turned out to be hoaxes.

In addition to complete episodes, extracts from some missing episodes have also been found. Some extracts from 'The Daleks' Master Plan' were discovered in 1992 during research for the BBC2 documentary *Resistance Is Useless*. It is rare that one has occasion to be thankful to censors, but in 1996 several 'trims' turned up courtesy of the Australasian television censors, who had removed certain offending shots. These include, for example, the controversial sequence at the end of the first part of 'The Underwater Menace' in which Polly is dragged forcibly into an operating theatre, and the poison-breathing Oak and Quill in 'Fury from the Deep'. It is ironic that the scenes unseen by Australian viewers are the only surviving extracts from those episodes.

As it stands, therefore, there are still significant gaps in the *Doctor Who* archive. Some serials are missing entirely, including 'Marco Polo' (the first, much-praised historical adventure), while others are represented only by a few short clips, such as 'The Power of the Daleks' (Troughton's first story). Others are represented at present by only one episode, including 'The Celestial Toymaker' (Episode 4), 'Evil of the Daleks' (Episode 2) and 'The Web of Fear' (Episode 1 – which fully deserves its reputation and in my opinion has a good claim to being the best individual *Doctor Who* episode.) 'The Crusade' and 'The Moonbase' are both half complete, while 'The Ice Warriors' (four of six episodes) and 'The Invasion' (six of eight) are complete enough to have been released on video, with linking narrative. Troughton is the 'Doctor Who' that has suffered most from the ravages of time: over half of his episodes (63 from a total of 119) currently do not survive. Hartnell is missing one third of his episodes (45 are still missing from a total of 134, or 135 if we also include the first recording of 'An Unearthly Child', which does survive). The most recent episode to be retrieved, in 2004, is 'Day of Armageddon', second episode of 'The Daleks' Master Plan'. It seems unlikely now that any of the completely lost serials will be retrieved.

The absence of 108 episodes of *Doctor Who* is not, however, an insurmountable problem for the researcher. In the first place the audio soundtracks for all episodes survive and are being released commercially on CD. Transcripts of the missing serials, furthermore, have been made available via the website *Earthbound Timelords: The Doctor Who Scripts Project* (http://homepages.bw.edu/~jcurtis/scripts_project.htm). In addition the BBC Written Archive Centre holds camera scripts for many episodes, while production stills, telesnaps (still photographs of episodes) and home movie footage (for example from the production of 'The Evil of the Daleks') provide some idea of what the episodes might have looked like. There are sufficient sources, therefore, to be able to analyse and discuss the 'lost' stories of *Doctor Who*.

Since the first edition of *Inside the Tardis* was published, two further complete episodes of *Doctor Who* have been recovered: Episode 3 of 'Galaxy 4' (which has the episode title 'Air Lock') and Episode 2 of 'The Underwater Menace'. Contrary to *Doctor Who Magazine*'s assertion that these 'would have been near the bottom of the list' of most-wanted episodes, the recovery of the episode of 'The Underwater Menace', in particular, is important because it allows us to contextualise the controversial cliffhanger at the end of Episode 1 (see p.59 for details). The recovery of these episodes means that, at the time of writing (January 2013), there are 106 missing episodes of *Doctor Who*.

Appendix II

Production Credits

Throughout the years that it was in continuous production between 1963 and 1989, there were 695 episodes *Doctor Who* comprising a total of 156 different stories. The internal BBC production documentation lists the serials according to an alphabetical and numerical code: A, B, C, D, AA, AAA, 4A, 5A, 6A, 7A etc. (In this system the first story is 'Serial A' and the last is 'Serial 7P'). For the sake of clarity, however, I have referred to the serials in numerical sequence from #1 to #156 in the main text and in this appendix. For the first three seasons of *Doctor Who* each episode had its own title until this policy was discontinued from Serial AA, 'The Smugglers'. Thus, strictly speaking, 'An Unearthly Child' is the title of the first episode but not the entire first serial. It became necessary for the BBC to devise, in retrospect, agreed titles for all serials. Throughout the book, and in this appendix, I have used the titles that are now 'official' accepted titles for the early serials. (There is still room for confusion: the second episode of the serial now known as 'The Dalek Invasion of Earth', for example, is 'The Daleks', which has since become the agreed title for the first Dalek story.) I have placed 'Shada' within the continuous run of serials, even though it was never broadcast. For each serial I have listed transmission dates, writer/s (W) and director/s (D). The 'new' *Doctor Who,* beginning in 2005, returned to Episode #1 in the official production schedule.

Doctor Who
BBC Television. 1963–1989.
Producers: Verity Lambert (1–19), John Wiles (20–23), Innes Lloyd (24–36, 38–40), Peter Bryant (37, 41–49), Derrick Sherwin (50–51), Barry Letts (52–75), Philip Hinchcliffe (76–91), Graham Williams (92–109), John Nathan-Turner (110–156).

Script Editors: David Whitaker (1–10), Dennis Spooner (11–16), Donald Tosh (17–22), Gerry Davis (22–36), Peter Bryant (36, 38–40), Victor Pemberton (37), Derrick Sherwin (41–45,49), Terrance Dicks (46–48, 50–74), Robert Holmes (75–95), Anthony Read (96–103), Douglas Adams (104–109), Christopher H. Bidmead (110–116), Antony Root (118,120, 122), Eric Saward (117, 119,121, 123–144), Andrew Cartmel (145–156).

Season 1 (42 weekly episodes)

1. 'An Unearthly Child' (23.11.1963–14.12.1963): Anthony Coburn (W), Waris Hussein (D).
2. 'The Daleks' (21.12.1963–01.02.1964): Terry Nation (W), Christopher Barry & Richard Martin (D).
3. 'The Edge of Destruction' (08.02.1964–15.02.1964): David Whitaker (W), Richard Martin & Frank Cox (D).
4. 'Marco Polo' (22.02.1964–04.04.1964): John Lucarotti (W), Waris Hussein & John Crockett (D).
5. 'The Keys of Marinus' (11.04.1964–16.05.1964): Terry Nation (W), John Gorrie (D).
6. 'The Aztecs' (23.05.1964–13.06.1964): John Lucarotti (W), John Crockett (D).
7. 'The Sensorites' (20.06.1964–01.08.1964): Peter R Newman (W), Mervyn Pinfield & Frank Cox (D).
8. 'The Reign of Terror' (08.08.1964–12.11.1964): Dennis Spooner (W), Henric Hirsch (D).

Season 2 (39 weekly episodes)

9. 'Planet of Giants' (31.10.1964–14.11.1964): Louis Marks (W), Mervyn Pinfield & Douglas Camfield (D).
10. 'The Dalek Invasion of Earth' (21.11.1964–26.12.1964): Terry Nation (W), Richard Martin (D).[1]
11. 'The Rescue' (02.01.1965–09.01.1965): David Whitaker (W), Christopher Barry (D).
12. 'The Romans' (16.01.1965–06.02.1965): Dennis Spooner (W), Christopher Barry (D).
13. 'The Web Planet' (13.02.1965–20.03.1965): Bill Strutton (W), Richard Martin (D).
14. 'The Crusade' (27.03.1965–17.04.1965): David Whitaker (W), Douglas Camfield (D).
15. 'The Space Museum' (24.04.1965–15.05.1965): Glyn Jones (W), Mervyn Pinfield (D).
16. 'The Chase' (22.05.1965–26.06.1965): Terry Nation (W), Richard Martin (D).

17. 'The Time Meddler' (03.07.1965–24.07.1965): Dennis Spooner (W), Douglas Camfield (D).

Season 3 (45 weekly episodes)

18. 'Galaxy 4' (11.09.1965–02.10.1965): William Emms (W), Derek Martinus (D).
19. 'Mission to the Unknown' (09.10.1965): Terry Nation (W), Derek Martinus (D).[2]
20. 'The Myth Makers' (16.10.1965–06.11.1965): Donald Cotton (W), Michael Leeston-Smith (D).
21. 'The Daleks' Master Plan' (13.11.1965–29.01.1966): Terry Nation & Dennis Spooner (W), Douglas Camfield (D).
22. 'The Massacre' (05.02.1966–26.02.1966): John Lucarotti & Donald Tosh (W), Paddy Russell (D).[3]
23. 'The Ark' (05.03.1966–26.03.1966): Paul Erickson & Lesley Scott (W), Michael Imison (D).
24. 'The Celestial Toymaker' (02.04.1966–23.04.1966): Brian Hayles (W), Bill Sellars (D).[4]
25. 'The Gunfighters' (30.04.1966–21.05.1966): Donald Cotton (W), Rex Tucker (D).[5]
26. 'The Savages' (28.05.1966–18.06.1966): Ian Stuart Black (W), Christopher Barry (D).
27. 'The War Machines' (25.06.1966–16.07.1966): Ian Stuart Black (W), Michael Ferguson (D).

Season 4 (43 weekly episodes)

28. 'The Smugglers' (10.09.1966–01.10.1966): Brian Hayles (W), Julia Smith (D).
29. 'The Tenth Planet' (08.10.1966–29.10.1966): Kit Pedler & Gerry Davis (W), Derek Martinus (D).
30. 'The Power of the Daleks' (05.11.1966–10.12.1966): David Whitaker (W), Christopher Barry (D).[6]
31. 'The Highlanders' (17.12.1966–07.01.1967): Gerry Davis & Elwyn Jones (W), Hugh David (D).
32. 'The Underwater Menace' (14.01.1967–04.02.1967): Geoffrey Orme (W), Julia Smith (D).
33. 'The Moonbase' (11.02.1967–04.03.1967): Kit Pedler (W), Morris Barry (D).
34. 'The Macra Terror' (11.03.1967–01.04.1967): Ian Stuart Black (W), John Davies (D).
35. 'The Faceless Ones' (08.04.1967–13.05.1967): David Ellis & Malcolm Hulke (W), Gerry Mill (D).

36. 'The Evil of the Daleks' (20.05.1967–01.07.1967): David Whitaker (W), Derek Martinus & Timothy Combe (D).

Season 5 (40 weekly episodes)

37. 'The Tomb of the Cybermen' (02.09.1967–23.09.1967): Kit Pedler & Gerry Davis (W), Morris Barry (D).
38. 'The Abominable Snowmen' (30.09.1967–04.11.1967): Mervyn Haisman & Henry Lincoln (W), Gerald Blake (D).
39. 'The Ice Warriors' (11.11.1967–16.12.1967): Brian Hayles (W), Derek Martinus (D).
40. 'The Enemy of the World' (23.12.1967–27.01.1968): David Whitaker (W), Barry Letts (D).[7]
41. 'The Web of Fear' (03.02.1968–09.03.1968): Mervyn Haisman & Henry Lincoln (W), Douglas Camfield (D).[8]
42. 'Fury from the Deep' (16.03.1968–20.04.1968): Victor Pemberton (W), Hugh David (D).
43. 'The Wheel in Space' (27.04.1968–01.06.1968): David Whitaker (W), Tristan de Vere Cole (D).[9]

Season 6 (44 weekly episodes)

44. 'The Dominators' (10.08.1968–07.09.1968): Norman Ashby (W), Morris Barry (D).[10]
45. 'The Mind Robber' (14.09.1968–12.10.1968): Peter Ling & Derrick Sherwin (W), David Maloney (D).
46. 'The Invasion' (02.11.1968–21.12.1968): Derrick Sherwin (W), Douglas Camfield (D).
47. 'The Krotons' (28.12.1968–18.01.1969): Robert Holmes (W), David Maloney (D).
48. 'The Seeds of Death' (25.01.1969–01.03.1969): Brian Hayles (W), Michael Ferguson (D).[11]
49. 'The Space Pirates' (08.03.1969–12.04.1969): Robert Holmes (W), Michael Hart (D).
50. 'The War Games' (19.04.1969–21.06.1969): Malcolm Hulke & Terrance Dicks (W), David Maloney (D).

Season 7 (25 weekly episodes)

51. 'Spearhead from Space' (03.01.1970–24.01.1970): Robert Holmes (W), Derek Martinus (D).[12]
52. 'Doctor Who and the Silurians' (31.01.1970–14.03.1970): Malcolm Hulke (W), Timothy Combe (D).[13]
53. 'The Ambassadors of Death' (21.03.1970–02.05.1970): David Whitaker (W), Michael Ferguson (D).

54. 'Inferno' (09.05.1970–20.06.1970): Don Houghton (W), Douglas Camfield (D).[14]

Season 8 (25 weekly episodes)

55. 'Terror of the Autons' (02.01.1971–23.01.1971): Robert Holmes (W), Barry Letts (D).

56. 'The Mind of Evil' (30.01.1971–06.03.1971): Don Houghton (W), Timothy Combe (D).

57. 'The Claws of Axos' (13.03.1971–03.04.1971): Bob Baker & Dave Martin (W), Michael Ferguson (D).

58. 'Colony in Space' (10.04.1971–15.05.1971): Malcolm Hulke (W), Michael Briant (D).

59. 'The Damons' (22.05.1971–19.06.1971): Guy Leopold (W), Christopher Barry (D).[15]

Season 9 (26 weekly episodes)

60. 'Day of the Daleks' (01.01.1972–22.01.1972): Louis Marks (W), Paul Bernard (D).

61. 'The Curse of Peladon' (29.01.1972–19.02.1972): Brian Hayles (W), Lennie Mayne (D).

62. 'The Sea Devils' (26.02.1972–01.04.1972): Malcolm Hulke (W), Michael Briant (D).

63. 'The Mutants' (08.04.1972–13.05.1972): Bob Baker & Dave Martin (W), Christopher Barry (D).

64. 'The Time Monster' (20.05.1972–24.06.1972): Robert Sloman (D), Paul Bernard (D).

Season 10 (26 weekly episodes)

65. 'The Three Doctors' (30.12.1972–20.01.1973): Bob Baker & Dave Martin (W), Lennie Mayne (D).

66. 'Carnival of Monsters' (27.01.1973–17.02.1973): Robert Holmes (W), Barry Letts (D).

67. 'Frontier in Space' (24.02.1973–31.03.1973): Malcolm Hulke (W), Paul Bernard (D).

68. 'Planet of the Daleks' (07.04.1973–12.05.1973): Terry Nation (W), David Maloney (D).

69. 'The Green Death' (19.05.1973–23.06.1973): Robert Sloman (W), Michael Briant (D).

Season 11 (26 weekly episodes)

70. 'The Time Warrior' (15.12.1973–05.01.1974): Robert Holmes (W), Alan Bromly (D).

71. 'Invasion of the Dinosaurs' (12.01.1974–16.02.1974): Malcolm Hulke (W), Paddy Russell (D).[16]

72. 'Death to the Daleks' (23.02.1974–16.03.1974): Terry Nation (W), Michael Briant (D).

73. 'The Monster of Peladon' (23.03.1974–27.04.1974): Brian Hayles (W), Lennie Mayne (D).

74. 'Planet of the Spiders' (04.05.1974–08.06.1974): Robert Sloman (W), Barry Letts (D).

Season 12 (20 weekly episodes)

75. 'Robot' (28.12.1974–18.01.1975): Terrance Dicks (W), Christopher Barry (D).[17]

76. 'The Ark in Space' (25.12.1975–15.02.1975): Robert Holmes (W), Rodney Bennett (D).

77. 'The Sontaran Experiment' (22.02.1975–01.03.1975): Bob Baker & Dave Martin (W), Rodney Bennett (D).

78. 'Genesis of the Daleks' (08.03.1975–12.04.1975): Terry Nation (W), David Maloney (D).

79. 'Revenge of the Cybermen' (19.04.1975–10.05.1975): Gerry Davis (W), Michael E. Briant (D).

Season 13 (26 weekly episodes)

80. 'Terror of the Zygons' (30.08.1975–20.09.1975): Robert Banks Stewart (W), Douglas Camfield (D).

81. 'Planet of Evil' (27.09.1975–18.10.1975): Louis Marks (W), David Maloney (D).

82. 'Pyramids of Mars' (25.10.1975–15.11.1975): Stephen Harris (W), Paddy Russell (D).[18]

83. 'The Android Invasion' (22.11.1975–13.12.1975): Terry Nation (W), Barry Letts (D).

84. 'The Brain of Morbius' (03.01.1976–24.01.1976): Robin Bland (W), Christopher Barry (D).[19]

85. 'The Seeds of Doom' (31.01.1976–06.03.1976): Robert Banks Stewart (W), Douglas Camfield (D).

Season 14 (26 weekly episodes)

86. 'The Masque of Mandragora' (04.09.1976–24.09.1976): Louis Marks (W), Rodney Bennett (D).

87. 'The Hand of Fear' (02.10.1976–23.10.1976): Bob Baker & Dave Martin (W), Lennie Mayne (D).

88. 'The Deadly Assassin' (30.10.1976–20.11.1976): Robert Holmes (W), David Maloney (D).[20]

89. 'The Face of Evil' (01.01.1977–22.01.1977): Chris Boucher (W), Pennant Roberts (D).

90. 'The Robots of Death' (29.01.1977–19.02.1977): Chris Boucher (W), Michael Briant (D).

91. 'The Talons of Weng-Chiang' (26.02.1977–02.04.1977): Robert Holmes (W), David Maloney (D).

Season 15 (26 weekly episodes)

92. 'Horror of Fang Rock' (03.09.1977–24.09.1977): Terrance Dicks (W), Paddy Russell (D).

93. 'The Invisible Enemy' (01.10.1977–22.10.1977): Bob Baker & Dave Martin (W), Derrick Goodwin (D).

94. 'Image of the Fendahl' (29.10.1977–19.11.1977): Chris Boucher (W), George Spenton-Foster (D).

95. 'The Sun Makers' (26.11.1977–17.12.1977): Robert Holmes (W), Pennant Roberts (D).

96. 'Underworld' (07.01.1978–28.01.1978): Bob Baker & Dave Martin (W), Norman Stewart (D).

97. 'The Invasion of Time' (04.02.1978–11.03.1978): David Agnew (W), Gerald Blake (D).[21]

Season 16 (26 weekly episodes)

98. 'The Ribos Operation' (02.09.1978–23.09.1978): Robert Holmes (W), George Spenton-Foster (D).

99. 'The Pirate Planet' (30.09.1978–21.10.1978): Douglas Adams (W), Pennant Roberts (D).

100. 'The Stones of Blood' (28.10.1978–18.11.1978): David Fisher (W), Darrol Blake (D).

101. 'The Androids of Tara' (25.11.1978–16.12.1978): David Fisher (W), Michael Hayes (D).

102. 'The Power of Kroll' (23.12.1978–13.01.1979): Robert Holmes (W), Norman Stewart (D).

103. 'The Armageddon Factor' (20.01.1979–24.02.1979): Bob Baker & Dave Martin (W), Michael Hayes (D).

Season 17 (20 weekly episodes)

104. 'Destiny of the Daleks' (01.09.1979–22.09.1979): Terry Nation (W), Ken Grieve (D).

105. 'City of Death' (29.09.1979–20.10.1979): David Agnew (W), Michael Hayes (D).[22]

106. 'The Creature from the Pit' (27.10.1979–17.11.1979): David Fisher (W), Christopher Barry (D).

107. 'Nightmare of Eden' (24.11.1979–15.12.1979): Bob Baker (W), Alan Bromly (D).
108. 'The Horns of Nimon' (22.12.1979–12.01.1980): Anthony Read (W), Kenny McBain(D).
109. 'Shada' (never transmitted): Douglas Adams (W), Pennant Roberts (D).[23]

Season 18 (28 weekly episodes)
110. 'The Leisure Hive' (30.08.1980–20.09.1980): David Fisher (W), Lovett Bickford (D).
111. 'Meglos' (27.09.1980–18.10.1980): John Flanagan & Andrew McCulloch (W), Terence Dudley (D).
112. 'Full Circle' (25.10.1980–15.11.1980): Andrew Smith (W), Peter Grimwade (D).
113. 'State of Decay' (22.11.1980–13.12.1980): Terrance Dicks (W), Peter Moffatt (D).
114. 'Warriors' Gate' (03.01.1981–24.01.1981): Steve Gallagher (W), Paul Joyce (D).
115. 'The Keeper of Traken' (31.01.1981–21.02.1981): Johnny Byrne (W), John Black (D).
116. 'Logopolis' (28.02.1981–21.03.1981): Christopher H. Bidmead (W), Peter Grimwade (D).

Season 19 (26 bi-weekly episodes)
117. 'Castrovalva' (04.01.1982–12.01.1982): Christopher H. Bidmead (W), Fiona Gumming (D).
118. 'Four to Doomsday' (18.01.1982–26.01.1982): Terence Dudley (W), John Black (D).
119. 'Kinda' (01.02.1982–09.02.1982): Christopher Bailey (W), Peter Grimwade (D).
120. 'The Visitation' (15.02.1982–23.02.1982): Eric Saward (W), Peter Moffatt (D).
121. 'Black Orchid' (01.03.1982–02.03.1982): Terence Dudley (W), Ron Jones (D).
122. 'Earthshock' (08.03.1982–16.03.1982): Eric Saward (W), Peter Grimwade (D).
123. 'Time-Flight' (22.03.1982–30.03.1982): Peter Grimwade (W), Ron Jones (D).

Season 20 (22 bi-weekly episodes and one `special')
124. 'Arc of Infinity' (03.01.1983–12.01.1983): Johnny Byrne (W),Ron Jones (D).

125. 'Snakedance' (18.01.1983–26.01.1983): Christopher Bailey (W), Fiona Gumming (D).
126. 'Mawdryn Undead' (01.02.1983–09.02.1983): Peter Grimwade (W), Peter Moffatt (D).
127. 'Terminus' (15.02.1983–23.02.1983): Steve Gallagher (W), Mary Ridge (D).
128. 'Enlightenment' (01.03.1983–09.03.1983): Barbara Clegg (W), Fiona Gumming (D).
129. 'The King's Demons' (15.03.1983–16.03.1983): Terence Dudley (W), Tony Virgo (D).
130. 'The Five Doctors' (25.11.1983): Terrance Dicks (W), Peter Moffatt (D).[24]

Season 21 (22 bi-weekly episodes and 2 weekly episodes)

131. 'Warriors of the Deep' (05.01.1984–13.01.1984): Johnny Byrne (W), Pennant Roberts (D).
132. 'The Awakening' (19.01.1984–20.01.1984): Eric Pringle (W), Michael Owen Morris (D).
133. 'Frontios' (26.01.1984–03.02.1984): Christopher H. Bidmead (W), Ron Jones (D).
134. 'Resurrection of the Daleks' (08.02.1984–15.02.1984): Eric Saward (W), Matthew Robinson (D).[25]
135. Planet of Fire' (23.02.1984–02.03.1984): Peter Grimwade (W), Fiona Gumming (D).
136. 'The Caves of Androzani' (08.03.1984–16.03.1984): Robert Holmes (W), Graeme Harper (D).
137. 'The Twin Dilemma' (22.03.1984–30.03.1984): Anthony Steven (W), Peter Moffatt (D).

Season 22 (13 weekly episodes)[26]

138. 'Attack of the Cybermen' (05.01.1985–12.01.1985): Paula Moore (W); Matthew Robinson (D).[27]
139. 'Vengeance on Varos' (19.01.1985–26.01.1985): Philip Martin (W), Ron Jones (D).
140. 'The Mark of the Rani' (02.02.1985–09.02.1985): Pip & Jane Baker (W), Sarah Hellings (D).
141. 'The Two Doctors' (16.02.1985–02.03.1985): Robert Holmes (W), Peter Moffatt (D).
142. 'Timelash' (09.03.1985–16.03.1985): Glen McCoy (W), Pennant Roberts (D).
143. 'Revelation of the Daleks' (23.03.1985–30.03.1985): Eric Saward (W), Graeme Harper (D).

Season 23 (14 weekly episodes)

144. 'The Trial of a Time Lord' (06.09.1986–06.12.1986): Robert Holmes, Philip Martin, Pip & Jane Baker (W); Nick Mallett, Ron Jones, Chris Clough (D).[28]

Season 24 (14 weekly episodes)

145. 'Time and the Rani' (07.09.1987–28.09.1987): Pip & Jane Baker (W), Andrew Morgan (D).

146. 'Paradise Towers' (05.10.1987–26.10.1987): Stephen Wyatt (W), Nicholas Mallett (D).

147. 'Delta and the Bannermen' (01.11.1987–16.11.1987): Malcolm Kohll (W), Chris Clough (D).

148. 'Dragonfire' (23.11.1987–07.12.1987): Ian Briggs (W), Chris Clough (D).

Season 25 (14 weekly episodes)

149. 'Remembrance of the Daleks' (05.10.1988–26.10.1988): Ben Aaronovitch (W), Andrew Morgan (D).

150. 'The Happiness Patrol' (02.11.1988–16.11.1988): Graeme Curry (W), Chris Clough (D).

151. 'Silver Nemesis' (23.11.1988–07.12.1988): Kevin Clarke (W), Chris Clough (D).

152. 'The Greatest Show in the Galaxy' (14.12.1988–04.01.1989): Stephen Wyatt (W), Alan Wareing (D).

Season 26 (14 weekly episodes)

153. 'Battlefield' (06.09.1989–27.09.1989): Ben Aaronovitch (W), Michael Kerrigan (D).

154. 'Ghost Light' (04.10.1989–18.10.2005): Marc Platt (W), Alan Wareing (D).

155. 'The Curse of Fenric' (25.10.1989–15.11.1989): Ian Briggs (W), Nicholas Mallett (D).

156. 'Survival' (22.11.1989–06.12.1989): Rona Munroe (W), Alan Wareing (D).

Doctor Who

BBC Worldwide/Universal Television. 1996.

Producer: Peter V. Ware.

'Doctor Who' (27.05.1996): Matthew Jacobs (W), Geoffrey Sax (D).

Doctor Who

BBC Wales. 2005–

Executive producers: Russell T. Davies (Series One–Four), Julie Gardner (Series One–Four), Mal Young (Series One), Steven Moffat (Series Five–), Piers Wenger (Series Five–Six), Beth Willis (Series Five–Six), Caroline Skinner (Series Seven).

Producers: Phil Collinson (Series One–Four), Tracie Simpson (Series Five),
     Peter Bennett (Series Six), Marcus Wilson (Series Six–).

Series One (13 weekly episodes)

1.1. 'Rose' (26.03.2005): Russell T. Davies (W), Keith Boak (D).

1.2. 'The End of the World' (02.04.2005): Russell T. Davies (W), Euros Lyn (D).

1.3. 'The Unquiet Dead' (09.04.2005): Mark Gatiss (W), Euros Lyn (D).

1.4. 'Aliens of London' (16.04.2005): Russell T. Davies (W), Keith Boak (D).

1.5. 'World War Three' (23.04.2005): Russell T. Davies (W), Keith Boak (D).

1.6. 'Dalek' (30.04.2005): Robert Shearman (W), Joe Ahearne (D).

1.7. 'The Long Game' (07.05.2005): Russell T. Davies (W), Brian Grant (D).

1.8. 'Father's Day' (14.05.2005): Paul Cornell (W), Joe Ahearne (D).

1.9. 'The Empty Child' (21.05.2005): Steven Moffat (W), James Hawes (D).

1.10. 'The Doctor Dances' (28.05.2005): Steven Moffat (W), James Hawes (D).

1.11. 'Boom Town' (04.06.2005): Russell T. Davies (W), Joe Ahearne (D).

1.12. 'Bad Wolf' (11.06.2005): Russell T. Davies (W), Joe Ahearne (D).

1.13. 'The Parting of the Ways' (18.06.2005): Russell T. Davies, Joe Aheane (D).

Series Two (Christmas Special + 13 weekly episodes)

2.X. 'The Christmas Invasion' (25.12.2005): Russell T. Davies (W), James
     Hawes (D).

2.1. 'New Earth' (15.04.2006): Russell T. Davies (W), James Hawes (D).

2.2. 'Tooth and Claw' (22.04.2006): Russell T. Davies (W), Euros Lyn (D).

2.3. 'School Reunion' (29.04.2006): Toby Whithouse (W), James Hawes (D).

2.4. 'The Girl in the Fireplace' (06.05.2006): Steven Moffat (W), Euros Lynn
     (D).

2.5. 'Rise of the Cybermen' (13.05.2006): Tom MacRae (W), Graeme Harper
     (D).[29]

2.6. 'The Age of Steel' (20.05.2005): Tom MacRae (W), Graeme Harper (D).

2.7. 'The Idiot's Lantern' (27.05.2006): Mark Gatiss (W), Euros Lyn (D).

2.8. 'The Impossible Planet' (03.06.2006): Matt Jones (W), James Strong (D).

2.9. 'The Satan Pit' (10.06.2006): Matt Jones (W), James Strong (D).

2.10. 'Love & Monsters' (17.06.2006): Russell T. Davies (W), Dan Zeff (D).

2.11. 'Fear Her' (24.06.2006): Matthew Graham (W), Euros Lyn (D).

2.12. 'Army of Ghosts' (01.07.2006): Russell T. Davies (W), Graeme Harper (D).

2.13. 'Doomsday' (08.07.2006): Russell T. Davies (W), Graeme Harper (D).

Series Three (Christmas Special + 13 weekly episodes)

3.X. 'The Runaway Bride' (25.12.2006): Russell T. Davies (W), Euros Lyn (D).

3.1. 'Smith and Jones' (31.03.2007): Russell T. Davies (W), Charles Palmer
     (D).

3.2. 'The Shakespeare Code' (07.04.2007): Gareth Roberts (W), Charles Palmer (D).

3.3. 'Gridlock' (14.04.2007): Russell T. Davies (W), Richard Clark (D).

3.4. 'Daleks in Manhattan' (21.04.2007): Helen Raynor (W), James Strong (D).

3.5. 'Evolution of the Daleks' (28.04.2007): Helen Raynor (W), James Strong (D).

3.5. 'The Lazarus Experiment' (05.05.2007): Stephen Greenhorn (W), Richard Clark (D).

3.7. '42' (19.05.2007): Chris Chibnall (W), Graeme Harper (D).

3.8. 'Human Nature' (26.05.2007): Paul Cornell (W), Charles Palmer (D).

3.9. 'The Family of Blood' (02.06.2007): Paul Cornell (W), Charles Palmer (D).

3.10. 'Blink' (09.06.2007): Steven Moffat (W), Hettie MacDonald (D).

3.11. 'Utopia' (16.06.2007): Russell T. Davies (W), Graeme Harper (D).

3.12. 'The Sound of Drums' (23.06.2007): Russell T. Davies (W), Colin Teague (D).

3.13. 'Last of the Time Lords' (30.06.2007): Russell T. Davies (W), Colin Teague (D).

Series Four (Christmas Special + 13 weekly episodes + 4 Specials)

4.X. 'Voyage of the Damned' (25.12.2007): Russell T. Davies (W), James Strong (D).

4.1. 'Partners in Crime' (05.04.2008): Russell T. Davies (W), James Strong (D).

4.2. 'The Fires of Pompeii' (12.04.2008): James Moran (W), Colin Teague (D).

4.3. 'Planet of the Ood' (19.04.2008): Keith Temple (W), Graeme Harper (D).

4.4. 'The Sontaran Stratagem' (26.04.2008): Helen Raynor (W), Douglas Mackinnon (D).

4.5. 'The Poison Sky' (03.05.2008): Helen Raynor (W), Douglas Mackinnon (D).

4.6. 'The Doctor's Daughter' (10.05.2008): Stephen Greenhorn (W), Alice Troughton (D).

4.7. 'The Unicorn and the Wasp' (17.05.2008): Gareth Roberts (W), Graeme Harper (D).

4.8. 'Silence in the Library' (31.05.2008): Steven Moffat (W), Euros Lynn (D).

4.9. 'Forest of the Dead' (07.06.2008): Steven Moffat (W), Euros Lynn (D).

4.10. 'Midnight' (14.06.2008): Russell T. Davies (W), Alice Troughton (D).[30]

4.11. 'Turn Left' (21.06.2008): Russell T. Davies (W), Graeme Harper (D).

4.12. 'The Stolen Earth' (28.06.2008): Russell T. Davies (W), Graeme Harper (D).

4.13. 'Journey's End' (05.07.2008): Russell T. Davies (W), Graeme Harper (D).

4.14. 'The Next Doctor' (25.12.2008): Russell T. Davies (W), Andy Goddard (D).

4.15. 'Planet of the Dead' (11.04.2009): Russell T. Davies & Gareth Roberts (W), James Strong (D).

4.16. 'The Waters of Mars' (15.11.2009): Russell T. Davies & Phil Ford (W), Graeme Harper (D).

4.17. 'The End of Time Part 1' (25.12.2009): Russell T. Davies (W), Euros Lyn (D).

4.18. 'The End of Time Part 2' (01.01.2010): Russell T. Davies (W), Euros Lyn (D).

Series Five (13 weekly episodes)[31]

5.1. 'The Eleventh Hour' (03.04.2010): Steven Moffat (W), Adam Smith (D).

5.2. 'The Beast Below' (10.04.2010): Steven Moffat (W), Andrew Gunn (D).

5.3. 'Victory of the Daleks' (17.04.2010): Mark Gatiss (W), Andrew Gunn (D).

5.4. 'The Time of Angels' (24.04.2010): Steven Moffat (W), Adam Smith (D).

5.5. 'Flesh and Stone' (01.05.2010): Steven Moffat (W), Adam Smith (D).

5.6. 'The Vampires of Venice' (08.05.2010): Toby Whithouse (W), Jonny Campbell (D).

5.7. 'Amy's Choice' (15.05.2010): Simon Nye (W), Catherine Morshead (D).

5.8. 'The Hungry Earth' (22.05.2010): Chris Chibnall (W), Ashley Way (D).

5.9. 'Cold Blood' (25.05.2010): Chris Chibnall (W), Ashley Way (D).

5.10. 'Vincent and the Doctor' (05.06.2010): Richard Curtis (W), Jonny Campbell (D).

5.11. 'The Lodger' (12.06.2010): Gareth Roberts (W), Catherine Morshead (D).

5.12. 'The Pandorica Opens' (19.06.2010): Steven Moffat (W), Toby Haynes (D).

5.13. 'The Big Bang' (26.06.2010): Steven Moffat (W), Toby Haynes (D).

Series Six (Christmas Special + 13 weekly episodes)[32]

6.X. 'A Christmas Carol' (25.12.2010): Steven Moffat (W), Toby Haynes (D).

6.1. 'The Impossible Astronaut' (23.04.2011): Steven Moffat (W), Toby Haynes (D).

6.2. 'Day of the Moon' (30.04.2011): Steven Moffat (W), Toby Haynes (D).

6.3. 'The Curse of the Black Spot' (07.05.2011): Stephen Thompson (W), Jeremy Webb (D).

6.4. 'The Doctor's Wife' (14.05.2011): Neil Gaiman (W), Richard Clark (D).

6.5. 'The Rebel Flesh' (21.05.2011): Matthew Graham (W), Julian Simpson (D).

6.6. 'The Almost People' (28.05.2011): Matthew Graham (W), Julian Simpson (D).

6.7. 'A Good Man Goes to War' (04.06.2011): Steven Moffat (W), Peter Hoard (D).

6.8. 'Let's Kill Hitler!' (27.08.2011): Steven Moffat (W), Richard Senior (D).

6.9. 'Night Terrors' (03.09.2011): Mark Gatiss (W), Richard Clark (D).

6.10. 'The Girl Who Waited' (10.09.2011): Tom MacRae (W), Nick Hurran (D).

6.11. 'The God Complex' (17.09.2011): Toby Whithouse (W), Nick Hurran (D).

6.12. 'Closing Time' (24.09.2011): Gareth Roberts (W), Steve Hughes (D).

6.13. 'The Wedding of River Song' (01.10.2011): Steven Moffat (W), Jeremy Webb (D).

Series Seven (13 weekly episodes + specials)[33]

7.X. 'The Doctor, the Widow and the Wardrobe' (25.12.2011): Steven Moffat (W), Farren Blackburn (D).

7.1. 'Asylum of the Daleks' (01.09.2012): Steven Moffat (W), Nick Hurran (D).

7.2. 'Dinosaurs on a Spaceship' (08.12.2012): Chris Chibnall (W), Saul Metzstein (D).

7.3. 'A Town Called Mercy' (15.12.2012): Toby Whithouse (W), Saul Metzstein (D).

7.4. 'The Power of Three' (22.12.2012): Chris Chibnall (W), Douglas Mackinnon (D).

7.5. 'The Angels Take Manhattan' (29.09.2012): Steven Moffat (W), Nick Hurran (D).

7.X. 'The Snowmen' (25.12.2012): Steven Moffat (W), Saul Metzstein (D).

7.6. 'The Bells of Saint John' (30.03.2013): Steven Moffat (W), Colm McCarthy (D).

7.7. 'The Rings of Akhaten' (06.08.2013): Neil Cross (W), Farren Blackburn (D).

7.8. 'Cold War' (13.04.2013): Mark Gatiss (W), Douglas Mackninnon (D).

7.9. 'Hide' (20.04.2013): Neil Cross (W), Jamie Payne (D).

7.10. 'Journey to the Centre of the Tardis' (27.04.2013): Stephen Thompson (W), Mat King (D).

7.11. 'The Crimson Horror' (04.05.2013): Mark Gatiss (W), Saul Metzstein (D).

7.12. 'Nightmare in Silver' (11.05.2013): Neil Gaiman (W), Stephen Woolfenden (D).

7.13. 'The Name of the Doctor' (18.05.2013): Steven Moffat (W), Saul Metzstein (D).

Torchwood

BBC Wales. 2006–2009.

BBC Wales/BBC Worldwide/Starz Entertainment. 2011.

Executive producers: Russell T. Davies (Series One–Four), Julie Gardner (Series One–Four), Jane Tranter (Series Four).

Producers: Richard Stokes (Series One–Two), Peter Bennett (Series Three), Kelly A. Manners (Series Four).

Series One (13 weekly or bi-weekly episodes)[34]

1.1. 'Everything Changes' (22.10.2006): Russell T. Davies (W), Brian Kelly (D).

1.2. 'Day One' (22.10.2005): Chris Chibnall (W), Brian Kelly (D).

1.3. 'Ghost Machine' (29.10.2006): Helen Raynor (W), Colin Teague (D).

1.4. 'Cyberwoman' (05.11.2006): Chris Chibnall (W), James Strong (D).

1.5. 'Small Worlds' (12.11.2006): Peter J. Hammond (W), Alice Troughton (D).

1.6. 'Countrycide' (19.11.2006): Chris Chibnall (W), Andy Goddard (D).

1.7. 'Greeks Bearing Gifts' (26.11.2006): Toby Whithouse (W), Colin Teague (D).

1.8. 'They Keep Killing Suzie' (03.12.2006): Paul Tomalin & Dan McCulloch (W), James Strong (D).

1.9. 'Random Shoes' (10.12.2006): Jacquetta May (W), James Erskine (D).

1.10. 'Out of Time' (17.12.2006): Catherine Tregenna (W), Alice Troughton (D).

1.11. 'Combat' (24.12.2006): Noel Clarke (W), Andy Goddard (D).

1.12. 'Captain Jack Harkness' (01.01.2007): Catherine Tregenna (W), Ashley Way (D).

1.13. 'End of Days' (01.01.2007): Chris Chibnall (W), Ashley Way (D).

Series Two (13 weekly or bi-weekly episodes)[35]

2.1. 'Kiss Kiss, Bang Bang' (16.01.2008): Chris Chibnall (W), Ashley Way (D).

2.2. 'Sleeper' (23.01.2008): James Moran (W), Colin Teague (D).

2.3. 'To the Last Man' (30.01.2008): Helen Raynor (W), Andy Goddard (D).

2.4. 'Meat' (06.02.2008): Catherine Tregenna (W), Colin Teague (D).

2.5. 'Adam' (13.02.2008): Catherine Tregenna (W), Andy Goddard (D).

2.6. 'Reset' (13.02.2008): J. C. Wilsher (W), Ashley Way (D).

2.7. 'Dead Man Walking' (20.02.2008): Matt Jones (W), Andy Goddard (D).

2.8. 'A Day in the Death' (27.02.2008): Joseph Lidster (W), Andy Goddard (D).

2.9. 'Something Borrowed' (05.03.2008): Phil Ford (W), Ashley Way (D).

2.10. 'From Out of the Rain' (12.03.2008): Peter J. Hammond (W), Jonathan Fox Bassett (D).

2.11. 'Adrift' (19.03.2008): Chris Chibnall (W), Mark Everest (D).

2.12. 'Fragments' (21.03.2008): Chris Chibnall (W), Jonathan Fox Bassett (D).

2.13. 'Exit Wounds' (04.04.2008): Chris Chibnall (W), Ashley Way (D).

Series Three (*Torchwood: Children of Earth*) (5 daily episodes)

3.1. 'Day One' (06.07.2009): Russell T. Davies (W), Euros Lyn (D).

3.2. 'Day Two' (07.07.2009): John Fay (W), Euros Lyn (D).

3.3. 'Day Three' (08.07.2009): Russell T. Davies & James Moran (W), Euros Lyn (D).

3.4. 'Day Four' (09.07.2009): John Fay (W), Euros Lyn (D).

3.5. 'Day Five' (10.07.2009): Russell T. Davies (W), Euros Lyn (D).

Series Four (*Torchwood: Miracle Day*) (10 weekly episodes)[36]

4.1. 'The New World' (14.07.2011): Russell T. Davies (W), Bharat Nalluri (D).

4.2. 'Rendition' (21.07.2011): Doris Egan (W), Billy Gierhart (D).

4.3. 'Dead of Night' (28.07.2011): Jane Espenson (W), Billy Gierhart (D).

4.4. 'Escape to LA' (04.08.2011): Jim Gray & John Shiban (W), Billy Gierhart (D).

4.5. 'The Categories of Life' (11.08.2011): Jane Espenson (W), Guy Ferland (D).

4.6. 'The Middle Men' (18.08.2011): John Shiban (W), Guy Ferland (D).

4.7. 'Immortal Sins' (25.08.2011): Jane Espenson (W), Gwyneth Horder-Payton (D).

4.8. 'End of the Road' (01.09.2011): Jane Espenson & Ryan Scott (W), Gwyneth Horder-Payton (D).

4.9. 'The Gathering' (08.09.2011): John Fay (W), Guy Ferland (D).

4.10. 'The Blood Line' (15.09.2011): Russell T. Davies & Jane Espenson (W), Billy Gierhart (D).

The Sarah Jane Adventures

BBC Wales for CBBC. 2007–2011.

Executive producers: Russell T. Davies (Series One–Five), Julie Gardner (Series One–Three), Phil Collinson (Series One–Three), Nikki Wilson (Series Four–Five)

Producers: Susie Liggat (1.X), Matthew Bouch (Series One), Nikki Wilson (Series Two–Three), Brian Minchin (Series Four–Five)

Series One (New Year Special + 10 weekly episodes)[37]

1.X. 'Invasion of the Bane' (01.01.2007): Russell T. Davies & Gareth Roberts (W), Colin Teague (D).

1.2. 'Revenge of the Slitheen' (24.09.2007–01.10.2007): Gareth Roberts (W), Alice Troughton (D).

1.3. 'Eye of the Gorgon' (08.10-2007–1510.2007): Phil Ford (W), Alice Troughton (D).

1.4. 'Warriors of Kudlak' (22.10.2007–29.10.2007): Phil Gladwin (W), Charles Marti (D).

1.5. 'Whatever Happened to Sarah Jane?' (05.11.2007–12.11.2007): Gareth Roberts (W), Graeme Harper (D).

1.6. 'The Lost Boy' (19.11.2007–26.11.2007): Phil Ford (W), Charles Martin (D).

Series Two (12 weekly episodes)

2.1. 'The Last Sontaran' (29.09.2008–06.10.2008): Phil Ford (W), Joss Agnew (D).

2.2. 'The Day of the Clown' (13.10.2008–20.10.2008): Phil Ford (W), Michael Kerrigan (D).

2.3. 'Secrets of the Stars' (27.10.2008–03.11.2007): Gareth Roberts (W), Michael Kerrigan (D).

2.4. 'The Mark of the Berserker' (10.11.2007–17.11.2008): Joseph Lidster (W), Joss Agnew (D).

2.5. 'The Temptation of Sarah Jane Smith' (24.11.2008–01.12.2008): Gareth Roberts (W), Graeme Harper (D).

2.6. 'Enemy of the Bane' (08.12.2008–15.12.2008): Phil Ford (W), Graeme Harper (D).

Series Three (12 bi-weekly episodes)

3.1. 'Prisoner of the Judoon' (15.10.2009–16.10.2009): Phil Ford (W), Joss Agnew (D).

3.2. 'The Mad Woman in the Attic' (22.10.2009–23.10.2009): Joseph Lister (W), Alice Troughton (D).

3.3. 'The Wedding of Sarah Jane Smith' (29.10.2009–30.10.2009): Gareth Roberts (W), Joss Agnew (D).

3.4. 'The Eternity Trap' (05.11.2009–06.11.2009): Phil Ford (W), Alice Troughton (D).

3.5. 'Mona Lisa's Revenge' (12.11.2009–13.11.2009): Phil Ford (W), Joss Agnew (D).

3.6. 'The Gift' (19.11.2009–20.11.2009): Rupert Laight (W), Alice Troughton (D).

Series Four (12 bi-weekly episodes)

4.1. 'The Nightmare Man' (11.10.2010–12.10.2010): Joseph Lidster (W), Joss Agnew (D).

4.2. 'The Vault of Secrets' (18.10.2010–19.10.2010): Phil Ford (W), Joss Agnew (D).

4.3. 'Death of the Doctor' (25.10.2010–26.10.2010): Russell T. Davies (W), Ashley Way (D).

4.4. 'The Empty Planet' (01.11.2010–02.11.2010): Gareth Roberts (W), Ashley Way (D).

4.5. 'Lost in Time' (08.11.2010–09.11.2010): Rupert Laight (W), Joss Agnew (D).

4.6. 'Goodbye, Sarah Jane Smith' (15.11.2010–16.11.2010): Gareth Roberts & Clayton Hickman (W), Joss Agnew (W).

Series Five (6 bi-weekly episodes)

5.1. 'Sky' (03.10.2011–04.10.2011): Phil Ford (W), Ashley Way (D).

5.2. 'The Curse of Clyde Langer' (10.10.2011–11.10.2011): Phil Ford (W), Ashley Way (D).

5.3. 'The Man Who Never Was' (17.10.2011–18.10.2011): Gareth Roberts (W), Joss Agnew (D).

Notes

For the endnotes books are referenced by the place of publication and the date of the edition used; full publication details can be found in the Bibliography. Where newspaper and magazine reviews are cited without a page number, the source is either the British Film Institute's microfiche collection or the *Doctor Who Cuttings Archive* (www.cuttingsarchive.org. uk). The abbreviation BBC WAC refers to the BBC Written Archives Centre, Caversham Park, Reading.

Introduction

1. '100 Greatest British Television Programmes', http://pedia.newsfilter. co.uk/wikipedia/10/100_greatest_british_television_programmes. html (accessed 17 November 2005). Covering light entertainment as well as drama, the top ten were (in order) *Fawlty Towers*, *Cathy Come Home*, *Doctor Who*, *The Naked Civil Servant*, *Monty Python's Flying Circus*, *Blue Peter*, *Boys from the Blackstuff*, *Parkinson*, *Yes, Minister* and *Brideshead Revisited*. Other 'telefantasy' series in the list included *The Avengers* (51st), *Thunderbirds* (60th) and *Quatermass and the Pit* (75th).

2. Matt Hills, 'Doctor Who', in Glen Creeber (ed.), *Fifty Key Television Programmes* (London, 2004), p.75.

3. John Tulloch and Manuel Alvarado, *Doctor Who: The Unfolding Text* (London, 1983), p.2.

4. Ibid, pp.5–6.

5. Aficionados insist that while the title of the series is *Doctor Who*, this is not the name of its main protagonist who is known as 'The Doctor'. In internal BBC documents, however, 'Doctor Who' is used interchangeably as the series' title and the name of the character. From the first episode until the end of the eighteenth season in 1981, the end credits of

each episode referred to 'Doctor Who' (or 'Dr. Who'), changing to 'The Doctor' at the beginning of the nineteenth season in 1982. In the 2005 series, the character is once again credited as 'Doctor Who'.

6.   Piers D. Britton and Simon J. Barker, *Reading Between Designs: Visual Imagery and the Generation of Meaning in 'The Avengers', 'The Prisoner', and 'Doctor Who* (Austin, 2003), p.133.

7.   Nicholas J. Cull, '"Bigger on the inside . . .": *Doctor Who* as British cultural history', in Graham Roberts and Philip M. Taylor (eds), *The Historian, Television and Television History* (Luton, 2001), p.103.

8.   The term 'science fiction' was coined by American magazines such as *Amazing Stories, Wonder Stories* and *Astounding Stories* during the 1920s, which specialised in futuristic adventure. In Britain, the term 'scientific romance' was used to refer to late nineteenth- and early twentieth-century writers such as H.G. [Herbert George] Wells (*The Time Machine, The War of the Worlds*) and Sir Arthur Conan Doyle (*The Lost World*). Many contemporary writers and critics prefer the term 'speculative fiction'. However it is labelled, the genre divides into more serious examples which respect the limits of scientific and technological plausibility (sometimes referred to as 'hard' science fiction) and more far-fetched 'space operas'. Some purists would insist that *Doctor Who* is not properly science fiction because its premise of travelling in time and space places it outside the bounds of plausibility. The abbreviation 'SF' is generally preferred by critics to the more familiar 'sci-fi', which tends to be used as a pejorative term for more juvenile fare.

9.   Tulloch and Alvarado, p.8; Britton and Barker, p.133.

10.   Britton and Barker, p.133.

11.   Anthony Weiner, 'Mean machines', *Sunday Telegraph*, 8 August 2004, p.23.

12.   Carole Ann Ford (Susan), Anneke Wills (Polly), Deborah Watling (Victoria), Wendy Padbury (Zoë), Katy Manning (Jo) and Nicola Bryant (Peri) have all told versions of this anecdote.

13.   'Lust in space?', *Evening Standard*, 8 August 1979.

14.   Richard Boston, 'Who's best', *The Observer*, 26 May 1974.

15.   Cull, p.99. Further unwitting evidence of the national association of the British police box is to be found in Britton and Barker, American-based academics, who refer to it as 'a police lock-up box (an oversized telephone booth used by police in early twentieth-century Britain for temporarily detaining suspects)', pp.133–4.

16.   John Thornton Caldwell, *Televisuality: Style, Crisis and Authorship in American Television* (New Brunswick, NJ, 1995), p.6.

17.   A.A. Gill, *Sunday Times*, 2 June 1996.

18.   The audience statistics in the text are expressed numerically in millions
        (calculated to the nearest 100,000) rather than as a percentage, though I
        have based them on the BBC's Audience Research Listening and Viewing
        Barometers (starting at BBC WAC R9/35/12 for 1963), which express
        them as a percentage of the United Kingdom population. These are
        estimates based on the number of people in the Viewing Sample watch-
        ing the programme. Independent television used a different method of
        quantitative analysis (JICTAR), based on the number of television sets
        switched on to the station rather than the number of people watching.
        BARB (Broadcasting Audiences Research Board) was set up partly so
        that audience research could be conducted on the same criteria.

1. A Space-Age Old Curiosity Shop (1963–1966)

1.   John R. Cook, 'Adapting Telefantasy: The *Doctor Who and the Daleks*
        films', in I.Q. Hunter (ed.), *British Science Fiction Cinema* (London,
        1999), p.115; Terrance Dicks and Malcolm Hulke, *The Making of Doctor
        Who* (London, 1976), p.8; Nicholas J. Cull, '"Bigger on the inside . . .":
        Doctor Who as British cultural history', in Graham Roberts and Philip
        M. Taylor (eds), *The Historian, Television and Television History* (Luton,
        2001), pp.95–6; John Tulloch and Manuel Alvarado, *Doctor Who: The Un-
        folding Text* (London, 1983), pp.50–1; Roger Fulton (ed.), *Encyclopedia
        of TV Science Fiction* (London, 2000), p.160; Lez Cooke, *British Television
        Drama: A History* (London, 2003), p.62; Daniel O'Brien, *SF:UK – How
        British Science Fiction Changed the World* (London, 2000), p.73; Asa
        Briggs, *The History of Broadcasting in the United Kingdom. Volume V:
        Competition 1955–1974* (Oxford, 1995), p.423.

2.   Briggs, p.1005.

3.   Linda Wood (ed.), *British Film Industry: A BFI Reference Guide* (London,
        1980), p.3A.

4.   Briggs, p.265.

5.   See John R. Cook, '"Between Grierson and Barnum": Sydney Newman
        and the development of the single television play at the BBC, 1963–7',
        Journal of British Cinema and Television, vol.1, no.2 (2004), pp.211–25.

6.   'ITV can expect a jolt when the BBC launches its "Dr Who"',
        Kinematograph Weekly, 24 October 1963, p.22.

7.   BBC WAC T5/647/1: Donald Baverstock to Eric Maschwitz, 14 May
        1962.

8.   Ibid.: 'Science Fiction', four-page report by Donald Bull and Alice Frick,
        undated but with an accompanying memorandum of 25 April 1962.

9.   See James Chapman, '*Quatermass* and the origins of British television

sf,' in John R. Cook and Peter Wright (eds), *British Science Fiction Television: A Hitch Hiker's Guide* (London, 2006), pp.21–51.

10.   See Joy Leman, 'Wise scientists and female androids: class and gender in science fiction', in John Corner (ed.), *Popular Television in Britain: Studies in Cultural History* (London, 1991), pp.108–24.

11.   BBC WAC T5/647/1: 'Science Fiction', by John Braybon and Alice Frick, 25 July 1962.

12.   Ibid.: C.E. Webber to Donald Wilson, 'Science Fiction', 29 March 1963.

13.   Ibid.: 'Discussion of Science Fiction series, held in Donald Wilson's office, 26 March 1963'. Present at the meeting were Wilson, Webber, Braybon and Frick.

14.   Ibid.: '"Dr Who": General Notes on Background and Approach', undated.

15.   Ibid.: '"Doctor Who": General notes on Background and Approach for an exciting adventure – Science Fiction Drama serial for Children's Saturday viewing', undated.

16.   Ibid.: Ayton Whitaker (Drama Group) to John Mair (Planning Department), 26 April 1963.

17.   Ibid.: Sydney Newman to Donald Wilson, 10 June 1963.

18.   Ibid.: Donald Wilson to Donald Baverstock, 10 October 1963.

19.   Ibid.: Richard Levin to Joanna Spicer, 13 June 1963.

20.   Ibid.: J.F. Mudie to John Mair, 20 June 1963.

21.   Ibid.: Sydney Newman to Joanna Spicer, 27 June 1963.

22.   Ibid.: David Whitaker to Ayton Whitaker, 8 August 1963.

23.   Ibid.: Donald Baverstock to Donald Wilson, 18 October 1963.

24.   BBC WAC T5/638/1: Donald Wilson to Editor, *Radio Times*, 5 November 1963.

25.   BBC WAC T5/647/1: David Whitaker to Verity Lambert, 'Doctor Who', 31 July 1963.

26.   As late as 16 September 1963, only three serials of the first season are identifiable in an outline of the series: Anthony Coburn's Stone Age adventure, John Lucarotti's Marco Polo story (third) and Terry Nation's Dalek story (fifth). Whitaker noted that 'in some cases items are subject to change'. 'The Daleks' was brought forward in the running order when another SF story, Anthony Coburn's 'The Masters of Luxor', was cancelled. This was later published as part of Titan Books' *Doctor Who: The Scripts* series in 1991. Whitaker hurriedly wrote two special episodes set entirely inside the TARDIS ('The Edge of Destruction' and 'The Brink of Disaster') to fill the gap.

27.   Quoted in 'Behind every Dalek there's this woman', *Daily Mail*, 28 November 1964.

28. BBC WAC T5/647/1: Verity Lambert to Jimmy Plater, 16 September 1963.

29. BBC WAC T5/638/1: David Whitaker to Verity Lambert, no date.

30. Michael Gowers, 'Dr Who', *Daily Mail*, 25 November 1963; 'Eerie weirdie', *Daily Worker*, 30 November 1963.

31. BBC WAC T5/638/1: Audience Research Report VR/63/412 'Dr Who', 30 December 1963.

32. David Whitaker, *Doctor Who in an exciting adventure with the Daleks* (London, 1964). This describes Ian and Barbara's first meeting and their encounter with the Doctor on a foggy Barnes Common and their intrusion into the police box. This was one of three novelisations published in the 1960s, the other two being *Doctor Who and the Crusaders*, again by Whitaker, and *Doctor Who and the Zarbi* by Bill Strutton.

33. BBC WAC T5/647/2: David Whitaker to Donald Wilson, 15 January 1964.

34. Ibid.: Donald Baverstock to Donald Wilson, 31 December 1963.

35. BBC WAC T5/647/1: Memorandum entitled 'Doctor Who' by David Whitaker, 16 September 1963.

36. See James Chapman, 'The BBC and the censorship of *The War Game* (1965)', *Journal of Contemporary History*, vol.41, no.1 (January 2006), pp.75–94.

37. On Nation's contribution to *Doctor Who*, see Jonathan Bignell and Andrew O'Day, *Terry Nation* (Manchester, 2004), *passim*.

38. BBC WAC T5/649/1: Letter from Mrs C.M. McConaghy (Phillip's mother). The request for a signed photograph was from Lorrain [*sic*] Hinson ('Dear Daleks . . .') and the birthday invitation came from Ian of High Wycomb ('There will be some nuts and bolts stewed oil drink and if you want our food that we eat'). A reply by Verity Lambert to one fan is sublime: 'The Daleks are very busy at the moment, but they have asked me to write and thank you for your Christmas card and they have agreed to suspend hostilities for one day on Christmas Day.' It was not only the Daleks who were popular. Three teenage girls asked 'if we could have a picture of those FABULOUS HANSOME [*sic*] Thais Alydon and Ganatus . . . I am sure that any picture will be joyfully received by many girls.'

39. Quoted in David J. Howe, Mark Stammers and Stephen James Walker, *Doctor Who: The Sixties* (London, 1992), p.27.

40. Raymond Cusick, 'How I created the Daleks' (letter), *Daily Telegraph*, 1 October 1994, p.14.

41. This point was picked up by some correspondents at the time. Eight-year-old M.J. Wright wrote to ask: 'I have watched your programme Dr Who, and I would like to know how the Daleks get up and down the

steps please.' Someone has annotated the letter: 'Do we know?' (BBC WACT5/649/1).

42.   Piers D. Britton and Simon J. Barker, *Reading Between Designs: Visual Imagery and the Generation of Meaning in 'The Avengers', 'The Prisoner', and 'Doctor Who'* (Austin, 2003), p.169.

43.   BBC WAC T5/649/1: Letters from Alistair Stewart (n.d.) and Shirley Sidlow (10 May 1964).

44.   T.C. Worsley, 'Spotting the winners', *Financial Times*, 6 January 1965; Mary Crozier, *The Guardian*, 18 January 1965; Peter Black, *Daily Mail*, 15 February 1965; John Holmstrom, 'Sigley's Rep', *New Statesman*, 16 April 1965.

45.   O'Brien, *SF: UK*, p.77.

46.   The average audiences for historical stories during the first three seasons were as follows: 'Marco Polo' (9.5 million), 'The Aztecs' (7.5 million), 'The Reign of Terror' (6.7 million), 'The Romans' (11.6 million), 'The Crusade' (9.4 million), 'The Time Meddler' (8.4 million), 'The Myth Makers' (8.4 million), 'The Massacre' (6.4 million) and 'The Gunfighters' (6.3 million). Averages for SF stories were: 'The Daleks' (9 million), 'The Keys of Marinus' (9 million), 'The Sensorites' (7 million), 'The Dalek Invasion of Earth' (12 million), 'The Web Planet' (12.5 million), 'The Space Museum' (9.2 million), 'The Chase' (9.4 million), 'Galaxy Four' (9.9 million), 'The Daleks' Master Plan' (9.4 million), 'The Ark' (6.5 million), 'The Celestial Toymaker' (8.3 million), 'The Savages' (5 million) and 'The War Machines' (5.2 million).

47.   BBC WAC T5/649/1: Donald Wilson to Pauline Ammesley (21 August 1964) in response to her letter of 18 August 1964.

48.   Ibid.: Letters from Barbara Johnson and Tony Priddy (30 November 1963) and M.M.G. Oborski (12 September 1964).

49.   Quoted in 'Behind every Dalek there's this woman', *Daily Mail*, 28 November 1964.

50.   BBC WAC T5/647/1: David Whitaker to Donald Wilson, 16 December 1963.

51.   Ibid.: A memo from John Crockett to David Whitaker (26 February 1964) suggests a long list of historical subjects, mostly, but not exclusively, British: the Peasants' Revolt or the Pilgrimage of Grace, Viking raids on Britain, the '45 and Bonnie Prince Charlie, Drake and the Armada, Raleigh and the colonisation of the Americas, the Globe Theatre, Australian convict settlement, the Roman invasion of Britain, Richard I and the Crusades, the downfall of Akhnaton, the Medicis or the Borgias, Benvento Cellini, Covered Wagons, Cornish smugglers and wreckers, and Boadicea. In the event only three of these topics became

serials: 'The Crusade' (#14), 'The Smugglers' (#28) and 'The Highlanders' (#31). 'The Time Meddler' (#17) features a Viking raid and 'The Daleks' Master Plan' (#21) includes a visit to Ancient Egypt and the time of the building of the pyramids. A story set in Roman Britain by Malcolm Hulke was planned for the first season (David Whitaker, 'Doctor Who', 16 September 1963) but was not commissioned.

52.   BBC WAC T5/1249/1: Innes Lloyd to Rex Tucker, 22 February 1966.

53.   Peter Haining, *Doctor Who: A Celebration – Two Decades Through Time and Space* (London, 1983), p.180.

54.   BBC WAC T5/1249/1: Audience Research Report VR/66/274, 'The O.K. Corral', 13 June 1966.

55.   Ibid.: Sydney Newman to Donald Wilson, 23 May 1966.

56.   BBC WAC T5/1238/1: Audience Research Report VR/65/150, 'The Centre', 23 April 1965, p.1.

57.   BBC WAC T5/647/1: David Whitaker to David Higham Associates Ltd, 23 September 1964.

58.   David Pringle (ed.), *The Ultimate Encyclopedia of Science Fiction* (London, 1996), p.23.

59.   BBC WAC T5/1238/1: 'The Web Planet – Promotion', undated.

60.   'Dennis Spooner Interview', *Doctor Who Monthly*, no.56 (September 1981), pp.21–4.

61.   BBC WAC T5/647/2: Donald Wilson to Head of Business, TV Enterprises, 24 February 1964.

62.   Cull, '"Bigger on the inside . . ."', p.101.

63.   BBC WAC T5/649/1: Mrs Patricia Stern to 'Programme Controller', 23 November 1964.

64.   BBC WAC T5/647/2: Letter from R. Taylor, 7 December 1964. Another correspondent wrote to request the prop sign stating 'It is forbidden to dump bodies in the river'!

65.   Philip Purser, *Sunday Telegraph*, 13 June 1965.

66.   BBC WAC T5/1246/1: Douglas Camfield to Tristram Gary, 20 July 1965.

67.   Ibid.: Audience Research Report VR/66/68, 'Destruction of Time', 8 March 1966.

68.   Ibid.: Audience Research Report VR/66/33, 'Escape Switch', 11 February 1966, p.1.

69.   Ibid.: Barry Learoyd to John Wiles, 23 November 1965.

70.   Ibid.: John Wiles to Barry Learoyd, 11 January 1966; Sydney Newman to Douglas Camfield, 11 January 1966.

71.   On the two Dalek films, see Cook, 'Adapting telefantasy', pp.113–27, and Richard Hollis, 'The Dalek movies', *Doctor Who Monthly*, no.84 (January

1984), pp.20–34. See also the documentary 'Dalekmania', directed by Kevin Davies for Lumiere Video in 1995, which is also included on Studio Canal's *Doctor Who Movie Collection* DVD (D5/Z1).

72.   Cook, p.119.

73.   *Films and Filming*, vol.12, no.12 (September 1966), p.7.

2. Monsters, Inc. (1966–1969)

1.   BBC WAC T5/1251/1: Derek Martinus to William Hartnell, 29 September 1966.

2.   BBC WAC T5/647/1: 'The New Dr Who', n.d. but from some time in the autumn of 1966.

3.   Quoted in Norman Hare, '"Tougher" Dr Who is chosen', *Daily Telegraph*, 2 September 1966.

4.   BBC WAC T5/647/2: 'The New Doctor Who', 28 November 1966.

5.   Ann Lawrence, 'Futurist', *Morning Star*, 25 January 1967.

6.   BBC WAC T5/647/1: Notes by Donald Tosh on a proposed serial 'The Playthings of Fo', no date.

7.   Stewart Lane, 'Better than "Who"', *Daily Worker*, 3 February 1966.

8.   BBC WAC T5/2532/1: Audience Research Report VR/67/419, 'The Evil of the Daleks' Final Episode, p.1.

9.   BBC WAC T5/1250/1: Innes Lloyd to Raymond London, 4 July 1966.

10.   BBC WAC T5/1271/1: Audience Research Report VR/69/141, 'The Seeds of Death' Part 6, p.2.

11.   BBC WAC T5/1249/1: Innes Lloyd to Rex Tucker, 10 May 1966.

12.   BBC WAC T5/1253/1: Audience Research Report VR/67/149, 'The Moonbase' Part 4, p.1.

13.   Francis Hope, 'Doctor When', *New Statesman*, 22 March 1968.

14.   See Nicholas J. Cull, 'Peter Watkins' *Culloden* and the alternative form in historical filmmaking', *Film International*, no.1 (2003), pp.48–53.

15.   BBC WAC T5/647/2: 'A comparison of the "Dr Who" audience during weeks 45–47 in 1964 and 1965', to Donald Tosh from unnamed source. It reported that in November–December 1964 'the audience was almost equally divided amongst children (that is, 5–14 year olds) (46%) and adults (54%). The comparative 1965 figures show that the proportion of children in the audience was lower (37%) and the proportion of adults higher (63%).'

16.   BBC WAC T5/647/2: 'The New Doctor Who', 28 November 1966.

17.   Ann Lawrence, 'Scientific', *Morning Star*, 22 February 1967.

18.   Virginia Ironside, *Daily Mail*, 5 August 1966.

19.   Hope, 'Doctor When', *New Statesman*, 22 March 1968.

20. BBC WAC T5/2536/1: C.M.H. Pedler to Gerry Carr, 2 February 1967 [*sic*] – though surely 1968, as 'The Tomb of the Cybermen' was not broadcast until September 1967 and the letter refers to its later screening on Australian television.

21. Julian Critchley, *The Times*, 4 September 1967.

22. BBC WAC T5/1271/1: Audience Research Report VR/69/141, 'The Seeds of Death' Part 6, p.2.

23. BBC WAC T5/1252/1: Nancy Safford to Innes Lloyd, 16 January 1967.

24. Ibid.: Innes Lloyd to Nancy Safford, 20 January 1967.

25. Lawrence, 'Scientific', *Morning Star*, 22 February 1967.

26. BBC WAC T5/1253/1: Audience Research Report VR/67/149, 'The Moonbase' Part 4, pp. 1–2.

27. BBC WAC T5/1271/1: Audience Research Report VR/69/141, 'The Seeds of Death' Part 6, p.1.

28. Stuart Hood, 'Who does it', *The Spectator*, 14 March 1969.

29. BBC WAC T5/1250/1: Audience Research Report VR/66/381, 'The War Machines' Part 4, p.1.

30. Quoted in David Banks, *Doctor Who: Cybermen* (London, 1988), p.25.

31. BBC WAC T5/1253/1: Innes Lloyd to Robin Scott, 27 January 1967.

32. Ann Lawrence, 'Monsters', *Morning Star*, 22 July 1967.

33. BBC WAC T5/1259/1: Derek Martinus to Martin Baugh, 3 October 1967.

34. Kenneth O. Morgan, *The People's Peace: British History 1945–1990* (London, 1990), p.285.

35. BBC WAC T5/1270/1: Audience Research Report VR/69/1, 'The Krotons' Part 1, p.1.

36. Ibid.: Robert Holmes to Donald Tosh, 25 April 1965. Holmes's original treatment was entitled 'Doctor Who and the Space Trap'. He submitted it again in May 1968 with this covering note: 'Cleaning out some old files this weekend, I came across the enclosed letter setting out the basis of a DR WHO adventure. I've no trace of a reply or any memory of discussing the idea further . . . I imagine that either Donald moved on or I became involved in something else around that time. Anyway, as it still seems to me to be a valid idea for the programme, I'm resubmitting the thing.' Holmes to Peter Bryant, 20 May 1968.

37. Ibid.: Audience Research Report VR/69/1, 'The Krotons' Part 1, p.1.

38. BBC WAC T5/2532/1: Derrick Sherwin to Peter Ling, 15 July 1968.

39. Ibid.: Audience Research Report VR/68/630, 'The Mind Robber' Part 5, p.1.

40. Ibid., pp.1–2.

41. BBC WAC T5/1267/1 contains statements of *Doctor Who* costs from 'The Underwater Menace' (GG) to 'The War Games' (ZZ). In the 1967/68

financial year ('The Underwater Menace' to 'The Web of Fear') total expenditure on *Doctor Who* was £157,614, an overspend of £10,189 on the allocated budget. In the 1968/69 financial year ('Fury from the Deep' to the first three episodes of 'The Space Pirates') total expenditure was £129,147, an underspend of £1,214 on the allocated budget. The average cost *per episode* during this period was £3,085. Indicative costs *per serial* are: 'The Underwater Menace' (£13,140 for four episodes), 'The Evil of the Daleks' (£20,534 for seven episodes and a further £7,274 for a repeat screening), 'The Tomb of the Cybermen' (£10,204 for four episodes), 'The Web of Fear' (£16,560 for six episodes), 'The Dominators' (£14,969 for five episodes), 'The Mind Robber' (£13,205 for five episodes), 'The Invasion' (£25,207 for eight episodes) and 'The Krotons' (£13,316 for four episodes). The costs for the first three episodes only of 'The War Games' are recorded (£11,146).

42. Ann Lawrence, 'Violence', *Morning Star*, 21 May 1969.

3. Earthbound (1970–1974)

1.   BBC WAC T65/64/1: Terrance Dicks to Terry Nation, 24 July 1972.

2.   BBC WAC T65/18/1: Terrance Dicks to Bob Baker and Dave Martin, 8 March 1972.

3.   Stewart Lane, *Morning Star*, 7 February 1970.

4.   Quoted in 'Why my monsters are marvellous', *Saturday Titbits*, 17 April 1971.

5.   Piers D. Britton and Simon J. Barker, *Reading Between Designs: Visual Imagery and the Generation of Meaning in 'The Avengers', 'The Prisoner', and 'Doctor Who* (Austin, 2003), p.149.

6.   Ibid. However, in an unattributed newspaper article from the summer of 1969, 'End of time for Dr Who' (www.cuttingsarchive.org.uk/news_mag/1960s/cuttings.htm), Pertwee is quoted as saying: 'I won't be wearing the Victorian clothes that the other Dr Whos have used. I will be in a modern day suit.'

7.   Stanley Reynolds, 'The metamorphoses of Who', *The Times*, 9 April 1973.

8.   John Tulloch and Manuel Alvarado, *Doctor Who: The Unfolding Text* (London, 1983), pp.210–13.

9.   BBC WAC T65/64/1: Terrance Dicks to Terry Nation, 1 August 1972.

10. BBC WAC T5/2561/1: Notes appended to script treatment, undated.

11. BBC WAC T65/20/1: 'New Characters', undated but probably summer 1970.

12. Asa Briggs, *The History of Broadcasting in the United Kingdom. Volume V: Competition 1955–1974* (Oxford, 1995), p.424.

13. Matthew Coady, 'The real enemies of Dr Who', *Daily Mirror*, 1 January 1972.

14. The UNIT stories are 'Spearhead from Space', 'Doctor Who and the Silurians', 'The Ambassadors of Death', 'Inferno', 'Terror of the Autons', 'The Mind of Evil', 'The Claws of Axos', 'The Dæmons', 'Day of the Daleks', 'The Time Monster', 'The Three Doctors', 'The Green Death' and 'Invasion of the Dinosaurs'. 'The Time Warrior' and 'Planet of the Spiders' both feature UNIT characters but neither are predominantly UNIT stories. The non-UNIT stories are 'Colony in Space', 'The Curse of Peladon', 'The Sea Devils', 'The Mutants', 'Carnival of Monsters', 'Frontier in Space', 'Planet of the Daleks', 'Death to the Daleks' and 'The Monster of Peladon'. However, 'The Sea Devils' follows the UNIT formula, except that on this occasion the UNIT role is taken by the Royal Navy.

15. Matthew Coady, 'The vintage nightmare', *Daily Mirror*, 27 January 1970.

16. Sylvia Clayton, *Daily Telegraph*, 18 January 1971; 'Dr Who gets back to his old routine', *The Sun*, 10 April 1971.

17. BBC WAC T65/64/1: Terrance Dicks to Terry Nation, 24 July 1972.

18. BBC WAC T65/3/1: Derrick Sherwin to David Whitaker, 11 August 1969.

19. Ibid.: Terrance Dicks to David Whitaker, 6 July 1970.

20. Nicholas J. Cull, '"Bigger on the inside...": *Doctor Who* as British cultural history', in Graham Roberts and Philip M. Taylor (eds), *The Historian, Television and Television History* (Luton, 2001), p.103.

21. BBC WAC T64/4/1: Don Houghton to Douglas Camfield, 23 June 1970.

22. Richard Last, *Daily Telegraph*, 28 December 1973 (review of a repeat of 'The Green Death').

23. BBC WAC T65/17/1: 'Doctor Who – Bridgehead from Space', 18 December 1972.

24. BBC WAC T65/16/1: 'Doctor Who and the Shape of Terror' by Brian Hayles, undated, with Dicks's handwritten annotations.

25. Ibid.: 'Doctor Who and the Brain-Dead' by Brian Hayles, undated.

26. BBC WAC T65/30/1: 'The Monster of Peladon', Episode 1 story breakdown, undated.

27. Ibid.: 'Argument', document appended to the treatment, undated.

28. BBC WAC T65/36/1: 'Doctor Who – Deathworld', undated.

29. BBC WAC T65/36/1: Terrance Dicks to Bob Baker and Dave Martin, 18 May 1972.

30. BBC WAC T65/32/1: Audience Research Report VR/74/351, 'Planet of the Spiders' Part 6, p.1.

4. High Gothic (1975–1977)

1.   On the Hinchcliffe-Holmes period of *Doctor Who*, see 'Serial Thrillers' on the DVD *Doctor Who: Pyramids of Mars* (BBCDVD 1350). The *Doctor Who – Dynamic Rankings* website includes an interactive poll of favourite stories which, as at 25 April 2005, included five Hinchcliffe-Holmes serials in the top ten: 'Genesis of the Daleks' (1st), 'The Talons of Weng-Chiang' (2nd), 'Pyramids of Mars' (5th), 'The Robots of Death' (6th) and 'The Deadly Assassin' (7th) (www.dewhurstdesigns.co.uk/dynamic/full/results.php).

2.   An indication of the special status of the twelfth season is that the scripts have been published in book form: *Doctor Who: The Scripts – Tom Baker 1974/5*, ed. Justin Richards (London, 2001).

3.   These were episode two of 'The Ark in Space' (13.6 million), episode three of 'The Deadly Assassin' (13 million) and episode three of 'The Robots of Death' (13.1 million). A compilation repeat of 'Pyramids of Mars' also attracted an audience of 13.7 million.

4.   BBC WAC T65/12/1: Robert Holmes to Gerry Davis, 23 July 1974.

5.   BBC WAC T65/63/1: Audience Research Report VR/76/545, 'Masque of Mandragora' Part 4, p.1.

6.   Shaun Usher, 'Vintage conventions', *Daily Mail*, 31 January 1977; Peter Fiddick, 'Doctor Who', *The Guardian*, 1 November 1976.

7.   BBC WAC T65/12/1: Carey Blyton to Philip Hinchcliffe, 10 July 1975.

8.   See John Peel and Terry Nation, *The Official Doctor Who and the Daleks Book* (New York, 1988) for an 'official' history of Dalek continuity and an imaginative, if laboured, attempt to resolve the discontinuities between 'Genesis' and earlier Dalek serials. In this narrative, the first Daleks (those encountered by the First Doctor and confined to their city) are the results of discarded experiments who have evolved independently and built their own city on a different part of Skaro.

9.   Nicholas J. Cull, '"Bigger on the inside…": *Doctor Who* as British cultural history', in Graham Roberts and Philip M. Taylor (eds), *The Historian, Television and Television History* (Luton, 2001), p.101.

10.   BBC WAC T65/10/1: Audience Research Report VR 75/215, 'Genesis of the Daleks' Part 6, p.1.

11.   Tom Baker, *Who on Earth is Tom Baker? An Autobiography* (London, 1997), p.202.

12.   BBC WAC T65/63/1: Audience Research Report VR/76/545, 'Masque of Mandragora' Part 4, p.1.

13.   Piers D. Britton and Simon J. Barker, *Reading Between Designs: Visual Imagery and the Generation of Meaning in 'The Avengers', 'The Prisoner', and 'Doctor Who'* (Austin, 2003), p.227 (their note 33).

14. Elizabeth Thomas, *New Statesman*, 24 January 1975; Martin Jackson, *Daily Mail*, 11 January 1975.

15. BBC WAC T5/2565/1: Audience Research Report VR/74/257, 'Robot' Part 1, 16 January 1975.

16. Quoted in Jackson, *Daily Mail*, 11 January 1975.

17. BBC WAC T65/12/1: Philip Hinchcliffe to Gerry Davis, 10 September 1974.

18. Peter Fiddick, 'Doctor Who', *The Guardian*, 1 November 1976.

19. Quoted in Martin Wainwright, 'The Why of Who', *Evening Standard*, 31 January 1977.

20. BBC WAC T65/33/1: Philip Hinchcliffe to Nan Greifer, 27 November 1974.

21. Ibid.: Robert Holmes to Lewis Greifer, 15 October 1974.

22. BBC WAC T65/60/1: Terrance Dicks to Robert Holmes, 22 September 1975.

23. Ibid.: Aidan Carlisle to 'Mr Robin Bland', 11 January 1976.

24. BBC WAC T65/65/1: Philippa Judge to 'Head of BBC Children's Television Programmes'.

25. BBC WAC T65/11/1: Audience Research Report VR/75/599, 'Planet of Evil' Part 4, p.1.

26. BBC WAC T65/63/1: Audience Research Report VR/76/545, 'Masque of Mandragora' Part 4, p.2.

27. For example, the first episode of 'The Android Invasion' cost £7969.10. The second highest component, after artists' fees and scripts (£4460.65), was 'scenery' (£2160). Visual effects accounted for only £397 (BBC WAC T5/2574).

28. Britton and Barker, p.143.

29. 'Fantasy v reality', letter from Alison Duddington and reply from Philip Hinchcliffe, *Radio Times*, 29 March–4 April 1975, p.74.

30. Hugh Whitton, 'Nothing scary about Dr Who say children', *Evening News*, 21 January 1975.

31. Quoted in Michael Tracey and David Morrison, *Whitehouse* (London, 1979). The authors identify this quotation as being from an address by Whitehouse to the Royal College of Nursing in 1970, but it refers to incidents from mid-1970s *Doctor Who:* 'strangulation . . . by obscene vegetable matter' and the reference to making a Molotov Cocktail would seem to suggest incidents in 'The Seeds of Doom'.

32. BBC T65/62/1: Mary Whitehouse to 'The Producer, *Dr Who*', 15 November 1976.

33. BBC WAC T65/63/1: Audience Research Report VR/76/545, 'Masque of Mandragora' Part 4, p.1.

34.   BBC WAC T65/62/1: Philip Hinchcliffe to Graeme McDonald, 12 June 1978.

35.   BBC WAC T65/65/1: Letters from 'John', Paul Kish (aged $7\frac{3}{4}$), Douglas Parker (8 years, 2 months) and Lucy Wilson ($7\frac{3}{4}$), with covering letter from headmaster A.C. Heslop, 21 February 1976; letters from Mrs J.M. Oliver, 21 February 1976 and Colin R. Thorpe, 22 February 1976; and letters addressed to Tom Baker from Valerie Wilkie of Fife, 22 February 1976, Sheridan Tongue, 6 March 1976, and John Smith of London, 11 March 1976.

36.   Ibid.: Philip Hinchcliffe to Colin R. Thorpe, 5 March 1976.

37.   BBC WAC T65/60/1: Robert Holmes to Aidan Carlisle, 13 January 1976.

38.   BBC WAC T65/65/1: Philip Hinchcliffe to Shaun Sutton, 20 February 1976.

39.   Stanley Reynolds, 'Dr Who', *The Times*, 10 October 1977.

40.   'Never mind what the other kids think about the lack of monsters in Dr Who. What I want to know is: when is Leela getting back into her original gear?' Letter from Ken Bayley '(aged 52)', *Radio Times*, 26 March–1 April 1977, p.59.

5. High Camp (1977–1980)

1.   Quoted in John Tulloch and Manuel Alvarado, *Doctor Who: The Unfolding Text* (London, 1983), p.158.

2.   BBC WAC T65/195: Graeme McDonald to Graham Williams, 25 April 1978.

3.   BBC WAC T65/211: Graeme McDonald to Graham Williams, 26 June 1979.

4.   BBC WAC T65/157: Graeme McDonald to Graham Williams, 9 February 1978.

5.   BBC WAC T65/208: Audience Research Report VR/77/664, 'The Sun Makers' Part 2, p.2.

6.   BBC WAC T65/201: Graham Williams to Anne Drabble, 19 November 1979.

7.   Ibid.: Graham Williams to Graeme McDonald, 12 July 1979.

8.   BBC WAC T65/157: 'Doctor Who (1977 Season)', by Graham Williams, 30 November 1976. The date of the document suggests that Williams had intended the Key to Time for the fifteenth season, his first in charge of the series, though in the event it had to wait another year.

9.   Richard Boston, *The Observer*, 25 September 1977.

10.   BBC WAC T65/188: Graham Williams to Graeme McDonald, 18 July 1979.

11. BBC WAC T65/158: Graeme McDonald to Anthony Read, 14 March 1978.

12. BBC WAC T65/201: Graeme McDonald to Graham Williams, 1 February 1979.

13. BBC WAC T65/156: Graham Williams to Graeme McDonald, 7 March 1978.

14. Tom Baker, *Who on Earth is Tom Baker? An Autobiography* (London, 1997), p.229.

15. See 'Dr Who and the Pilgrims of Horror', *Daily Express*, 15 February 1978; and Andrew Pixley, 'Doctor Who: Invasion, USA 1978 AD', *In Vision*, no.30 (March 1991), pp.10–11.

16. Quoted in Tulloch and Alvarado, p.159.

17. Baker, pp.211–12.

18. BBC WAC T65/195: Publicity notes for 'The Stones of Blood', undated.

19. BBC WAC T65/208: Audience Research Report VR/77/664, 'The Sun Makers' Part 2, p.2.

20. BBC WAC T65/157: 'Doctor Who (1977 Season)', by Graham Williams, 30 November 1976.

21. BBC WAC T65/206: Graeme McDonald to Graham Williams, 21 February 1977.

22. BBC WAC T65/155: Publicity notes for 'Underworld', undated.

23. BBC WAC T65/208: Audience Research Report VR/77/664, 'The Sun Makers' Part 2, p.1.

24. See M.J. Simpson, 'Counterpointing the Surrealism of the Underlying Metaphor in *The Hitchhiker's Guide to the Galaxy*', in John R. Cook and Peter Wright (eds), *British Science Fiction Television: A Hitch Hiker's Guide* (London, 2006), pp.219–39.

25. Jonathan Bignell and Andrew O'Day, *Terry Nation* (Manchester, 2004), p.82.

6. New Directions (1980–1984)

1. On the reign of *Doctor Who's* longest-serving producer, 'JN-T', see 'Doctor Who: A Decade of Producing', *Starburst Yearbook 1989– 90* (Winter 1990), pp.46–9, and David Darlington, 'From Brighton to Perivale . . .', *TV Zone*, no.152 (July 2002), pp.23–6. See also the documentary 'A New Beginning' on the DVD *Doctor Who: The Leisure Hive* (BBCDVD 1351).

2. 'The New Dr Who', *Starburst*, vol.3, no.3 (1979), p.19.

3. *Doctor Who Monthly*, no.52 (May 1981), p.56.

4.   The continuity references in Season 18 tend to be visual, such as the Doctor's 'Sherlock Holmes' costume from 'The Talons of Weng-Chiang' and Romana's schoolgirl hat from 'City of Death' seen in the TARDIS. In 'The Keeper of Traken', Geoffrey Beevers, as the Master, was made up in the same way as Peter Pratt in 'The Deadly Assassin'. Verbal references such as the galactic co-ordinates of Gallifrey (ten zero eleven zero zero by zero two) mentioned in 'Logopolis' were consistent with 'Pyramids of Mars'. These sorts of references, unnoticed by casual viewers, pleased the series' fans. By the mid 1980s, however, they would become almost a fetish.

5.   Quoted in David J. Howe, Stephen James Walker and Mark Stammers, *The Handbook: The Unofficial and Unauthorised Guide to the Production of Doctor Who* (Tolworth, 2005), p.522.

6.   Piers D. Britton and Simon J. Barker, *Reading Between Designs: Visual Imagery and the Generation of Meaning in 'The Avengers', 'The Prisoner', and 'Doctor Who'* (Austin, 2003), p.183.

7.   Ibid., p.183.

8.   Nigel Robinson, 'Doctor Who', *Time Out*, 27 November–3 December 1981, p.94.

9.   Justin Richards, *Doctor Who: The Legend – 40 Years of Time Travel* (London, 2003), p.287.

10.   Quoted in Margaret Forwood, 'Two for Who', *The Sun*, 27 June 1981.

11.   Margaret Forwood, 'Dr Who needs a timer switch!', *The Sun*, 25 March 1982.

12.   'In at the deep end' [interview with Eric Saward], *Doctor Who Magazine*, no.346 (August 2004), p.18.

13.   'Tardis lands on the wrong day', *The Guardian*, 4 January 1982, p.10.

14.   Britton and Barker, p.172.

15.   'The New Dr Who', *Starburst*, vol.3, no.3 (1979), p.19.

16.   *The Scotsman*, 17 March 1984, p.3.

17.   'Earthshock' includes flashbacks to 'The Tenth Planet', 'Tomb of the Cybermen' and 'Revenge of the Cybermen', suggesting that it came later in the Cyber chronology, though 'Revenge' is set centuries after the Cyber Wars. Unlike the Daleks, the Cybermen do not possess time travel ability, though they do acquire a time ship in 'Attack of the Cybermen'. See David Banks, *Doctor Who: Cybermen* (London, 1990). Banks played the Cyber Leader in 'Earthshock', 'The Five Doctors', 'Attack of the Cybermen' and 'Silver Nemesis'.

18.   Speaking on *Doctor Who: 30 Years in the TARDIS* (BBC1, 1993).

19.   Quoted in John Tulloch and Manuel Alvarado, *Doctor Who: The Unfolding Text* (London, 1983), p.270.

20.   Ibid., p.269.

21.   'What the fanzines said . . .', *In Vision*, no.57 (May 1995), p.13.

22.   Quoted in *In Vision*, no.73 (August 1997), p.4.

23.   'What the fanzines said . . . ,' *In Vision*, no.73 (August 1997), p.14.

24.   Quoted in Howe, Walker and Stammers, p.541.

25.   Tom Baker, *Who on Earth is Tom Baker? An Autobiography* (London, 1997), p.219.

7. Trials of a Time Lord (1985–1989)

1.   Andrew Pixley, 'Too short a season', *Doctor Who Magazine*, no.346 (August 2004), pp.26–31.

2.   Reports of the suspension of *Doctor Who* are characterised by an inverse proportion of accuracy and hysteria. See: 'Dr Who is axed in a BBC plot', *The Sun*, 28 February 1985, p.2; 'Beeb's shock for Dr Who', *Daily Star*, 28 February 1985, p.7; 'Dr Who down-Graded', *Daily Mail*, 28 February 1985, p.3; 'BBC cash curbs ground Dr Who', *Daily Telegraph*, 28 February 1985, p.1; 'BBC Daleks threaten the Doctor with hibernation', *The Scotsman*, 28 February 1985, p.1; 'Grade: Why the Doctor had to go', *Daily Mail*, 2 March 1985, p.19; 'Baddies of the Beeb', *Daily Star*, 1 March 1985, p.8; 'Time Lord will rematerialise, BBC chief tells followers', *The Scotsman*, 2 March 1985, p.5; 'Carry on Doctor', *Daily Star*, 2 March 1985, p.5.

3.   'Temporary time warp for Dr Who', *The Times*, 28 February 1985, p.3.

4.   Kevin Davies and Jeremy Bentham, 'Armageddon Factors', *In Vision*, no.90 (June 2000), p.5.

5.   *Daily Express*, 23 March 1984, p.18.

6.   *Sunday Express*, 25 March 1985, p.22.

7.   'TV "nasty" lands a nice role – as new Dr Who', *Western Mail*, 20 August 1983, p.1; 'Time Lord with six appeal', *Daily Express*, 17 March 1984, p.19.

8.   'Naughty Nicola!', *Daily Star*, 26 January 1985, p.13.

9.   Simon Hoggart, 'Who's Who', *New Society*, 24 January 1985, p.138.

10.   'One last chance for timeless Dr Who', *Daily Mail*, 14 August 1986, p.5.

11.   'The Doctor on trial in new television series', *The Times*, 30 August 1986, p.23.

12.   Maureen Patton, 'Time warps even the Doctor's case', *Daily Express*, 2 December 1986, p.24.

13.   'One last chance for timeless Dr Who', *Daily Mail*, 14 August 1986, p.5.

14.   'Rebel Dr Who gets the sack', *The Sun*, 13 December 1986, p.13; 'Time runs out for Dr Who star', *Evening Standard*, 18 December 1986, p.13; 'Who will be the next Doctor?', *Today*, 18 December 1986, p.13; 'Material

dilemma for Dr Who', *The Guardian*, 19 December 1986, p.4. It is widely believed within *Doctor Who* fandom that Grade bore a personal animosity towards Baker.

15.   'Lies, damned lies, and statistics', *In Vision*, no.90 (June 2000), p.4.

16.   See also an illuminating article by Stephen James Walker, 'Wolves at the Door', *In Vision*, no.103 (August 2002), pp.29–32.

17.   'Dr Who killed by the Street, *The Sun*, 21 October 1989, p.15; 'Rovers pulling power exterminates Dr Who', *Today*, 5 February 1990, p.25; 'Dr Who zapped', *Daily Mirror*, 5 February 1990, p.3.

18.   Minette Marrin, *Daily Telegraph*, 8 September 1987, p.12; *The Scotsman*, 17 December 1988, p.6.

19.   Andrew *Cartmel, Script Doctor: The Inside Story of Doctor Who 1986–89* (London, 2005), p.81.

20.   Ibid., pp. 134–5.

21.   'MacGuffin' was Alfred Hitchcock's term for the plot object – 'the device, the gimmick, if you will, or the papers the spies are after . . . it doesn't matter what it is.' See Francois Truffaut, with Helen G. Scott, *Hitchcock* (London, 1978), pp.191–2.

22.   Cartmel, p.163.

23.   Ibid., p.146.

24.   Extracts from the correspondence between Bassett Foods plc and the BBC is printed in *In Vision*, no.97 (August 2001), p.10.

25.   Cartmel, p.78. This reference can only be to *Doctor Who: The Unfolding Text*.

26.   Piers D. Britton and Simon J. Barker, *Reading Between Designs: Visual Imagery and the Generation of Meaning in 'The Avengers', 'The Prisoner', and 'Doctor Who* (Austin, 2003), p.157.

27.   'Doctor to go private?', *Daily Telegraph*, 1 December 1989, p.18; 'Look Who's for sale', *Today*, 2 December 1989, p.11; 'A diagnosis of sick series syndrome', *Sunday Telegraph Magazine*, 14 January 1990, p.10; 'Mass protest planned over "extermination of Dr Who"', *The Independent*, 30 November 1990, p.2; 'Will Doctor Who ever rematerialise?', *Daily Telegraph*, 29 July 1991, p.13; 'BBC thwarts the return of Dr Who', *Mail on Sunday*, 4 August 1991, p.21; 'A suitable case for treatment', *The Independent*, 14 September 1991, p.30.

8. Millennial Anxieties (1996)

1.   The television movie is sometimes given the unofficial title of 'The Enemy Within' by certain sections of the fan community; others refer to it simply as *Doctor Who – The Movie*.

2.   On the BBC during this period, see Georgina Borne, *Uncertain Vision: Birt, Dyke and the Reinvention of the BBC* (London, 2004).

3.   Adrian Rigelsford, *The Doctors: 30 Years of Time Travel* (London, 1994), p.149.

4.   'Dr Who lands in the middle of a £22m lawsuit', *The Times*, 15 February 1997, p.4; 'BBC faces £14m lawsuit after Dr Who film plan scrapped', *The Guardian*, 15 February 1997, p.8; 'BBC sued for pulling out of Dr Who feature film', *The Independent*, 15 February 1997, p.2.

5.   'Dr Who gets Spielberg call to Hollywood', *Sunday Times*, 6 March 1994, p.3.

6.   'Dr Who takes off in £5m TV revival', *Daily Telegraph*, 11 January 1996, p.5; 'Bad news for Daleks as the doctor is reincarnated', *The Times*, 11 January 1996, p.3; 'Keep the Dalek basher', *Daily Telegraph*, 13 January 1996, p.12; Andrew Beech, 'The New Adventures of . . . Doctor Who?', *Starburst*, no.210 (February 1996), pp.10–13; 'Who News', *Starburst*, no.211 (March 1996), p.8; Garry Jenkins, 'Who Meets Planet Hollywood', *Times Magazine*, 25 May 1996, pp. 18–20; Nigel Kendall, 'Whose Who?', *Time Out*, 29 May 1996, p.15.

7.   'Philip Segal Interview 2001' on the DVD *Doctor Who: The Movie* (BBCDVD 1043). See also Garry Jenkins, 'The Saviour of Doctor Who', *Starburst*, no.212 (April 1996), pp.10–13.

8.   Matthew Norman, 'Selling out and alienating everyone', *Evening Standard*, 28 May 1996, p.45; Max Davidson, *Daily Mail*, 28 May 1996, p.43; Matthew Bond, 'Welcome back, Doctor, whoever you are', *The Times*, 28 May 1996, p.39; Stuart Jeffries, *The Guardian*, 28 May 1996, p.8; John Diamond, *New Statesman*, 31 May 1996, p.35; Kim Newman, 'Dr Who has been exterminated', *The Independent*, 19 May 1996, p.16; Serena Mackesy, *The Independent*, 28 May 1996, p.28; letter from Derek Crawthorne, *The Independent*, 31 May 1996, p.17.

9.   Letter from Mark Unsworth, *The Independent*, 31 May 1996, p.17; Newman, *The Independent*, 19 May 1996, p.15.

10.   Newman, *The Independent*, 19 May 1996, p.15; Jeffries, *The Guardian*, 28 May 1996, p.8.

11.   Mackesy, *The Independent*, 28 May 1996, p.28.

12.   Jeffries, *The Guardian*, 28 May 1996, p.8.

13.   Ibid.

14.   Ibid.; Kendall, 'Whose Who?', *Time Out*, 29 May 1996, p.15.

15.   Geoff King, *Spectacular Narratives: Hollywood in the Age of the Blockbuster* (London, 2000), p.156.

16.   Tom Cussock, 'That essential "Whoishness"', *Sunday Telegraph*, 2 June 1996, p.28.

17.   Jenkins, 'Who Meets Planet Hollywood', *Times Magazine*, 25 May 1996,
       p.18.
18.   Sean Day-Lewis, 'A Time Lord's place is in the past', *Daily Telegraph*, 28
       May 1996, p.35.

9. Second Coming (2005)

1.   Nicholas J. Cull, '"Bigger on the inside . . .": *Doctor Who* as British
       cultural history', in Graham Roberts and Philip M. Taylor (eds), *The
       Historian, Television and Television History* (Luton, 2001), p.108; Mark
       Campbell, *Doctor Who: The Pocket Essential* (Harpenden, 2000), p.7. See
       also Rob Morris, 'Doctor Who: Animated cadaver or run forever?', *TV
       Zone* Special no.36 (March 2000), pp.54–7.
2.   'Doctor Who and the Curse of Fatal Death', written by Steven Moffat,
       comprised four five-minute episodes broadcast on BBC1 during the
       Comic Relief special on the evening of 12 March 1999. Rowan Atkinson,
       Richard E. Grant, Jim Broadbent, Hugh Grant and Joanna Lumley were
       Doctors 9–13, suggesting that the Doctor had reached his thirteenth
       incarnation and the BBC was symbolically killing him (or her) off.
       The choice of Lumley as the final Doctor was a fan-pleasing gesture
       as suggestions that the Doctor should be reincarnated as a woman
       have persisted ever since Tom Baker left *Doctor Who*. Baker himself
       hosted BBC2's '*Doctor Who* Night' on 13 November which featured
       a series of sketches written and performed by Mark Gatiss and David
       Walliams: one was about the origin of *Doctor Who* with Sydney Newman
       (Walliams) selling a 'pitch' to 'Mr Borusa' (Gatiss), another had Peter
       Davison kidnapped by an obsessed fan. 'The Web of Caves' features the
       Doctor (Gatiss) meeting a less-than-terrifying alien (Walliams).
3.   See Lance Parkin, 'Canonicity matters: defining the *Doctor Who* canon',
       in David Butler (ed.), *Time and Relative Dissertations in Space: Critical
       Perspectives on 'Doctor Who'* (Manchester, 2007), pp.246–62. See also
       Lance Parkin and Lars Pearson, *AHistory: An Unauthorised History of the
       'Doctor Who' Universe* (Des Moines, IA, 3rd edn, 2012), which attempts
       to fit all *Doctor Who* stories – including spin-off novels and Big Finish
       audios as well as television episodes – into an overall chronology.
4.   See Matt Hills, 'Televisuality without television? The Big Finish audios
       and discourses of "tele–centic" *Doctor Who*', in Butler, *Time and Relative
       Dissertations in Space*, pp.280–95.
5.   The four webcasts were: 'Death Comes to Time' (13 episodes: 13 July
       2001–3 May 2002) featuring Sylvester McCoy and Sophie Aldred as the
       Seventh Doctor and Ace; 'Real Time' (6 episodes: 2 August–6 September

2002) with Colin Baker as the Sixth Doctor; 'Shada' (6 episodes: 2 May–6 June 2003), a remake of the untransmitted Douglas Adams story with Paul McGann's Eighth Doctor and Lalla Ward as Romana II; and 'Scream of the Shalka' (6 episodes: 13 November–18 December 2003) with an animated Richard E. Grant as a Ninth Doctor. These adventures are now generally regarded as non-canonical, especially 'Scream of the Shalka'.

6.   'Who dares, wins', *The Guardian: G2*, 23 March 2004, p.4.

7.   'Dr Who to return to BBC', *Broadcast*, 20 September 2002, p.3.

8.   Quoted in Matt Hills, *Triumph of a Time Lord: Regenerating 'Doctor Who' in the Twenty-First Century* (London, 2010), pp.48–9.

9.   'Production Notes', *Doctor Who Magazine*, no.368 (April 2006), p.66.

10.   'Dr Who to return to BBC', *Broadcast*, 20 September 2002, p.3.

11.   'Saturday night TV least popular', *BBC News*, 29 August 2003: http://news.bbc.co.uk/1/hi/entertainment/3190783.stm (accessed 17.12.2012).

12.   'How Saturday night television rediscoved its magic touch', *The Observer*, 21 September 2008: http://www.guardian.co.uk/media/2008/sep/21/television (accessed 17.12.2012).

13.   'Heggessey's Legacy', *Doctor Who Magazine*, no.356 (May 2005), p.9.

14.   Frank Collins, 'Doctor Who: The Transmedia Experience', *Television Heaven*, n.d.: http://www.televisionheaven.co.uk/doctor_who.htm (accessed 27.01.2013).

15.   The URL for Clive's website (http://www.whoisodoctorwho.co.uk) was still active as of January 2013, though it now links to another website entitled *Defending the Earth* which suggests that Mickey Smith took over editing it following Clive's death.

16.   The authorship discourse in television studies is exemplified by MUP's 'The Television Series' which includes volumes on Alan Bennett, Alan Clarke, Andrew Davies, Tony Garnett, Trevor Griffiths, Troy Kennedy Martin, Terry Nation, Jimmy Perry and David Croft, Lynda La Plante and Jack Rosenthal. To date the only book-length study of Davies, surprisingly, is Mark Aldridge and Andy Murray, *T is for Television: The Small Screen Adventures of Russell T. Davies* (London, 2008).

17.   'Duckie Who: Time Lord has gay show writer', *The Sun*, 27 September 2003, p.33.

18.   Hills, *Triumph of a Time Lord*, p.27.

19.   See, for example, Andy Murray, 'The talons of Robert Holmes', in Butler, *Time and Relative Dissertations in Space*, pp.217–32.

20.   *Sunday Times: Culture*, 6 March 2005, pp.6–7.

21.   Steven Moffat wrote 'Doctor Who and the Curse of Fatal Death'. Mark Gatiss wrote the straight-to-video unofficial *Doctor Who* spin-off *P.R.O.B.E.* in the early 1990s, as well as four *Doctor Who* novels for

Virgin's 'New Adventures' and 'Missing Adventures', and (to date) two Big Finish audio dramas. Robert Shearman had written several Big Finish audios, including 'The Holy Terror' (2000), 'The Chimes of Midnight' (2002) and 'Jubilee' (2003). Paul Cornell has written *Doctor Who* across several media, including a dozen novels, Big Finish audios and comic strips for *Doctor Who Magazine*.

22.   Eccleston is credited as 'Doctor Who' on the end credits – as were the first four Doctors. David Tennant later insisted on being credited as 'The Doctor'.

23.   'Carry On Doctor', *Sunday Herald Magazine*, 13 March 2005, p.6.

24.   Andrew Spicer, *Typical Men: The Representation of Masculinity in Popular British Cinema* (London, 2001), p.195.

25.   'Oh Lord, he's still stuck in the past', *Sunday Times: Culture*, 27 March 2005, p.12.

26.   'Marketing *Doctor Who*', *Ariel*, 21 June 2005, p.4.

27.   'Production Notes', *Doctor Who Magazine*, no.356 (May 2005), p.66.

28.   'First Series Audience Research', *Outpost Gallifrey: Doctor Who News Page*: http://www.gallifreyone.com/news–archives.php?id=7-2005 (accessed 13.07.2005).

29.   'Alien resurrection', *The Guardian*, 13 June 2005: http://www.guardian .co.uk/media/2005/jun/13/mondaymediasection7 (accessed 27.01.2013).

30.   An analysis of overnight and consolidated viewing figures for the 2005 series is provided in J. Shaun Lyon, *Back to the Vortex: The Unofficial and Unauthorised Guide to Doctor Who 2005* (Tolworth, 2005), pp.400–7. See also Andrew Pixley, 'Scheduled for Success', *Doctor Who Magazine*, no.367 (March 2006), pp.50–5.

31.   'Doctor prescribes a cure for Beeb's terminal misery', *Sunday Express*, 27 March 2005, p.62.

32.   *The Stage*, 4 April 2005, p.18.

33.   'Blitz and species', *Daily Mail*, 27 May 2005, p.53.

34.   This quotation is from a review of 'Dalek' archived with others from the old *Outpost Gallifrey* website at: http://web.archive.org.web/ 2008020911301/ http://www.gallifreyone.com/news-archives.php?id+ 5–2005#newsitem (accessed 30.01.2013).

35.   '2005 Season Survey', *Doctor Who Magazine*, no.363 (December 2005), pp.32–7.

36.   'Doctor Who finally makes the Grade', *The Guardian*, 21 June 2005: http://www.guardian.co.uk/media/2005/jun/21broadcasting.bbc (accessed 30.01.2013).

37.   'Doctor Who "too scary" say parents', *The Guardian*, 14 April 2005: http://www.guardian.co.uk/media/2005/apr/14/bbc.broadcasting (accessed 30.01.2013).

38.   'Cut, the scene that was too scary even for Dr Who', *Daily Mail*, 19 May 2005, p.20.

39.   'Let's not be beastly to the Daleks', *The Times*, 16 May 2005, p.3.

40.   'Dandified Daleks', *The Times*, 16 May 2005, p.15.

41.   'Bad Wolf' is a sly reference to *Buffy the Vampire Slayer*, where each season's menace was referred to as the 'Big Bad': hence 'Big Bad Wolf'.

42.   John Thornton Caldwell, *Televisuality: Style, Crisis and Authorship in American Television* (New Brunswick, NJ, 1995), p.261.

43.   Jan Johnson-Smith, *American Science Fiction TV: 'Star Trek', 'StarGate' and Beyond* (London, 2005), p.10.

44.   'Tooth and Claw: The Russell T. Davies Interview', *Doctor Who Magazine*, no.360 (September 2005), p.13.

45.   'The City on the Edge of Forever' was the penultimate episode of the first season of *Star Trek* in 1966–1967. Captain Kirk (William Shatner) and Mr Spock (Leonard Nimoy) are transported back in time to 1930s New York on the trail of Dr McCoy (De Forest Kelley), who has accidentally been injected with a drug overdose. McCoy's presence in the past has already changed the future so that the Starship *Enterprise* no longer exists. Kirk meets and falls in love with Edith Keeler (Joan Collins), a progressive social worker. Spock uses his tricorder to project two possible futures for Edith: either she will be killed in a traffic accident, or she will lead a pacifist movement that will delay America's entry into the Second World War resulting in victory for the Axis powers. At the crucial moment Kirk deliberately prevents McCoy from saving Edith's life when she is struck by a lorry and the future is restored to its proper course. The script, by SF writer Harlan Ellison, won an award from the Writers' Guild of America in 1968.

46.   'Elevate, exterminate: Daleks conquer stairs in new Doctor Who', *The Times*, 6 March 2005, p.14.

47.   Paul Hawkins, 'The Reasons and Functions behind the use of *Deus ex Machina* in Series One of the New *Doctor Who*', in Simon Bradshaw, Antony Keen and Graham Sleight (eds), *The Unsilent Library: Essays on the Russell T. Davies Era of the New Doctor Who* (London, 2011), p.35.

48.   'Editor's Letter', *Doctor Who Magazine*, no.356 (May 2005), p.3.

49.   'Eccleston quits Doctor Who role', *BBC News*, 31 March 2005: http://news.bbc.co.uk/2/hi/entertainment/4395849.stm (accessed 27.01.2013).

50.   Russell T. Davies, with Benjamin Cook, *Doctor Who: The Writer's Tale – The Untold Story of the BBC Series* (London, 2008), p.134.

10. Love and Monsters (2006–2009)

1.   Matt Hills, *Triumph of a Time Lord: Regenerating 'Doctor Who' in the Twenty-First Century* (London, 2010), p.227. Other critical studies

focusing wholly or largely on this period include Simon Bradshaw, Antony Keen and Graham Sleight (eds), *The Unsilent Library: Essays on the Russell T. Davies Era of the New 'Doctor Who'* (London, 2011), and Ross P. Garner, Melissa Beattie and Una McCormack (eds), *Impossible Worlds, Impossible Things: Cultural Perspectives on 'Doctor Who', 'Torchwood' and 'The Sarah Jane Adventures'* (Newcastle-upon-Tyne, 2010).

2. These are the consolidated series averages including the BBC3 Sunday repeats and those who recorded to watch later. As with the classic series, the season averages conceal some fluctuations. Series Two, for example, had a highest audience of 9.2 million for 'Tooth and Claw' and a low of 6.1 million for 'The Satan Pit'. There was less fluctuation during Series Three and Series Four. The highest consolidated ratings for individual episodes during the Davies/Tennant era were for 'Voyage of the Damned' (13.3 million), 'The Next Doctor' (13.1 million), 'The End of Time Part 1' (12 million), 'The End of Time Part 2' (12.2 million), 'Journey's End' (10.6 million) and 'The Waters of Mars (10.3 million). All bar 'Journey's End' were 'Specials'. Several of the *Doctor Who* websites publish the viewing figures for the new series: caution should be exercised to ensure that overnight and consolidated statistics are not conflated. Perhaps the most user-friendly website is *The Mind Robber*: http://www.themindrobber.co.uk/ratings.html (accessed 15.01.2013).

3. 'Brave New Worlds', *Doctor Who Magazine*, no.373 (September 2006), p.32.

4. 'BBC Worldwide revenues exceed £1bn for the first time', *BBC Press Office*, 14 July 2009: http://www.bbc.co.uk/pressoffice/bbcworldwide/worldwidestories/pressreleases/2009/07_july/annual-review.0809.stm (accessed 27.01.2013).

5. 'Time Lord handed permanent home', *BBC News*, 27 July 2006: http://news.bbc.co.uk/1/hi/wales/5222610.stm (accessed 30.01. 2013).

6. This includes two episodes where he is credited as co-writer: 'Planet of the Dead' (4.15) and 'The Waters of Mars' (4.16).

7. Russell T. Davies, with Benjamin Cook, *The Writer's Tale: The Untold Story of the BBC Series* (London, 2008), p.134.

8. Gareth Roberts had written several Virgin 'New Adventures' and 'Missing Adventures' novels. He went on to write original novels for the Ninth (*Being Human*, 2005) and Tenth Doctors (*I Am A Dalek*, 2006) and a novelisation of the untransitted Fourth Doctor story *Shada* (2012). He has also written several Big Finish audios and comic strips for *Doctor Who Magazine*. Matt Jones was a former contributor to *DWM* and author of *Bad Therapy* (1996) and *Beyond the Sun* (1997) for the Virgin 'New Adventures' range.

9.   'Brave New Worlds', pp.31–2.

10. Davies, *The Writer's Tale*, p.287.

11. Ibid., p.125.

12. Ibid., p.287.

13. 'Cost "keeps Doctor Who on earth"', *BBC News*, 19 September 2006: http://news.bbc.co.uk/1/hi/entertainment/5359552.stm (accessed 30.01.2013).

14. An 'SFX day' refers to the amount of effects work undertaken by one person in one day: twenty people working for two days each would equal forty SFX days.

15. Davies, *The Writer's Tale*, p.283.

16. Ibid., p.458.

17. 'Favourite Doctor', *Doctor Who Magazine*, no.414 (November 2009), p.21. Tennant (with 25.6 per cent of the votes) narrowly shaded Tom Baker (24.7 per cent) in a survey that included 6,700 respondents. When broken down by age group, Tennant was a clear favourite with the under-18s (37 per cent) while Baker was the preferred choice for those over 35 (28 per cent) with the middle (18–35) group very narrowly favouring Tennant. Christopher Eccleston came sixth overall (with 5.7 per cent) but was third favourite with the under-18s (11 per cent).

18. 'From Time Lord to antic prince: David Tennant is the best Hamlet . . .', *The Guardian*, 6 August 2008: http://www.guardian.co.uk/stage/2008/aug/06/theatre.rsc (31.01.2013).

19. 'The David Tennant Interview', *Doctor Who Magazine*, no.375 (November 2006), p.21.

20. Ibid., p.23.

21. Laura Mead, 'David Tennant's Bum', in Deborah Stanish and L. M. Myles (eds), *Chicks Unravel Time: Women Journey Through Every Season of 'Doctor Who'* (Des Moines, 2012), pp.141, 139.

22. John Paul Green, 'The Regeneration Game: *Doctor Who* and the Changing Faces of Heroism', in Garner *et al.*, *Impossible Worlds, Impossible Things*, p.16.

23. 'Christians protest as Doctor Who is portrayed as messiah', *The Times*, 21 December 2007: http://entertainment.timesonline.co.uk/tol/arts_and_entertainment/tv_and_radio/article3080608.ece (accessed 29.01.2013).

24. Neil Clarke, 'Holy Terror and Fallen Demigod: The Doctor as Myth', in Anthony Burdge, Jessica Burke and Kristine Larsen (eds), *The Mythological Dimensions of 'Doctor Who'* (Crawfordville, FL, 2010), p.42.

25. Davies, *The Writer's Tale*, p.496.

26. There are some continuity issues with 'School Reunion' in relation to classic *Who* in that it makes no reference to the events of either 'The

Five Doctors' or *K9 and Company* (though to be fair the latter is best forgotten). See Antony Keen, 'Whatever Happened to Sarah Jane?', in Bradshaw *et al.*, *The Unsilent Library*, pp.63–79.

27. Davies, *The Writer's Tale*, pp.488–9.

28. Letters from Paul Shearman and Paisley Boyd (aged 15), *Doctor Who Magazine*, no.384 (July 2007), p.11.

29. '2007 Awards', *Doctor Who Magazine*, no.389 (December 2007), p.40.

30. Davies, *The Writer's Tale*, p.319.

31. Graham Sleight, 'The Big Picture Show: Russell T. Davies' Writing for *Doctor Who*', in Bradshaw *et al.*, *The Unsilent Library*, p.21.

32. This revelation seems to have been a late addition to the script and might not have been planned as part of the story arc. The Ninth Doctor had met the Face of Boe in 'The End of Time' (1.2) before meeting Jack in 'The Empty Child' (1.9). There again what would *Doctor Who* be without a contradictory internal continuity?

33. 'Production Notes', *Doctor Who Magazine*, no.368 (April 2006), p.67.

34. 'DW Mail', *Doctor Who Magazine*, no.376 (December 2006), p.10.

35. Una McCormack, 'He's Not the Messiah: Undermining Political and Religious Authority in New *Doctor Who*', in Bradshaw *et al.*, *The Unsilent Library*, p.55.

36. The 'celebrity historicals' are discussed in Hills, *Triumph of a Time Lord*, pp.106–11. See also Antony G. Keen, 'Sideways Pompeii!: The Use of a Historical Period to Question the Doctor's Role in History', in Garner *et al.*, *Impossible Worlds, Impossible Things*, pp.94–117.

37. Davies, *The Writer's Tale*, p.72.

38. Frank Collins, *The Pandorica Opens: Exploring the Worlds of the Eleventh Doctor* (Cambridge, 2010), p.33.

39. 'Brave New Worlds', p.34.

40. Davies, *The Writer's Tale*, pp.32–3.

11. Aliens of Cardiff (2006–2011)

1. Stephen James Walker, *Inside the Hub: The Unofficial and Unauthorised Guide to 'Torchwood' Series One* (Tolworth, 2007), p.50. The phrase 'Torchwood' – which of course is an anagram of 'Doctor Who' – was apparently first used on the pre-transmission tapes of *Doctor Who* in 2005 in order to safeguard against theft. Davies's original name for the series is referenced as an in-joke in 'Kiss Kiss, Bang Bang' (2.1) when Captain John remarks 'Not Excalibur?' when Jack mentions the name of his organisation.

2.   Quoted in 'Jumping Jack', *Doctor Who Magazine*, no.363 (December 2005), p.4.

3.   'BBC Three digital channel launches', *BBC News*, 10 February 2003: http://news.bbc.co.uk/1/entertainment/tv_and_radio/2738245.stm (accessed 24.01.2013).

4.   'Torchwood is beacon of success for BBC3', *Broadcast*, 27 October 2006, p.5.

5.   'First for Torchwood as it moves to BBC1', *Broadcast*, 6 June 2008, p.3.

6.   'Davies' love letter to Cardiff', *BBC News*, 19 October 2006: http://news.bbc.co.uk/1/hi/wales/6063480.stm (accessed 24.01.2013).

7.   '*Doctor Who* showrunner Russell T. Davies talks about *Torchwood* spin-off series', *SFX*, no.136 (November 2005), p.14.

8.   Quoted in 'Jumping Jack', p.4.

9.   There are 'bum shots' of actor Kai Owen in 'Out of Time' and 'End of Days'. However, audiences would have to wait until episode two of *Children of Earth* for a glimpse of John Barrowman's bottom.

10.   *Daily Telegraph*, 23 October 2006, p.30.

11.   *Daily Telegraph*, 29 October 2006, p.18.

12.   *The Independent*, 26 October 2006, p.22.

13.   *Evening Standard*, 23 October 2006, p.42.

14.   Sue Short, *Cult Telefantasy Series: A Critical Analysis of 'The Prisoner', 'Twin Peaks', 'The X-Files', 'Buffy the Vampire Slayer', 'Lost', 'Heroes', 'Doctor Who' and 'Star Trek'* (Jefferson, NC, 2011), p.180.

15.   Andrew Ireland, 'Introduction: Reading the Rift', in *Illuminating Torchwood: Essays on Narrative, Character and Sexuality in the BBC Series* (Jefferson, NC, 2010), pp.1–2.

16.   Graeme Burk, 'The Ten Commandments of Doctor Who Spinoffs', in *Time Unincorporated: The Doctor Who Fanzine Archives. Vol.3: Writings on the New Series* (Des Moines, IA, 2011), p.204.

17.   See Barbara Creed, 'Horror and the Monstrous–Feminine: An Imaginary Abjection', *Screen*, vol.27, no.1 (1986), pp.44–70.

18.   Elspeth Kydd, 'Cyberwomen and Sleepers: Rereading the Mulatta Cyborg and the Black Woman's Body', in Ireland, *Illuminating Torchwood*, p.191.

19.   This idea is explored further R. C. Neighbors, 'Existentialism and Christian Symbolism', in Ireland, *Illuminating Torchwood*, pp.22–9.

20.   'Hundreds of complaints over Torchwood gay sex scenes', *Pink News*, 30 August 2011: http://www.pinknews.co.uk/2011/08/30 (accessed 31.01.2013).

21.   'Jack of Hearts', *Gay Times* , no.337 (October 2006), p.37.

22.   Christopher Pullen, '"Love the coat": Bisexuality, the Female Gaze and

the Romance of Sexual Politics', in Ireland, *Illuminating Torchwood*, p.136.

23.   Sherry Ginn, 'Sexual Relations and Sexual Identity Issues: Brave New World or More of the Old One?', in Ireland, *Illuminating Torchwood*, p.167.

24.   'Plans for new Torchwood revealed', *BBC News*, 30 June 2008: http://news.bbc.co.uk/1/hi/entertainment/7582511.stm (accessed 31.01.2013).

25.   There is a reference to Martha Jones being on honeymoon in the first episode of *Children on Earth*. The coda to the *Doctor Who* Special 'The End of Time', broadcast six months after *Children of Earth*, reveals that Martha and Mickey Smith are married and appear to be working as freelance alien-fighters. Martha had previously been engaged to Dr Tom Milligan ('The Sontaran Stratagem'/'The Poison Sky').

26.   'Torchwood: Children of Earth: Day Five', *The Guardian*, 11 July 2009: http://www.guardian.co.uk/culture/tvandradioblog/3009/jul/10 (accessed 31.01.2013).

27.   'Torchwood: interview with Russell T. Davies', *BBC Press Office*, 7 July 2011: http://.www.bbc.co.uk/pressoffice/pressreleases/stories/2011/07_july/torchwood2.shtml (accessed 31.01.2013).

28.   'The Doctor takes on Ant & Dec again (and beats them – again!)', *Doctor Who Magazine*, no.440 (November 2011), p.12.

29.   'Have you been watching . . . Torchwood?', *The Guardian*, 1 September 2011: http://www.guardian.co.uk/tv-and-radio/tvandradioblog/2011/sep/01 (accessed 31.01.2013).

30.   'Russell T. Davies on the future of Torchwood', *Den of Geek*, 20 November 2012: http://www.denofgeek.com/tv/torchwood/23238 (accessed 31.01.2013).

12. Sarah Jane and Company (2007–2011)

1.   The pilot of *K9 and Company*, written by Terence Dudley, was entitled 'A Girl's Best Friend' and was broadcast on BBC1 on 28 December 1981.

2.   Elisabeth Sladen with Jeff Hudson, *The Autobiography* (London, 2011) p.245.

3.   Tom Baker, *Who On Earth is Tom Baker?: An Autobiography* (London, 1997), p.212.

4.   Sladen, *The Autobiography*, p.257.

5.   Ibid., p.265.

6.   Gary Russell, *Doctor Who: The Inside Story* (London, 2006), p.252.

7.   Sladen, *The Autobiography*, p.314.

8.   The first series of *The Sarah Jane Adventures* (24 September–19 November 2007) was broadcast weekly on BBC1 on Mondays at 5.05 pm.

Each episode was immediately followed by the next on CBBC. From the second series (29 September–8 December 2008) episodes were broadcast first on CBBC at 5.15 pm and one week later on BBC1 at 4.35 pm. This pattern recognised the fact that more people watched on CBBC than on BBC1. In 2009 *The Sarah Jane Adventures* moved to twice-weekly broadcast on Thursdays and Fridays for the third series (15 October–20 November 2009) and Mondays and Tuesdays for the fourth (11 October–16 November 2010) and fifth series (3–18 October 2011).

9. 'Sarah Jane's success', *Doctor Who Magazine*, no.389 (December 2007), p.5.

10. 'The Sarah Jane Adventures', *The Telegraph*, 29 November 2007: http://www.telegraph.co.uk/culture/3674553.html (accessed 16.02.2013).

11. 'Russell T. Davies creates new series for CBBC, starring Doctor Who's Sarah Jane Smith', BBC Press Office, 14 September 2006, BFI Library.

12. This view was best captured by the website *The Spoof!*, which at the start of the second series of *Torchwood* ran an item headlined 'BBC to "sex up" *The Sarah Jane Adventures*' declaring: 'Used to a diet of soft porn aliens, flashes of nipple and unnecessary swearing, *Torchwood* enthusiasts are said to have found Sarah-Jane's stories too funny, exciting and grown-up for their tastes.' *The Spoof!*, 2 January 2008: http://www.thespoof.com/news/entertainment-gossip/27516 (accessed 16.02.2013).

13. Phil Ford wrote 11 stories (22 episodes) and Gareth Roberts was sole or joint writer of 9 (17 episodes including 'Invasion of the Bane', which he wrote with Davies, and 'Goodbye, Sarah Jane Smith', co-written with Clayton Hickman). The other writers were Joseph Lidster (three stories), Rupert Leight (two) and Phil Gladwin (one).

14. *The Sarah Jane Adventures* is replete with visual references to *Doctor Who* that are sometimes only apparent after repeated viewing. To take just one example: in 'Warriors of Kudlack' the film posters visible in Lance Metcalf's bedroom are the same titles as the DVDs on which the Doctor recorded messages for Sally Sparrow in 'Blink'.

15. 'Favourite Companion', *Doctor Who Magazine*, no.414 (November 2009), p.21.

16. 'Production Notes', *Doctor Who Magazine*, no.375 (November 2006), p.66.

17. 'The Sarah Jane Adventures are going to be fun', *The Guardian*, 25 September 2007: http://www.guardian.co.uk/culture/tvandradioblog/2007/sep/25 (accessed 16.02.2013).

18. 'The Doctor's *not* in the house', *The Times: The Knowledge*, 27 September 2008, p.34.

19.   'The Sarah Jane Adventures are going to be fun'.

20.   'Filling in for the Doctor', *Daily Telegraph*, 25 September 2007, p.30.

21.   Ross P. Garner, '"Don't You Forget About Me": Intertextuality and Generic Anchoring in *The Sarah Jane Adventures*', in Ross P. Garner, Melissa Beattie and Una McCormack (eds), *Impossible Worlds, Impossible Things: Cultural Perspectives on 'Doctor Who', 'Torchwood' and 'The Sarah Jane Adventures'* (Nescastle upon Tyne, 2010), p.172.

22.   'Sarah Jane adventures end after Elisabeth Sladen death', *CBBC Newsround*, 5 May 2011: http://www.bbc.co.uk/cbbcnews/hi/newsid_9475600/9475643.stm (16.02.2013).

23.   'Children's programming comes to an end on BBC One', *BBC News*, 21 December 2012: http://www.bbc.co.uk/news/entertainment-arts-20809627 (16.02.2013).

13. Golden Anniversary (2010–2013)

1.   For commentary on this period, see Frank Collins, *Doctor Who: The Pandorica Opens: Exploring the Worlds of the Eleventh Doctor* (Cambridge, 2010), and Andrew O'Day (ed.), *Doctor Who – The Eleventh Hour: A Critical Celebration of the Matt Smith and Steven Moffat Era* (London, forthcoming).

2.   'Doctor Who BBC Worldwide's biggest selling TV show internationally', *The Guardian*, 12 July 2011: http://www.guardian.co.uk/media/2011/jul/12/ (accessed 27.01.2013).

3.   'Can Matt Smith's Doctor Who conquer America?', *Daily Telegraph*, 21 April 2011: http://www.telegraph.co.uk/culture/tvandradio/8464245 (accessed 27.01.2013).

4.   'Doctor Who ratings break BBC America record', *The Huffington Post*, 25 April 2005: http://www.huffingtonpost.com/2011/04/25/85356.html (accessed 27.01.2013).

5.   'Doctor Who boss not worried by budget cuts', *BBC News*, 23 March 2010: http://www. bbc.co.uk/1/hi/entertainment/8580299.stm (accessed 27.01.2013).

6.   'New Doctor Who episode billed as scariest ever sees ratings fall by 1.5m', *Mail Online*, 23 April 2011: http://www.dailymail.co.uk/tvshowbiz/article–1380150.html (accessed 05. 02.2013); 'New Doctor Who scares off another one million viewers', *Mail Online*, 3 May 2011: http://www.dailymail.co.uk/tvshowbiz/article-1382802 (accessed 05.02.2013).

7.   'New Doctor Matt Smith is turn-off for Tennant fans', *The Week*, 29 June 2010 http://www.theweek.co.uk/13629 (accessed 05.02.2013).

8.   'Viewers choose to "timeshift" as ratings stay strong', *Doctor Who Magazine*, no.436 (July 2011), p.11.

9.   'Series split for 2011', *Doctor Who Magazine*, no.426 (September 2010), p.5.

10.   'Steven Moffat on "Doctor Who", "Sherlock" and his BAFTA Special Award', *Digital Spy*, 19 May 2012: http://www.digitalspy.co.uk/tv/s7/doctor-who/news/a38247 (accessed 30.01.2013).

11.   Ibid.

12.   'Moffat promises new Who monsters', *BBC News*, 29 July 2008: http://www.bbc.co.uk/1/hi/entertainment/7531310.stm (accessed 30.01.2013).

13.   'Doctor Who guru steps down', *BBC News*, 20 May 2008: http://www.bbc.co.uk/1/hi/entertainment/7411177.stm (accessed 30.01.2013).

14.   'Dr Who writer denies Tintin row', *BBC News*, 21 July 2008: http://www.bbc.co.uk/1/hi/entertainment/7517423.stm (accessed 30.01.2013).

15.   'Steven Moffat: The man with a monster of a job', *The Guardian*, 22 March 2010: http://www.guardian.co.uk/media/2010/mar/22 (accessed 30.01.2013).

16.   'Casting the Eleventh Doctor', *Doctor Who Magazine*, no.405 (March 2009), p.8.

17.   'Matt Smith to see in the 50th anniversary', *Doctor Who Magazine*, no.436 (July 2011), p.7.

18.   'When Matt "met" Pat', *Doctor Who Magazine*, no.450 (September 2012), pp.16–25.

19.   Letter from Mrs Joan M. Drain, *Doctor Who Magazine*, no.423 (July 2010), p.14.

20.   'A Good Man Goes to War', *Doctor Who Magazine*, Special Edition no.30: 'The Doctor Who Companion: The Eleventh Doctor: Volume 4' (2011), pp.27–35.

21.   'Steven Moffat talks Doctor Who future', *DigitalSpy*, 1 November 2009: http://www.digitalspy.co.uk/tv/s7/doctorwho/tubetalk/a184561.html (accessed 30.01.2013).

22.   'Doctor Who: Episode 2: Day of the Moon', *Daily Telegraph*, 20 April 2011: http://www.telegraph.co.uk/culture/tvandradio/8479708 (accessed 27.01.2013).

23.   See Richard Burley, 'Philosophies of Time Travel in the New *Doctor Who*', in Simon Bradshaw, Antony Keen and Graham Sleight (eds), *The Unsilent Library: Essays on the Russell T. Davies Era of the New 'Doctor Who'* (London, 2011), pp.135–47.

24.   'Moffat promises new Who monsters'.

25.   'Doctor Who: Asylum of the Daleks', *The Guardian*, 15 August 2012: http://www. guardian.co.uk/tv–and–radio/tvandradioblog/2012/aug/15 (accessed 05.02.2013).

26.   'Snakes on a plane' was the pitch tag-line for an unmade film screenplay known first as *Venom* and later as *Pacific Air Flight 121* that became

something of an Internet sensation in 2004. The film was commissioned when Samuel L. Jackson agreed to star in the film, on the condition that it was called *Snakes on a Plane*. New *Doctor Who* has included several episodes where the title sounds like a basic story idea in the absence of anything better: 'Daleks in Manhattan' (3.4) and 'Let's Kill Hitler!' (6.8) are other examples.

27.   Collins, *The Pandorica Opens*, p.32.

28.   Nicholas J. Cull, 'Tardis at the OK Corral: *Doctor Who* and the USA', in John R. Cook and Peter Wright (eds), *British Science Fiction Television: A Hitch Hiker's Guide* (London, 2005), pp.52–70.

29.   'Doctor Who could make BBC money forever, says Steven Moffat', *The Guardian*, 25 August 2012: http://www.guardian.co.uk/media/2012/aug/25 (accessed 31.01.2013).

Appendix II

1.   The working title for 'The Dalek Invasion of Earth' during production was 'The Return of the Daleks'. *Doctor Who* has not (to date) used 'Return of . . .' as a story title.

2.   'Mission to the Unknown' is the only *Doctor Who* episode not to feature the character of the Doctor himself. It was a single-episode 'teaser' for the forthcoming epic 'The Daleks' Master Plan', added when the production schedule required an extra week.

3.   'The Massacre' is sometimes referred to as 'The Massacre of St Bartholomew's Eve'.

4.   'The Celestial Toymaker' was reportedly inspired by a play by Gerald Savory entitled *George and Margaret* and had to be rewritten twice, first by Donald Tosh and again by Gerry Davis.

5.   'The Gunfighters' was the last *Doctor Who* serial to use individual episode titles.

6.   'The Power of the Daleks' was the first Dalek story not to be written, or co-written, by Terry Nation.

7.   Episode 3 of 'The Enemy of the World' was the first *Doctor Who* to be recorded on 625-line videotape rather than 405-line.

8.   'The Web of Fear' marked the first appearance of Nicholas Courtney as Colonel (later Brigadier) Lethbridge-Stewart. Courtney had previously played Bret Vyon in 'The Daleks' Master Plan'.

9.   'The Wheel in Space' was followed by a repeat screening of 'The Evil of the Daleks', as the Doctor shows new companion Zoë one of his previous adventures by dint of mental projection onto the TARDIS monitor screen. This meant that *Doctor Who* was broadcast almost continuously throughout the summer break in 1968.

10. 'Norman Ashby' was a pseudonym for Mervyn Haisman and Henry Lincoln, authors of the two Yeti serials.

11. Terrance Dicks seems to have contributed significantly to writing 'The Seeds of Death': he is in fact credited as co-writer on the 1985 VHS release of this serial (BBCV 4072), though not on the 2003 DVD release (BBCDVD 1151).

12. 'Spearhead from Space' was not only the first *Doctor Who* serial in colour, but also the only one to be shot entirely on 16-millimetre film when a strike closed Television Centre.

13. This was the only serial to feature the words 'Doctor Who' in the title.

14. Barry Letts took over direction of 'Inferno' when Douglas Camfield fell ill during recording.

15. 'Guy Leopold' was a pseudonym for Barry Letts and Robert Sloman. Coincidentally Sloman also wrote the concluding adventure of each of the next three seasons: 'The Time Monster', 'The Green Death' and 'Planet of the Spiders'.

16. In order to keep the appearance of the dinosaurs a surprise, the first episode of this serial was just called 'Invasion'. This was much to the chagrin of Malcolm Hulke, who never wrote for the series again.

17. Terrance Dicks's claim that he 'invented' a tradition whereby the out-going script editor wrote the first story for his successor is not correct. David Whitaker ('The Rescue'), Dennis Spooner ('The Time Meddler') and Gerry Davis ('The Tomb of the Cybermen') had all done so.

18. 'Stephen Harris' is a pseudonym: the original scripts by Lewis Greifer were extensively rewritten by Robert Holmes.

19. 'Robin Bland' is another pseudonym: on this occasion the original scripts by Terrance Dicks were rewritten by Robert Holmes.

20. 'The Deadly Assassin' is the Doctor's only solo adventure in that he is not accompanied by a regular companion.

21. 'David Agnew' was a pseudonym for Graham Williams and Anthony Reed.

22. On this occasion 'David Agnew' was a pseudonym for Graham Williams and Douglas Adams.

23. 'Shada' was never completed due to a technicians' strike at the BBC. The location filming had already been completed and a few sequences were later used in 'The Five Doctors'.

24. 'The Five Doctors' was broadcast as part of BBC1's *Children in Need*.

25. 'Resurrection of the Daleks' was shot as four 25–minute episodes, but broadcast in two episodes of 50 minutes.

26. Season 22 comprised 45–minute episodes rather than the usual 25 minutes.

27. 'Paula Moore' was a pseudonym for several writers, including Eric Saward, Paula Woolsey and Ian Levine.

28. 'The Trial of a Time Lord' was the umbrella title for the whole season. The individual segments are sometimes referred to as 'The Mysterious Planet' (Episodes 1–4), 'Mindwarp' (Episodes 5–8), 'Terror of the Vervoids' (Episodes 9–12) and 'The Ultimate Foe' (Episodes 13–14).

29. Graeme Harper was the first – and to date only – director to have worked on both the classic series and the new series. He had directed the classic *Who* stories 'The Caves of Androzani' and 'Revelation of the Daleks'.

30. 'Midnight' was a late replacement for an episode to have been written by Tom MacRae. In the original schedule it was to have been Episode 8, with 'Silence in the Library'/'Forest of the Dead' as Episodes 9–10. I have listed the episodes in order of broadcast.

31. The internal BBC designation for this series was 'Series 1', though for the DVD release it reverted to 'Series 5'.

32. Series Six was split into a 'Part 1' of seven episodes in the spring ('The Impossible Astronaut' to 'A Good Man Goes to War') and a 'Part 2' of six episodes in the early autumn ('Let's Kill Hitler!' to 'The Wedding of River Song').

33. Series Seven was similarly split into a 'Part 1' of five episodes in the early autumn of 2012 ('Asylum of the Daleks' to 'The Angels Take Manhattan') with a 'Part 2' of eight episodes scheduled for the late spring/early summer of 2013. An additional Special was confirmed for the fiftieth anniversay on 23 November 2013.

34. Transmission dates for Series One of *Torchwood* are for the first broadcast on BBC3.

35. Transmission dates for Series Two of *Torchwood* are for the first broadcast on BBC2.

36. Transmission dates for *Torchwood: Miracle Day* are for the first UK broadcast on BBC1, which came six days after the first US broadcast on Starz.

37. The transmission dates for *The Sarah Jane Adventures* refer to the first screening on BBC1. From the second episode of 'Revenge of the Slitheen' the next episode was broadcast immediately afterwards on CBBC, meaning that episodes aired one week earlier on CBBC. The official BBC numbering has separate codes for each episode of the two-part serials, hence 'Revenge of the Slitheen' was 2.1. and 2.2. However, for the sake of clarity, I have numbered each serial rather than each episode.

Bibliography

BBC Written Archives

The BBC Written Archives Centre at Caversham Park, Reading, has extensive holdings of production documentation relating to *Doctor Who*. These comprise two general files relating to the origins of the series (T5/647/1–2), one file of correspondence from viewers (T5/649/1) and production files covering most of the serials (T5/1232–T5/2622 and T/65/1–T/65/272). At the time of my research, the files for the 1980s were not available. The Listening and Viewing Barometers (R9/35/12–R9/39/11) provide a breakdown of the estimated audience expressed as a percentage of the total United Kingdom population.

Published scripts

In the late 1980s and 1990s selected *Doctor Who* scripts were published by Titan Books, London, edited and introduced by John McElroy. The series comprises (in production order): *The Tribe of Gum* (January 1988), *The Masters of Luxor* (August 1992), *The Daleks* (December 1989), *The Crusade* (November 1994), *Galaxy 4* (July 1994), *The Power of the Daleks* (March 1993), *The Tomb of the Cybermen* (August 1989), *The Dæmons* (October 1992) and *The Talons of Weng-Chiang* (November 1989). *The Masters of Luxor*, by Anthony Coburn, was an unused story from the early history of the series. The complete scripts of the twelfth season, with extensive annotations, have been published as *Doctor Who The Scripts: Tom Baker 1974/5*, eds Justin Richards and Andrew Pixley (London: BBC Books, 2001). The shooting scripts of the 2005 series have also been published as *Doctor Who: The Shooting Scripts*, ed. Charlotte Lochhead (London: BBC Books, 2005).

Newspapers and periodicals

I have drawn upon reviews and articles from the following newspapers and periodicals: *Ariel, Broadcast, Daily Express, Daily Mail, Daily Mirror, Daily Star, Daily Telegraph, Daily Worker, Evening Standard, Financial Times, Gay Times, The Guardian, The Independent, Kinematograph Weekly, Mail on Sunday, Morning Star, New Society, New Statesman, The Observer, Radio Times, Saturday Titbits, The Scotsman, SFX, The Spectator, Starburst, Sun, Sunday Express, Sunday Herald, Sunday Telegraph, Sunday Times, Televisual, Time Out, The Times, Today, TV Zone* and *Western Mail*. Specific reviews and articles are identified in the endotes. The British Film Institute's Reuben Library at BFI Southbank holds an extensive digitised collection of press clippings. However, *The Doctor Who Cuttings Archive* (formerly at http://www.cuttingsarchive.org) no longer seems active as of January 2013.

Fan magazines

Doctor Who has given rise to an extensive fan literature and a wide range of magazines and newsletters. The two principal fanzines are *Doctor Who Magazine* (founded in 1979 as *Doctor Who Monthly*) and *In Vision: The Making of a Television Series*, edited by the doyen of *Doctor Who* historians, J. Jeremy Bentham, which documents the production history of each serial. Since the relaunch of *Doctor Who* in 2005, the special editions of *Doctor Who Magazine* (*DWM*) have more or less taken over from *In Vision* in chronicling the production history of the new series. The World Wide Web (see below) has now replaced many of the small-circulation fan magazines as a source of information and discussion about the series.

Websites

The seemingly infinite expansion of the World Wide Web provides a vast resource for fans of cult television – though websites tend to come and go faster than the Doctor's regenerations in 'The Curse of Fatal Death'. In 2013 a Google search for 'Doctor Who' turned up 847 million hits, compared to 28 million when I was completing the first edition of *Inside the Tardis* in 2005. The BBC's official *Doctor Who* website (http://www.bbc.co.uk/doctorwho) is useful for facts and figures, though is really best understood as a promotional site for the franchise. Unofficial fan sites proliferate, and compete with each other for the honour of being the most visited or most authoritative, though most fans recognise *Gallifrey Base* (http://www.gallifreybase.com) – formerly known as *Outpost Gallifrey* – as a reliable source of factual information about both the classic and new series, as well as a forum for discussion and debate (which can, variously, be passionate, pedantic, irritating, and at its best highly insightful and knowledgeable about all things *Who*). *Earthbound Timelords: The Doctor Who Scripts Project* (http://www.bw .edu/~jcurtis/Scripts/scripts_project.htm) is an invaluable research resource for all those interested in the classic series, as it includes dialogue transcripts of the missing serials from the 1960s. Uninitiated web browsers should be warned that some websites (though none of those listed above) are devoted to what is known as 'slash fiction' (unofficial fan-generated stories about fictional characters) that can be sexually explicit and even pornographic in content.

Biographies and autobiographies

Baker, Tom, *Who on Earth Is Tom Baker? An Autobiography* (London: HarperCollins, 1997)

Bale, Bernard, *Jon Pertwee: The Biography* (London: Andre Deutsch, 2000)

Carney, Jessica, *Who's There? The Life and Career of William Hartnell* (London: Virgin Books, 1996)

Courtney, *Nicholas, Five Rounds Rapid! The Autobiography of Nicholas Courtney, Doctor Who's Brigadier*, ed. John Nathan-Turner (London: Virgin, 1998)

Letts, Barry, *Who & Me: The Memoir of 'Doctor Who' Producer Barry Letts 1925– 2009* (West Midlands: Fantom Publishing, 2009)

Pertwee, Jon, and David J. Howe, *I Am the Doctor: Jon Pertwee's Final Memoir* (London: Virgin, 1996)

Sladen, Elisabeth, with Jeff Hudson, *Elisabeth Sladen: The Autobiography* (London: Aurum Press, 2011)

Troughton, Michael, *Patrick Troughton: The Biography of the Second Doctor Who* (Andover: Hirst Publishing, 2012)

Books

Aldridge, Mark, and Andy Murray, *T Is For Television: The Small Screen Adventures of Russell T. Davies* (Richmond: Reynolds & Hearn, 2008)

Banks, David, with Adrian Rigelsford, *Doctor Who – Cybermen* (London: W.H. Allen, 1988)

Bentham, Jeremy, *Doctor Who; The Developing Art – Programme Notes for NFT Weekend Screenings October 29/30 1983* (London: British Film Institute, 1983)

Bignell, Jonathan, and Andrew O'Day, *Terry Nation* (Manchester: Manchester University Press, 2004)

Bignell, Richard, *Doctor Who on Location* (London: Reynolds & Hearn, 2001)

Borne, Georgina, *Uncertain Vision: Birt, Dyke and the Reinvention of the BBC* (London: Secker & Warburg, 2004)

Bradshaw, Simon, Antony Keen and Graham Sleight (eds), *The Unsilent Library: Essays on the Russell T. Davies Era of the New 'Doctor Who'* (London: The Science Fiction Foundation, 2011)

Briggs, Asa, *The History of Broadcasting in the United Kingdom. Volume V: Competition 1955–1974* (Oxford: Oxford University Press, 1995)

Britton, Piers D., *TARDISbound: Navigating the Universes of 'Doctor Who'* (London: I.B.Tauris, 2011)

———, and Simon J. Barker, *Reading Between Designs: Visual Imagery and the Generation of Meaning in 'The Avengers', 'The Prisoner' and 'Doctor Who'* (Austin: University of Texas Press, 2003)

Butler, David (ed.), *Time and Relative Dissertations in Space: Critical Perspectives on 'Doctor Who'* (Manchester: Manchester University Press, 2007)

Burdge, Anthony, Jessica Burke and Kristine Larsen (eds), *The Mythological Dimensions of 'Doctor Who'* (Crawfordville FL: Kitsune Books 2010)

Burk, Graeme, and Robert Smith? (eds), *Time Unincorporated: The Doctor Who Fanzine Archives. Vol. 1: Lance Parkin* (Des Moines IA: Mad Norwegian Press, 2009)

———(eds), *Time Unincorporated: The Doctor Who Fanzine Archives. Vol. 2: Writings on the Classic Series* (Des Moines IA: Mad Norwegian Press, 2010)

———(eds), *Time Unincorporated: The Doctor Who Fanzine Archives. Vol. 3: Writings on the New Series* (Des Moines IA: Mad Norwegian Press, 2011)

Cabell, Craig, *The Doctors Who's Who: The Story Behind Every Face of the Iconic Time Lord* (London: John Blake, 2010)

Caldwell, John Thornton, *Televisuality: Style, Crisis and Authorship in American Television* (New Brunswick, NJ: Rutgers University Press, 1995)

Campbell, Mark, *The Pocket Essential Doctor Who* (Harpenden: Pocket Essentials, 2000)

Cartmel, Andrew, *Script Doctor: The Inside Story of Doctor Who 1986–89* (London: Reynolds & Hearn, 2005)

———, *Through Time: An Unauthorised and Unofficial History of 'Doctor Who'* (New York: Continuum, 2005)

Clapham, Mark, Eddie Robson and Jim Smith, *Who's Next: An Unofficial and Unauthorised Guide to Doctor Who* (London: Virgin, 2005)

Collins, Frank, *Doctor Who – The Pandorica Opens: Exploring the Worlds of the Eleventh Doctor* (Cambridge: Classic TV Press, 2010)

Cook, Benjamin, *Doctor Who: The New Audio Adventures – The Inside Story* (Maidenhead: Big Finish, 2003)

Cook, John R., and Peter Wright (eds), *British Science Fiction Television: A Hitch Hiker's Guide* (London: I.B.Tauris, 2005)

Cooke, Lez, *British Television Drama: A History* (London: British Film Institute, 2003)

Cornell, Paul, Martin Day and Keith Topping, *The Guinness Book of Classic British TV* (Enfield: Guinness Publishing, 2nd edn, 1996)

Couch, Steve, Tony Watkins and Peter S. Williams, *Back in Time: A Thinking Fan's Guide to 'Doctor Who'* (Milton Keynes: Damaris Books, 2005)

Creeber, Glen (ed.), *The Television Genre Book* (London: British Film Institute, 2001)

——(ed.), *Fifty Key Television Programmes* (London: Edward Arnold, 2004)

Davies, Russell T., and Benjamin Cook, *The Writer's Tale: The Untold Story of the BBC Series* (London: BBC Books, 2008)

Davis, Glyn, *Queer as Folk* (London: British Film Institute, 2007)

Dicks, Terrance, and Malcolm Hulke, *The Making of Doctor Who* (London: Tandem, 1976)

Fiddy, Dick, *Missing Believed Wiped: Searching for the Lost Treasures of British Television* (London: British Film Institute, 2001)

Fulton, Roger (ed.), *Encyclopedia of TV Science Fiction* (London: Boxtree, 2000)

Garner, Ross P., Melidda Beattie and Una McCormack (eds), *Impossible Worlds, Impossible Things: Cultural Perspectives on 'Doctor Who', 'Torchwood' and 'The Sarah Jane Adventures'* (Newcastle-upon-Tyne: Cambridge Scholars Publishing, 2010)

Haining, Peter, *Doctor Who: A Celebration – Two Decades Through Time and Space* (London: W.H. Allen, 1983)

——, *Doctor Who: 25 Glorious Years* (London: Virgin, 1988; 1990 edn)

——, *Doctor Who: The Time-Travellers' Guide* (London: W.H. Allen, 1987)

Harper, Graeme, with Adrian Rigelsford, *Calling the Shots: Directing the New Series of 'Doctor Who'* (Richmond: Reynolds & Hearn, 2007)

Hickman, Clayton (ed.), *The Brilliant Book of 'Doctor Who'* (London: BBC Books, 2010)

Hills, Matt, *Triumph of a Time Lord: Regenerating 'Doctor Who' in the Twenty-First Century* (London: I.B.Tauris, 2010)

Hochscherf, Tobias, and James Leggott (eds), *British Science Fiction Film and Television: Critical Essays* (Jefferson, NC: McFarland, 2011)

Howarth, Chris, and Steve Lyons, *Doctor Who: The Completely Unofficial Encyclopedia* (Des Moines IA: Mad Norwegian Press, 2006)

Howe, David J, Stephen James Walker and Mark Stammers, *The Handbook: The Unofficial and Unauthorised Guide to the Production of 'Doctor Who'* (Tolworth: Telos, 2005)

Ireland, Andrew (ed.), *Illuminating 'Torchwood': Essays on Narrative, Character and Sexuality in the BBC Series* (Jefferson, NC: McFarland, 2010)

Irvine, Matt, *Doctor Who Special Effects* (London: Hutchinson, 1986)

Johnson, Catherine, *Telefantasy* (London: British Film Institute, 2005)

Johnson-Smith, Jan, *American Science Fiction TV: 'Star Trek', 'StarGate' and Beyond* (London: I.B.Tauris, 2004)

King, Geoff, *Spectacular Narratives: Hollywood in the Age of the Blockbuster* (London: I.B.Tauris, 2000)

Lofficier, Jean-Marc, *The Doctor Who Programme Guide* (London: W. H. Allen, 1981)

Leach, Jim, *Doctor Who* (Detroit: Wayne State University Press, 2009)

Lewis, Courtland, and Paula Smithka (eds), *Doctor Who and Philosophy: Bigger on the Inside* (Chicago: Open Court, 2010)

Lukins, Jocelyn, *The Fantasy Factory: Lime Grove Studios, London 1915–1991* (London: Venta Books, 1996)

Lyon, J. Shaun, *Back to the Vortex: The Unofficial and Unauthorised Guide to 'Doctor Who' 2005* (Tolworth: Telos Publishing, 2005)

Miles, Lawrence, and Tat Wood, *About Time: The Unauthorized Guide to 'Doctor Who' 1975–1979: Seasons 12 to 17* (Des Moines IA: Mad Norwegian Press, 2004)

———, *About Time: The Unauthorized Guide to 'Doctor Who 1980–1984: Seasons 18 to 21* (Des Moines IA: Mad Norwegian Press, 2004)

Morgan, Kenneth O., *The People's Peace: British History 1945–1990* (Oxford: Oxford University Press, 1990)

Morton, Alan, *The Complete Directory to Science Fiction, Fantasy and Horror Television Series: A Comprehensive Guide to the First 50 Years 1946 to 1996* (Peoria IL: Other Worlds Books, 1997)

Muir, John Kenneth, *A Critical History of 'Doctor Who' on Television* (Jefferson, NC: McFarland, 1999)

Newman, Kim, *Doctor Who* (London: British Film Institute, 2005)

O'Brien, Daniel, *SF:UK – How British Science Fiction Changed the World* (London: Reynolds & Hearn, 2000)

Parkin, Lance, and Lars Pearson, *AHistory: The Unauthorised History of the 'Doctor Who' Universe* (Des Moines IA: Mad Norwegian Press, 2012)

Peel, John, and Terry Nation, *The Official Doctor Who and the Daleks Book* (New York: St Martin's Press, 1988)

Phillips, Mark, and Frank Garcia, *Science Fiction Television Series: Episode Guides, Histories, and Casts and Credits for 62 Prime Time Shows, 1959 through 1989* (Jefferson NC: McFarland, 1996)

Pringle, David (ed.), *The Ultimate Encyclopedia of Science Fiction* (London: Carlton, 1996)

Rigelsford, Adrian, *The Doctors: 30 Years of Time Travel* (London: Boxtree, 1994)

Richards, Justin, *Doctor Who: The Legend – 40 Years of Time Travel* (London: BBC Books, 2003)

Road, Alan, *Doctor Who: The Making of a Television Series* (London: Andre Deutsch, 1983)

Robb, Brian J., *Timeless Adventures: How 'Doctor Who' Conquered TV* (Harpenden: Kamera Books, 2009)

Russell, Gary, *Doctor Who: The Inside Story* (London: BBC Books, 2006)

———, *Doctor Who: The Encyclopedia – The Definitive Guide to the Hit BBC Series* (London: BBC Books, 2011)

Schuster, Mark, and Tom Powers, *The Greatest Show in the Galaxy: The Discerning Fan's Guide to 'Doctor Who'* (Jefferson NC: McFarland, 2007)

Short, Sue, *Cult Telefantasy Series: A Critical Analysis of 'The Prisoner', 'Twin Peaks', 'The X-Files', 'Buffy the Vampire Slayer', 'Lost', 'Heroes', 'Doctor Who' and 'Star Trek'* (Jefferson, NC: McFarland, 2011)

Spicer, Andrew, *Typical Men: The Representation of Masculinity in Popular British Cinema* (London: I.B.Tauris, 2001)

Stanish, Deborah, and L. M. Myles, (eds), *Chicks Unravel Time: Women Journey Through Every Season of 'Doctor Who'* (Des Moines, IA: Mad Norwegian Press, 2012)

Thomas, Lynda M., and Tara O'Shea (eds), *Chicks Dig Time Lords: A Celebration of 'Doctor Who' by the Women Who Love It* (Des Moines, IA: Mad Norwegian Press, 2011)

Tracey, Michael, and David Morrison, *Whitehouse* (London: Macmillan, 1979)

Tribe, Steve, *Doctor Who: The Tardis Handbook* (London: BBC Books, 2010)

——— and James Goss, *Doctor Who: The Dalek Handbook* (London: BBC Books, 2011)

Truffaut, François, with Helen G. Scott, *Hitchcock* (London: Paladin, 1978)

Tulloch, John, and Manuel Alvarado, *Doctor Who: The Unfolding Text* (London: Macmillan, 1983)

Tulloch, John, and Henry Jenkins, *Science Fiction Audiences: Watching 'Doctor Who' and 'Star Trek'* (London: Routledge, 1995)

Walker, Stephen James, *Inside the Hub: The Unofficial and Unauthorised Guide to 'Torchwood' Series 1* (Tolworth: Telos, 2007)

————, *Something in the Darkness: The Unofficial and Unauthorised Guide to 'Torchwood' Series 2* (Tolworth: Telos, 2008)

Wood, Linda (ed.), *British Film Industry: A BFI Reference Guide* (London: British Film Institute, 1980)

Wood, Tat, and Lawrence Miles, *About Time: The Unauthorized Guide to 'Doctor Who 1963–1966: Seasons 1 to 3* (Des Moines IA: Mad Norwegian Press, 2006)

————, *About Time: The Unauthorized Guide to 'Doctor Who' 1966–1969: Seasons 4 to 6* (Des Moines IA: Mad Norwegian Press, 2006)

————, *About Time: The Unauthorized Guide to 'Doctor Who' 1970–1974: Seasons 7 to 11* (Des Moines: Mad Norwegian Press, 2006)

Wood, Tat, with Lars Pearson, *About Time: The Unauthorized Guide to 'Doctor Who' 1985–1989: Seasons 22 to 26, The TV Movie* (Des Moines IA: Mad Norwegian Press, 2007)

Articles and chapters

Amy-Chinn, Dee, 'Rose Tyler: The ethics of care and the limits of agency', *Science Fiction Film and Television*, vol.1, no.2 (2008), pp.231–47

Bignell, Jonathan, 'Space for "quality": negotiating with the Daleks', in Jonathan Bignell and Stephen Lacey (eds), *Popular Television Drama: Critical Perspectives* (Manchester, 2005), pp.76–92

Bould, Mark, 'Science Fiction Television in the United Kingdom', in J. P. Telotte (ed.), *The Essential Science Fiction Television Reader* (Lexington: University Press of Kentucky, 2008), pp.209–30

Chapman, James, 'The BBC and the censorship of *The War Game* (1965)', *Journal of Contemporary History*, vol.41, no.1 (January 2006), pp.75–94

Charles, Alec, 'War Without End?: Utopia, the Family, and the Post-9/11 World in Russell T. Davies' *Doctor Who*', *Science Fiction Studies*, vol.35, no.3 (2008), pp.450–65

Chen, Ken, 'The Lovely Smallness of *Doctor Who*', *Film International*, no.32 (2008), pp.52–9

Cook, John R., 'Adapting telefantasy: The Doctor Who and the Daleks films', in I.Q. Hunter (ed.), *British Science Fiction Cinema* (London: Routledge, 1999), pp.113–27

Cook, John R., '"Between Grierson and Barnum": Sydney Newman and the development of the single television play at the BBC, 1963–7', *Journal of British Cinema and Television*, vol.1, no.2 (2004), pp.211–25

Cull, Nicholas J., '"Bigger on the inside . . .": *Doctor Who* as British cultural history', in Graham Roberts and Philip M. Taylor (eds), *The Historian,*

Television and Television History (Luton: University of Luton Press, 2001), pp.95–111

———, 'Peter Watkins' Culloden and the alternative form in historical film-making', *Film International*, no.1 (2003), pp.48–53

Fiske, John, '*Doctor Who*: ideology and the reading of a popular narrative text', *Australian Journal of Screen Theory*, nos. 14–15 (1983)

Hills, Matt, 'The Dispersible Television Text: Theorising moments of the new *Doctor Who*', *Science Fiction Film and Television*, vol.1, no.1 (2008), pp.35–44

Leman, Joy, 'Wise scientists and female androids: class and gender in science fiction', in John Corner (ed.), *Popular Television in Britain: Studies in Cultural History* (London: British Film Institute, 1991), pp.108–24

McKee, Alan, 'Which is the best Doctor Who story? A case study in value judgements outside the academy', *Intensities: The Journal of Cult Media*, no.1 (2001) (available at: http://www.cult-media.com/issue1/Amckee.htm)

———, 'Is *Doctor Who* political?', *European Journal of Cultural Studies*, vol.7, no.2 (2004), pp.201–17

MacMurraugh-Kavanagh, M.K., 'The BBC and the birth of The Wednesday Play, 1962–66: "institutional containment" versus "agitational contemporaneity"', *Historical Journal of Film, Radio and Television*, vol.17, no.3 (August 1997), pp.367–81

Perryman, Neil, '*Doctor Who* and the convergence of media: a case study of "transmedia storytelling", *Convergence: The International Journal of Research into New Media Technologies*, vol.14, no.1 (2008), pp.21–39

Tulloch, John, '*Doctor Who*: Similarity and difference', *Australian Journal of Screen Theory*, nos. 11–12 (1982), pp.8–24

Index